PRODUCTIVITY IN THE
U.S. SERVICES SECTOR

PRODUCTIVITY IN THE U.S. SERVICES SECTOR

New Sources of Economic Growth

JACK E. TRIPLETT

BARRY P. BOSWORTH

BROOKINGS INSTITUTION PRESS
Washington, D.C.

Library of Congress Cataloging-in-Publication data

Triplett, Jack E.
  Productivity in the U.S. services sector : new sources of economic growth /
Jack E. Triplett and Barry P. Bosworth.
      p.   cm.
  Includes bibliographical references and index.
  ISBN 0-8157-8335-3 (pbk. : alk. paper)
  1. Service industries—Labor productivity—United States.   2. Industrial
productivity—United States—Measurement.   I. Bosworth, Barry, 1942–   II. Title.
  HD9981.5.T74 2004
  338.4'5'0973—dc22   2004013859

9 8 7 6 5 4 3 2 1

The paper used in this publication meets minimum requirements of the
American National Standard for Information Sciences—Permanence of Paper
for Printed Library Materials: ANSI Z39.48-1992.

Typeset in Adobe Garamond

Composition by R. Lynn Rivenbark
Macon, Georgia

Printed by R. R. Donnelley
Harrisonburg, Virginia

Contents

Foreword

After many years of slow growth, the U.S. economy has experienced a remarkable improvement in labor productivity that began in the mid-1990s but continued through the 2001–02 recession and has now lasted for nearly a decade. This book undertakes a detailed assessment of the resurgence of productivity growth. It demonstrates the dominant role played by the services-producing industries in recent U.S. productivity performance. This is a great turnaround from the past view of services industries. In the old view of services, they were stagnant and unprogressive sectors that slowed overall economic growth. In the new view presented in this book, they are revealed as dynamic and innovative sectors that are significant sources of economic growth.

The study makes a particular effort to measure the contributions of the new information technologies (IT) at the level of individual industries. IT is a major driver of improvements in services productivity. The authors also estimate improvements in multifactor productivity, in addition to the more traditional labor productivity growth.

The book is in many respects a product of a series of sixteen workshops on the measurement of output and productivity in services held at the Brookings Institution between 1998 and 2003. Those workshops document the substantial progress that has been made in improving measures of output and prices in the services industries. At the same time they highlighted areas where further work is needed. The authors are heavily indebted to the representatives of the statistical agencies and academic researchers who participated in the workshops.

The workshops and the research that went into the preparation of this volume were made possible through major grants from the Alfred P. Sloan Foundation, with additional support provided by the Bureau of Economic Analysis, U.S. Department of Commerce, and the Bureau of Labor Statistics, U.S. Department of Labor. The authors greatly appreciate the support of Harry Freeman, a long-time member of the Brookings Council, who funded the planning phase of the project.

STROBE TALBOTT
President
Brookings Institution

Washington, D.C.
July 2004

Acknowledgments

The authors would like to thank Emil Apostolov, David Gunther, Helen E. Kim, Jane J. Kim, and Kristin Wilson for their excellent research assistance. At Brookings, Kathleen Elliott Yinug and Theo Merkle were instrumental in organizing the workshops. Eileen Hughes and Theresa Walker edited the manuscript, and Stephen Robblee checked the volume for accuracy. Carlotta Ribar provided proofreading and Julia Petrakis indexing services.

PRODUCTIVITY IN THE U.S. SERVICES SECTOR

CHAPTER ONE

Introduction

The United States has a services-based economy. Over the past half-century, the share of the nation's output accounted for by goods-producing industries has fallen by nearly half, and the services-producing industries now account for more than three-quarters of GDP and a comparable proportion of total employment.

Yet services industries have long been disparaged as sources of low-skill, low-wage jobs, and they often are characterized as part of a stagnant sector marked by low productivity growth and only limited opportunities for innovation. Some economists have contended that, over the long term, the need to devote an ever-increasing share of employment to services would drag down the rate of aggregate economic growth (Baumol 1967).

Our fundamental motivation for writing this book was the growing realization of how much things have changed. The services-producing industries have emerged as the dominant engines of U.S. economic growth. During the 1990s, services were responsible for 19 million additional jobs, while employment in the goods-producing sector stagnated.

Even more striking, productivity growth in the services industries, as we show, has fueled the post-1995 expansion of labor productivity in the United States. Labor productivity in services-producing industries advanced 2.6 percent a year between 1995 and 2001, exceeding the 2.3 percent growth in productivity in goods-producing industries (see chapter 2). Though the margin for services industries might appear small, it represents a tremendous contrast from

earlier years, when labor productivity growth in services industries lagged far
behind that in the goods-producing sector.

Services now lead the way, indicating how much things have changed. We
estimate that services industries accounted for 73 percent of post-1995 labor
productivity growth in the United States and 76 percent of aggregate U.S. multifactor productivity growth. This is not a portrait of a stagnant sector.

Moreover, the services industries are the primary consumers of information
technology (IT) capital. It has been widely reported by others (Jorgenson and
Stiroh 2000; Oliner and Sichel 2000) that IT has been a major contributor to
recent U.S. productivity growth. We confirm this at the industry level and show
in addition that the productivity-enhancing contributions of IT took place in
the services industries. IT in services industries accounted for 80 percent of the
total IT contribution to U.S. labor productivity growth between 1995 and
2001. As with labor productivity growth and multifactor productivity growth,
the IT revolution in the United States is a services industry story.

Services industries have emerged as one of the most dynamic and innovative
sectors of the U.S. economy. That was the basis of one of our previous studies
(Triplett and Bosworth 2002), which proclaimed that "Baumol's Disease has
been cured." The characterization of services as a drag on aggregate growth is no
longer valid.

The U.S. statistical system also has changed. The trend toward services
claiming a growing share of the economy was long ignored by a statistical system originally structured to report the production and consumption of goods.
For many years the outputs of major services-producing industries were estimated by making simple extrapolations of their past relationships to employment or some similar partial indicator. The research reported in this book high-
lights the progress that has been made in the U.S. statistical system in expanding
the range of surveys of the services-producing industries and in developing an
improved methodology for measuring both the output of services and the contribution of critical new high-technology products. We have benefited from the
emergence of new government data sets that have enabled us to measure labor
productivity and the growth in multifactor productivity (MFP) at the level of
individual industries. Labor productivity is simply the ratio of output per unit
of labor input, which is defined as persons or hours. However, with the new
data, we can measure the growth in MFP, defined as output per unit of input
when input is expanded to include labor, purchased inputs, and different forms
of capital. Multifactor productivity is a far more comprehensive measure of the
efficiency of resource use.

Our research employs data for twenty-nine services sector industries—at approximately the two-digit level of the old U.S. SIC (Standard Industrial Classification) system—and for fifty-four industries overall. The United States now has a comprehensive set of data on the output, value added, purchased inputs, capital services, and employment of all fifty-four industries. Our conclusion that accelerating labor productivity and MFP in services industries played a crucial part in the post-1995 growth in U.S. productivity would not have been possible without the improvements in the U.S. industry database. We know of no other country that has a comparable database.[1]

Our broad conclusions about the improved productivity of the services-producing industries are developed in chapter 2. We find that the bulk of the post-1995 acceleration of productivity growth was within the services-producing industries. In the period after 1995, labor productivity in the goods-producing industries improved, but not nearly so much as it did in the services-producing industries. Multifactor productivity, moreover, accelerated strongly in services-producing industries (we measured it at 0.3 percent a year before 1995 and at 1.5 percent a year for the 1995–2001 period) but hardly at all in the goods-producing sector.

However, the services sector encompasses a diverse range of industries, including various forms of transportation and communications, wholesale and retail trade, financial services, and business, personal, and professional services. The patterns of productivity change are equally diverse—seventeen of the twenty-nine services industries in our database showed an acceleration of multifactor productivity growth after 1995. Though large industries (retail trade, wholesale trade, finance) accounted for much of the contribution to aggregate growth after 1995 (because they advanced and they are large), the improvement in services productivity growth was broad based: twenty-four of the twenty-nine services industries in our analysis had positive growth in labor productivity after 1995.

The growing awareness of the importance of services in creating job opportunities and raising productivity and real income has arisen from the improvements that have been made in the statistical reporting system. Some economists still believe that government statistics on services are too poor to be used or believed—but that belief, like the belief that services inherently are not susceptible to productivity improvements, is outdated.

This is a book on developments in the productivity of the services sector, but it is also a book on measurement. Measuring economic variables has long been a

1. The closest examples would be O'Mahony and Van Ark (2003) and Jorgenson and Lee (2001).

major part of productivity research in the United States because accurate and relevant measurements are so important in forming conclusions about productivity growth.

In subsequent chapters we examine the behavior of measured productivity for individual industries, with a particular focus on issues of measurement. We also report and incorporate the results of a Brookings Institution research program on measuring output and productivity in the services sector. Many of the twenty-nine services industries for which we compute labor and multifactor productivity growth in chapter 2 were subjects of a series of fifteen Brookings economic measurement workshops. The workshops and presentations are listed in appendix B of this volume.[2]

Our examination of individual industries allows us to identify some of the factors that lie behind the acceleration of U.S. aggregate productivity growth. In transportation, for example, we can readily observe the impacts of deregulation, which led to major internal reorganization in railroads and in trucking. The surge of output and labor productivity in communications and finance can be traced directly to the rapid adoption of new information and communications technologies. A combination of changes in information technology (scanners and computers) and organizational changes led to substantial efficiency improvements in retailing. What emerges is a picture of services that is at sharp variance with the old picture.

In several cases, the changed perspective can be traced to new and improved ways of measuring output in services. In particular, the shift away from a focus on value added to gross output (sales or revenues) in Bureau of Economic Analysis (BEA) industry accounts has led to measures of output that better reflect what is actually produced. In banking, for example, the measurement of output now includes use of more convenient automated teller machines and the provision of services over the Internet. The Bureau of Labor Statistics (BLS) also has greatly expanded the coverage of the producer price index (PPI) program to cover a large proportion of services. It was not so long ago that the PPI was restricted to goods alone. The Census Bureau now produces annual surveys of most services-producing industries.

However, our examination of individual industries also provides an opportunity to point out some of the areas where the concepts and data are still inadequate or anomalies need to be resolved. Despite the surge in productivity in services as a whole, in some industries measured growth in labor and multifactor

2. A list also is available at the Brookings website (www.brookings.edu/es/research/projects/productivity/productivity.htm [March 25, 2004]).

productivity has been negative over sustained periods of time. Those results suggest that there are still significant measurement problems. We spend a fair amount of our space and an entire chapter (chapter 11) on improvements that we think are still needed in services statistics.

Zvi Griliches (1992, 1994) suggested that even in the "old days" before the IT and managerial revolutions, productivity in services industries might not have been as bad as it appeared because the statistics that existed at the time were so inadequate.[3] Innovations in services—changes in organization, delivery, and variety—often are more difficult to identify than the new products offered in the goods-producing sector, and too few resources were put into measuring services industries. Only recently have statistics emerged that allow us to identify and track the changes in these industries. Economists, including us, owe Griliches a great debt for calling attention to the need for services sector data and the implications for productivity analysis. In many ways, this book commemorates Griliches' foresight.

3. Marimont (1969) indicates that there were "old, old" days when nearly the only information on services concerned employment; at that time BEA estimated services industry output in part by labor extrapolation with a labor productivity adjustment based on manufacturing productivity. When direct information on services output became available for some industries, the methodology changed to combining the direct measures with labor extrapolation in the other industries, but without any productivity adjustment. It is significant that implied productivity in services from the "old, old" BEA data, before the 1970s, exceeded the implied productivity for the following period.

CHAPTER TWO

Overview:
Industry Productivity Trends

I n this chapter we report measures of labor and multifactor productivity
(MFP) for U.S. industries at roughly the two-digit SIC (Standard Industrial
Classification) level. The productivity estimates are based on gross output, using
a combination of government databases from the Bureau of Economic Analysis
(BEA) and the Bureau of Labor Statistics (BLS)—and implicitly the Census
Bureau, since the other two agencies' compilations rest heavily on data originally
collected by the Census Bureau's "economic directorate." Our database is a relatively new one that has not previously been employed for productivity research.
With the new database, we can compare productivity trends in the goods-
producing and services-producing industries, estimate sources of labor productivity growth, and aggregate the industry productivity estimates to be consistent
with the aggregate productivity estimates that have appeared in "macro" studies
such as Oliner and Sichel (2000, 2002), Baily and Lawrence (2001), Gordon
(2000, 2002), and Jorgenson and Stiroh (2000). We cover the 1987–2001
period, for which the data are complete, though information for many industries extends back to 1977 (we used the 1977–87 data, where available, in our
earlier paper).[1]

---

1. Several industry-level studies of U.S. labor and multifactor productivity have appeared following our earlier work (Triplett and Bosworth 2002). Stiroh (2002a) preceded our work; he estimated
labor productivity for manufacturing industries in the BEA industry data file (without including the

Table 2-1. *Labor Productivity and MFP Growth, Sectoral Estimates,
Goods-Producing and Service-Producing Industries*
Least-squares annual trend growth[a]

Measure	1987–95	1995–2001	Change
Labor productivity			
Private nonfarm business	1.0	2.5	1.5
Goods-producing industries	1.8	2.3	0.5
Service-producing industries	0.7	2.6	1.8
Multifactor productivity			
Private nonfarm business	0.6	1.4	0.9
Goods-producing industries	1.2	1.3	0.1
Service-producing industries	0.3	1.5	1.1

Source: Table A-2 in appendix A. As explained in this chapter, the aggregate productivity numbers differ from those published by BLS.
a. Based on value added per worker, BEA industry accounts.

It is now well known that aggregate U.S. labor productivity and multifactor productivity accelerated after 1995, with the amount of the acceleration understandably depending on the end period. For example, labor productivity rose at a 2.8 percent annual rate between 1995 and 2002, while data for the 1995–2001 period show that it rose 2.4 percent (2001 was a recession year). In order to reduce the sensitivity of our results to these end-point issues, we present in this chapter mainly least-squares trend rates of change, which give 2.5 percent a year for trend labor productivity growth for the 1995–2001 interval (table 2-1) and 1.0 percent for 1987–1995.

Our first major finding is that over the post-1995 period, labor productivity in the services-producing sector advanced more rapidly than labor productivity in the goods-producing sector. Table 2-1 presents a sector-level summary: for three sectors (the private nonfarm, goods-producing, and services-producing sectors) aggregated value added taken from the BEA industry accounts is used to

Bureau of Labor Statistics capital services data). Jorgenson, Ho, and Stiroh (2002) employ a different industry output series that is based on data from the BLS economic projections program and their own estimates of capital services. Basu and others (2003) use our earlier data set (Triplett and Bosworth 2002), plus U.K. data to compare U.S. and U.K. productivity growth. O'Mahony and Van Ark (2003) compare U.S. and European industry productivity performance using OECD data; the U.S. portion comes from BEA, but the OECD data include only value added from the BEA file, not output, and the OECD database does not include the BLS capital services.

calculate the growth in labor productivity and MFP from aggregated inputs at the corresponding sector level.[2] Labor productivity in services advanced at a 2.6 percent trend rate in 1995–2001, while productivity in the goods-producing sector advanced at a rate of 2.3 percent a year. The post-1995 acceleration in the services sector, 1.8 percentage points, also far exceeded the acceleration of labor productivity growth in the goods-producing sector, 0.5 points (see table 2-1).

Similarly, post-1995 MFP growth in the services sector exceeded MFP growth in the goods-producing sector (1.5 percent compared with 1.3 percent a year). As with labor productivity, the services-producing sector accounted for nearly all of the acceleration in U.S. MFP growth, because there was minimal acceleration in MFP growth in the goods-producing sector taken as a whole (only 0.1 percentage point).

The aggregations conceal much heterogeneity among the industries. We compute industry labor productivity and MFP for twenty-five goods-producing industries and twenty-nine services-producing industries. In these industries, productivity is computed using a measure of gross output rather than value added as in some past industry-level studies. In both the goods-producing and services-producing sectors, some industries experienced very high labor productivity growth, such as electronics in the goods-producing industries and security and commodity brokers in the services industries. Labor productivity growth in the goods-producing sector was restrained by low productivity growth in mining and negative productivity growth in construction in the 1995–2001 period. A number of services also had negative productivity growth, including hotels, amusement and recreation services, and education. It is important to recognize that the *net change* in sector productivity reflects the behavior of productivity in the individual industries within the sector and that within both the services- and the goods-producing sectors, there were industries with negative as well as positive productivity growth.

Our conclusions about services industry productivity conflict with a widely cited *interpretation* of previous macro-level studies. In those studies, researchers "backed out" (subtracted) from the macro productivity change the contribution of IT-producing industries. They concluded that the MFP contribution of IT-producing industries accounted for all or nearly all of the post-1995 acceleration of U.S. MFP growth and said (or have been interpreted as saying) that no improvement in MFP growth took place in the other industries.

---

2. As explained later in the chapter, these aggregations do not agree precisely with BLS published productivity numbers.

We show in this chapter that the post-1995 resurgence in MFP growth was evident in many non–IT-producing industries and that it was especially evident in a number of services industries. We do not disagree that MFP in the IT-producing industries was very high, as emphasized by other studies. It contributed greatly to the tremendous fall in IT prices and thus to the surge in IT investment (and therefore in turn to labor productivity growth through the standard channel of capital deepening). However, as we show later, there is no inconsistency in finding strong MFP contributions from both IT production and from services industries, because the total contributions of industries that have growing productivity are greater than the *net productivity growth* in the aggregate or sector (because of the offsets from industries that make negative contributions and because of reallocations across industries).

In the second major strand of our research, we estimate the contributions of IT capital to labor productivity growth. We confirm the finding of others about the strong contribution of IT capital deepening. We add to previous research the finding that IT made strong contributions to labor productivity growth in the services industries; services are the industries where IT intensity is greatest. This helps resolve a rather confused debate about whether the effects of IT can be found in the IT-using sectors.

The Industry Database and Aggregate Nonfarm Business Productivity Estimates

We used for this book the recently expanded industry accounts of BEA and combined them with data on capital services flows from the Bureau of Labor Statistics. The BEA industry data set has been improved substantially in recent years in ways that make it more suitable for productivity analysis. The data set now includes measures of output and purchased inputs to go with the previous measures of value added (formerly somewhat confusingly called "gross product") by industry. The industry-specific price indexes have been improved, particularly for the services-producing industries, because of expansion of price measures for services industries in the BLS producer price index program. The database improvements are documented in Yuskavage (1996) and in Lum, Moyer, and Yuskavage (2000). An evaluation of the current data set and plans for its extension are outlined in Yuskavage (2001) and in Moyer and others (2004).[3]

---

3. The BEA-BLS industry data set is an alternative to that developed by Dale Jorgenson and his various coauthors. While they share many of the same sources, the BEA data offer more disaggregation of the services-producing industries. On the other hand, the Jorgenson data are available for a

The BEA industry accounts are constructed to be fully consistent with the estimates of aggregate GDP—or rather, with the income side of the national income and product accounts (NIPA). They are published annually for sixty-six industries at roughly the two-digit industry level of the old SIC classification system. After excluding government and the farm sector and combining some industries for which the BLS does not estimate separate information on capital services, we had fifty-four industries (twenty-five in goods and twenty-nine in services) within the private nonfarm business sector spanning the 1987–2001 period.

We constructed measures of labor and multifactor productivity for each of the fifty-four industries and various subaggregates. We also estimated growth accounts for each of the industries in order to analyze the contributions of capital and materials deepening and multifactor productivity to the growth and acceleration of labor productivity. Those calculations are based on the following model:

(1) $d\ln \text{LP} = w_{K_{IT}} d\ln(K_{IT}/L) + w_{K_N} d\ln(K_N/L) + w_M d\ln(M/L) + d\ln \text{MFP}.$

Within this model, capital services (K) are disaggregated into IT capital (K_{IT}) and non-IT capital (K_N); intermediate inputs—combined energy, materials, and purchased services—are designated M. The share of each input in total output, averaged over the current and preceding period, is denoted by w. The change in logarithms is shown as $d\ln$.

Our industry labor productivity and MFP estimates obviously will reflect the nature of the BEA database, so we need to emphasize several aspects of it. As we show, labor productivity and MFP at the aggregate, private nonfarm business level, *estimated using the data from the BEA industry accounts*, grows more rapidly after 1995 than the corresponding aggregate productivity numbers published by BLS. The reasons involve differences in both the output measure and the labor input measure.

Most important, BLS begins with aggregate GDP as measured from the *expenditure side* of the national accounts and excludes several sectors. In contrast, our measure of private nonfarm business is the result of aggregating the value added of individual industries as measured by the *income side* of the national accounts. The difference between the income and expenditure sides is the statistical discrepancy, which has grown in recent years. The statistical dis-

---

longer time period, and they include measures of labor quality. As discussed later, there often are considerable differences between the two data sets in the growth rates of output at the level of individual industries.

crepancy added an average of 0.3 percentage points annually to the growth of nonfarm business output over the 1995–2001 period, measured from the income side, which means that our productivity measures for the aggregate nonfarm sector grow faster than the BLS labor productivity and MFP measures.[4]

In addition, the difference between the estimates of aggregate price change obtained from the expenditure-side measure of GDP and the double deflation of industry value added is another frequently overlooked source of difference. The expenditure-side estimate of the GDP price index is based on a chain index in which the weights are the shares of individual components of final demand. In contrast, the industry measure of price change for value added is the difference between two chain indexes, gross output and purchased inputs. Each of those two indexes is based in turn on the composition of the industry's sales (final and intermediate) and purchases. The nonfarm sector is then an aggregation of these industry value-added estimates. Not surprisingly, the two measures of aggregate real output and price change are not identical. These differences in deflation procedures add another 0.1 point to the annual growth of the BEA nonfarm aggregate. However, much of the difference is actually accounted for by a few cases where the deflators are different.[5]

As shown in table 2-2, aggregate nonfarm value added grew 4.3 percent annually after 1995 according to the industry-based measure (second column of table 2-2), while it grew 3.8 percent a year with the BLS measure.[6] The industry-based measure also shows more post-1995 acceleration, 1.4 compared with 0.9 percentage points a year, because 1987–95 income-side and product-side growth were the same.[7]

Because reliable measures of hours of work are not available for many of the services industries, we used the labor input in the BEA data set—the number of persons engaged in production, which equals full-time equivalent employees

4. However, in the December 2003 benchmark revision to GDP, the product side of the accounts was revised up relative to the income side, which implies that our income-side productivity estimates stand up. The new GDP data were released too late to incorporate into this book, and in any case they have yet to be translated into the BEA industry data files.

5. Communication with Marshall Reinsdorf of BEA, in late 2003. See also Moyer, Reinsdorf, and Yuskavage (2004).

6. This comparison table uses actual changes, as opposed to least-squares trend changes, so as not to confuse the comparison of the basic data.

7. We also show the growth rate of the aggregation of industry gross output (first column of the lower panel of table 2-2). Although aggregated industry gross output may not be appropriate for computing aggregate productivity, it is useful to note that its overall growth (3.9 percent after 1995) is actually closer to the BLS value added measure after 1995 than is aggregated industry value added.

Table 2-2. *Alternative Measures of Nonfarm Business Output and Productivity, 1987–2001*[a]

Average annual rate of change

Period	Output		Labor	Capital	Value added per worker	Multi-factor productivity
	Gross output	Value added				
Bureau of Labor Statistics						
1987–2001	n.a	3.3	1.5	4.0	1.8	1.0
1987–1995	n.a	2.9	1.5	3.0	1.4	0.9
1995–2001	n.a	3.8	1.5	5.3	2.3	1.1
Change	n.a	0.9	0.0	2.3	0.9	0.2
Industry aggregate (BEA/BLS data)						
1987–2001	3.4	3.5	1.8	3.9	1.6	1.0
1987–1995	3.1	2.9	1.7	2.9	1.1	0.7
1995–2001	3.9	4.3	1.9	5.2	2.3	1.3
Change	0.8	1.4	0.2	2.2	1.2	0.5

Source: Authors' calculations using data from the BLS labor productivity program (upper panel) and the BLS multifactor productivity program (lower panel) and the BEA industry data file.

a. The BLS published measures of the labor input and MFP have been adjusted to exclude changes in labor quality. The industry aggregate is an income-side measure that excludes the statistical discrepancy of the national accounts. The industry data set measures labor as persons; BLS uses hours.

plus the self-employed.[8] This is an incomplete adjustment for variations in hours of work. At the level of total nonfarm business, it results in an index of labor services that grows slightly faster than that of the BLS—1.8 percent a year over the 1987–2001 period compared with 1.5 percent (table 2-2, column 3)— and it accelerates slightly, whereas the BLS measure shows the same rate of growth before and after 1995. This implies that hours have been falling relative to full-time equivalent employment growth.

We adjusted the labor income data to include the compensation of the self-employed. One approach is to simply assume that the self-employed earn a wage equal to that of employees in the industry. However, that adjustment produces a negative residual estimate of capital income in several industries. The BLS makes a proportionate adjustment based on the average of two algorithms: equal rates of labor compensation and a rate of return on noncorporate capital

8. The adjustment for full-time equivalents is done by multiplying total employment by the ratio of hours for all employees to hours for those on full-time schedules. Our measure differs from the treatment in Stiroh (2002a), where the labor measure excludes the self-employed.

equal to the rate for corporations in the same industry—eliminating the possibility of a negative return to either factor. We adopted the BLS estimate of the factor shares.

The measures of capital services are obtained directly from the BLS. Therefore the small discrepancies between the two aggregates (table 2-2, column 4) are due solely to the minor differences in the industries that are included in the aggregate measures.

Columns 5 and 6 of table 2-2 quantify the implications for labor productivity and MFP of differences in the data. The upper panel presents the published BLS data for the nonfarm business sector. The lower panel presents the estimates of nonfarm business labor productivity and MFP obtained when the value-added aggregate is formed from the BEA industry accounts and the labor input is employment rather than hours.

Labor productivity growth based on aggregating the BEA industry accounts is significantly lower than that of BLS for the 1987–95 period because of faster growth in the labor input in our data (the two output measures being the same). However, the two series are very similar after 1995 (both at 2.3 percent a year), when the higher rate of growth in aggregated industry value added is offset by more rapid growth in the labor input. Thus the aggregated BEA industry accounts produce a significantly larger estimate of the post-1995 acceleration, 1.2 compared with 0.9 percent a year (column 5 of table 2-2). This result complements the research of Baily and Lawrence (2001) and Baily (2002), who estimated productivity from an average of the income and product sides of the accounts, but our measure shows a larger acceleration than the estimates in other studies that start from the BLS aggregate numbers.

A comparison of alternative aggregate MFP estimates is also presented in column 6. In addition to the other differences in output and labor input already discussed, the published BLS measure of MFP incorporates an adjustment for improvement in the quality of the workforce. Improvements in labor quality account for about 0.4 percentage point of the increase in labor productivity over the 1987–2001 period, with an offsetting reduction in the residual estimate of MFP. However, we did not have the information required to distribute those labor quality improvements among the fifty-four industries. Instead, to gain comparability we adjusted the published BLS MFP measure of labor inputs to exclude the effect of improvements in workforce quality. On this adjusted basis, growth in the BLS measure of MFP was virtually the same overall (1987–2001) as that using the aggregated BEA industry data, as table 2-2 shows. But, as with labor productivity, differences between the two subperiods result in a larger MFP acceleration after 1995 in the industry-based aggregate than in the published BLS numbers.

Manufacturing Productivity

The BLS also publishes estimates of labor and multifactor productivity growth for durable and nondurable manufacturing. Because several studies (Oliner and Sichel 2002 and Gordon 2002) have contended that large portions of the acceleration in productivity were within manufacturing (particularly semiconductors and computers), it is important to assess the comparability of BLS and BEA manufacturing measures. In the manufacturing case, the BEA industry-based measures yield slower productivity growth after 1995 and less acceleration, especially in durables, than do the BLS published numbers.

Table 2-3 compares growth rates for output and labor productivity.[9] BLS relies on the same basic Census Bureau data as BEA, and both the BLS and BEA measures of manufacturing output are based on the concept of gross output, not value added, so the statistical discrepancy is not an issue. As shown in the top portion of the table, BLS estimates somewhat greater output growth after 1995 in both durables and nondurables manufacturing (0.2 and 0.3 percentage point respectively). In constructing its gross output measure for manufacturing, BLS removes an estimate of intra- and inter-industry shipments within manufacturing to get an unduplicated total, while we have aggregated the BEA industry data without this adjustment. A comparison of the nominal values of the BEA and BLS output measures for total manufacturing suggests that the intra-industry shipments could be around one-third of total output. The adjusted measure will grow faster than the unadjusted one when intramanufacturing shipments are growing more slowly than shipments to destinations outside of manufacturing, but it is not evident that this was the case. Both measures, as we understand them, add to industry output growth the BEA estimate of own-account software production, which is treated as investment in the national accounts. Therefore we do not know why the output measures differ. The patterns are similar before 1995 (that is, the BLS output measure grows more rapidly than our aggregation of the BEA data). However, the accelerations (decelerations for nondurables) in the two output measures turn out to differ more than do the growth rates within each of the periods.

We also report in table 2-3 a comparison with the Federal Reserve Board's (FRB) indexes of industrial production for durables and nondurables manufacturing. The FRB index agrees closely with the BEA measure for nondurables, but it shows a considerably larger acceleration of durables output growth after

9. The BLS estimates of multifactor productivity are available only through 2000.

Table 2-3. *Alternative Measures of Manufacturing Output and Labor Productivity, 1987–2001*[a]

Average annual rate of change

Period	Durables			Nondurables		
	BLS	BEA	FRB	BLS	BEA	FRB
Output index						
1987–2001	3.6	3.7	4.7	1.5	1.0	1.0
1987–1995	3.1	3.5	3.9	2.1	1.5	1.4
1995–2001	4.1	3.9	5.8	0.7	0.4	0.4
Change	1.0	0.4	1.9	−1.4	−1.1	−1.0
Labor productivity						
1987–2001	3.9	4.1	n.a	2.3	1.8	n.a.
1987–1995	3.2	4.0	n.a	1.9	1.4	n.a.
1995–2001	4.8	4.2	n.a	2.7	2.2	n.a.
Change	1.6	0.2	n.a	0.8	0.8	n.a.

Source: Authors' calculations from data obtained from the Board of Governors of the Federal Reserve System, BLS, and BEA.

a. Output measures are based on gross output. Labor productivity is an hours-based measure for BLS; and for the BEA data, we use full-time equivalent employees plus the self-employed. No productivity estimates are made with the FRB industrial production indexes.

1995. In fact, the FRB durables index grows more rapidly over the full 1987–2001 period than either the BEA or BLS measures.

The important point to carry away from these comparisons is that the BLS measures of manufacturing labor productivity grow more rapidly after 1995 than similar measures that we constructed from the BEA data (by 0.6 percentage point in durables and 0.5 point in nondurables—see the bottom panel of table 2-3). Moreover, the BLS measures show substantially more acceleration in durables: the BLS measures indicate accelerating labor productivity of 1.6 percentage points (4.8 minus 3.2), whereas the BEA data indicate very little acceleration after 1995 (only 0.2 percentage point). This reflects not only differences in the output measures but also in the input measures: the BLS uses hours, whereas we rely on full-time equivalent workers. For nondurables, both BLS and BEA measures show about the same acceleration in labor productivity (0.8 percentage point for each). Taking durables and nondurables together, the BLS measures imply a slightly faster growth rate for output and labor productivity for total manufacturing over the whole period and substantially more acceleration after 1995.

The finding of greater acceleration in the aggregate nonfarm productivity measures—and less acceleration in manufacturing—in the BEA data is an important consideration in evaluating the detailed industry productivity measures that are reported in the following sections. It also is a factor in our comparison with other studies that are based on the aggregate nonfarm measures. In our subsequent discussion of the aggregation of industry contributions to productivity growth and in comparing our results with other studies, the aggregated labor productivity (LP) and MFP numbers in the lower panels of table 2-2 are our "targets"—that is, the aggregation of BEA industry data that corresponds to the income side of the national accounts.

Trends in Labor Productivity and MFP at the Industry Level

In this section we report our estimates of labor productivity and MFP for the industries in the BEA industry database. We have constructed industry productivity measures using both gross output and value added, but we emphasize the results based on gross output at the industry level.[10]

Labor productivity (Q) is the output index divided by a simple index of the labor input. Multifactor productivity is the ratio of the output index divided by a weighted average of the inputs, K, L, and M (capital, labor services, and intermediate inputs), so the rate of change in gross output MFP is defined as:

$$(2) \qquad d\ln \text{MFP} = d\ln Q - \{(1 - v)[s_l d\ln L + s_k d\ln K] + v d\ln M\},$$

where inputs include intermediate purchases (M) in addition to labor (L) and capital services (K); v equals the two-period average share of intermediate purchases in gross output; and s_l and s_k are the two-period averages of the share of capital and labor income in value added. We compute a Tornqvist chain index of the weighted annual changes in the logarithm of the inputs ($d\ln$).[11] As noted earlier, we separate the capital input into IT and non-IT capital.

Tables 2-4A and 2-4B provide a detailed view of the changes in labor and multifactor productivity for the services-producing industries. We focus on

---

10. Estimates of gross output back to 1977 are incomplete for services industries, largely because early economic censuses and surveys collected very limited information from services-producing firms. See our earlier paper (Triplett and Bosworth 2002), which carried out separate analyses for the services industries for which data extend to 1977. The information on industry value added extends back to 1947 for the nominal measures and 1977 for real values.

11. The output data of the BEA are aggregated using Fisher indexes. We switched to Tornqvist indexes only to take advantage of a slightly simpler algorithm.

these industries because they played such a dominant role in the post-1995 resurgence in productivity, and it is in this sector that the industry analysis offers an interpretation of the resurgence that differs from that of the macroeconomic analysis. The full set of growth accounts for all fifty-four industries, using gross output and value added, are provided in appendix A, tables A-1 through A-4.

In the services sector, the overall growth in labor productivity and MFP camouflages a wide disparity of trends within the individual two-digit industries. Advancing labor productivity in four large services industries—telephone, wholesale trade, retail trade, and finance (both brokerage and depository institutions)—drove the overall sector improvement. Labor productivity gains in these industries ranged from 3 to more than 10 percent a year after 1995, in all cases representing acceleration over the corresponding rate before 1995. These four industries represent more than one-quarter of total value added in the private nonfarm business sector.

However, growth in services sector labor productivity affected more than a small number of large industries. Of the twenty-nine detailed industries, twenty-four experienced labor productivity growth after 1995, and of the positive-growth industries, seventeen experienced acceleration.[12] In two industries, accelerations or decelerations were marginal (only 0.1 percentage point), so they might better be defined as zero-acceleration industries. Negative labor productivity growth occurred after 1995 in five industries (two fewer than before 1995), but in one of them labor productivity actually accelerated—that is, the negative productivity growth became less negative.

Multifactor productivity growth showed a more mixed picture in services industries (table 2-4B). The 2001 recession was not a factor in this, as a similar mix was found in our previous paper, in which the post-1995 period ended with 2000. MFP growth was actually negative in twelve of the twenty-nine industries after 1995 (three marginally so), but MFP grew rapidly in others. Strong MFP growth in a number of large industries—retail and wholesale trade and finance—was sufficient to offset negative productivity growth in other large services, including hotels, health, education, entertainment/recreation, and "other services" (a combination of several two-digit SICs).

More than half of the services industries experienced accelerating MFP after 1995. Acceleration after 1995 was associated with large swings from negative to positive MFP growth in several industries (see for example, local transit, pipelines,

---

12. This contrasts with the goods-producing sector, where post-1995 labor productivity growth was positive in twenty-four of twenty-five industries but accelerated in only fourteen of the twenty-four.

Table 2-4A. *Growth in Labor Productivity in Twenty-Nine Service Industries,*
1987–2001

Least-squares annual trend growth[a]

Industry	Value added weight	Trend growth in output per worker		
		1987–95	*1995–2001*	*Change*
Railroad transportation	0.4	6.2	2.1	−4.1
Local and interurban passenger transit	0.2	−1.7	−0.6	1.1
Trucking and warehousing	1.6	3.4	0.8	−2.7
Water transportation	0.2	1.7	1.0	−0.7
Transportation by air	1.1	0.0	0.4	0.4
Pipelines (except natural gas)	0.1	−0.7	1.2	1.8
Transportation services	0.4	2.0	3.5	1.5
Telephone and telegraph	2.6	5.5	7.9	2.5
Radio and television	0.7	0.0	1.8	1.8
Electric, gas, and sanitary services	3.4	2.1	2.0	−0.1
Wholesale trade	8.5	3.4	4.2	0.8
Retail trade	11.3	1.3	3.4	2.2
Depository institutions	4.0	2.9	3.1	0.2
Nondepository institutions	0.6	2.4	1.9	−0.6
Security and commodity brokers	1.4	7.2	10.3	3.2
Insurance carriers	1.9	−0.6	−1.7	−1.0
Insurance agents, brokers, and service	0.8	−3.3	2.8	6.1
Real estate (excluding owner-occupied housing)	6.6	2.7	1.7	−1.0
Hotels and other lodging places	1.0	1.0	−0.6	−1.6
Personal services	0.8	1.0	1.5	0.5
Business services	5.2	2.9	3.6	0.7
Auto repair, services, and parking	1.1	0.9	1.5	0.6
Miscellaneous repair services	0.4	1.9	1.8	−0.1
Motion pictures	0.4	0.1	0.3	0.1
Amusement and recreation services	0.9	1.6	−0.4	−2.0
Health services	7.1	−0.7	0.9	1.6
Legal services	1.7	0.0	1.5	1.5
Educational services	0.9	0.2	−1.0	−1.1
Other services	4.9	−0.4	2.0	2.4

Source: Appendix tables A-1 and A-5.

a. Based on gross output.

Table 2-4B. *Growth in Multifactor Productivity in Twenty-Nine Service Industries, 1987–2001*

Least-squares annual trend growth[a]

| Industry | Domar weight | Trend growth in multifactor productivity | | |
		1987–95	1995–2001	Change
Railroad transportation	0.7	3.4	1.5	−1.9
Local and interurban passenger transit	0.4	−1.0	1.3	2.3
Trucking and warehousing	3.4	0.9	−0.1	−1.0
Water transportation	0.6	1.6	0.2	−1.4
Transportation by air	1.9	2.5	−0.5	−2.9
Pipelines (except natural gas)	0.1	−2.8	1.6	4.4
Transportation services	0.6	−0.3	0.2	0.5
Telephone and telegraph	4.3	1.7	1.2	−0.5
Radio and television	1.2	1.6	−4.5	−6.2
Electric, gas, and sanitary services	5.6	0.5	−0.6	−1.1
Wholesale trade	12.4	1.5	3.1	1.6
Retail trade	17.4	0.2	2.9	2.7
Depository institutions	5.6	0.2	1.5	1.3
Nondepository institutions	1.4	−0.2	2.1	2.4
Security and commodity brokers	2.4	3.1	6.6	3.5
Insurance carriers	4.1	−0.1	0.0	0.2
Insurance agents, brokers, and service	1.3	−3.6	−0.1	3.5
Real estate (excluding owner-occupied housing)	11.2	0.4	1.4	1.0
Hotels and other lodging places	1.7	0.0	−1.3	−1.3
Personal services	1.4	−0.9	0.4	1.3
Business services	7.8	0.9	−0.6	−1.5
Auto repair, services, and parking	1.9	−1.4	1.4	2.8
Miscellaneous repair services	0.7	−1.1	−1.6	−0.5
Motion pictures	0.9	−1.2	0.2	1.4
Amusement and recreation services	1.6	0.1	−1.1	−1.2
Health services	10.7	−1.7	−0.5	1.2
Legal services	2.2	−0.8	0.9	1.7
Educational services	1.6	−0.2	−0.8	−0.5
Other services	8.5	−0.3	−0.1	0.2

Source: Appendix table A-1.

a. Based on gross output.

auto repair, and legal services) and strong MFP growth in the big industries of trade and finance. However, the acceleration of MFP growth in medical care (though growth is still negative!) is one area where the result was influenced by a methodological break in the index of real output because new PPI measures of price changes begin in 1991. Methodological breaks also occur in other industries, such as miscellaneous repair services.

Aggregation of Industry Productivity Measures

The fifty-four industries in the data set vary widely in size. Therefore, while tables 2-4A and 2-4B report the changes in labor productivity and MFP at the industry level, it is not evident which of the industries made the largest contributions to the post-1995 surge of aggregate productivity growth. In this section, we aggregate the industry productivity measures and show the contributions of the productivity of individual industries to aggregate and sector-level productivity measures. We find that the industries within the services sector accounted for the bulk of U.S. productivity growth after 1995, both labor productivity and MFP, and for all of the post-1995 acceleration. The goods-producing industries, taken together, made no net contribution to the recent acceleration in growth of U.S. productivity.

Industry and Aggregate Productivity Relations

Previously we discussed measures of productivity that were based on aggregating data on industry outputs and inputs up to the level of total goods- and services-producing sectors. The productivity measures were then computed from the aggregate data (table 2-1). We call such measures "direct" aggregate-level (or sector-level) productivity measures.

Computing industry productivity first and then aggregating the results raises a set of issues that we need to confront in order to compare our industry productivity figures with the direct aggregate-level productivity numbers and with sector-level productivity measures, such as those for the goods-producing and services-producing sectors, durables manufacturing, and so forth. In this section, it is important to bear in mind that the aggregate productivity numbers to which our industry productivity numbers correspond are those "targets" in the lower panel of table 2-2—that is, the direct aggregate-level productivity estimates formed by aggregating inputs and outputs in the BEA industry accounts, not the published BLS aggregate numbers in the top panel.

First, aggregate productivity is not just the aggregation of productivity changes within the individual industries. Aggregate productivity can also change because of reallocations across industries. As we (and others, including Stiroh 2002a and Jorgenson, Ho, and Stiroh, 2002) show, aggregated industry productivity estimates generally exceed direct aggregate-level productivity change because of reallocation of resources across industries. These reallocation effects are an important and interesting part of the productivity resurgence story that has been overlooked in some macro productivity studies.

A second issue concerns combining gross output productivity at the industry level with value added productivity at the aggregate level. Gross output is preferred for production analysis at the industry level because it requires the fewest restrictions on the relationship between intermediate inputs and output. The construction of a production relationship based on value added requires that the components of value added be separable from those of purchased inputs.[13] The value added construct at the industry level also implies a specific way that productivity or technical change affects economies in the use of capital and labor on one hand and of savings in intermediate inputs on the other.

Yet value added is the appropriate focus at the level of the aggregate economy. As Gollop (1979) put it, the objective is to maximize society's deliveries to final demand—which corresponds with aggregate value added for a closed economy—subject to the constraint of limited supplies of the primary inputs. At this level, intermediate purchases net out (except for imports), and the aggregation of the industry gross outputs would involve repeated double counting. Therefore full consideration of the implications of productivity developments at the level of individual industries requires a means of linking gross output productivity at the industry level to the value added concept of the aggregate.

Recent discussions of the aggregation of labor productivity are found in Nordhaus (2002) and Stiroh (2002a). We rely on Stiroh's formula that relates the industry measures of gross output labor productivity to aggregate value added per worker:

$$(3) \qquad d ln\, LP^{V} = \left[\sum_i w_i\, d ln\, LP_i^{Q} \right] + \left[\sum_i w_i\, d ln\, L_i - d ln\, L \right] - \left[\sum_i m_i (d ln\, M_i - d ln\, Q_i) \right],$$

13. Gross output at the industry level can be represented as

$$Q = f[K, L, M, t],$$

where Q is output; and K, L, and M are capital, labor, and purchased inputs, respectively. Excluding purchased inputs and focusing on value added is equivalent to assuming

$$Q = f[g(K, L, t_1), M, t_2],$$

where g is separable from M, and t_1 and t_2 represent (different) shift factors.

where

LP^V = aggregate value added per worker,

LP$_i^Q$ = gross output per worker in industy i,

w_i = the two-period average of the share of industry i's nominal value added in aggregate value added, and

m_i = the two-period average of the ratio of industry i's nominal purchased inputs to aggregate value added.

L and M, of course, are the standard notations for labor and intermediate inputs. In this formulation, we can think of $d \ln$ LP^V as the direct aggregate-level labor productivity growth already discussed and displayed in table 2-2. Equation (3) shows that the direct aggregate-level labor productivity estimate is a combination of an industry productivity effect equal to the weighted sum of the growth in the industry productivities, where the weights are the industry shares of total value added, and reallocation terms that capture the shift of output among industries with variations in their levels of labor productivity and intermediate input intensity.[14]

As an intuitive example, suppose industry A contracts out a portion of its activities to industry B. This intermediate inputs deepening ($d \ln$ M$_i$ > $d \ln$ Q$_i$) may raise labor productivity in industry A (presuming that industry A rids itself of labor employed in its own less-productive activities), because less labor is required per unit of output in industry A. But contracting out cannot by itself raise aggregate labor productivity; it will cause aggregate labor productivity to rise only if industry B is more productive in the contracted activities than was industry A. The reallocation terms capture this effect. They will be positive when shifts in economic activity go from industries with lower productivity growth toward industries with higher productivity growth, and they will be negative in the opposite case.

Domar (1961) provided the link to aggregating industry gross output MFP by expressing the rate of aggregate MFP growth as a weighted average of the industry MFP growth rates, with weights equal to the ratios of industry gross output to aggregate value added. That framework was generalized and developed more fully in Hulten (1978) and Gollop (1979). The important point is that productivity improvements at the industry level contribute to the aggregate economy in two ways—first, through direct cost reductions for the industries'

14. This formulation differs from that of Nordhaus (2002) because it uses chain index weights (the w_i terms), eliminating what Nordhaus labeled the Baumol effect. It also adds an additional source of reallocation by measuring labor productivity at the industry level with gross output instead of value added.

outputs that are part of final demand, and second, through reductions in the cost of intermediate inputs for other industries.

For the aggregation of MFP, we have relied on the generalization of the Domar weights given in Jorgenson, Gollop, and Fraumeni (1987):

$$(4) \quad d\ln \text{MFP}^V = \left[\sum_i v_i d\ln \text{MFP}_i^Q\right] + \left[\sum_i v_i s_i^k d\ln \text{K}_i - s^k d\ln \text{K}\right] +$$
$$\left[\sum_i v_i s_i^l d\ln \text{L}_i - s^l d\ln \text{L}\right],$$

where

v_i = two-period average of the ratio of industry i's gross output to aggregate value added (Domar weights), and

s_i = the two-period average share in industry i of the designated factor's (K or L) income in nominal gross output.

The framework differs from Domar's because it does not net out the intra-industry shipments and because in the case of labor, the total is simply the sum of employment at the industry level rather than being weighted by the industry share of total compensation. In addition, our aggregations of both labor productivity and MFP use Tornqvist chain indexes—that is, the weights are averages of adjacent periods, not single-period or base-period weights.[15] The Domar weights (the first element of equation 4) can best be thought of as the product of two steps in the aggregation: the scaling up of the change in MFP at the industry level by the ratio of gross output to value added at the industry level, and the aggregation using value added weights.[16]

Sector Aggregates of Industry Productivity

Table 2-5 shows a summary of the industry contributions to the growth in the direct aggregate value added measures of labor productivity (shown in bold) and MFP, using equations (3) and (4). A more complete accounting is given in appendix tables A-5 and A-6.

The aggregation of industry labor productivity estimates (the within-industry effects, shown in italics in table 2-5) more than accounts for the growth of aggregate productivity in both periods. The contributions of industry productivity changes are offset by resource reallocations (the among-industries effects)

15. Domar (1961) assumed a Cobb-Douglas function, which implies base period weights in a logarithmic index.

16. At the level of individual industries, MFP computed from the gross output framework will always be less that MFP computed from the value added data (see appendix tables A-1 and A-2); however, the contribution to the aggregate MFP is the same for both concepts.

Table 2-5. *Aggregation of Industry Contributions to Labor and Multifactor Productivity Growth, Nonfarm Business Sector, 1987–2001*

Least-squares annual trend growth[a]

	Growth rate		
Component	1987–95	1995–2001	Change
Labor productivity			
Direct aggregate level[b]	1.01	2.46	1.45
Intermediate inputs reallocation	–0.48	0.14	0.62
Labor reallocation	–0.44	–0.31	0.13
Value added weighted industry aggregate	1.93	2.63	0.70
Multifactor productivity			
Direct aggregate level	0.56	1.44	0.88
Input reallocation	–0.09	–0.14	–0.04
Domar weighted industry aggregate	0.66	1.58	0.92

Source: Equations (3) and (4) of text and appendix tables A-5 and A-6.

a. Except where noted.

b. Note that the values differ from those in table 2-2 because the current table reports trend rates of change.

that reduce the aggregate gain. For example, for the 1987–95 period, the aggregation of industry labor productivity yields 1.93 percent growth a year, nearly twice as much productivity growth as is recorded at the aggregate level (1.01 percent). Reallocations reduce aggregate labor productivity growth by 0.92 percentage point.

On the other hand, more of post-1995 labor productivity growth within the industries feeds through to the aggregate level because the reallocation terms have had a less negative influence in recent years—the weighted industry productivity changes (2.63 percent a year) total only 0.17 point more than the direct aggregate estimate (2.46 percent). Put another way, the aggregate post-1995 acceleration of 1.45 (2.46 – 1.01) percentage points a year in labor productivity growth was boosted by changes in—that is, by less negative—reallocation terms. Because reallocations are smaller after 1995, the (1.45 point) aggregate productivity growth acceleration is roughly twice as large as the acceleration that is evident from a straight aggregation of the fifty-four individual industries (0.70 point a year).[17]

17. This variation between the aggregate and the industry results is largely due to changes in the relationship between gross output and value added—what we have labeled reallocation of the intermediate inputs. If labor productivity is measured at the industry level using value added, the

The lower part of table 2-5 indicates that the reallocation terms are less important in the aggregation of the industry measures of MFP growth. The aggregation of industry MFP is formed by using Domar weights, as indicated in equation (4). The aggregation of industry MFPs is larger than direct aggregate-level MFP for both periods, but the reallocation term is small (only –0.14 for 1995–2001). Moreover, the acceleration in MFP is the same (about 0.9 point), whether calculated from the direct aggregate or by aggregating industry MFPs.

Industry Contributions to Aggregate Productivity Growth

We can now turn to the contributions of individual industries to aggregate productivity growth. These are shown, for all twenty-nine services industries and for the major aggregates, in table 2-6. The industry contributions in table 2-6 equal the totals given by the first terms in equations (3) and (4)—that is, the aggregations of the industry productivity growth rates in the top line of table 2-6 repeat the two italicized lines of table 2-5. As we have already noted, the total industry productivity contribution is larger than the direct aggregate-level productivity change shown in table 2-5 for the nonfarm business aggregate because the direct industry contributions are gross of reallocation effects.

Similarly, the sector aggregations in table 2-6 are the sums of the industry contributions within the sector. One should interpret industry (and sector) contributions in table 2-6 in the following way: they show the contribution of industry i (or the industries in sector j) to the total of all industry contributions to productivity change. Thus of the 2.63 percent a year aggregated industry labor productivity growth for 1995–2001, goods-producing industries contributed 0.71 percentage point and services-producing industries 1.92 percentage points—services industries accounted for 73 percent of the total industry labor productivity growth. The post-1995 resurgence in labor productivity can be traced largely to productivity growth in the services-producing industries. A similar statement applies to MFP growth: services industries accounted for 76 percent of the 1.58 percent a year growth in MFP after 1995.

Table 2-6 shows that the two machinery industries (within which are located computer and semiconductor manufacturing) contributed about 17.5 percent of the total industry increase in labor productivity [(0.15 + 0.31) / 2.63] between 1995 and 2001 and 32 percent [(0.22 + 0.29) / 1.58] of the total industry MFP growth. In contrast, four large services industries—retail and wholesale trade, finance (specifically, brokerage firms), and a miscellaneous

---

reallocation term is limited to changes in the distribution of labor among the industries, which does not change very much before and after 1995.

Table 2-6. *Industry Contributions to Labor and Multifactor Productivity Growth, Nonfarm Business Sector, 1987–2001*

Least-squares annual trend growth

Industry	Aggregate	Labor productivity				Multifactor productivity			
		Value added weight	Contribution			Domar weight	Contribution		
			1987–95	1995–2001	Change		1987–95	1995–2001	Change
Private nonfarm business	Yes	100.0	1.93	2.63	0.70	186.9	0.66	1.58	0.92
Goods-producing industries	Yes	29.6	0.77	0.71	-0.06	73.1	0.39	0.38	-0.01
Agricultural services, forestry, and fishing	No	0.6	-0.00	0.01	0.01	0.9	-0.01	0.00	0.01
Mining	Yes	1.9	0.07	0.01	-0.06	3.1	0.04	-0.03	-0.06
Construction	No	5.3	-0.01	-0.06	-0.05	9.3	0.02	-0.05	-0.07
Manufacturing	Yes	21.7	0.72	0.76	0.04	59.7	0.34	0.45	0.11
Durable goods	Yes	12.3	0.58	0.60	0.02	31.7	0.35	0.59	0.23
Industrial machinery and equipment	No	2.32	0.15	0.15	0.00	5.5	0.10	0.22	0.12
Electronic equipment and instruments	No	3.25	0.28	0.31	0.04	7.2	0.20	0.29	0.09
Nondurable goods	Yes	9.4	0.14	0.16	0.02	28.1	-0.01	-0.13	-0.12
Service-producing industries	Yes	70.4	1.16	1.92	0.76	113.8	0.27	1.20	0.93
Transportation	Yes	4.0	0.08	0.04	-0.04	7.8	0.10	0.01	-0.10
Communications	Yes	3.4	0.15	0.22	0.07	5.6	0.09	0.00	-0.09
Telephone and telegraph	No	2.6	0.15	0.21	0.05	4.3	0.07	0.06	-0.01
Radio and television	No	0.7	0.00	0.02	0.01	1.2	0.02	-0.06	-0.08
Electric, gas, and sanitary services	No	3.4	0.07	0.06	-0.01	5.6	0.03	-0.03	-0.07

Wholesale trade	No	8.5	0.31	0.36	0.05	12.4	0.18	0.38	0.20
Retail trade	No	11.3	0.15	0.38	0.23	17.4	0.04	0.50	0.46
Finance and insurance	Yes	8.7	0.18	0.31	0.13	14.8	0.01	0.34	0.32
Depository institutions	No	4.0	0.12	0.13	0.01	5.6	0.01	0.09	0.08
Nondepository institutions	No	0.6	0.01	0.01	-0.00	1.4	-0.01	0.04	0.05
Security and commodity brokers	No	1.4	0.09	0.18	0.10	2.4	0.06	0.21	0.15
Insurance carriers	No	1.9	-0.01	-0.04	-0.02	4.1	-0.00	0.00	0.00
Insurance agents, brokers, and service	No	0.8	-0.02	0.02	0.05	1.3	-0.04	-0.00	0.04
Real estate (excluding owner-occupied housing)	No	6.6	0.16	0.11	-0.05	11.2	0.05	0.16	0.11
Other service industries	Yes	24.6	0.05	0.43	0.38	39.1	-0.23	-0.15	0.08
Hotels and other lodging places	No	1.0	0.02	-0.01	-0.02	1.7	0.00	-0.02	-0.02
Personal services	No	0.8	0.00	0.01	0.01	1.4	-0.01	0.01	0.02
Business services	No	5.2	0.11	0.22	0.11	7.8	0.06	-0.07	-0.12
Auto repair, services, and parking	No	1.1	0.01	0.02	0.01	1.9	-0.03	0.03	0.05
Miscellaneous repair services	No	0.4	0.01	0.01	0.00	0.7	-0.01	-0.01	-0.00
Motion pictures	No	0.4	0.00	0.00	0.00	0.9	-0.01	0.00	0.01
Amusement and recreation services	No	0.9	0.01	-0.00	-0.02	1.6	0.00	-0.02	-0.02
Health services	No	7.1	-0.07	0.06	0.14	10.7	-0.18	-0.06	0.13
Legal services	No	1.7	-0.01	0.02	0.03	2.2	-0.02	0.02	0.04
Educational services	No	0.9	-0.00	-0.01	-0.01	1.6	-0.00	-0.01	-0.01
Other services	No	4.9	-0.02	0.10	0.13	8.5	-0.03	-0.01	0.01

Source: Apppendix tables A-5 and A-6.

grouping of other services that includes business services[18]—contributed 56 percent [(0.36 + 0.38 + 0.31 + 0.43) / 2.63] of the total labor productivity growth and 87 percent [(0.38+ 0.50 + 0.34 + 0.16) / 1.58] of the MFP growth. Each of the first three of these large services subsectors contributed as much or more to aggregate post-1995 productivity growth as either industrial machinery or electrical machinery, which have received so much attention because of their electronics components.

Turning now to sources of acceleration after 1995 (that is, comparing industry productivity growth after 1995 with growth in the previous period), these same four services industries provided 70 percentage points of the post-1995 aggregate acceleration in labor productivity (see the "Changes" column of table 2-6), and the next ten most important contributors to the acceleration (all of which are in services) added only 30 percentage points. Improvements in MFP growth also were dominated by the gains in the services-producing industries, which contributed 0.93 point of the net 0.92 point of MFP acceleration (that is, more than the total). The top contributors to the post-1995 MFP acceleration (retail trade, wholesale trade, brokerage firms, and health) were all in services, closely followed by industrial machinery, which includes computers.[19] As shown in the table, the contribution of durable goods manufacturing to the improvement is large, but it is offset by declines in other goods-producing industries, including nondurables manufacturing.

Twenty-seven of the industries show a post-1995 acceleration of the trend growth in MFP, and seventeen are services-producing industries. Despite the similarity of the large contributing industries, the cross-industry correlation between the post-1995 acceleration of labor productivity and MFP is a surprisingly low 0.33.

There is also a large change in the role of business services, which was a major source of the rise in labor productivity, but it makes a negative contribution to the improvement in overall MFP growth. Its positive contribution to labor productivity is largely the result of a rapid increase in its weight; labor productivity growth was high but not accelerating after 1995. However, a large increase in purchases of intermediate inputs results in a post-1995 decline in MFP.

18. As mentioned in the prior section, we believe that the improvements in health services and other services are partly due to changes in the methodology for measuring the price deflators for output.

19. The large positive contribution of health arises because the MFP change is less negative after 1995.

The Role of IT Capital

A number of studies have reported that increasing use of IT capital contributed to the acceleration of labor productivity after 1995, in the standard paradigm of capital deepening, but that non-IT capital per worker did not accelerate after 1995 (see, for example, Oliner and Sichel 2002). Using the labor productivity decomposition in equation (1) and applying it to the nonfarm value added data, we find the same result: overall, increasing IT capital per worker contributes 0.8 point to growth in labor productivity (value added per worker) after 1995 and 0.5 percentage point to acceleration (line 1 of table 2-7, and appendix table A-2). Non-IT capital services contribute positively to growth, but only a little less than 0.1 point to acceleration.

Most of the effect of IT capital deepening in the U.S. economy in recent years shows up in its contribution to labor productivity growth in the services industries. Again, as with so many aspects of recent U.S. productivity performance, most of the action is in the services industries. As shown on the left of table 2-7, the increased use of IT contributes 0.6 percentage point of labor productivity growth in the services-producing industries after 1995, which was 0.4 point more than the contribution of IT capital in the previous period. In contrast, IT contributes only 0.1 point to the acceleration in the goods-producing industries.[20]

Furthermore, if we use the Domar weights to compute the contribution of IT capital in individual industries (the right side of table 2-7), we find that the services-producing industries are responsible for 80 percent (0.62/0.77) of the contribution of IT capital to post-1995 productivity growth in the nonfarm economy. The contributions were particularly large from wholesale trade, finance, and other services (primarily business services and health).

The contributions data also are useful for exploring the role of IT capital in the productivity revival. Following Stiroh (2002a), we rank industries by the proportion of capital services that are derived from IT capital.[21] We use the values for 1995, but they are essentially the same as the 1987–95 average, a correlation coefficient of 0.96. We can then relate this measure of IT capital services intensity to the growth of productivity after 1995.

20. As shown in Triplett and Bosworth (2002), the services-producing industries are also more intensive users of IT than the goods-producing industries (appendix table A-7).

21. For our earlier paper (Triplett and Bosworth 2002), we computed several different measures of IT capital intensity, using alternative definitions of IT and IT intensity. The industry rankings do vary according to IT definition or to intensity measure, but the top industries appear on all the lists.

Table 2-7. Contributions of IT Capital to Labor Productivity Growth, Nonfarm Business Sector, 1987–2001

Least-squares annual trend growth

Industry	Domar weight	Contribution to industry			Contribution to aggregate		
		1987–95	1995–2001	Change	1987–95	1995–2001	Change
Private nonfarm business	186.9	0.36	0.85	0.49	0.38	0.77	0.39
Goods-producing industries	73.1	0.12	0.19	0.07	0.09	0.15	0.06
Mining	3.1	0.09	0.24	0.15	0.00	0.01	0.00
Construction	9.3	0.06	0.09	0.03	0.01	0.01	0.00
Manufacturing	59.7	0.11	0.18	0.07	0.09	0.13	0.05
Durable goods	31.7	0.12	0.24	0.12	0.04	0.08	0.04
Nondurable goods	28.1	0.15	0.23	0.08	0.04	0.06	0.01
Service-producing industries	113.8	0.23	0.59	0.37	0.28	0.62	0.34
Transportation	7.8	0.13	0.31	0.17	0.01	0.02	0.01
Communications	5.6	0.86	1.29	0.43	0.05	0.07	0.02
Electric, gas, and sanitary services	5.6	0.25	0.25	0.00	0.01	0.01	0.00
Wholesale trade	12.4	0.49	1.42	0.93	0.06	0.18	0.12
Retail trade	17.4	0.11	0.26	0.15	0.02	0.05	0.03
Finance and insurance	14.8	0.62	1.09	0.48	0.08	0.13	0.05
Real estate (excluding owner-occupied housing)	11.2	-0.01	0.02	0.04	-0.00	0.00	0.00
Other service industries	39.1	0.14	0.47	0.33	0.05	0.16	0.11

Source: The direct estimates of the contribution to labor productivity in individual inudstries are from the gross-output estimates of table A-1, except for the nonfarm aggregates, which are value added estimates from table A-2. The contributions to the aggregate, shown in the right-hand columns, are computed using Domar weights at the industry level and aggregating up to the subsector and sector level.

Using the cross-industry averages of trend labor productivity growth from 1995–2001, we obtain a statistically significant correlation of 0.26 with the intensity of IT use. This is very much in line with the results reported by Stiroh, and it is essentially the same if we use the actual changes over the 1995–2001 period. It suggests, as we should expect, that the contribution to overall labor productivity growth has been more rapid in industries that made extensive use of IT capital.

However, if we now apply the same analysis to the post-1995 growth of MFP, the evidence of a correlation with IT capital vanishes and the correlation coefficient declines to 0.05. This too is as expected. If IT capital investments earn a normal return and there are no substantial externalities associated with such investments, then IT capital should not be associated with MFP, which is after all the residual after all other inputs (including IT inputs) are taken into account. This is also the conclusion of Stiroh (2002b), who examined the manufacturing industries.

Growth accounting analyses of productivity change (of the type we apply to industry productivity analysis) apply the assumption that IT capital earns normal returns. This has often been criticized on various "IT capital is special" grounds. The lack of correlation between IT and MFP supports the view that IT can be analyzed in the same way as any other capital good.

Consistency with Other Studies: IT-Producing and Services Industries

Studies using macro approaches, including Oliner and Sichel (2000) and Gordon (2000, 2002), find MFP acceleration in the United States after 1995 but also estimate (in somewhat indirect ways) that two-thirds to all of the aggregate acceleration is accounted for by MFP acceleration in the industries that produce IT investment goods. For example, Gordon (2002) concludes: "There has been no acceleration of MFP growth outside of computer production and the rest of durable manufacturing."[22]

The view that all recent MFP growth is in the IT-producing industries suggests that the post-1995 productivity acceleration is fragile, because it rests entirely in a single set of goods-producing industries. In addition, it suggests that recent U.S. productivity performance differs from that of Europe mainly because the United States has a larger IT-producing sector. In contrast, our finding that MFP acceleration is broadly—though not universally—based on

22. Gordon (2002, p. 65).

services industries leads to the view that something significant did change in the U.S. economy. Moreover, changes in IT-using industries probably explained a good amount of the recent productivity differences between the United States and western Europe. Therefore reconciling the apparently conflicting findings has considerable importance.

Existing macro and industry studies differ from ours in three dimensions: the output measures, the labor measures, and the estimates of MFP in IT-producing industries. We discuss these below. But first, we address an essential methodological point.

A Note on "Exhausting" Total MFP

The macro studies back out, or subtract, estimates of the contribution of MFP in IT-producing industries from the growth of *direct aggregate-level MFP*. Doing so seems to exhaust or nearly exhaust total MFP growth and to leave little "room" for MFP growth in the rest of the economy. For example, backing out Oliner and Sichel's IT MFP estimate (0.77 percent a year) from the trend BLS MFP growth estimate (1.17 percent a year) appears to leave only 0.40 percent a year MFP growth outside the IT-producing industries (see the first column of table 2-8, row 5).[23] This calculation is the basis for Gordon's statement, quoted above. If one backs out the same IT estimate from the growth in the direct aggregate-level MFP measure from BEA data (which is greater, for the reasons discussed previously), MFP growth outside IT appears a little greater because the overall MFP growth estimate is larger in the BEA database, as explained earlier.

However, we showed that the sum of all industries' MFP growth exceeds growth in the direct MFP measure because of reallocations. If one wants to determine whether non-IT industries contribute to MFP growth, clearly the starting point is the aggregation of industry MFP growth rates, not the direct aggregate-level measure that includes reallocations. As the third column of table 2-8 shows, that backing-out exercise leaves more room for non-IT MFP. To illustrate, backing out our industry IT MFP measure (0.51) from the sum of the industry MFP changes (1.58) leaves a contribution of 1.07 percent a year to net MFP growth from industries outside the IT-producing sector, more than twice the amount that originates inside the IT-producing sector.

---

23. For comparability, we show trend rates of MFP growth in table 2-8. Using Oliner and Sichel's average annual rate of MFP growth—0.99 percent from 1995 to 2001, the recession year—yields only 0.23 percentage point for the contribution of non-IT industries. The 0.77 percent acceleration in IT industry MFP is the sum of the contribution of semiconductors, computer hardware and software, and communications equipment in table 1 of Oliner and Sichel (2002).

Table 2-8. *Alternative "Backing Out" Exercises for Comparisons of MFP of IT-Producing and Other Industries, 1995–2001*
Least-squares annual trend growth[a]

		BEA data set		
Category	BLS MFP	Direct MFP estimate	Sum of industry MFPs	Sum of positive industry MFPs
1. Nonfarm business MFP (table 2-5)	1.17	1.44	1.58	2.09[a]
Contribution of				
2. Machinery industries MFP (table 2-6)	0.51	0.51	0.51	0.51
3. Oliner and Sichel (2002) IT-industry MFP	0.77	0.77	0.77	0.77
4. Remainder (row 1 – row 2 = MFP outside IT)	0.66	0.93	1.07	1.58
5. Remainder (row 1 – row 3 = MFP outside IT)	0.40	0.67	0.87	1.32

Source: Authors' computations.
a. Sum of positive (only) industry MFP growth, from table 2-6.

One might think of column 3 as the answer to the question "Has there been any *net* MFP growth outside the IT sector?" But if one really wants to determine whether there has been *any* MFP growth outside the IT sector, then the starting point should be the sum of all the industries having positive MFP growth. This is shown in the last column of table 2-8. Positive MFP growth in industries outside the IT-producing sector contributes three times as much to the total as MFP growth in the IT industries, using our measure of IT MFP growth, and twice as much as the IT contribution using Oliner and Sichel's IT estimate. By any measure of MFP in IT production, MFP growth outside IT production is substantial, and it exceeds the contribution of IT production to MFP.

There is no necessary conflict between our finding of substantial MFP growth in services industries and the finding of high MFP growth in the IT-producing industries. The misinterpretation arises because some researchers, observing a large MFP contribution from the production of IT, have concluded incorrectly that there can be no other similar contributions of equal size from other industries. Jorgenson, Ho, and Stiroh (2002) make the same point: The "conclusion . . . that all productivity growth originates in these two IT-producing industries . . . would be highly misleading, since the sum of the contributions of . . . agriculture and wholesale trade . . . also exhaust productivity growth for the economy as a whole."[24]

Reconciliation

Two major alternatives to our study are the macro study by Oliner and Sichel (2002) and the industry study by Jorgenson, Ho, and Stiroh (2002). With respect to the contributions of IT capital deepening and of MFP in the IT-producing industries, Gordon's influential study relies on the estimates of Oliner and Sichel (O&S), though he also buttresses them with independent calculations of his own (Gordon 2002). Accordingly, we focus on the O&S and the Jorgenson, Ho, and Stiroh (JH&S) studies, since our analysis of Oliner and Sichel also applies to Gordon's estimates.

Our study differs from the others in its output measure and its labor input measure, both of which are tied to our use of the BEA industry database. As already described, the O&S study relies on the BLS output measure (from the expenditure side of the accounts), which means that their output measure grows less rapidly after 1995 than our income-side measure. Other things being equal, the income side gives more labor productivity after 1995 and more MFP growth. The benchmark revision to GDP that was released in December 2003 raised the product-side estimate more than the income-side estimate; if that carries over to the private nonfarm estimates, it implies that our product-side productivity measure is better. Jorgenson, Ho, and Stiroh (2002) use a wider definition of output (including both government and household sectors) than that employed in our study or by Oliner and Sichel. It grows somewhat more slowly, implying less MFP growth, other things being equal (partly because the way government output is measured ensures low productivity growth in the government sector).

In addition, the labor input in our study does not include a labor quality adjustment, and it is based on employment rather than hours. When labor quality is growing, we record it as MFP growth, because the contribution of the mismeasured input falls into MFP.[25]

All studies estimate capital deepening and distinguish IT capital deepening from improvements in the non-IT capital-labor ratio. The estimates of capital deepening and IT capital deepening in Jorgenson, Ho, and Stiroh are by far the

---

24. Jorgenson, Ho, and Stiroh (2002, p. 43).

25. As noted earlier, the differences in output measures and labor measures coincidentally offset each other after 1995 (but not before 1995), so labor productivity is similar in the two data sets after 1995.

largest, mainly because of their different output concept (the growth in IT capital services in the household "industry" after 1995 is the largest of any industry). Our estimate of IT capital deepening in the 1995–2001 period, 0.85 in table 2-7, is slightly smaller than the 1.02 percentage points of contribution obtained by Oliner and Sichel. We do not know why, but this is not a major factor in the comparisons.[26] More capital deepening, of course, diminishes their aggregate MFP estimate relative to ours.

Putting all this together, these three factors—difference in output measure, difference in estimates of IT capital deepening, and our omission of labor quality—cause our aggregate MFP estimate, 1.44 in table 2-5, to exceed that of Oliner and Sichel by 0.45 percentage point after 1995.[27] Our MFP estimate is more than twice that of Jorgenson, Ho, and Stiroh, mostly because of the effects of including the household and government sectors in their estimates.

MFP in High-Tech Industries

The remaining point to consider is our smaller estimates of MFP in the IT-producing industries compared with the O&S estimate, which is also relied on by Gordon. We do not actually estimate MFP at the level of the computer, communications equipment, and semiconductor industries (which are three- and four-digit SIC classifications) because we work with two-digit industry detail. However, the IT data used in other studies are embedded in two of our two-digit industries.

In the old U.S. industry classification system (SIC 1987), computer production was located in SIC 35 (industrial machinery) and semiconductors and communications equipment were located in SIC 36 (electronic and electrical machinery). The old SIC system combined computers with drill bits and semiconductors with Christmas tree lights. This means that the electronics-producing industries, which are of major interest in analyzing the post-1995 economy, are buried within broad industrial categories that have little to do with electronics, the new economy, or high technology. The BEA industry database is still constructed around SIC 1987 (which is far more than fifteen years out of date) because BLS, the laggard among the statistical agencies, is just beginning to convert its statistical series to the new NAICS classification system, which has an electronics sector.

26. We are both using the data on capital services from BLS, and our two non-IT capital deepening estimates are the same.

27. In addition, our estimate is computed from trend rates of change and that of Oliner and Sichel from end-period average annual rates, which will differ to an extent because 2001 was a recession year.

Table 2-9. *Estimates of MFP for Computers, Semiconductors,*
and Other Machinery, 1995–2000[a]
Average annual rate of change

Industry	JHS (1995–2000)			This study (1995–2000)	
	Domar weight	MFP growth	Output growth	MFP growth	Output growth
1. Industrial machinery, except computers	0.034	0.23	3.88	n.a.	1.1
2. Computers	0.012	16.75	31.5	n.a.	34.4
3. Total, industrial machinery	0.046	4.40	n.a.	4.19	9.4
4. Other electrical machinery	0.017	0.93	3.56	n.a.	0.4
5. Communications equipment	0.007	–0.38	14.52	n.a.	18.8
6. Electrical components (including semiconductors)	0.011	18.00	28.65	n.a.	34.0
7. Total, electrical machinery	0.035	5.66	n.a.	n.a.	18.0
8. Total, electrical machinery and instruments	n.a.	n.a.	n.a.	4.68	13.2

Sources: Lines 1, 2, 4, 5 and 6: Jorgenson, Ho, and Stiroh (2002), table 18. Lines 3 and 7: computed by the authors, using sum of the Domar weights to define the two-digit industry total. This study: computed as the average annual rate of change over the period 1995–2000. Note that the values differ from the least squares trends of table A-1, which are for 1995–2001.

a. This study, compared with Jorgenson, Ho, and Stiroh (2002).

Jorgenson, Ho, and Stiroh (2002) have extracted the lower-level IT-producing industries from their concealment within the non–high-tech sectors. We have aggregated their MFP estimates to produce two-digit machinery industry estimates comparable with our own (table 2-9). The table also compares output growth rates for relevant categories. As table 2-9 shows, the MFP rate for the industrial machinery industry implied by Jorgenson, Ho, and Stiroh (4.4 percent a year) is two-tenths of a point greater than ours for the same 1995–2000 interval. The Census Bureau shipments data that underlie the BEA industry data show that computer output growth in our data and in the JH&S data are quite comparable, at more than 30 percent a year (ours is slightly more rapid). In both data sets, nearly all the growth in industrial machinery between 1995 and 2000 was in computers. Indeed, Jorgenson, Ho, and Stiroh record very little MFP growth for noncomputer industrial machinery. Our MFP estimate for industrial machinery thus incorporates the rapid growth in computer output that appears in the JH&S data, and our contribution to MFP from this two-digit industry (in table 2-7) also incorporates the computer MFP that is explicitly estimated in Jorgenson, Ho, and Stiroh.

Jorgenson, Ho, and Stiroh's implied MFP rate for the electrical machinery industry, at 5.7 percent, is about a point higher than ours (4.7 percent). However, we combined instruments (SIC 38) with electrical machinery (SIC 36) because of changes in the SIC classifications in the 1980s (Jorgenson, Ho, and Stiroh combined instruments with miscellaneous manufacturing). Because the Census Bureau shipments data show that the output of the instrument industry grew more slowly than did the output of the electrical machinery industry (see line 7 of table 2-9), the inclusion of instruments probably reduces the MFP of our sector. Note that the output of communications equipment and semiconductors in BEA data corresponds fairly closely with JH&S output data (the BEA growth is actually a little larger). Of course, these high-tech sectors far outstripped in output growth the other types of electrical equipment, in both data sets.

Thus the output of each of the three high-tech manufacturing industries (computers, semiconductors, and communications equipment) grows slightly faster using our data than the JH&S data set. Their MFP estimates for two-digit high-tech goods-producing industries are somewhat larger than our estimates, but not by a great amount. From this, we conclude that our estimate for the contribution of industrial and electrical machinery to MFP (0.51—see table 2-8) is consistent with the very rapid MFP growth in IT production estimated by Jorgenson, Ho, and Stiroh and with their estimate of the (narrower) IT-producing sector's contribution (0.41 point for 1995–2000, as reported in their table 2) to total MFP growth.

We next need to ask whether our and the JH&S industry MFP estimates for IT production are consistent with the indirect IT estimate of macro-oriented studies. Two indirect approaches have been used. Baily and Lawrence recalculated constant price GDP with IT deflators set to the same rate of price change as the other components of GDP (rather than falling 20 to 30 percent a year, as do the national accounts IT deflators) and compared the results with constant price GDP as estimated by BEA (Baily and Lawrence 2001; see also Baily 2002). This is equivalent to estimating IT MFP by the ratio of the decline in IT prices to other prices.

Oliner and Sichel (2002) do this more explicitly: they infer relative MFP in IT-producing industries (they identify computers, communications equipment, software, and semiconductors) by the ratio of the respective IT prices to the prices of non-IT sectors—that is, $MFP_i / MFP_j = (P_i / P_j) - C$, where C is an index of other input prices and all symbols should be interpreted as rates of change. They then calculate the MFP contribution from, for example, comput-ers by applying Domar weights to this MFP number.[28] Gordon (2002) uses the Oliner-Sichel results.[29]

The major alternative is, accordingly, the IT MFP growth estimate of Oliner and Sichel (2002). We think that their indirect estimate is imprecise and inferior to estimating MFP for high-tech production directly at the industry level. How-ever, they may also use somewhat better deflators for semiconductors.

Oliner and Sichel rely on the "dual" productivity estimation procedure for "high-tech" products in Triplett (1996a). The innovation in Triplett is not the dual procedure itself, because using that procedure to estimate productivity (that is, using input and output price indexes to estimate productivity change) dates back at least to Copeland and Martin (1938). Rather, the innovation might be called "one-price dual" estimation: in a chain of user-supplier indus-tries, Triplett estimated MFP change in the computer industry from only the price index for semiconductors as an input to the computer industry and the price index for the output of computers. Other input prices to computers, semi-conductors, and semiconductor manufacturing equipment industries (for exam-ple, wages and energy costs) were assumed to be dominated by national forces outside the three industries. Put another way, whatever differences existed in price movements for nontechnological inputs to these three industries, *they were minor in comparison with changes in semiconductor and computer prices*, which were falling at prodigious rates, on the order of 20 to 30 percent a year. Other input prices therefore could be neglected, because the error from neglecting them would be small.[30]

Oliner and Sichel apply Triplett's one-price dual method to industries that relate, not as links in a vertical supply chain but horizontally. That has some appeal: the relative price change in computers must be related to overall price change, as is the relative MFP change in computer production to aggregate MFP. But the assumption that other input prices move together and can be ne-

28. The contribution of IT is computed from table 1 of Oliner and Sichel (2002).

29. In addition, Gordon's nonfarm MFP growth incorporated a cyclical correction that made it smaller than the growth rate that others had estimated, and because he did not remove any cyclical component from manufacturing durables, durables made up more of the MFP total than they otherwise would. Gordon's cyclical correction has been controversial, but his cyclically cor-rected estimate of post-1995 labor productivity growth agrees exactly with our estimated trend (2.46 percent a year). We estimated the trend from data that included the recession year 2001, which Gordon of course did not have when he made his original trend estimate. See our table 2-5 and Gordon (2002), table 3.2, line 3.

30. Triplett shows that the procedure is very sensitive to input shares, but that is not the is-sue here.

Table 2-10. *Post-1995 MFP Estimates, IT-Producing Industries*
Average annual rate of change

Study	Computers	Communications equipment	Semi-conductors	Software
Jorgenson, Ho, and Stiroh				
MFP	16.75	–0.38	18.00[a]	–2.79[b]
Contribution	0.16	0.01	0.12[a]	–0.01[b]
Domar weight	0.012	0.007	0.011[a]	0.013[b]
Oliner and Sichel				
MFP	14.0	2.5	45.2	4.3
Contribution	0.19	0.05	0.42	0.11
Domar weight	0.0132	0.0183	0.0091	0.027

Sources: Computed by the authors from Jorgenson, Ho, and Stiroh (2002) and Oliner and Sichel (2002).
a. Electronic components.
b. Computer services.

glected is more tenuous the more remote the industries for which the calculation is done and the greater the difference in their input mixes.

In table 2-10, we compare the MFP estimates, Domar weights, and contributions to aggregate MFP for computers, semiconductors, and communication equipment from Oliner and Sichel and Jorgenson, Ho, and Stiroh. For computers, both MFP estimates and Domar weights (and therefore contributions) are similar in both studies.[31] However, for communications equipment and software, Oliner and Sichel's contributions are positive and so swell IT MFP, whereas those of Jorgenson, Ho, and Stiroh are negative and shrink it. Oliner and Sichel's estimate for semiconductor MFP is very large, so their contribution from semiconductors is 3.5 times that of Jorgenson, Ho, and Stiroh. For semiconductors, Oliner and Sichel use unpublished deflators from the industrial production index (see Aizcorbe, Flamm, and Khurshid 2002) that decline more rapidly[32] and that therefore would yield more MFP in semiconductor manufacturing.

In sum, the O&S estimate of the contribution of MFP in computer production is close to the industry estimate, despite their indirect method. However, they find far greater MFP in production of semiconductors, communications

31. The greater output in the numerator of Jorgenson, Ho, and Stiroh's MFP is balanced by the rapid growth of household IT.
32. Communication with Daniel Sichel, in late 2003.

equipment, and software than is evident in the industry data. A portion of this difference appears consistent with the concerns we expressed above about the accuracy of the indirect method. Another portion stems from more rapidly declining semiconductor deflators. In all, this suggests that the O&S estimate that IT MFP accounted for three-fourths of the total is somewhat too high, as it is also in Gordon (2002), who depends on the O&S research; however, to the extent that it arises because of their use of better semiconductor deflators, the O&S estimate is preferable.

Conclusion

There is more acceleration in our measure of the private, nonfarm business economy than is present in other studies (therefore we have more "room" in our income-side measure for contributions from both IT-producing and services industries). In addition, our omission of labor quality from the input side swells our aggregate MFP, again producing more room for MFP in the services industries. Within that aggregate MFP measure, our estimates of industry MFP are consistent with the rapid growth in IT MFP (and therefore in durable goods manufacturing) that has emerged in the JH&S industry study but perhaps somewhat lower than the O&S estimate.

However, despite the large contribution of IT production to aggregate MFP, it is also true that net MFP in the goods-producing industries has not grown. Net MFP growth in the services industries, on the other hand, has been a strong contributor to recent economic growth.

Discussion of Productivity Trends and Measurement Issues in Services Industries

The last decade has been an exciting time for productivity analysts. After more than twenty years of relatively slow productivity growth, the U.S. economy suddenly reversed course in 1995 and productivity accelerated substantially. This allowed economists to turn from the decidedly dismal task of explaining the productivity slowdown to the much more appealing job of explaining the productivity revival. Given the issue's importance, potential answers poured in: fundamental technological progress in the production of information technology, capital deepening related to information technology use, cyclical effects, changes to workplace practices and firm organization, and competitive forces driven by deregulation and globalization all were nominated as possible causes.

The work of Barry Bosworth and Jack Triplett has been in the middle of this research debate, and this chapter uses detailed, industry-level data to address several basic questions surrounding the resurgence of U.S. productivity growth. Where, precisely, did the productivity growth originate? How important was the formerly moribund services sector? What role did the production and use of information technology (IT) play? And, finally, how reliable are the industry data? This note briefly reviews the main findings of the Triplett and Bosworth study on industry productivity and raises several caveats and issues about their interpretation and conclusions.

Primary Findings

The U.S. productivity revival began after 1995, when both labor productivity (LP) and multifactor productivity (MFP) showed substantial acceleration. To better understand this phenomenon, Triplett and Bosworth combined detailed output and labor data from the Bureau of Economic Analysis with capital services data from the Bureau of Labor Statistics to generate estimates of industry-level LP and MFP growth. They report estimates for the twenty-nine services-producing industries and twenty-five goods-producing industries that constitute the U.S. economy with the primary goals of tracing the aggregate gains back to industry sources and identifying the industries that drove the aggregate productivity revival.

The most important conclusion is that the services-producing industries— defined broadly to include transportation, communications, trade, finance, and other services industries—saw much more dramatic productivity gains after 1995 than the goods-producing industries. In terms of LP growth, the services-producing industries showed an increase from 0.7 percent for 1987–95 to 2.6 percent for 1995–2001, while the goods-producing industries showed an increase from 1.8 percent for 1987–95 to 2.3 percent for 1995–2001.[33] For MFP growth for the same periods, the growth rates increased from 0.3 percent to 1.5 percent for services-producing industries and from 1.2 percent to 1.3 percent for goods-producing industries, respectively.

Within each set of industries, however, there is considerable heterogeneity: some industries in each broad sector show acceleration in LP or MFP, while others show deceleration. Related to this heterogeneity, Triplett and Bosworth show that LP and MFP gains were not found solely in the relatively small portion of the U.S. economy that produces high-tech IT assets, but rather spread throughout both the services-producing and the goods-producing industries. The clear implication is that looking simply at the aggregate data can hide important information about the underlying origins and fundamental causes of the U.S. productivity revival.

Issues

This section raises several issues relating to the estimation and interpretation of the results reported by Triplett and Bosworth. In particular, I discuss the relative importance of the services-producing industries, the role of industry hetero-

---

33. All growth rates are for average annual growth estimated using the trend growth rates.

geneity and the contributions of particular industries, and the implications and interpretation of the negative productivity growth reported for some industries.

Importance of Services

One of the authors' consistent themes is that the services-producing industries are the force driving the U.S. productivity gains. For example, they report that services-producing industries accounted for 73 percent of the LP growth after 1995, 76 percent of the MFP growth after 1995, and 80 percent of the IT capital-deepening contribution. The services-producing industries, however, produced about three-quarters of output and accounted for nearly three-quarters of employment in this period, so this is not particularly surprising.

It is only when one examines the post-1995 productivity acceleration that it appears that these industries made a disproportionate contribution. In fact, the authors estimate that the services-producing industries account for all of the net gains in both LP and MFP when 1987–95 is compared to 1995–2001. However, this partially reflects the relatively large size of the services-producing industries, and there is less systematic difference when looks at a "typical" services-producing and goods-producing industry. For example, eighteen of the twenty-nine services-producing industries (62 percent) showed LP gains after 1995, while fourteen of twenty-five goods-producing industries (56 percent) did. For MFP, the services-producing industries do better, with seventeen of the twenty-nine industries (58 percent) showing gains after 1995, compared with only eleven of twenty-five (44 percent) goods-producing industries (appendix table A-1). While this type of comparison raises some questions about the specifics, it is nonetheless clear that services-producing industries have emerged from their productivity slowdown to play a substantial role in the revival of aggregate U.S. productivity.

Heterogeneity and Industry Contributions

A second consistent theme is the importance of recognizing heterogeneity across industries, and Triplett and Bosworth document a wide divergence in both LP and MFP growth rates. For the twenty-nine services-producing industries, for example, they report a range of trend LP growth for 1995–2001 from –1.7 percent for insurance carriers to 10.3 percent for security and commodity brokers. Similar variation exists for MFP growth, as well as within the goods-producing industries.

From a microeconomic perspective, this variation reflects basic differences across industries in the ability to make new investments and apply new technologies, in the regulatory environment, and in the structure, competition, and organization of the industry. From a macroeconomic perspective, the key point is that aggregate productivity estimates, which are in some sense "net" numbers that may reflect offsetting contributions of different industries, cannot tell the whole story. In a world with positive and negative growth rates for different industries, one can only get a clear picture of the underlying sources of productivity gains by moving beneath the aggregate data and examining the evolution of productivity on an industry-by-industry basis.

A related point is that aggregate productivity data reflect two distinct types of forces—the direct contribution of particular industries and the reallocation of production inputs as they move between industries. These reallocations are real economic forces that reflect the gains to society as inputs are successfully transferred from low- to high-productivity activities. Triplett and Bosworth emphasize that any attempt to isolate the contribution of a particular industry or set of industries—for example, the IT-producing industries—will leave a net remainder that includes the contributions of other industries as well as these reallocation terms. For short periods, the reallocation terms may be quite large and therefore will provide a misleading view of the relative importance of the remaining industries.

Negative Productivity Growth

A final issue that has troubled some productivity analysts recently is the observation that certain industries have shown measured productivity growth that is negative, often for long periods of time. One potential explanation is that output growth and therefore productivity growth are systematically mismeasured and biased downward.

In their analysis, the authors identify six industries (education, amusement and recreation, hotels, insurance carriers, local transit, and construction) with negative LP for 1995–2001 and suggest that measurement problems may play a role here. To be clear, they do not argue that negative productivity is impossible and that it is entirely a reflection of measurement error, but rather that one should use such information as a starting point for a detailed examination of industry-specific trends, data issues, and conceptual or statistical problems. This seems totally reasonable, and the Brookings economic measurement workshops, organized by Bosworth and Triplett and summarized in other chapters in this volume, have shown it to be enormously fruitful work.

One difficulty, however, is that this signal does not appear particularly robust. Of the six industries identified by the authors as showing negative LP growth for 1995–2001, only three (insurance carriers, construction, and local transit) also had negative LP growth for 1987–95. Moreover, there are another seven industries (air transportation, printing, lumber, health, pipelines, other services, and insurance agents) that posted negative LP growth for 1987–95 but positive LP growth for 1995–2001 (appendix table A-1). This type of variation would require a very specific pattern of measurement error, and it suggests that additional factors are at work.

An alternative method for evaluating measurement problems would be to develop ex ante objective indicators of industries in which systematic mismeasurement is most probable. These indicators would likely be informed by data collection issues and statistical agencies' observations and could then be compared with observed productivity growth rates. While a difficult task, it would prevent the somewhat circular solution of identifying productivity mismeasurement by low measured productivity.

Conclusions

The U.S. productivity revival has renewed interest in the sources of U.S. economic growth and returned attention to the fundamental importance of understanding the evolution of productivity at a more disaggregated level. Only by moving beneath the aggregate data and identifying those industries that have shown the largest productivity gains and declines can analysts begin to understand the dynamic economic forces and policies that are driving the economy. For example, the main conclusion of Triplett and Bosworth, that the services-producing industries are driving the U.S. productivity revival, is apparent only with detailed industry-level data like those compiled and analyzed in chapter 2.

One critical question lingers, however. If services-producing industries were largely responsible for the post-1973 productivity slowdown, as argued by Griliches (1994), and if services-producing industries drove the post-1995 productivity revival, as documented here, one is left with a key question: Why does services-sector productivity growth fluctuate so wildly? Put another way, what economic, technological, or policy factors cause productivity growth to be more stable in the goods-producing industries than in the services-producing industries? With the facts established by this book and others, productivity analysts must now turn to this challenging question.

CHAPTER THREE

Output and Productivity in the Transportation Sector

The transportation sector has been of considerable interest in productivity research. Major portions of the sector were long subject to regulation, which resulted in the collection of a wealth of data on their operations. More recently, much of the industry has been deregulated and economists have been very interested in the impact of that change on the efficiency of its three major components—rail, truck, and air transport.[1] Here we examine the nature of productivity change in the transportation industry as revealed by the existing data. What are the patterns of change in labor productivity and multifactor productivity? What can we infer about the quality of the statistics that underlie those patterns? We also compare the measures of output and productivity change produced by the industry programs of the Bureau of Economic Analysis (BEA) and the Bureau of Labor Statistics (BLS).

Overview

The transportation sector represented 3.3 percent of GDP in 2001. Its share has steadily declined from about 5 percent in the 1950s, but it appeared to stabilize over the 1990s. The industry composition of nominal output (total revenue),

---

1. For a prior examination of productivity in the transportation industry that includes an extensive bibliography, see Gordon (1992). This chapter illustrates the changes in the statistical measures that have occurred since the Gordon study.

Table 3-1. *Composition of the Transportation Sector, 1999*

Category	Gross output[a]	Value added[a]	Intermediate purchases[a]	Employment[b]
Total transportation	603.0	306.1	296.9	4.6
Composition[c]				
Railroads	7.1	8.4	5.8	4.1
Local and interurban passenger transit	4.9	6.2	3.6	11.2
Trucking and warehousing	47.2	41.2	53.4	44.1
Water transportation	7.5	5.1	10.0	4.2
Air transportation	23.4	26.2	20.4	26.0
Pipelines (except natural gas)	1.3	2.1	0.6	0.3
Transportation services	8.6	10.7	6.4	10.1

Source: BEA industry data set.
a. Billions of dollars.
b. Millions of workers.
c. Percent.

value added, purchase of intermediate materials, and employment in 2001 is summarized in table 3-1.[2] The three industries that are examined in more detail (railroads, trucking, and airlines) account for three-quarters of the sector as measured by both value added and employment.

One important limitation of the BEA data set is that the measures of the nominal value of gross output (revenues) extend back only to 1977 (or in a few cases to 1987) and the estimates of both real gross output and real value added begin in 1977 or later. This is a significant limitation for any analysis of the behavior of the transportation industry before and immediately after the global productivity slowdown of the early 1970s, and the BEA data do not provide much of a historical reference period prior to the deregulation of the late 1970s. Historical information on output and labor productivity over a longer time span is available from the industry productivity program of BLS for specific components of these industries (line-haul railroads, long-distance trucking, and airlines.) However, with the changeover to NAICS (North American Industry Classification System), their current data also are limited to the post-1987 period.[3]

2. In its industry accounts, BEA refers to value added as gross product. To avoid confusing gross product and gross output, we will normally refer to the former as value added.
3. Most recently, the industry productivity program has produced a multifactor productivity measure for the large scheduled-service airlines, but its more general focus is on labor productivity and unit labor costs.

Summary measures of the growth in labor productivity and multifactor productivity (MFP) are reported in table 3-2.[4] The table includes indexes of productivity based on both the gross output and value added estimates of BEA and a comparable gross output measure from the BLS. The top portion of the table shows the growth in the real value of gross output and value added of the BEA and the output measure of the BLS for railroad, trucking, and air transport. The BLS measures of output and employment reflect significant differences in industry coverage that will be explained later.

In the decade following the passage of the Staggers Rail Act of 1980, the railroad industry achieved very large gains in labor productivity. Sharply reduced regulation allowed the railroads to abandon unprofitable lines and eliminate excess staff. However, the railroad industry's rate of growth in all three measures of labor productivity declined, and as a result, it did not contribute to the acceleration of productivity growth after 1995. The estimate of multifactor productivity, shown near the bottom of the table, accounts for more than half of the growth in labor productivity and also indicates a substantial deceleration after 1995. The contributions of intermediate inputs and capital services are both relatively small. There is some increase in capital intensity, but the larger gains are from increased purchased inputs per worker—perhaps reflecting more outsourcing.

The trucking industry shows less convincing evidence of productivity gains from deregulation. The growth in labor productivity is particularly low for the BEA concept based on value added because of a decline in the value added share of output during the 1980s. The BLS measure, which is limited to interstate trucking, shows a higher rate of productivity increase after 1980, but both the BEA and BLS productivity measures show a deceleration of growth in labor productivity after 1995. Both BEA output concepts imply very modest rates of growth in multifactor productivity, and that growth turned negative in the post-1995 period. Further, it appears that most of the gain in labor productivity was the result of substitution of purchased inputs. There is only a minor increase in capital intensity over the 1977–2001 period.

The airline industry has had very strong output growth over the past quarter-century, but its rate of growth in labor productivity has been much less than that of railroads and comparable to that of trucking. There is a sharp post-1995 drop in labor productivity growth, which in the BEA measure is largely due to the collapse of air travel in 2001, but it stretches over more years in the BLS

4. The calculation of MFP is explained in chapter 2. It is a Tornqvist index in which the factor income shares are from the BLS and are adjusted to reflect the capital and labor income of self-employed workers. The index of capital services is provided by the productivity division of BLS, based on the capital stock estimates of BEA. The output and employment measures are those of BEA.

data. The BEA data also show substantial swings in the purchase of intermediate inputs, but there is little or no contribution from an increase in capital intensity. The poor performance of productivity in recent years seems surprising in view of the trend toward larger aircraft and high rates of capacity utilization. However, capital intensity may be understated, because a significant share of commercial aircraft is leased from financial institutions and business services firms. Those inputs would appear as purchased services (intermediate inputs) rather than own capital. However, the gross output measure actually shows an increase in MFP in excess of labor productivity in 1987–95, implying a negative contribution from the substitution of the other factors for labor.

In the following sections, the methodologies used by BEA and BLS to generate the above estimates are examined in more detail. Since the BLS program estimates multifactor productivity only for airlines, the comparison is limited to the procedures used to compute estimates of nominal and real gross output and the measures of employment.

Railroad Industry

The railroad industry achieved dramatic improvements in productivity after 1980, and many of those gains appear to be a response to deregulation. That was not unexpected; in earlier years political pressures on the regulators led to the continuing uneconomic operation of large portions of the rail network. As mentioned above, labor productivity in the years after deregulation, as measured by either BEA or BLS, soared. Yet, at least since 1992, the two agencies have used quite different methods to estimate output growth, resulting in a significant difference in their estimates of the growth in labor productivity. For the 1995–2001 period, BEA reports a 2.6 percent annual rate of growth in output per worker, while the BLS reports a rate of 3.6 percent (table 3-2).

Since the railroad industry has long been subject to regulation and is dominated by a very small number of companies, the data required to construct measures of productivity are relatively complete. Furthermore, coverage differences between the BEA and BLS data for railroads are quite small. The BEA includes all of SIC 40, which is composed of two industry groups: 4011 (line-haul operations) and 4013 (switching and terminal establishments). The BLS limits its analysis to SIC 4011. The BLS and BEA estimates of employment are very similar, and although the BLS measures labor input in terms of hours, the differences in labor productivity are dominated by methodological differences in the construction of their measures of real output.

The method used by BLS to estimate output is quite straightforward. It divides the industry's activities between freight and passenger operations and

Table 3-2. *Comparison of Alternative Measures of Output and Productivity Growth in the Transportation Sector*
Average annual percent change

Measure	Railroads			Trucking			Air transportation		
	1977–87	1987–95	1995–2001	1977–87	1987–95	1995–2001	1977–87	1987–95	1995–2001
Output									
BEA output	1.6	3.6	0.3	3.8	5.7	2.9	8.3	3.6	3.3
BEA value added	2.7	3.0	1.6	2.5	3.6	2.3	7.0	8.1	3.7
BLS	0.4	3.0	1.6	-0.6	3.7	3.1	7.4	3.4	2.9
Employment									
BEA	-6.2	-2.8	-2.2	1.9	2.2	2.4	4.5	3.5	3.1
BLS	-6.0	-3.0	-1.9	-3.8	0.9	1.6	3.1	1.3	3.5
Labor productivity									
BEA output	8.3	6.5	2.6	1.9	3.4	0.5	3.6	0.0	0.2
BEA value added	9.5	5.9	4.0	0.5	1.3	-0.1	2.4	4.4	0.5
BLS	6.7	6.2	3.6	3.4	2.8	1.5	4.1	2.0	-0.6
Contributions of									
Capital per worker	1.1	0.3	0.3	0.2	0.0	0.2	-0.0	-0.2	0.7
Intermediate inputs	1.8	2.9	0.4	1.6	2.9	0.6	2.5	-2.3	-0.2
Multifactor productivity									
BEA output	5.3	3.3	1.9	0.1	0.5	-0.2	1.1	2.6	-0.4
BEA value added	7.7	5.5	3.3	0.3	1.3	-0.5	2.5	4.7	-0.7

Source: Authors' calculations based on BEA and BLS industry data sets. Calculation of the contributions of capital and intermediate inputs are based on the BEA gross output measure.

uses total ton-miles as the basic measure of real output growth in the freight component. However, BLS adjusts the index for shifts in the commodity mix. Because of a shift toward lower-value freight, the adjusted index grew at a 1.6 percent annual rate in the 1977–2001 period; in comparison, the unadjusted index grew at a rate of 2.5 percent. The BLS overall index is a Tornqvist aggregation of the passenger and freight revenue miles using operating expense weights.[5]

In constructing its estimates of nominal gross output and value added, the BEA begins with a focus on the benchmark years for which it has constructed input-output (I-O) tables. Those tables in turn depend heavily on information collected in the five-year economic censuses. Various interpolators are then used to obtain estimates for the years between benchmarks and to extrapolate beyond the last benchmark year, currently 1992. The BEA approach is designed to provide complete coverage of the economy in a format that can be integrated with the national accounts. However, although the benchmark I-O tables are the primary input for the estimates of industry gross output, value added is not constrained to match the estimates from the I-O tables. Instead, the value added estimates are tied into the income side of the national accounts.[6] Thus the nominal value of intermediate inputs is obtained by subtraction, and their composition is largely based on information from the I-O tables. Quantity indexes of gross output and intermediate inputs are then used to obtain an estimate of the real value of value added. The comprehensive structure of the BEA estimates often requires rather heroic assumptions to cover gaps in information.[7]

The basic procedure used by BEA to estimate freight output is summarized in table 3-3. The first line shows the estimate of nominal gross output for each of the benchmark years, beginning in 1977. It is estimated largely from the same sources used to put together the benchmark I-O tables. The second line is total operating revenues of class I railroads as reported by the Association of American Railroads (AAR). The ratio of these two series is interpolated between benchmark years and used to compute an annual measure of the nominal value of gross output. Thus between 1977 and 1992, the BEA measure of nominal freight output grows 12 percent faster than revenues reported by the AAR, and

5. Passenger travel represents only 8 percent of total costs, and it is only 3 percent of revenues in the BEA index.

6. Obviously, it would be desirable for the national accounts, industry gross product, and the I-O tables to be fully consistent with one another, but that goal is still hampered by data limitations (Yuskavage 2000).

7. An alternative data set on industry gross output that covers a longer time span has been used at the BLS to analyze trends in MFP. An example of those results is provided by Gullickson and Harper (1999).

Table 3-3. *Derivation of Nominal Output of Railroads*

Category	Benchmark years			
	1977	*1982*	*1987*	*1992*
Freight[a]				
Benchmark gross output (BEA)	20,767	28,338	29,029	32,769
Total revenue (AAR)	20,090	27,504	26,622	28,349
Passenger[a]				
Benchmark gross output (BEA)	622	918	1,096	1,226
Total revenue (Amtrak)	415	631	974	1,325
Adjustment ratio[b]				
Freight	1.00	1.00	1.05	1.12
Passenger	1.00	0.97	0.75	0.62

Source: Authors' calculations based on data provided by the Bureau of Economic Analysis.
a. Millions of dollars.
b. 1977 = 1.0.

after 1992 the two measures are assumed to move in parallel. A similar calculation is made for passenger output using operating revenues of Amtrak as the interpolator. However, in this case the benchmark series declines relative to the interpolator, as Amtrak absorbs the passenger operations of other railroads.

For the years before 1992, freight and passenger revenues, together with indexes of ton-miles and passenger miles, are used to compute implicit price deflators that are applied to the BEA measures of nominal gross output to create the indexes of real gross output. The ton-mile measure, however, is not adjusted for changes in the commodity mix, as is done by BLS. Using a combination of the benchmark adjustment of nominal revenues and an unadjusted index of ton-miles leads to an output growth rate in the freight component of the BEA series of 2.2 percent a year over the 1977–92 period, compared with a rate of only 1 percent for the BLS.

Beginning in 1992, however, the BEA made a major change in its methodology when it switched to using the producer price index of BLS to compute an output price deflator.[8] The use of the PPI implies a much slower rate of real output growth than would have resulted from the use of the index of ton-miles. For

8. The shift from physical volume measures of output to greater reliance on price indexes to deflate nominal revenues in a major shift in the BEA methodology for measuring many industries, such as transportation and communications. A discussion of the choice between physical output measures and price indexes is provided in Baily and Zitzewitz (2001).

Figure 3-1. *Alternative Price Indexes for Railroad Output*

Index[a]

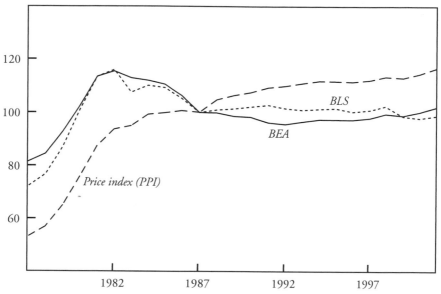

Source: The price index is for haul railroads (SIC 4011) from the producer price index. The BEA and BLS indexes are both implicit deflators computed by dividing an index of nominal output by an index of real output.
a. 1987 = 100.

example, in the 1992–2001 period, output as measured under the new procedure rose at an annual rate of 1.5 percent, compared with 3.5 percent for an index based on ton-miles and passenger miles, cutting the growth rate by more than half.

The importance of the change in the BEA's methodology is highlighted in figure 3-1. Although the PPI is only used to compute the real output index after 1992, it extends back to 1969. It is evident that there was a large discrepancy in the early 1980s between the estimated rate of price increase as reported in the PPI and the implicit deflators based on freight revenue per ton-mile. In the period immediately after deregulation, revenue per ton-mile declined dramatically while the PPI for rail freight continued to rise. For the longer period of 1977–92, revenues per adjusted ton-mile rose by only 28 percent, compared with the 107 percent reported in the PPI—a very large discrepancy. If BEA had employed the PPI index over the full 1977–92 period, its measure of real output growth would have decreased from a 40 percent gain to a gain of only 15 percent. The differences are much less significant after 1992, but the PPI reports an average annual rate of increase between 1992 and 2001 of 0.7 percent, whereas the BLS adjusted measure of revenue per ton-mile shows a decline of 0.6 percent a year.

Why are the differences so large? Since deregulation, both the railroad and trucking industries have faced new competition, which has substantially shifted the composition of the freight services that each provides. Those changes are underrepresented in a Laspeyres index such as the PPI, for which the weights are updated infrequently. The sample for the PPI was altered in 1984 when BLS moved away from the use of waybill statistics, but it remained unchanged until 1996.[9]

With deregulation, the railroads were free to adjust rates to bring them more in line with costs. The result was a major change in the structure of rates across commodities, with lower rates for bulk products, such as coal, whose rail costs were low, and rate increases for those services for which the previous rate system in effect required subsidies (Winston and others 1990). Consequently, there was a large increase in the share of freight traffic composed of commodities for which the rates were reduced.

In addition, some of the rate changes were introduced as new services; therefore the PPI would not capture the initial rate reduction, though it would track future changes. For example, following deregulation and the merger of railroads, there was a doubling of the share of traffic accounted for by unit train services between central collection and distribution points. There was an equally dramatic expansion of intermodal shipments of trailers and containers, which doubled between 1980 and 1990 (Association of American Railroads 2003).

Finally, in the BLS sample a significant number of the rates quoted were for moving a particular commodity between two specific geographic locations, a service that no longer existed after deregulation. In those cases, the carriers were asked to estimate what the rate would be if the service existed. In a world of growing reliance on long-term contracts with volume and other discounts, it is not evident that the quotes reflected actual transaction prices.[10]

9. Normally the producer price indexes would be reweighted on a five-year cycle following the economic census, but the Census Bureau does not collect detailed product information for railroads, and the weights are drawn from trade association sources.

10. Our examination of the sources of difference between the PPI and the measure of revenues per ton-mile has benefited greatly from conversations with Scott Dennis of the Bureau of Transportation Statistics.

Some of these issues have been addressed in a Tornqvist price index using current revenue weights that has been constructed by the Surface Transportation Board.[11] That index declined by 20 percent between 1984 and 1999, in a nearly identical match with the BLS measure. It may be that the factors that gave rise to the differences between the PPI and the various measures of revenues per ton-mile are less important now that the adjustment to deregulation is largely complete, but the historical experience suggests some caution in using the PPI measures and reinforces the value of having an alternative methodology to provide a check on the reasonableness of the results. Furthermore, analysts need to be aware of the shift in the methodology used by BEA because it has created a break in the data that will affect comparisons based on pre- and post-1992 measures of real output and productivity.

The railroad industry also is one of a select number of industries for which BLS has constructed estimates of multifactor productivity. The BLS and BEA measures are compared in figure 3-2. While the BLS measure extends only through 1999, the two measures of the change in MFP are very similar in indicating a sharp acceleration of growth after 1980 and a slowdown after 1995. In both cases, gains in MFP account for the bulk of the growth in labor productivity. The MFP gains can be attributed in turn to passage of the Staggers Rail Act, which made it easier to abandon underutilized tracks, expedited mergers, and facilitated reorganization of the industry. Rail consolidation resulted in fewer interchanges between lines, reducing transit time and labor costs. Changes in work rules further reduced labor requirements. However, the adjustment to a less-regulated environment was largely complete by the mid-1990s.

Both the BEA-based growth accounts of table 3-2 and the BLS measures indicate a relatively large contribution of purchased inputs and little or no role for increased capital per worker. This reflects a shift in which a large number of rail cars now are owned by shippers; the percentage of freight cars owned by the railroads declined from 74 percent in 1980 to 48 percent in 2001. Because the information available on the ownership of capital by the industry is limited, it is doubtful that shifts of this magnitude between capital and purchased inputs are accurately captured in the industry accounts. Although railroads have benefited from the introduction of new electronic sensor devices, the industry is not a major user of IT capital. Therefore a slowing of growth in labor productivity and MFP after 1995 is not surprising.

11. Surface Transportation Board (2000). The index is based on the board's waybill sample of revenues per ton-mile by detailed commodity groups. The STB also experimented with alternative measures that ignore distance (revenues/ton), with little measurable impact on the index.

Figure 3-2. *Alternative Estimates of Multifactor Productivity Growth in Railroads, 1977–2001*

Index[a]

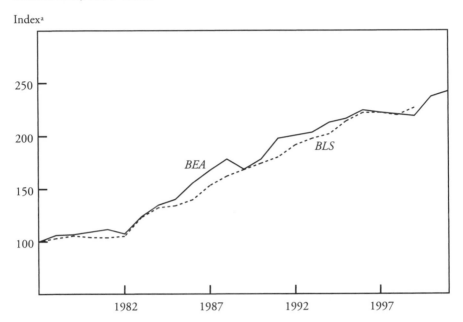

Sources: BEA industry data file and BLS industry productivity program.
a. 1977 = 100.

Trucking and Warehousing

The structure of the trucking industry, with its thousands of carriers, creates a number of difficulties in any effort to measure its output, let alone its productivity. As shown in table 3-4, the industry includes a large number of companies, particularly in local markets. In addition, it is a dynamic industry with considerable company turnover. Therefore administrative records, such as those that were available from the regulatory agencies, are unlikely to provide a representative picture of the industry, and reliable information can be collected only in a well-designed, representative survey. The Census Bureau (CB) has conducted a survey of the industry, benchmarked to the economic census, on an annual basis since 1982. The survey now provides the primary source of information for both the BEA and the BLS measures of industry output and productivity.

Before its 2000 revision, the BEA dealt with the industry at the aggregate level of SIC 42 (trucking and warehousing). The annual revenues from the Cen-

Table 3-4. *Structure of the Trucking Industry, 1992*

Category	SIC code	Establish-ments[a]	Output[b] Census Bureau	BEA	BLS
Trucking and warehousing	42	110.9	143.8	165.8	
Local trucking without storage	4212	49.9	33.6 ⎫		
Trucking except local	4213	40.8	78.4 ⎬ 136.8		78.4
Local trucking with storage	4214	4.5	4.2 ⎭		
Courier services except by air	4215	6	19.3	19.4	
Public warehousing	422	9.7	8.3	9.7	
Benchmark adjustments	*1977*	*1982*	*1987*	*1992*	
Benchmark gross output (BEA)[b]	47.8	73.4	114.2	165.8	
Operating revenue (Census Bureau)[b]	52.8	75.6	103.7	143.8	
Adjustment ratio[c]					
Operating revenue (nominal output)	1.000	1.073	1.216	1.274	

Source: Authors' calculations based on data from the Bureau of Census, the industry accounts of BEA, and the productivity division of BLS.

a. Thousands.

b. Billions of dollars.

c. 1977 = 1.0.

sus Bureau survey were used to interpolate between benchmark years and combined with an index of interstate ton-miles to develop a price index.[12] The CB data on revenues are compared to the BEA benchmark in the lower portion of table 3-4. It is evident that the relationship between the two estimates of industry revenues has changed substantially over time. Between the 1977 and 1992 benchmarks, the BEA reports an additional 27 percent increase in nominal gross output relative to that in the CB survey.[13]

Currently however, BEA employs a more disaggregated approach, dividing the industry into courier services, public warehousing, and an amalgam of local and intercity trucking. It continues to use the Census Bureau survey to extrapolate the nominal values, but it employs indexes from the PPI to deflate operating revenues at the level of the three industries. Indexes from the PPI are available

12. No information on ton-miles is available for local trucking, a serious limitation on the quality of the data. Also, until 1990, the annual survey of the Census Bureau did not separate local and intercity trucking. In effect, the BEA methodology assumed that the real output of SIC 42 moves in parallel with the intercity component.

13. The comparable adjustment between the benchmark and the interpolator was 12 percent for railroads (table 3-3).

only from 1992, and the BEA relies on the old, more aggregated methodology for earlier years.

The BLS restricts its analysis to the "trucking, except local" (SIC 4213) portion of the industry, and in 1992, this interstate component composed about half of the total industry (table 3-4). Under the new NAICS categorization, the size of the long-haul component is estimated at $64 billion in 1992, whereas under the SIC classification the estimate is $78.2 billion. Since 1992, BLS has estimated real output by deflating revenue data from the Census Bureau survey with a price index from the PPI. However, unlike the BEA, the BLS makes no adjustment to the census data for drift between benchmark years.[14] For the years prior to 1992, the BLS series is based on ton-miles from a variety of sources, and it was possible to adjust for some changes in the composition of freight by class of service, such as "less-than-truckload."

The BLS index does have the advantage of providing a measure of output and labor productivity back to 1960. In the two decades ending in 1980, labor productivity in the intercity component grew at an annual rate of 2.5 percent. In the subsequent ten years, prior to the change in methodology, labor productivity rose at a rate of 3.7 percent a year, implying an annual improvement of about 1 percentage point after deregulation.

Alternative measures of real output growth are shown in panel A of figure 3-3. The relationship between the two series is very different before and after 1992. In the early period, the broad industry grows more rapidly than the long-haul portion measured by BLS, but after 1992, the two indexes move in parallel, even though the industrial coverage is really quite different. Trends in employment are reported in panel B. Again the correspondence between the BEA and BLS data is very different before and after 1992. The BLS series shows very large employment declines in the long-haul portion of the industry before 1992 and increases that largely parallel those in the BEA series after 1992. Given that the long-haul component represents about half of the total, the divergent behavior in the pre-1992 period is puzzling. Both measures include self-employed workers. In the BEA series, part-time employees are converted to full-time equivalents. For the total industry, the self-employed increase from about 5 percent of the workforce prior to deregulation to 15 percent in the 1990s. However, because the differences in the trends of output and employment are largely offsetting, the BEA and BLS data yield similar estimates of the trend in labor productivity (panel C).

_____

14. Since the BEA has not yet introduced the 1997 benchmark, the drift factor is of no consequence in a comparison of the output measures from BEA and BLS for the post-1992 period.

Figure 3-3. *Output, Employment, and Labor Productivity in the Trucking Industry, 1977–2001*

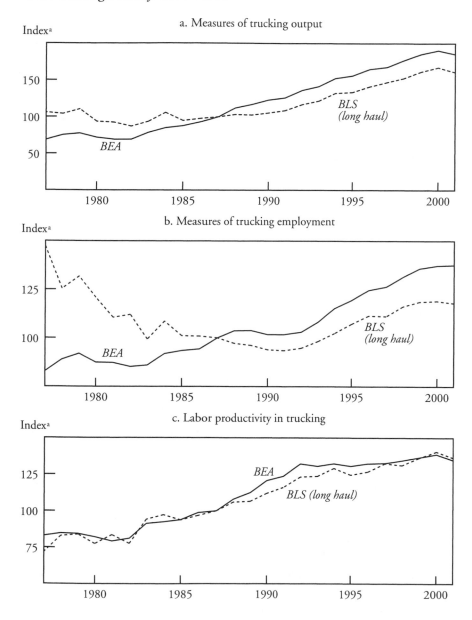

a. Measures of trucking output

Index^a

BLS (long haul)

BEA

b. Measures of trucking employment

Index^a

BEA

BLS (long haul)

c. Labor productivity in trucking

Index^a

BEA

BLS (long haul)

Source: Computed by the authors from the BLS and BEA industry data files.
a. 1987 = 100.

A large portion of the discrepancy between the BEA and BLS data prior to 1992 appears to be related to the limited coverage of the BLS series. The long-haul segment was most affected by deregulation and most of the statistical reporting system focused on the large carriers that provided less-than-truckload (LTL) service. The 1980 Motor Carrier Act concentrated on liberalizing entry into the industry, and most of the new firms were small class III firms offering truckload service.[15] One consequence was a large decline in the number of class II carriers after 1980. It seems likely that the BLS data reflect the decline of class I and II carriers without fully capturing the growth of the smaller class III. Given the possibility of differing coverage for the output and employment estimates, we can have little confidence in the measures of labor productivity.

Overall, the new BEA methodology for computing output of the trucking sector represents an improvement over the pre-1992 measures. At the same time, we really have no basis for evaluating the quality of the producer price indexes. Trucking would seem to raise many of the same concerns about measuring prices that were reported previously for railroads: do the indexes capture the changes in composition of the industry's output? A second concern is that the benchmark adjustments that BEA makes to the annual census survey seem disconcertingly large and variable; the two sources imply much different patterns of growth in nominal revenues over time. Third, the data now exist to carry the new BEA methodology one step further, to separate local and long-haul trucking. These two components would seem to have significantly different technology (truck size) and cost trends.

Finally, none of the measures of inputs include an estimate of changes in highway capital. The development of the interstate highway system has been critical to the growth of the long-haul segment. Purchased inputs include the fuel taxes and tolls that the industry pays for the use of the highways, but changes in tax rates will be classified as a price increase rather than reflect growth in the highway network. At the same time, the industry is strongly affected by changes in roadway congestion. An extension of the growth accounting framework to incorporate both capital improvements in highways and the cost of congestion would be very useful. A measure of average speed or trip time, for example, would weigh both factors, but a national measure is not available.

The estimates of MFP growth, reported in table 3-2, suggest very little improvement within the trucking industry. Instead, the gains in labor productivity are attributed to increased reliance on purchased inputs, particularly in the years prior to 1995. There also is very little growth in the amount of capital per

15. Winston and others (1990, pp. 9–13).

worker. Compared with railroads, trucking emerges as a relatively stagnant industry in term of improvements in its economic efficiency. The measures of labor productivity and MFP all show a deceleration of growth after 1995.

Airline Transportation

Deregulation has had an enormous impact on the structure of the airline industry, yet it is not evident that the changes have increased productivity. According to the BLS, labor productivity growth in the large scheduled airlines averaged 2.4 percent a year in the first ten years after deregulation (the 1980s), compared with 4.4 percent in the prior decade. That is a sharp contrast to the results for railroads and trucking. However, because of the structural changes, a simple focus on labor productivity may provide an inadequate measure of trends in efficiency. MFP, which takes account of changes in the intensity of capital use, purchased inputs, and outsourcing, is a broader measure of efficiency. The wealth of information available for air travel has led the BLS to produce estimates of MFP that can be compared with the estimates that we have constructed from the BEA industry data (BLS 2003). However, these two measures differ in the scope of their coverage: BEA uses a very broad definition of air transport (SIC 45), which includes SIC 4512, scheduled air (passenger and freight); SIC 4513, air couriers (mail and parcels); SIC 4522, nonscheduled transport (cargo, charter, and so forth); and SIC 4581, support services (airports and services). The BLS measure, on the other hand, is restricted to the large certificated carriers. A comparison of the two approaches also illustrates some important issues of methodology.

While the Census Bureau has expanded the information that it collects in the economic censuses, most of the data on revenue and miles flown are obtained from reports filed with the Department of Transportation and published by the Bureau of Transportation Statistics (BTS). Large certificated carriers (those that operate aircraft with a capacity of more than sixty seats and 18,000 pounds of freight or that conduct international flights) file a Form 41, and smaller regional-commuter airlines file a Form 238c. However, a significant amount of unscheduled charter and freight-hauling flights by small aircraft is not included in the statistics.

OUTPUT. Primary measures of the industry's output are produced by the BEA, BLS, and the Census Bureau. Comparative values are shown in table 3-5 for the 1992 benchmark. The BEA divides the revenue of the air transport industry into three categories: passenger, freight, and support services. As with trucking, the BEA estimate of output in 1992 is larger than that reported by the Census Bureau, although the difference is less pronounced, about 8 percent.

Table 3-5. *Alternative Measures of Airline Gross Output, 1992*
Billions of dollars

	Output		
Category	*BEA*	*BLS*	*Census Bureau*
Passenger	66.1	60.9	n.a.
Freight	16.5	4.3	n.a.
Support services	6.9	n.a.	6.2
Subtotal	89.3	65.2	82.7
Tax	4.5	n.a.	n.a.
Total	93.7		
Benchmark adjustment (BEA)	*1977*	*1982*	*1987*	*1992*
Passenger				
Gross output (BEA)	18.5	33.3	51.3	66.1
Revenues (BTS)	16.9	31.1	46.0	61.0
Freight				
Gross output (BEA)	2.2	5.1	16.9	16.5
Revenues (BTS)	2.2	3.4	7.8	8.8
Adjustment ratios[a]				
Passenger	1.000	0.974	1.014	0.984
Freight	1.000	1.467	2.138	1.845

Source: Authors' estimates from data provided by BEA and BLS. BLS definitions are based on the NAICS and exclude air couriers.
   a. 1977 = 1.0.

The BEA also includes all operating revenues of the large certificated air carriers, the smaller regional-commuter airlines that report on Form 238c, an estimate for unscheduled transport, the support services in SIC 4581, and taxes.

The BLS restricts its analysis to the large certificated carriers who report to the BTS (Form 41). Also, in the changeover to the NAICS, BLS removed air couriers, which are now recorded in their own industry group.[16] As shown in table 3-5, the BEA estimates of both the passenger and freight components are considerably larger because they include operating revenues of the large carriers that are not directly allocated to passenger or freight in the Form 41 reports and because they include activities of the smaller carriers. The differences are particularly large for freight, where the BEA estimate is more than three times that of

16. The BLS has extended its estimates back to 1972, but the old measures of output and productivity that included air carriers are available back to 1947.

the BLS. The Census Bureau uses Form 41 as its source for the large carriers and conducts a survey of the smaller carriers.

In estimating real output, the BEA and BLS use identical source data up to 1992. Indexes of total passenger and freight ton-miles are constructed from the Form 41 reports of the large certificated carriers. To compute its index, BLS also splits the data into domestic and foreign operations. Since the Form 41 carriers are the universe for the BLS estimates, the output measure is simply a Tornqvist index using revenue shares of the four categories (passenger and freight transport, foreign and domestic) as weights.

The BEA introduces the additional step of adjusting the nominal data to conform to its benchmark estimates at five-year intervals, using nominal revenues from Form 41 as interpolators. The magnitudes of those adjustments are shown at the bottom of table 3-5. As the doubling of the adjustment ratio between 1977 and 1987 indicates, a major portion of freight services are performed by non–Form 41 carriers, and that share has changed substantially since 1977; however, the adjustments for passenger travel are quite small. International and domestic data are combined and converted to constant prices using a price deflator constructed from the revenue and ton-mile data of Form 41. Beginning in 1992, the BEA uses PPIs to deflate the output measure for freight and airport services, but it has continued to use miles as the basic measure of output for the passenger segment of the industry. Prior to 1992, the implicit deflator for airport services is based on an index of wages. The resulting aggregate measure for airlines is a Laspeyres index.

While the BEA and BLS measures of output differ in scope, they have very similar trends, shown in table 3-6. The BEA index grows more rapidly in the pre-1992 period because of the greater weight assigned to the fast-growing freight sector.

EMPLOYMENT. BEA obtains an estimate of employment in the air transport industry from the reports of the state unemployment insurance programs. Those reports are the basic source for all of the BEA employment data, and they provide the annual benchmark for the monthly establishment employment estimates of BLS. Part-time employees are converted to full-time equivalents and combined with an estimate of self-employed workers, which is insignificant for the air transport industry. There is also a break in the employment estimates for the total industry in 1988, when air couriers were reclassified from trucking to air transportation, raising industry employment by nearly one-third. There is no real means of making the classification adjustment for the years before 1988. Therefore we simply extended the adjustment as a percent of air transport employment back in time and subtracted that amount from trucking.

Table 3-6. *Alternative Estimates of Labor and Multifactor Productivity in Air Transportation, 1977–2001*
Average annual percent change

Measure	BEA			BLS		
	1977–87	*1987–95*	*1995–2001*	*1977–87*	*1987–95*	*1995–2001*
Output	8.3	3.6	3.3	7.3	3.4	2.9
Employment	4.5	3.5	3.1	3.1	1.3	3.5
Output per worker	3.6	0.0	0.2	4.0	2.0	–0.6
Contribution of capital	–0.0	–0.2	0.7	0.1	0.3	0.0
Intermediate purchases	2.5	–2.3	–0.2	1.1	0.5	–1.4
Multifactor productivity	1.1	2.6	–0.4	2.7	1.2	0.7

Source: BEA and BLS industry data sets. The measures of BEA refer to all of SIC 45. The BLS measure is limited to the large carriers, excluding air couriers.

Because the BLS limits its analysis to Form 41 carriers, it obtains its employment estimate directly from that form. Employment of Form 41 carriers was only 47 percent of the industry total in 2001, and their share has been slowly declining over time. There was a particularly sharp slowing of growth compared with the BEA estimate of total industry growth in the 1987–95 period.

PRODUCTIVITY. The estimated rates of growth for labor productivity and its components in both the BEA and BLS measures are shown in table 3-6. The two estimates of the change in labor productivity for the total industry (BEA) and the major carriers (BLS) are quite similar in indicating a slowing of growth over the past quarter-century, but there is a significant discrepancy in the 1987–95 period. There also is an interesting contrast in the methods of estimating the contributions of capital and purchased inputs. The BEA data are based on a perpetual-inventory estimate of the capital stock in which the different types of investment are allocated among using industries and cumulated with assumed rates of depreciation. The BLS data, in contrast, are based on actual counts of the types of aircraft in operation in each year, aggregated with purchase prices as weights.[17] As shown in table 3-6, the estimates of the capital con-

17. The details of the BLS methodology are reported in BLS (2003). The purchase prices are renormalized to a standard base year using the PPI for aircraft. While there is no systematic adjustment for differences in aircraft quality beyond that embedded in the PPI, the post-1977 period comes well after the biggest changes in aircraft characteristics.

tribution are quite similar, but it appears that the BLS data are able to capture the withdrawal of aircraft from operation during periods of recession, implied by a significantly smaller increase in capital per worker in 1995–2001. However, neither the BLS nor the BEA estimates incorporate any adjustment for the argument of Gordon (1990) that the price indexes for aircraft incorporate an inadequate adjustment for quality improvements.

Furthermore, the BLS can obtain direct information on purchased inputs from the Form 41 reports, whereas BEA must estimate its measure by subtracting value added from gross output. Since the measures of value added and gross output are built on much different data sources, the residual estimate of purchased inputs has a large potential for measurement error. The comparison of the two approaches is imperfect because the BEA measure of the industry is much broader than that of the BLS, but it is notable that the largest discrepancies between the two estimates of productivity are in the contribution of purchased inputs. For this industry, the BLS methodology, with its emphasis on direct measurement of capital and purchased inputs, seems preferable.

The BLS data also extend back to 1972, permitting comparison of the pre- and post-1980 changes in MFP for evidence of any impact of deregulation. The annual rate of growth of MFP declines from 3.3 percent in the 1972–80 period to 2.1 percent in 1980–88. The lack of efficiency gains in the airline industry following deregulation contrasts with our findings for railroads and trucking but matches the conclusion of Gordon (1992).

PRICES. The most difficult aspect of measuring the output of the airline industry revolves around the issue of quality changes in air travel. Both the BEA and BLS measures of productivity rely on passenger miles as the fundamental measure of output change, yet the quality of air travel has changed in many dimensions. The hub-and-spoke system that emerged after deregulation offered increased frequency of service for many passengers, and the increased emphasis on jet service greatly reduced travel time.[18] On the other hand, increased loads have led to reduced passenger comfort as many airlines altered leg room and cut back on other dimensions of service. Greater travel has also resulted in significant increases in congestion and travel delays. None of these quality issues are reflected in a simple index of passenger miles.

In general, the difficulties of aggregating quantities have translated into a preference for measuring an aggregate of price changes, which can then be used to deflate a nominal measure of output. The assumption was that prices are more likely to move together. Therefore, in developing its industry data, BEA

18. Morrison and Winston (1986 and 1995).

Figure 3-4. *Alternative Price Indexes for Air Travel, 1977–2001*

Index[a]

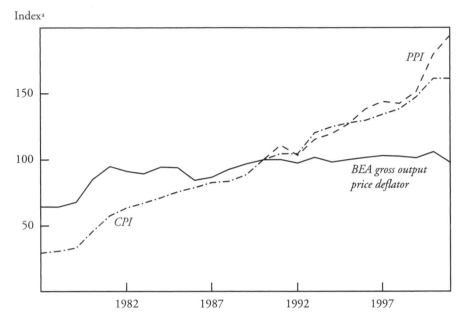

Sources: The gross output price deflator is taken from the BEA industry data file. The consumer and producer price indexes are obtained from the BLS website (www.bls.gov). The producer price index for air travel begins in 1990. All three indexes are converted to use 1990 as the base year.
  a. 1990 = 100.

has moved toward progressively greater reliance on price indexes as produced by the PPI program of BLS. However, in the case of air travel, the market prices seem even more disparate than the quantities, largely because of the growing use of price discrimination as a tool for extracting more of the consumer surplus.

Some of the important distinctions between the use of price and quantity indicators can be illustrated by comparing an index of directly measured prices with an index based on dividing revenues by a physical measure of output. Three alternative measures of the price of airline travel are shown in figure 3-4. The BEA implicit price deflator for gross output is essentially an index of revenue per passenger mile. Both the CPI and the PPI are based on direct measures of prices: the CPI uses prices listed by the airlines in the SABRE system, a reservation system used by travel agents; the PPI collects the information directly from the airlines.

These alternatives present dramatically different pictures of the trend in airfares. Between 1977 and 2001, the annual rate of increase of the CPI averaged

7.4 percent, compared with only 1.6 percent for revenue per passenger mile.[19] The PPI measure begins only in 1990, but it has closely tracked the CPI since its introduction. If the CPI or PPI were used to deflate passenger revenues to arrive at an index of real output, we would be showing sharply declining levels of labor productivity and MFP in the airline industry.[20]

Since revenue per passenger mile is a relatively hard number, the price indexes imply a large decline in the quality of air travel, something with which some travelers might agree. But the magnitude of deterioration in the quality of travel seems implausible. There has been some increase in the length of flights, which might be an argument that the revenue-per-mile measure fails to adequately reflect the higher fixed costs of landings, takeoffs, and terminal facilities.[21] However, the change has been too small to account for the magnitude of the price differences. Instead, it appears that the methodology for collecting representative prices fails to capture the growing importance of discount tickets and the use of frequent flier miles. In fact, few of the usual notions of quality change are captured in the price indexes, which are based on measuring changes in a large market basket of fares between pairs of cities.[22] For example, travel is negatively affected by larger loads, reduced seat space, and the increased hassle of security checkpoints, but it has been enhanced by more frequent service and the reduced travel time associated with jet aircraft. None of these aspects are captured in the current price indexes. While the revenue-per-mile measure also misses many of the quality aspects of air travel, it does have the important advantage of capturing the frequent flier programs, though not on an accrual basis.

Some of these issues are addressed in a recent analysis by Janice Lent and Alan Dorfman of the Bureau of Labor Statistics (BLS 2002). They make use of a quarterly data file compiled by the U.S. Department of Transportation that contains a 10 percent sample of airline tickets with information on the actual fare

19. Gross output includes business travel, an intermediate product, whose price may have varied substantially from the prices included in the CPI; however, over the period as a whole, business prices would be presumed to have increased faster than those paid by consumers.

20. There are similar differences between the two approaches for measuring freight output. Revenue per ton-mile declined by 12 percent between 1988 and 1998, whereas the PPI for freight transport rose by 3 percent.

21. Morrison and Winston (1995), especially chapter 4.

22. Since 1999, the CPI for airfares has been computed as a geometric mean. As part of its creation of a historical series that incorporates a consistent methodology (the Research Series), the BLS estimated a geometric mean version of the airfare index for the 1991–97 period. Over that period the rate of price increase dropped from 3.6 percent a year to 2.2 percent. However, that is still well above the corresponding rate of change in revenue per passenger mile.

and the sequence of airports, carriers, and class of service from origin to final destination. They matched the fares over time, first by those with identical itineraries, airlines, and class of service and then by apportioning the cost of segments of multisegment itineraries using matching single-segment itineraries. They compute unit-value indexes for each individual category and aggregate that information to an overall price index using a variety of different formulas (Laspeyres, Paasche, Fisher, Tornqvist, and Jevons). Their experimental indexes indicate rates of fare increase substantially below those of the CPI and PPI and close to the simple revenue-per-mile measure used by BEA. Presumably, the differences arise because the official price indexes fail to capture fully the importance of restricted discount fares and frequent flier awards.[23]

The value of time is the most important aspect of quality that currently goes unmeasured in the price indexes. Gordon (1992) pointed out that the largest reductions in travel time were associated with the introduction of jet travel but that most of that transformation was completed prior to the mid-1970s. He did analyze the change in travel time associated with the shifts in routes following deregulation, concluding that there had been a net increase in travel times equivalent to a 4 percent increase in fares between 1978 and 1989. In addition, Gordon (1990 and 1992) proposed measures to account for variations in seat space and speed.

Other researchers have investigated the use of hedonic methods to measure changes in the quality dimensions of air travel (Good, Sickles, and Weiher 2001). However, much of the variation in fares appears to be part of an effort to discriminate among users with different price elasticities. Therefore, having measured a price differential in a quality dimension, we do not know whether it reflects a difference in quality or in consumers. It also is difficult to interpret the coefficients on various measures of quality in the hedonic regressions. The resulting measures of change in ticket prices concur with the finding of some upward bias in the current CPI for air fares, but the hedonic approach does not yet provide a feasible alternative to the CPI.

Recently the hassle of air travel has been significantly reduced by the ability to book tickets and obtain boarding passes over the Internet. Some of that change was reflected in fares when the airlines reduced their payments to travel agents, and in a competitive market those cost savings would be passed forward to consumers. However, the fees that travel agents now routinely charge non-Internet users to book flights are probably not incorporated in the price indexes.

---

23. They also report that their comparisons of alternative index formulas suggest that the Jevons formula, which is currently employed in the CPI for air travel, is biased downward compared with the Fisher and Tornqvist indexes.

The Role of Information Technology Capital in the Transportation Sector

The contribution of information technology capital to productivity growth in the BEA/BLS industry data set was summarized in table 2-7 (chapter 2). In that comparison of the fifty-four industries that make up the nonfarm sector, IT capital made a below-average contribution to productivity growth within the transportation industries over the 1987–2001 period. For the three industries that we have focused on—airlines, railroads, and trucking—IT capital purchases have been particularly small.

These results contrast, however, with Hubbard (2001), who used individual firm data from the Census Bureau's 1992 and 1997 vehicle inventory and use surveys to examine the relationship between the use of on-board computers (OBC) and labor productivity.[24] He found an average gain of 13 percent in capacity utilization for trucks equipped with advanced OBCs. The improvements appear to result from improved communication between dispatchers and drivers. The study provides a direct link between the use of IT technologies and productivity.

Yet our calculations for the aggregate trucking industry show a very small contribution from increases in capital per worker throughout the 1990s and a deceleration of MFP growth after 1995. The differences arise in part from the treatment of the on-board computers in the aggregate accounts, where capital is allocated to the purchasing industry, which may differ from the using industry. It is common for the OBC service to be leased from telecommunications firms because of its reliance on wireless technology. Therefore its use would be recorded as a capital investment of telecommunications and an increase in purchased inputs for the trucking industry. We note that there is substantial growth in purchased inputs in the 1987–95 period (table 3-2), which according to the Hubbard study coincides with the period when the OBC technology was being introduced. Furthermore, it is notable that the use of IT capital was more significant in the transportation services industry—travel agencies and freight agents—where we would anticipate a substantial role for IT.

Summary

In the 1990s, major progress was made, particularly at the BEA, in developing a consistent data framework for analyzing productivity at the level of individual

24. A preliminary version of this paper was presented at a Brookings workshop, "Transportation Output and Productivity," in May 2001.

services industries. We now have integrated estimates of gross output, gross product (value added), and intermediate inputs for all of the National Income and Product Accounts (NIPA) industry groups. When that information is combined with the data on the capital stock and capital services (BLS) by industry, we are able to compute estimates of the contributions of labor, capital, purchased inputs, and multifactor productivity to growth. That is certainly a major step forward compared with the situation even ten years earlier.

The transportation sector provides a useful opportunity to examine the industry data and the methodologies used to generate it in greater detail. More source data are available for these formerly regulated industries than for most services industries. We also have the opportunity to compare the data and methodology of both the BEA and the BLS. While we can account for the differences between the BEA and BLS estimates of output and employment in these industries and relate those differences to different decisions on data sources and methodology, they often add up to significant divergences in the final results.

Overall, the emergence of a comprehensive accounting framework at the BEA is of great value in providing a means of relating developments at the industry level to the more commonly discussed developments in the aggregate economy, the lack of which is a limitation of the selective-industries approach employed at the BLS. Yet the BLS approach allows for greater tailoring of methods to the unique characteristics of particular industries. Therefore there is much to be gained from a closer integration of the two agencies' work on industry-level output and productivity.[25] The focus of the effort should be on improving the quality of a single industry data set, rather than on trying to join pieces that do not fit together.

The examination of output estimates in the transportation sector also raises questions about the use of some PPIs to obtain estimates of real output. There are surprisingly large differences compared with results of an older methodology that relied on physical indicators, such as ton-miles, to project output. While some of the difference is undoubtedly due to changes in the quality of a passenger mile or ton-mile of travel, the magnitude often seems improbable. Significant work needs to be done to evaluate the quality of the PPIs being produced for the transportation sector. Finally, the adoption of a new methodology in the mid-1990s created a major statistical break in the BEA series on output growth that needs to be incorporated in any discussion of past trends.

25. A good example of such cooperation is the work undertaken by the BLS to use the BEA capital stock estimates to develop industry-specific measures of capital services.

CHAPTER FOUR

Output and Productivity Growth in the Communications Industry

Since the historic court ruling in 1984 that opened the long-distance telephone market, long dominated by AT&T, to competition, the communications industry has experienced dramatic economic and technological change. The Telecommunications Act of 1996 went further, promoting competition in all telecommunications sectors, including the provision of local telecommunications services. Technological and economic changes have included the introduction of fiber-optic cable, the expansion of cable services from 10 million subscribers in 1975 to 68 million in 2000, the surge in cellular phone subscribers from only 5 million in 1990 to 128 million in 2001, and regular access to the Internet for more than half of American households. New consumer and business services appear almost daily, among them different types of broadband services and Internet-enabled wireless phones, and the potential is great for large Internet-related efficiency gains in industry (Litan and Rivlin 2001). The pace of change has been particularly fast since 1995.

Our primary interest in the telecommunications sector is to examine the extent to which the rapid innovations in this sector have been captured by the statistical system. How have the innovations and new services affected the growth of output, labor productivity, and multifactor productivity? How are the service

We are indebted to Daniel Sichel, who prepared an overview of developments in the communications industry for the Brookings workshop "Communications Output and Productivity" in February 2001.

innovations reflected in the measures of price change? Has the communications industry played a significant role in the post-1995 acceleration of productivity growth? The communications industry also stands out as one of the most important examples of IT-using industries.

The revenues of the communications sector have been increasing as a percentage of GDP: in 2001 they were 5.6 percent, compared with 3.9 percent in 1990. The distribution of the industry's revenues is summarized in table 4-1. The telecom sector represents about 75 percent of the total, and it is undergoing a dramatic transformation as wireless communications claim a rapidly growing share of the total. Long-distance service over fixed-wire carriers declined by 20 percent between 1998 and 2001, while local service continued to grow. However, cellular revenue more than doubled in size in that brief three-year period. Broadcasting is a relatively stable share of total communications, but since 1998, its growth has been completely dominated by cable programming, which accounted for 60 percent of the industry in 2001. Traditional television broadcasting has experienced little revenue growth.

Growth in Output and Productivity

The rapid innovation within the communications industry has been reflected in high rates of real output growth in the telecommunications portion of the industry and strong productivity gains overall. Surprisingly, there was only a modest acceleration of labor productivity gains after 1995, and MFP growth, as measured by output, has slowed in telecommunications and turned negative in broadcasting. The basic trends are reported in table 4-2. The BEA industry data set distinguishes between telecommunications and the broadcasting (including cable) portion of SIC 48, the classification for the entire communications industry. The BLS productivity program has converted to NAICS, under which communications is part of a larger grouping of information-related industries (NAICS 51). BLS provides measures of labor productivity at the levels of wired (5171) and wireless (5172) telecommunications, radio and television broadcasting (5151), and cable programming (5152).[1] We have combined the four BLS series into two categories, telecommunications and broadcasting, even though they exclude some elements of the BEA aggregates.

The rapid output growth in telecommunications and its acceleration after the mid-1990s is clearly evident at the top of table 4-2, where both the BEA and

1. Internet service providers and publishers are part of the information sector in NAICS (industries 516 and 5181), but they had no specific assignment in the SIC.

Table 4-1. *Revenues of the Communications Sector, 1992, 1998, and 2001*
Billions of dollars

Industry	1992 Revenue	1992 Percent	1998 Revenue	1998 Percent	2001 Revenue	2001 Percent
Communications services	232.2	100.0	388.1	100.0	495.9	100.0
Telephone and telegraph	174.9	75.3	294.4	75.9	378.1	76.3
Cellular and other radiophone	9.2	4.0	41.9	10.8	84.2	17.0
Wired and other	165.7	71.4	252.5	65.1	293.9	59.3
Radio and television	57.3	24.7	93.6	24.1	117.7	23.7
Radio broadcasting	7.0	3.0	11.6	3.0	13.7	2.8
Television broadcasting	22.8	9.8	32.8	8.4	33.9	6.8
Cable programming	27.5	11.8	49.3	12.7	70.1	14.1
Addenda						
Internet service providers[a]			11.4		29.7	

Source: Census Bureau, *Annual Survey of the Communications Sector, 1998* and *Annual Survey of Information Sector Services, 2001*. Data for 2001 are converted to an SIC basis using Census Bureau conversions for 1998.

a. NAICS industry 514191 in the 2002 Census Bureau annual survey.

BLS data show growth rates in excess of 10 percent. In fact, the underlying BLS data for wireless communications have an average growth rate of 25 percent a year for the full 1987–2001 period. At the same time there has been a notable acceleration of growth in broadcasting, which is entirely due to cable programming. However, the growth of value added in broadcasting differs substantially from that of gross output because of large fluctuations in the ratio of value added to gross output.

The two agencies use very similar methods to estimate real output for both telecommunications and broadcasting, deflating nominal sales measures by various price indexes obtained from the CPI, PPI, and private industry. However, because of differences in the level of detail at which they do the deflation and some differences in the choice of price deflators, their indexes of output growth are not identical. The BEA measure of gross output grows significantly faster than the comparable BLS concept after 1995. However, there is less growth in the value added measure due to a fall in the nominal share of value added in gross output.

Both BEA and BLS estimates of labor productivity show rapid rates of increase in telecommunications. However, the BEA measure of gross output per

Table 4-2. *Output and Productivity Growth in the Communications Sector,*
1977–2001

Annual percent rates of change

Measure	Telecommunications			Radio and television		
	1977–87	1987–95	1995–2001	1977–87	1987–95	1995–2001
Output						
BEA output	6.7	5.4	13.2	4.6	2.3	5.0
BEA value added	5.8	4.6	10.3	0.3	9.0	1.4
BLS	n.a	5.8	11.7		2.6	4.6
Employment						
BEA	0.2	−0.4	4.5	3.7	2.1	3.2
BLS	n.a	0.8	4.6		2.7	4.4
Labor productivity						
BEA output	6.4	5.8	8.4	0.9	0.2	1.7
BEA value added	5.6	5.0	5.6	−3.3	6.7	−1.8
BLS		5.0	6.8		−0.1	0.2
Contributions of						
Capital per worker	2.2	1.6	1.2	1.1	1.8	3.2
IT capital per worker	1.1	0.9	1.0	0.7	1.0	2.3
Intermediate inputs	2.4	2.5	5.6	3.4	−3.4	3.2
Multifactor productivity						
BEA output	1.7	1.6	1.4	−3.5	1.9	−4.4
BEA value added	2.4	2.5	3.2	−5.4	3.3	−6.7

Source: Authors' calculations based on BEA and BLS industry data sets. Calculation of the contributions of capital and intermediate inputs are based on the BEA gross output measure. The BLS aggregates
were calculated by the authors from underlying detail.

worker shows significant acceleration in recent years, while the BLS reports high
but steady rates of productivity growth before and after 1995. These differences
are largely due to the larger acceleration of output growth in the BEA measure.
Both data sets indicate very low rates of labor productivity growth in broadcasting. In fact, the BEA value-added measure is negative in two subperiods and the
BLS reports zero growth over the 1987–2001 period.

  The lower portions of table 4-2 display the decomposition of labor productivity growth into the contributions of increased capital per worker, increased intensity in the use of purchased inputs, and multifactor productivity growth (MFP).

These measures are available only for the BEA data set. For telecommunications, all three elements are important, but the large contribution of purchased inputs is a surprise. A possible explanation would be the rapid expansion of intra-industry transactions following deregulation. They are included in the BEA data, and as a form of double counting, they would contribute to higher growth of both revenues and costs. The large contribution of capital is anticipated since telecommunications is a very capital-intensive industry; furthermore, the 1990s boom in wireless communications and the growth of competitive local exchange carriers (CLECs) after passage of the 1996 Telecommunications Act resulted in a very large expansion of the capital base. Growth in capital services and purchased inputs is sufficient to account for all of the post-1995 acceleration of labor productivity, and we find no increase in the pace of change in the output-based measure of MFP and only a small acceleration for the value added concept.

The decomposition of productivity growth for broadcasting also shows a large capital contribution, particularly after 1995, which reflects increased investment in cable systems as they upgrade in order to provide digital services. However, in this case the role of intermediate purchases (primarily programming costs) is very unstable, growing rapidly up to 1987, declining as a share of output up to 1995, and increasing again more recently. The result is a highly variable residual measure of MFP and a very negative rate of change after 1995.

For both telecommunications and broadcasting, the purchase of intermediate inputs has a major influence on the calculation of MFP. The inputs are a rapidly growing share of total output in telecommunications, and they fluctuate widely in broadcasting. It is possible that these changes accurately reflect changes in industrial structure. However, it also is important to note that inconsistencies may be introduced by relying on separate data sources to derive the estimates of gross output and value added. As discussed more fully in chapter 11 and Yuskavage (2000), this is a major concern with the BEA industry data set. BEA calculates intermediate materials as the residual difference between the estimates of gross output and value added, in contrast with the input-output accounts, which provide direct estimates of both gross output and purchased inputs, with value added being the residual.

The estimates of gross output are increasingly drawn from census surveys of individual industries, with benchmark adjustments in order to align with the input-output (I-O) accounts at five-year intervals. The data sources for the construction of the value added measures are similar to those used on the income side of the national accounts. Particularly for capital-type income, the data are reported to the IRS on a company basis. Therefore the assignment of incomes to specific industries requires conversion to an establishment basis. There are no good ways to make the conversion, and BEA apportions the income by using a cross-classification of employment by enterprise and establishment and assuming that capital income per employee for an establishment-based industry does not vary by industry of ownership.

In a world of constantly changing corporate structures, there are likely to be significant inconsistencies between the estimates of value added and gross output. However, the alternative approach—estimating value added as the residual of gross output less purchased inputs—is frustrated by the lack of comprehensive source data on intermediate inputs, which is a problem for services-producing industries in particular.

We have constructed alternative estimates of purchased inputs from the annual Census Bureau (CB) surveys of the communications industry (an industry for which reasonably good information on purchased inputs does exist) for the period 1990–2001. While the definitions are not identical to those of the BEA accounts, the pattern of change in the relationship between purchased inputs and output should be similar in the industry accounts and the CB surveys. We define purchased inputs from the surveys as operating expenses less wages and salaries, supplemental wage benefits, and depreciation.

The ratios of purchased inputs to total revenue from the Census Bureau and BEA data are shown in figure 4-1. There is a steadily rising trend in the share of purchased inputs in the BEA data for telecommunications that is not evident in the survey. It arises because the estimate of value added from the income-side sources of the national accounts increases more slowly than gross output, which is largely obtained from the CB survey. For broadcasting, the BEA data indicate a large decline in the share of purchased inputs over the first half of the 1990s, followed by a sharp rise in subsequent years. Again, that pattern of change is not evident in the Census Bureau data.

Further efforts to compare the CB and BEA data indicate similar estimates of labor costs but very different patterns of change in the estimates of capital income (defined in the Census Bureau data as revenue less operating income plus depreciation). This result is very much in accord with the argument of Yuskavage (2000), which states that it is increasingly difficult to apportion the income of large corporate firms to the specific industries in which they operate. Broadcasting, for example, has gone through a wave of corporate mergers between the broadcasters and the firms that supply their programming. In corporate accounts, the distribution of income between the subsidiaries and the parent can be quite arbitrary.

Figure 4-1. *Comparison of Purchased Input Shares for the Communications Sector, BEA, and Census Bureau, 1990–2001*[a]

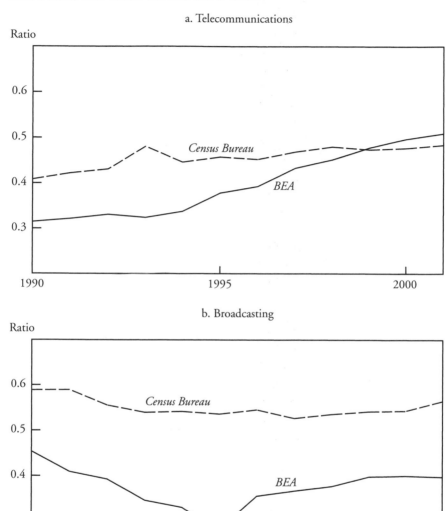

a. Telecommunications

Ratio

b. Broadcasting

Ratio

Source: Authors' calculations from BEA industry data and Census Bureau, *Service Annual Survey, 2001* and prior years.

a. Purchased inputs defined as operating expenses less wage and salary, wage supplements, and depreciation.

BEA is currently engaged in a program to more closely integrate and reconcile its estimates of industry value added with the benchmark I-O accounts. An integrated system has become more feasible with the expansion of survey data from the Census Bureau on revenues and operating expenses of services-producing industries. In the meantime, the potential inconsistency between the industry apportionment of capital income and the measures of gross output does create problems for the residual estimates of purchased inputs. These problems are most troublesome for efforts to estimate the contribution of multifactor productivity. Therefore we are skeptical about the accuracy of the decomposition of labor productivity growth shown in table 4-2. A slower rate of increase in purchased inputs would have a direct impact on the estimates of MFP growth, for which estimates of negative change over multiple years do not seem credible.

Prices

The rapid rate of innovation in the communications sector has created particular problems for the price index programs. New services must be introduced into the system on a timely basis, and rapid changes in market share can quickly outdate the weights that are used to aggregate the price indexes. Furthermore, with deregulation the telecom companies adopted very complex pricing schemes combining increases in basic rates with a wide variety of discount plans.

The CPI measure of telephone charges extends back for several decades, and it distinguishes between local and long-distance service. However, a measure of cellular phone services was not incorporated until 1998. Over the period from deregulation up to 1995, the CPI provided the only price index covering long-distance phone service, and it used a methodology that was not well suited to the post-1995 period because it did not fully reflect the growth of discount plans. To begin with, a fixed-weight index would not capture the increased share of the market that was claimed by the discount plans in the period between sample revisions. Also, the shift from a standard to a discount plan is linked out of the index since it is a new specification or new product—that is, it is treated as a quality change rather than a price decline.

The potential magnitude of this problem is illustrated in the top panel of figure 4-2 and in table 4-3, which provide comparisons of the change in the CPI for interstate toll calls with an index based on average revenues per minute from the Federal Communications Commission (FCC). The FCC measure shows a much more rapid annual rate of decline over the 1985–2001 period

Figure 4-2. *Comparison of Alternative Measures
of Telecommunications Charges, 1985–2001*

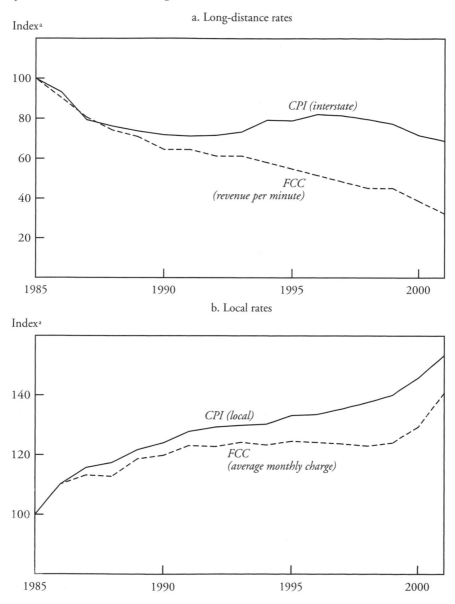

a. Long-distance rates

Index[a]

CPI (interstate)

FCC
(revenue per minute)

b. Local rates

Index[a]

CPI (local)

FCC
(average monthly charge)

Source: FCC measures are from *Trends in Telephone Service, 2003*, tables 13.1 and 13.4. The CPI components are for the U.S. city average.
 a. 1985 = 100.

Table 4-3. *Price Trends for Telecommunications*

Average annual rate of change

Period	Long distance			Local charge		
	FCC revenue per minute	CPI interstate	PPI	FCC	CPI	PPI
1985–1995	−5.8	−2.3		2.2	2.9	
1995–2001	−8.5	−2.3	−3.3	2.1	2.4	0.4
1985–2001	−6.8	−2.3		2.2	2.7	

Year	Revenue per conversation minute		
	International	Interstate	Overall
1992	1.01	0.15	0.19
1993	1.02	0.15	0.19
1994	0.93	0.14	0.18
1995	0.91	0.13	0.17
1996	0.76	0.12	0.16
1997	0.69	0.11	0.15
1998	0.58	0.11	0.14
1999	0.54	0.11	0.14
2000	0.52	0.09	0.12
2001	0.35	0.08	0.1

Sources: PPI and CPI indexes from the BLS; revenue per minute from Federal Communications Commission, *Trends in Telephone Service, 2003*, table 13.4

than the CPI measure, 6.8 percent compared with 2.3 percent. The comparison may overstate the problem for consumer prices because we do not have measures of revenue per minute that distinguish between business and consumer uses. It often is argued that reduced regulation resulted in the shifting of a portion of the costs of long-distance service from business to residential consumers. Competition and technological changes invalidated the old system, under which high charges to business provided a cross-subsidy to households. In contrast, the CPI and FCC measures of the cost of local phone service are more similar (table 4-3).

Some observers also have questioned the appropriate treatment of the discount plans. To some extent, they reflect differences in the quality of service: for example, restrictions on time of use and the lack of operator assistance. In other cases, the differences reflect efforts to capture unsophisticated consumers.

Therefore the adjustment for quality is not straightforward. It is important to note that the FCC data, shown in figure 4-2, do not distinguish between peak and off-peak usage, implicitly attaching equal value to calls made at all times of the day.

The PPI began to include telephone services in 1995, and wireless was introduced in 1999. The BLS uses a mix of methods to compute price changes, but they all involve an effort to initially price a homogeneous set of services and then aggregate them by using fixed base-period weights, creating a Laspeyres index (Gerduk 2001). In constructing the PPI for telecommunications, BLS has emphasized a unit-value calculation: computing revenues per minute within detailed homogeneous service categories, such as peak and off-peak minutes, call-forwarding, and so forth. In many cases, BLS has been able to obtain data from all providers rather than rely on a probability-based sample. That method is used for all wireless and a growing proportion of toll-based long-distance communications. For local service, they use a method that samples the rates that make up a telephone bill of fixed characteristics. In principle, the PPI should capture changes in the structure of the various phone plans, but it still relies on base-period weights that may lag in capturing the changing composition of the market.

In the period after 1996, the PPI for telephone service shows substantial declines in long-distance charges for businesses that are much greater than those reported for residential usage. For example, the PPI for residential toll calls declined by 17 percent between 1995 and 2002, compared with 38 percent for business calls. The charges for local service are shown as roughly constant, in contrast to the increases reported by the CPI and the FCC. However, the CPI and the PPI both indicate substantial declines in cellular phone charges for the few years for which data have been collected.

The BEA measure of the price change for gross output of the telecom industry has been based on components of the PPI since 1995. For the 1977–87 period, it largely follows movements in the CPI, and for the 1987–95 period, it is based on unpublished measures from the PPI; therefore it is likely that it underestimates the growth in telecom output prior to 1995. However, as shown in figure 4-3, both the BLS and BEA price indexes for telecommunications output have declined substantially compared with the CPI.

Several observers have also suggested that the available price indexes understate the overall rate of decline in telecom prices because they fail to incorporate some of the new services, such as broadband. Gilder (2000), for example, has argued that the availability of infinitely abundant bandwidth at low prices is an

Figure 4-3. *Comparison of Alternative Output Price Deflators for Telecommunications, 1985–2001*

Index[a]

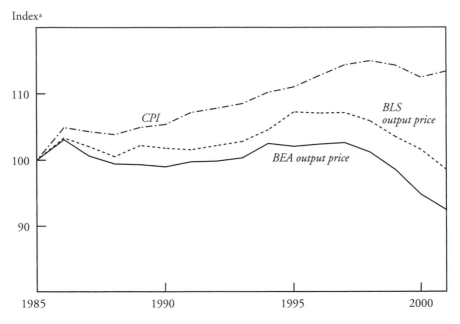

Source: Computed by the authors from data provided by BEA and BLS.
a. 1985 = 100.

innovation of revolutionary importance. Bandwidth, which plays a particularly critical role in the transmission of large amounts of data, has been an area of rapid technological innovation that, with the introduction of fiber-optic cable and improved switching and routing devices, rivals the rate of innovation in computers.

Galbi (2000), who examined trends over the 1990s in the price of bandwidth, pointed out the importance of properly defining the unit of broadband service to be priced. Broadband service is geographically specific—for example, offered between New York to Chicago; therefore he needed to control for both bandwidth and distance. Using data filed with the FCC for sales within local exchanges, he found that prices had dropped about 20 percent in the first part of the 1990s, but, surprisingly, there was very little change after 1995. Galbi's result, together with the small size of the broadband market in terms of revenue, suggests that broadband is not currently a large source of error in the construc-

Table 4-4. *Net Capital Stock of the Communications Sector, 2001*
Billions of dollars

Capital items	Telecommunications		Broadcasting and cable	
	Stock	Percent	Stock	Percent
Total capital	693.1	100.0	166.4	100.0
Equipment	326.8	47.1	80.4	48.4
Computer equipment and software	22.5	3.3	3.5	2.1
Communication equipment	216.1	31.2	56.4	33.9
Transport	26.4	3.8	6.6	4.0
Electrical transmission and distribution	20.7	3.0	3.5	2.1
Other equipment	41.0	5.9	10.4	6.3
Structures	366.4	52.9	85.9	51.6
Telecommunications structures	255.5	36.9	45.8	27.5
Other structures	110.9	16.0	40.1	24.1

Source: Bureau of Economic Analysis, *Fixed Asset Tables* (www.bea.doc.gov/bea/dn/home/fixedassets.htm [November 2003]).

tion of telecom price indexes, but these types of new services are likely to require continual innovation in the price measurement programs.

Role of IT Capital

Among the fifty-four industries that constitute the nonfarm sector in the BEA data file, telecommunications and broadcasting rank first and second respectively in the intensity of use of IT capital. We define capital intensity as the average share of IT capital income in value added or gross output over the 1987–2001 period. In this case, the choice between value added and gross output is of little consequence in the rankings. On average, the income of IT capital accounted for one-third of value added in telecommunications and about one-fourth in broadcasting. However, as shown in table 4-2, the growth of the contribution of IT capital to labor productivity in telecommunications was high but was not accelerating over that period. In contrast, the contribution of IT capital in broadcasting grew dramatically, particularly in the post-1995 period and primarily in the cable segment.

The distribution of the capital stock in telecommunications and broadcasting at the end of 2001 is shown in table 4-4. Both computer equipment and software and communications equipment are part of the category of information-

Figure 4-4. *Price Indexes for Total Producer Durable Equipment and Software and Communications Equipment, 1980–2001*

Index[a]

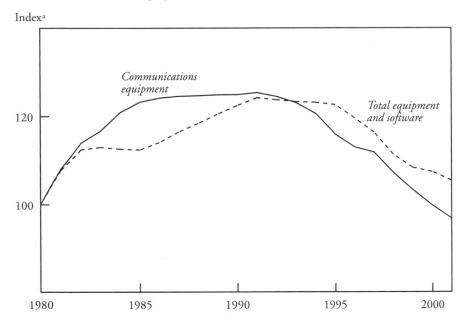

Source: Bureau of Economic Analysis, *National Income and Product Accounts*, table 7.8.
a. 1980 = 100.

processing equipment (IT capital), but the share of computers is quite small. On the other hand, communications equipment represents about one-third of the capital stock in both telecommunications and broadcasting.

The fact that communications capital typically is included with computers in the discussion of IT capital has led some observers to expect that the quality-adjusted price of communications equipment should follow that of computers. In the first half of the 1990s, computer equipment prices fell at a 14 percent annual rate, accelerating to more than 20 percent in the 1996–2000 period. In contrast, prices of communications equipment have been falling at a rate of only about 3 percent per year. As shown in figure 4-4, the price of communications equipment has closely followed that of the total category of equipment and software.

Like computers, telecommunications equipment is a heavy consumer of semiconductors, which are the source of much of the decline in computing costs. Therefore Jorgenson and Stiroh (2000) and others have suggested that the rate of price decline in communications capital may be severely understated. Doms (2003) also noted that the large volume of new patents in communications identifies it as an area of rapid innovation.

Several recent studies have examined prices of communications equipment for evidence that the rate of decline is understated in the official statistics. These studies and some additional work are summarized in Doms (2003).[2] He concludes that a conservative interpretation of the results would suggest that communications equipment prices have been declining at about twice the annual rate shown in the official statistics between 1995 and 2000. While the difference is substantial, the rate of price decline is still much less than that of computers. One explanation for the slower rate of decline is given by Aizcorbe, Flamm, and Khurshid (2002), who argue that semiconductors are less important for communications equipment than for computers and that the prices of the specific semiconductors used in communications equipment have fallen less dramatically. They suggest that the difference in the use of semiconductors in computers and communications equipment could explain a divergence in the change in equipment prices of about 12 percent annually.

Summary

The communications industry has experienced very rapid output growth led by the expansion of wireless telecommunications and cable systems in the broadcast segment. The gains in labor productivity have been very rapid in telecommunications but surprisingly slow in broadcasting. Both segments show rapid growth in capital per worker, driven by increased use of IT capital. However, we believe that the estimates of improvements in multifactor productivity may be unreliable because of problems in accurately measuring purchased inputs.

With respect to the measurement of prices, the new PPI measures for telecom services provide reliable measures of price change since 1995, but there is some evidence that the price indexes missed a significant portion of the decline in long-distance charges prior to 1995. Furthermore, the adequacy of the measures of communications equipment is an area of considerable uncertainty. To

---

2. Some of the major studies are Doms and Forman (2003) on LAN equipment, Grimm (1996) for telephone switches, and Aizcorbe, Flamm, and Kurshid (2002). Preliminary versions of the papers by Aizcorbe, Flamm, and Khurshid and by Doms and Forman were presented at the Brookings workshop "Communications Output and Productivity" in February 2001. Doms (2003) extends the work to cover fiber-optic equipment and modems.

date, the research suggests that the rate of price decline is understated for many types of communications capital, but the rate is considerably less than that for computers. Overall, this review suggests that the rates of output and labor productivity growth are currently being measured quite well, though they may have been understated prior to 1995. However, because of problems with the measures of purchased inputs and capital goods prices, the estimates of MFP growth are very tentative.

COMMENT BY ROBERT J. GORDON

Discussion of the Transportation and Communications Industries

The Triplett-Bosworth chapters on transportation and communications are admirable. The authors do the best job to date of untangling what the BEA and BLS data actually show and why they differ, and they bring together evidence on the reasons for acceleration and deceleration of productivity growth at the sectoral level. Moreover, their book is impressive in recognizing past research and linking their results to this inheritance. The main thrust of these comments is to praise the progress that the authors have made in reconciling measurement differences but to criticize them on two quite different grounds. First, they display output and productivity measures for the BEA gross output and value added concepts of output as if these were equally important and equally reliable; I argue that several aspects of the BEA intermediate materials estimates are implausible and that future work on productivity in transportation, communications, and indeed the entire economy should place much greater weight on gross output measures when those measures differ from estimates of value added. Second, the chapters are long on measurement discussion and short on substantive answers to significant questions, such as why productivity growth disappeared in airlines and trucking after 1995 and why MFP growth was significantly negative in broadcasting just when labor productivity and MFP growth in the overall economy experienced a marked revival.

Transportation

My comparative advantage is in the substantive and measurement issues involving transportation, and my discussion remarks here are confined primarily to that sector. My point of departure is the analysis of output and productivity measurement issues in the transportation sector (Gordon 1992), which the authors generously cite. I will take on the task, which they set themselves at the beginning of the transportation chapter, of evaluating what we have learned about productivity in the transportation sector since 1992.

The first reason why the BLS and BEA publish different growth rates for productivity in the transportation sector is that their coverage is different. There are no significant differences for railroads, but the BLS covers only about three-quarters of the BEA output universe for airlines and a bit less than half for trucking. Table 3-4 provides for trucking an exact mapping of coverage by the BEA, BLS, and Census Bureau to particular SIC codes, and this together with table 3-5 provides a much clearer explanation of the subsector location of coverage differences than I achieved in 1992. Typically the BLS chooses to cover a subset of a sector, limiting itself to those activities that are easiest to measure, whereas the BEA must strive for broader coverage in order to achieve a complete breakdown of GDP by industry, including any subsector no matter how difficult the task of measuring its output.

Let me add equal praise for the basic presentation of results in table 3-2. Here it is transparent that the BEA provides two measures of output (gross output and value added) while the BLS provides one (gross output), each provides an estimate of employment, and only the BEA provides estimates of capital and intermediate inputs. As a result, only the BEA publishes multifactor productivity (MFP) at this level of industry detail, and there are two MFP growth rates listed at the bottom of table 3-2, one corresponding to BEA gross output and the other to BEA value added.

The most surprising result in the transportation chapter is the disappearance of productivity growth in the airline industry during 1995–2001 (for three measures of labor productivity and two measures of MFP) after a very robust, rapid rate of productivity growth starting in 1930 and lasting up until the mid 1970s. The chapter does not cover output before 1977, because the BEA has chosen not to publish current estimates of output by industry for the earlier decades of the postwar era due to discontinuities in methodology. But it is possible to compare the results in this chapter with previously published BEA and BLS estimates for the period prior to 1977. My 1992 paper had combined earlier estimates and reported annual labor productivity growth rates for airlines of 8.25 percent for 1929–48, 5.33 percent for 1948–73,[3] followed by 3.04 percent for 1973–87. The latter number corresponds relatively closely to Triplett and Bosworth's airline growth rate for BEA value added labor productivity for 1977–87, 2.4 percent (table 3-2).

Therefore one overriding question is why airline (and trucking) productivity growth ground to a halt in the 1995–2001 period while productivity growth in much of the rest of the economy was reviving. Before turning to substantive issues, we should note that the timing of this volume, with its final data points in 2001, distorts the results for airlines perhaps more than for any other industry. Output in the year 2001 was held down artificially by the grounding of the airlines in the few days after September 11 and by the artificial depression in travel for months after that. By the end of the year 2001, airlines had only just begun to rationalize their fleets and employment in response to the new post-9/11 environment. This rationalization was largely accomplished by early 2004. To take one dramatic example, United Airlines flew 41 percent more seat miles per full-time-equivalent employee in the first quarter of 2004 than in the first quarter of 2001, an annual (log) growth rate of output per employee of 11.4 percent.[4]

My first substantive point applies to the transportation sector as a whole. Why should we expect any MFP growth at all in the transportation industry? The transportation industry buys big boxes—trucks, railroad cars, airplanes—and it buys engines to make the boxes move. Then it puts stuff inside the boxes. The transportation industry does no research and development. It is all done by the makers of the big boxes. General Electric makes both locomotives and aircraft engines, and it performs a lot of R&D. Boeing makes aircraft and also does a lot of R&D. In the trucking industry, most of the technical change is coming from companies like Detroit Diesel and Cummins, which make the engines that propel the trucks.

Thus much if not most of the changes in MFP for the transportation industry reflect errors in measuring the quality of the boxes and the engines, and the leading example of error is the airlines. The biggest contributor to labor productivity growth, except for the invention of the airplane itself, occurred in the transition from piston to jet engines, which occurred between 1958 and 1969

3. Gordon (1992, table 10.1).
4. Source for 2001 is the *Airline Database Full-Year 2001 Edition* (UBS Warburg, June 18, 2002). Source for 2004 is a United Airlines press release dated April 29, 2004.

for the major airlines. Output per employee in the airline industry grew at a remarkably steady 7.0 percent over half-decade subintervals from 1935 to 1969,[5] and it then began its slowdown toward the zero percent exhibited in Triplett and Bosworth's table 3-2. Why did this occur? Innovation in the aircraft-producing industry and the engine industry basically ceased in the late 1960s. We are still flying in 747s that are only marginally different from the early models introduced in 1969.

The only important improvements in aircraft technology in the last thirty-five years have been in fuel economy and in the distance that a plane can go without refueling, neither of which translates directly into improvements in measured productivity. Computerized cockpits may ease the workload on pilots and may improve safety, but airline output per pilot depends almost entirely on the size of the plane and on the length of the flight. Two pilots in a 747 flying to Tokyo produce many more seat miles per pilot than two pilots in a regional jet flying from Washington to Raleigh-Durham. The move from large 747s to smaller 767s on international routes, and from 737s to smaller regional jets on many domestic routes, provides at least one substantive answer to the puzzle of declining airline productivity growth in the past decade. That is, compositional changes can be major drivers of acceleration and deceleration in productivity growth.

There is no discussion at all in the chapter about price indexes for aircraft, locomotives, or for trucks. What is the nature of the errors in measuring the quality of these capital inputs to transportation? Have the errors grown larger or smaller over time? My 1992 paper had an extensive discussion of changes in input and output quality in the airline industry and concluded that failure to correct capital input for quality changes, particularly before 1970, causes official measures of airline MFP growth in the earlier period—and thereby the recent slowdown—to be overstated.[6]

A few comments are in order about changes in the quality of airline output, which the authors briefly discuss. Most of the change in seating density, which they rightly treat as a reduction in airline quality, occurred between 1975 and 1982 and is not relevant for the more recent behavior of output quality. In fact, two large airlines, American and United, reduced seating density and thus raised output quality in the 1999–2001 period, and a start-up (JetBlue) has done so more recently. There are no comments in the chapter about such intangible improvements in airline output quality as the value of frequent flyer awards, the

5. Gordon (1992, table 10.6).
6. Gordon (1992, pp. 386–408).

introduction of in-flight entertainment, Internet booking and check-in, and other kinds of conveniences having to do with airlines. Going in the opposite direction, as a reduction in output quality there is the padding of flight times to deal with congestion; flight times on transcontinental flights are now thirty minutes longer or more than in the late 1970s.

One problem in using a value-added measure for airline productivity is that airlines keep switching back and forth between the use of purchased inputs and their own employees. In the 1990s travel agent commissions were virtually eliminated, and airlines switched to using their own reservation agents, which were replaced in part by their own and third-party Internet sites after 1995. More recently, especially since 2001, draconian cost cutting has shifted maintenance work from highly unionized airline labor to lower-cost third-party providers.

My characterization of airline productivity as having been achieved mainly by the manufacturers of aircraft and engines may be an accurate characterization for the period between the 1930s and 1980s, but airlines are now obtaining significant benefits from the "new economy" revolution of the post-1995 period. Websites have sharply cut the cost of reservation and ticketing per passenger, and that is true particularly for the low-cost carriers (Southwest, JetBlue) that do not participate in third-party websites at all, thus forcing their customers to go to the airlines' proprietary websites. A major post-1995 innovation is the airline lobby e-kiosk and at-home self check-in, both of which use third-party web-based technology and would not have been possible before the commercialization of the web after 1995. Lobby e-kiosks have virtually eliminated lines in many airports and have allowed airlines to reduce substantially the staffing of departure lobbies, although post-9/11 security line congestion may have offset those gains at some airports and at some times of day.

Turning to trucking, there have been three types of capital improvements. First of all, fuel economy has improved, which of course reduces the need for purchased fuel. IT capital has had a minor role, which is briefly discussed by Triplett and Bosworth, in that trucks can be located by a global positioning system and sent to pick up return loads in a way that was not feasible before. But overwhelmingly, the most important role of capital in the trucking industry is government-financed highway capital. Perhaps the most important creator of productivity growth in the trucking industry was the invention and development of the interstate highway system, starting in 1958. Particularly for trucking and less so for airlines and railroads, a measure of government-owned capital should be added to provide a useful measure of MFP growth.

There is more to running a transportation company than just buying boxes and engines. Airline managers are well aware of the trade-off between better productivity and better service. If you want to cut the check-in line or cut the line waiting at the gate to board the plane, put on two employees instead of one. You cut the lines, but you reduce productivity by hiring more workers. It is precisely this productivity-versus-service trade-off curve that has been shifted by the invention of airline websites and self check-in.

Communications

My comments on the communications chapter are very brief. There is an analogy to transportation in my main first point, which is that almost all of the output is being produced by purchased capital input. A typical TV station has lights, cameras, wires, microphones. Over the years there have been enormous improvements in electronic switching devices, the lights are now less hot, and all sorts of computerized special effects are possible. Even the use of portable video cameras for routine use in local TV news is a development of the past twenty-five years. Everything is being purchased from the outside, and all the R&D is being done by the suppliers.

The communications chapter has a nice discussion of what little we know about price deflators for capital in the communications industry, but there is no parallel discussion about capital input in broadcasting. So we need a bit of caution regarding productivity in the broadcast TV or radio industry. My backyard was dug up for digital cable about 1998. There was an enormous investment, as the chapter notes, in the late 1990s to extend digital cable for that last mile to the individual customer. To attribute the decline in MFP in broadcasting to investment (or overinvestment) in the late 1990s implies to me that there has been mismeasurement of the distinction between investment and capital input, and perhaps use of overly high depreciation rates. My cable TV provider also supplies my Internet service. My monthly charges are outrageously high, and virtually no employees are needed once the basic installation is complete. Productivity in the cable TV industry must now be growing at very high rates.

The Problem of Value Added and Intermediate Inputs

The book suffers from the authors' impartial presentation of productivity and MFP measures based on the BEA measures of gross output versus value added, as if these were equally reliable. In their display of value added results, the authors do not heed their own warnings, which are so well developed in the communications chapter. There they provide a blistering indictment of the BEA's methodology for measuring value added.

Capital-type income reported to the IRS is reported on a company basis. The assignment of this income requires its conversion to an establishment basis. There is no good way to make this conversion. There are likely to be significant inconsistencies between estimates of value added and gross output. Perhaps an even more important problem is the "inconsistent residual problem" involved in the difference between the methods of calculating nominal and real value added. As the authors point out, there are insufficient data to provide reliable estimates of nominal intermediate materials inputs, and so these are calculated as a residual by subtracting income-based value added measures (with the company-versus-establishment dilemma that they pose) from gross output. However, in the calculation of real value added, the location of the residual is reversed. Gross output and intermediate materials inputs are deflated separately; then real value added is calculated as a residual. There are multiple sources of errors in calculating real value added that do not apply to real gross output, a much more straightforward concept.

To see some of the problems, turn to figure 4-1 in the communications chapter. The BEA measure of purchased input shares bears no resemblance to the Census Bureau's input shares. One of the more important contributions of the communications chapter is its presentation of an alternative measure of purchased inputs from the Census Bureau that can be used as an alternative to the BEA measure. The Census Bureau purchased input shares in gross output are very stable. This means that any evidence that value added is growing at a substantially different rate from gross output has got to be a measurement error, not a fact about the economy, and that applies across the board to the entire economy, not just to transportation and communications.

There is other evidence that the BEA value added measures of productivity and MFP are unreliable. In the airline industry intermediate inputs grew at 2.5 percent a year, or 25 percent a decade, from 1977 to 1987. But then in the next eight years it was almost all reversed. Is there any technological counterpart of this? It probably has something to do with capital income and profits.

Returning now to the themes of measurement accuracy and the overall quality of the industry data, I fear that the BEA has been moving backward, in contrast to the situation in the late 1980s and early 1990s. The first draft of my 1992 transportation paper was presented at a conference in 1989, when the BEA airline output data grew at implausibly low rates due to the use of PPI-based deflators that ignored the existence of discount fares. In its January 1991 benchmark revision of the industry data, the BEA switched from use of these erroneous deflators for all of transportation to a volume-based measure such as the one the BLS had been using all along. Presto, many of the previous discrepancies between the BLS and BEA productivity measures were eliminated, and between the conference and the 1992 publication of my paper, I had to redo everything. Suddenly the BEA, instead of saying that airline productivity had fallen at 4 percent a year, said that it had risen at 4 percent a year. At least in some industries it now appears that the BEA has moved backward to the use of flawed PPIs for deflation. The Triplett-Bosworth treatment of railroads in the transportation chapter includes an excellent criticism of the BEA's use of the PPI.

Conclusion

The authors' conclusion is a bit bland. They recommend a closer integration of the work of the BLS and BEA. I would reach a different and stronger conclusion: there are significant and perhaps unavoidable flaws in BEA measures of real value added that should lead both the BEA and productivity analysts to put primary weight on productivity and MFP measures based on gross output, not value added. In their excellent discussion in the communications chapter, Triplett and Bosworth place primary emphasis on the difficulty of translating company-based estimates of capital income to an establishment basis. I would add to this company-versus-establishment difficulty two further elements, to create a trilogy of near-fatal problems. The second flaw is the "double residual" method wherein nominal intermediate inputs are calculated as a residual, while real value added is calculated as a residual in a subsequent step that is subject to magnification of any errors in the deflation of intermediate inputs. The third flaw is the apparent use in some industries, like the railroad industry, of a PPI that implies output changes that are not consistent with available data on volume changes.

This leaves us, then, with the dilemma of how to divide up total GDP by industry. In census years this is done in nominal terms as part of the construction of input-output tables. The issue is how to go between census years and how to extrapolate beyond them, both in nominal and real terms. Triplett and Bosworth's figure 4-1 points the way toward an answer: shares of real intermediate input use should be assumed—that is, forced—to evolve at a steady rate, not to jump around, as is implied for some industries by the BEA method, or to reverse themselves for no apparent reason, as in the airline industry.

CHAPTER FIVE

Overview: Productivity and Measurement in the Finance and Insurance Sector

I n some services industries, the concept of real output is unclear. When it is difficult to measure the output of an industry, it is also difficult to measure its price change and productivity. The finance and insurance sector is filled with those difficult-to-measure industries.

For goods, the concept of output is usually straightforward. What the industry produces—an automobile or a computer, for example—is usually obvious and implies the unit in which output is measured. Of course, measuring the output of automobiles or computers involves much more than just counting the units, because in both cases quality change is nearly as important a contributor to output growth as change in units produced and, in the case of computers, perhaps more important. But conceptually, one counts the output of the automobile or computer industry in units that are "quality-adjusted" cars or computers, and one has the intellectual security of a unit with which to start.

The finance and insurance sector has no equivalent agreed-on unit, and for that reason this volume includes two chapters that review the conceptual issues—issues that are both old and contentious—in defining the output of the banking and insurance industries. An oversimplification, which nevertheless is not inaccurate, is that the output measures for finance and for insurance that are favored by national accountants are not the output measures that are used in most economic analyses of these industries. We discuss these issues in detail in chapters 6 and 7. We are mostly critical of national accounts conventions. It happens that BEA is introducing changes in the way it measures the output of both the finance and the insurance industries in the National Income and Product Accounts (NIPA) benchmark revisions of 2003 (Chen and Fixler 2003; Fixler, Reinsdorf, and Smith 2003); the BEA changes, however, do not address our criticisms of the old conventions.

In this chapter we first review recent trends in the output and productivity of the finance and insurance sector, using data from the BEA industry accounts for consistency with our analyses of other industries. The BEA industry accounts employ, naturally enough, national accounts definitions of output for insurance and finance; those definitions are the old ones, not the new ones introduced in 2003.

Output and Productivity Trends in Finance and Insurance

The rapidly expanding finance and insurance sector's share of gross domestic product, only 6 percent fifteen years ago, is now 9 percent (table 5-1). In the old Standard Industrial Classification system, the finance and insurance sector comprised six industries: depository institutions (banks, SIC 60); nondepository credit institutions (SIC 61); security and commodity brokers, dealers, exchanges, and services (SIC 62); insurance carriers (SIC 63); insurance agents, brokers, and services (SIC 64); and holding and other investment offices (SIC 67). We exclude the latter.[1]

Among the six is the "nondepository credit institutions" industry (SIC 61)—or "nondepository credit intermediation" (NAICS 5222)—an industry that is awkwardly named and awkwardly defined. It consists of financial firms that "are engaged in extending credit or lending funds raised by credit market borrowing, such as issuing commercial paper or other debt instruments or by borrowing from other financial intermediaries."[2] By this definition they conduct one part of the output activity of banking (lending), but they do not provide transactions services, the other major output activity of banks (see chapter 7). Examples of financial firms classified in this industry are Fannie Mae (formerly the Federal National Mortgage Association), consumer finance

---

1. The new NAICS classifications, which will be used in a future revision of the BEA industry accounts, bring changes to the financial industries. Insurance industries were less extensively changed. Insurance carriers (NAICS 5241) is approximately the same as SIC 63 less some pension and other funds, formerly treated as insurance companies, that were moved into separate industries. Insurance agents and brokers (NAICS 5242) is the same as the old SIC 64.

2. Office of Management and Budget (1998, p. 520).

Table 5-1. *Finance and Insurance Sector, Percent of Gross Domestic Product*

SIC Code	Category	1987	1992	1997	2000	2001
	Finance and insurance	6.3	6.6	7.8	8.7	9.0
60	Depository institutions	3.0	3.2	3.3	3.7	3.6
61	Nondepository institutions	0.4	0.4	0.6	0.7	0.9
62	Security and commodity brokers	0.9	0.9	1.5	1.5	1.7
63	Insurance carriers	0.9	1.3	1.8	1.9	1.7
64	Insurance agents and brokers	0.6	0.6	0.6	0.6	0.7
67	Holding and other investment offices	0.4	0.1	0.1	0.3	0.4

Source: Bureau of Economic Analysis, "GDP by Industry" (www.bea.doc.gov/bea/dn2/gpo.htm [October 17, 2003]).

companies, motor vehicle manufacturers' finance companies, finance leasing, mortgage bankers, and loan brokers. As the examples show, some of the economic units classified in this industry do not lend. In addition, because some banks also do not take deposits and finance their lending activities partly through nondepository sources, the classification of the firms and the measurement of output may not have caught up with the dynamism of the financial industry.

Banking and insurance account for about two-thirds of the total in table 5-1. However, the nondepository financial institution and security and commodity broker industries have had substantially higher output growth rates, especially in recent years (table 5-2). For example, the securities industry's real output in 2000 was five times as high as it was in 1987. The nondepository financial institutions industry has grown substantially more rapidly than the banking portion of finance, and the amount of finance that is nondepository in nature has grown even faster because the portion of banks' financial activity that relies on nondepository sources of funds has also been increasing.

Table 5-3 presents an overview of output and input shares for the three major financial services industries and the two insurance industries. In a number of respects, changes in the banking industry differ from trends in the other two finance industries. Banking has the lowest rate of growth, and its value added share in gross output is stable or rising. In the nondepository and brokerage industries, substantial fluctuation in the share of intermediate inputs took place, with consequent fluctuation in the ratio of value added to output.

Table 5-2. *Output Growth of Finance and Insurance Industries*
Average annual percent change[a]

SIC Code	Category	1987–92	1987–95	1992–2001	1995–2001
60	Depository institutions	0.7	1.5	2.7	2.7
61	Nondepository institutions	2.6	8.2	12.0	9.0
62	Security and commodity brokers	4.9	9.5	15.9	15.1
63	Insurance carriers	−1.1	0.7	0.9	−0.5
64	Insurance agents, brokers, and services	−2.3	−1.8	1.2	2.3

Source: Authors' calculations based on Bureau of Economic Analysis, "GDP by Industry" (www.bea.doc.gov/bea/dn2/gpo.htm [October 17, 2003]).
a. Chain-type quantity indexes for gross output.

Fluctuation in the share of property income is especially marked in securities brokerage firms, apparently caused by unusual trading gains and losses.[3] Fluctuation in the measured capital share is a major and neglected problem in estimating industry productivity to which we return later in this chapter.

Productivity Growth in Finance

Financial services industries not only have high output growth, they have very high productivity growth rates. Indeed, their productivity growth rates are at or near the top of those for all services industries (see table 5-4 and figures 5-1 and 5-2).

Much recent analysis of productivity acceleration in the United States uses 1995 as the "break year" (Jorgenson and Stiroh 2000, Oliner and Sichel 2000, Stiroh 2002a). Examination of the data for the financial industries suggests that 1992 is a better year to mark productivity acceleration. As evidence of this, the post-1987 output growth in these industries is substantially stronger if computed with 1995 as the end period rather than 1992 (see the comparisons in table 5-2). However, the choice of break year has no important substantive implications: numerical magnitudes of the average annual growth rates are affected by it, but the qualitative results and conclusions are not; for that reason and to facilitate comparison with other studies, we present productivity trends using 1995 as the break year.

3. Communication from Brian Moyer of BEA, October 29, 2003.

Table 5-3. *Economic Structure of Finance and Insurance Industries,*
1987, 2000, and 2001

Billions of dollars[a]

	1987		2000		2001	
Nominal value	*Value*	*Percent*	*Value*	*Percent*	*Value*	*Percent*
Depository institutions						
Gross output	203.3	100.0	476.1	100.0	482.4	100.0
Value added	143.9	70.8	361.1	75.8	359.8	74.6
Indirect taxes	6.7	3.3	9.5	2.0	10.0	2.1
Labor	87.3	42.9	218.5	45.9	216.2	44.8
Capital	49.9	24.6	133.1	28	133.6	27.7
Intermediate inputs	59.4	29.2	115	24.2	122.5	25.4
Nondepository institutions						
Gross output	36	100.0	164.7	100.0	167.4	100.0
Value added	17.9	49.7	69.5	42.2	88.8	53.0
Indirect taxes	1.6	4.5	5.4	3.3	5.6	3.3
Labor	6.1	16.9	23.4	14.2	30.0	17.9
Capital	10.2	28.3	40.8	24.8	53.2	31.8
Intermediate inputs	18.2	50.6	95.2	57.8	78.6	47.0
Security dealers and brokers						
Gross output	61.9	100.0	330.7	100.0	274.6	100.0
Value added	41.3	66.7	150.8	45.6	175	63.7
Indirect taxes	0.7	1.2	4.7	1.4	5.0	1.8
Labor	36.8	59.5	131.2	39.7	151.8	55.3
Capital	3.7	6.0	14.9	4.5	18.2	6.6
Intermediate inputs	20.6	33.3	179.9	54.4	99.6	36.3
Insurance carriers						
Gross output	131.4	100.0	296.7	100.0	308.6	100.0
Value added	43.6	33.2	182.4	61.5	170.1	55.1
Indirect taxes	9.1	6.9	14.8	5.0	15.1	4.9
Labor	27.8	21.2	124.9	42.1	115.1	37.3
Capital	6.7	5.1	42.6	14.4	39.9	12.9
Intermediate inputs	87.8	66.8	114.3	38.5	138.6	44.9
Insurance agents, brokers, and services						
Gross output	48.3	100.0	106.6	100.0	103.4	100.0
Value added	30.4	62.9	61.6	57.8	66.5	64.3
Indirect taxes	0.4	0.7	0.9	0.9	1.0	0.9
Labor	27.8	57.6	55.1	51.6	59.4	57.5
Capital	2.2	4.6	5.6	5.2	6.1	5.9
Intermediate inputs	17.9	37.1	45	42.2	36.9	35.7

Source: Bureau of Economic Analysis, "GDP by Industry" (www.bea.doc.gov/bea/dn2/gpo.htm
[October 17, 2003]).

a. Value in current prices.

Table 5-4. *Finance and Insurance Industries, Output per Worker, Input and MFP Growth, 1987–2001*

Least squares trend growth rate

Measure	1987–1995	1995–2001
Depository institutions		
Output per worker	2.91	3.12
Intermediate inputs	1.27	0.30
Capital contribution	1.46	1.36
IT contribution	0.85	1.24
MFP	0.19	1.47
Nondepository institutions		
Output per worker	2.44	1.86
Intermediate inputs	2.31	−2.04
Capital contribution	0.38	1.78
IT contribution	1.10	1.61
MFP	−0.25	2.12
Security dealers and brokers		
Output per worker	7.17	10.35
Intermediate inputs	3.55	3.37
Capital contribution	0.50	0.35
IT contribution	0.06	0.20
MFP	3.12	6.63
Insurance carriers		
Output per worker	−0.63	−1.66
Intermediate inputs	−1.08	−2.56
Capital contribution	0.57	0.87
IT contribution	0.31	0.63
MFP	−0.13	0.03
Insurance agents, brokers, and services		
Output per worker	−3.35	2.79
Intermediate inputs	0.13	2.35
Capital contribution	0.10	0.54
IT contribution	0.07	0.25
MFP	−3.58	−0.10

Source: Authors' calculations.

Figure 5-1. *Nondepository Financial Institutions Industry,*
Sources of Growth in Gross Output per Worker

Index[a]

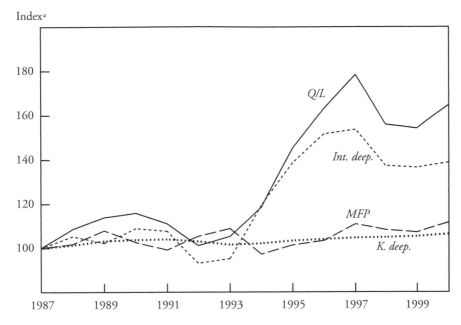

a. 1987 = 100.
Q/L = Output per worker.
MFP = Multifactor productivity.
Int. Deep. = Contribution of intermediate inputs.
K. Deep. = Contribution of capital inputs.

As table 5-4 shows, output per worker—our measure of labor productivity (LP)—grew after 1995 at 3.1 percent for banks and 1.9 percent for nondepository institutions. The rates of productivity growth for brokerage are striking—10.3 percent a year for labor productivity and 6.6 percent for multifactor productivity (MFP). With the exception of LP in nondepository institutions, LP and MFP growth rates are substantially higher than in the previous period (1987–95) in all three finance industries. We also computed value added per worker, which also accelerates after 1992, so the productivity acceleration is apparent with either measure of labor productivity. For the rest of the analysis, we use the standard measure of output per person.

As explained in chapter 2, we use the usual Solow labor productivity decomposition model, in which LP growth is accounted for by changes in inputs and multifactor productivity (equation 2-1). The contributions data for each industry are arrayed in table 5-4.

Figure 5-2. *Security Dealers Industry, Sources of Growth in Gross Output per Worker*

Index[a]

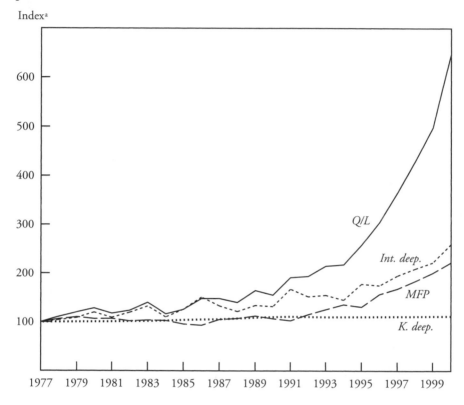

a. 1977 = 100.
Q/L = Output per worker.
MFP = Multifactor productivity.
Int. Deep. = Contribution of intermediate inputs.
K. Deep. = Contribution of capital inputs.

With respect to capital deepening, investment in information technology (IT) capital has yielded a substantial and somewhat accelerating contribution to labor productivity in banking—1.2 points of the 3.1 percent annual increase after 1992, or around 40 percent of LP growth in banking. Information technology also contributes strongly to LP growth in nondepository institutions, which is seemingly and somewhat inexplicably held down by reductions in intermediate inputs. IT makes a nil contribution to the brokerage industry, partly because the capital share is small.

Multifactor productivity contributes substantially to LP growth in all three industries, and its contribution is larger in the most recent period than it was before 1995. In nondepositories, MFP went from being negative to strongly positive.

Thus, in a general way, the trends for financial services industries repeat the trends for services industries as a group, reported in chapter 2. For services industries as a group, LP and MFP accelerated in the 1990s. Capital services generated by IT equipment made a substantial contribution to LP growth. Because the contribution of IT services to LP in services industries was prominent before the 1990s acceleration, IT contributed less to the acceleration than to post-1995 growth, but it was still a factor in the acceleration. And in a number of services industries, though not all, intermediate input deepening was associated with improvements in LP, as was the case in the brokerage industry.

Insurance Input Shares and Productivity Growth

Insurance industries, on the other hand, are not among the services industries with high productivity growth. As table 5-4 shows, labor productivity in the insurance carrier industry, which already was negative before 1995, regressed after 1995. Multifactor productivity growth in insurance carriers is minuscule, essentially zero. Although LP accelerated strongly in the insurance agent industry, the major contributor was a substantial and puzzling increase in intermediate inputs, and its MFP growth remains negative in both periods, though far less so after 1995. The relatively small contributions of IT capital in these two industries also seem surprising, since it is clear that many insurance operations have benefited from computerization. The large and volatile contributions of intermediate inputs look suspect—note, particularly, the large negative contribution of intermediate inputs in the insurance carrier industry, which seems to balance their large positive contribution in the insurance agent industry.

When one encounters odd behavior in an industry's productivity measures, the usual suspects are data problems. First, in the BEA data, insurance carriers' output is defined as net premiums earned minus claims, which differs from the output concept (risk-adjusted premiums) that is used for most research on insurance. Second, there is the perennial problem of the output deflators. We discuss these two problems below, and the conceptual one is discussed at length in chapter 6, where we also develop new output and productivity growth estimates for insurance carriers.

Third, we are not sure that the flows between insurance carriers and their agents are well measured or that they are handled appropriately. The irregular and seemingly offsetting movements in intermediate inputs in the two industries are suggestive of measurement error, but we do not assess this point.

BEA Measurement of Output in the Finance and Insurance Industries

In 1999, BEA made a number of changes to GDP methodology that increased output growth in the financial services industries (Moulton, Parker, and Seskin 1999). The revised BEA industry database incorporated these GDP changes in 2000 (Lum, Moyer, and Yuskavage 2000). At the end of 2003, BEA again changed its methodology for the finance and insurance sector (Chen and Fixler 2003; Fixler, Reinsdorf, and Smith 2003).

Considering that output in the financial services industries is hard to measure, it is well worth asking whether the post-1992 acceleration in these industries was somehow caused by changes in the statistical methodology. This is, of course, a question that can also be asked of services industry productivity measures in general. The rest of the chapter presents what we have been able to draw together on measurement issues in the financial services and insurance industries. In brief, the changes have raised output and productivity growth measures, but there is no break in series.

Tables 5-5A and 5-5B summarize BEA methods for estimating real output and value added for financial services industries and for insurance. The tables summarize the status of the BEA industry program at two points in time, 1996 and 2000, which are the relevant points for this discussion.

In 1996, GDP data by industry were updated and improved (Yuskavage 1996). By 1996, output (in national accounts jargon, "gross output") information was included in the GDP-by-industry database for forty-four industries, but the complete database was constructed only for what is essentially value added (which BEA formerly and confusingly called gross product; BEA now calls it "GDP originating").

In 2000, two additional improvements were made. First, double-deflation methodology for value added was extended to all sixty-one industries in the BEA program; second, that meant that measures of output were developed for all sixty-one industries. With these changes, input and output measures became available for an additional seventeen services industries, permitting industry productivity analysis of these industries (for example, Stiroh 2002a; Triplett and Bosworth 2002; Basu and others 2003; and Bosworth and Triplett 2003).

Two of the additional seventeen industries were financial industries—banks and nondepository institutions. Output data for the brokerage industry were

Table 5-5A. *Financial Services: Methodologies for Real Output and Value Added*

Source and date	GDP originating	Gross output[a]
Yuskavage (1996, tables 7 and 8)		
Depository (banks)	Extrapolate by L[b]	Not available
Nondepository	Extrapolate by L[b]	Not available
Brokerage	Double deflation	Securities (Q): number of trades
		Mutual funds (P): IPD for commissions
		Underwriting (Q): number of new registrations
		Other revenue, 1977–87 (P): BEA price index for merger fees
		All other components (P): GDP deflator
Lum, Moyer, and Yuskavage (2000, table K)		
Depository (banks)	Double deflation	NIPA price index for imputed services (implied by BLS Q index for banking)
Nondepository	Double deflation	PCE price index for priced services, wages, and salaries
		PCE price index for vehicle leasing
Brokerage	Double deflation	Same as 1996, except other revenue (post-1987) composite PCE price index for brokerage. Also, the investment advice portion of mutual funds was changed (see text); this is in brokerage.

Source: Bureau of Economic Analysis, "GDP by Industry" (www.bea.doc.gov/bea/dn2/gpo.htm [October 17, 2003]).

a. Q = quantity index; P = deflated.
b. L = persons engaged in production (BEA labor measure).

available in the earlier period, and the 2000 methodology required few changes from what was used previously. We first review the depository and nondepository institution industries, then the brokerage and insurance industries.

Output Measurement of Depository and Nondepository Institution Industries

As indicated in table 5-5A, in 1996 output for both banking (SIC 60) and nondepository institutions (SIC 61) was still extrapolated by the BEA labor measure,

Table 5-5B. *Insurance: Methodologies for Real Output and Value Added*

Source and date	GDP originating	Gross output[a]
Yuskavage (1996, tables 7 and 8)		
Insurance carriers	Double deflation	Non-life: premiums minus claims (Q)
		Life: expense for handling (Q)
		Health and life: PCE IPD (P)
		Other: IPD for workers' comp (P)
		+ CPI for auto and homeowner insurance (P)
Insurance agents	Double deflation	IRS receipts (Q)
		Same as insurance carriers, but weighted by commissions (P)
Lum, Moyer, and Yuskavage (2000, table K)		
Insurance carriers	Double deflation	Same as 1996
Insurance agents	Double deflation	Same as 1996

Source: Bureau of Economic Analysis, "GDP by Industry" (www.bea.doc.gov/bea/dn2/gpo.htm [October 17, 2003]).

a. Q = quantity index; P = deflated.

persons engaged in production (PEP)—indicated in the table with the notation "L." In the census or benchmark year, the level of banking output consisted of interest received minus interest paid (viewed in U.S. national accounts as a proxy for unpriced *depositor* services), plus direct fee revenues. Value added (the output concept that was extrapolated in 1996) was the net interest measure as defined in the previous sentence, less the usual range of purchased intermediate materials and services, as in any other industry. For nondepository institutions, calculating benchmark year value added was more complicated, but its extrapolation was the same, by labor input. Note that in 1996, the gross output of banks and nondepository institutions was not actually included in the BEA industry accounts, only value added.

Considering that annual real value-added measures were constructed by extrapolating labor input in both cases, it is not surprising that measured value added per employee for these two industries did not increase in the old BEA data. It is somewhat surprising that measured labor productivity growth was actually negative in the old BEA data, although it accelerated after 1992 (that is, labor productivity growth became less negative).[4]

In the 2000 revision of the BEA industry database, labor extrapolation of value added in finance was replaced by direct deflation of gross output. In addition, a number of methodological and measurement changes in the benchmark GDP revision released in October 1999 altered the output measures for financial services industries in the 2000 version of the BEA industry database. Earlier changes were made in the output definition for nondepository institutions that were not part of the 1999 GDP changes. These changes affected the current price output (sometimes called "nominal output") measures as well as what BEA calls the "chain" output measures (sometimes called "real output"). A partial list of these GDP changes includes the following:

—The treatment of "own-account" software as investment. This was part of the capitalization of all software expenditures as investment in GDP.

—A new extrapolator for banking output that explicitly measured transactions, such as checks cleared, deposits, ATM transactions, and so forth, in the form of a quantity index of banking operations.

—A redefinition of the output of "regulated investment companies" (mutual funds).

—Redefinition of the output of nondepository institutions.

As the following paragraphs explain, all four of these changes raised the rate of output growth in financial services industries.

SOFTWARE. Finance and insurance industries are major producers of own-account software—software that is developed by the user rather than purchased. When these expenditures are treated as investment in the BEA industry accounts, it raises the industry's output because the industry is treated as producing software as well as financial services. Because own-account software is added to the industry's capital stock of software, it will eventually show up as increased industry consumption of software capital services. In the short run, however, the change might reduce the apparent industry use of software, because in the previous methodology all software was expensed—implying that it was used entirely in the year produced, rather than yielding services over a number of years.[5]

---

4. Negative value added/labor growth implies that property income shrinks. It does not imply that output/labor growth is negative.

5. Consider $1 of own-account software. Under the previous methodology, this was simply $1 of expense in the industry. Under the revised methodology, the $1 is treated as investment and therefore

The methodological change was extended back, so the time series is consistent before 1992 and after. Software expenditures grew rapidly after 1992 (own-account software production doubled economywide between 1992 and 2000), so capitalizing own-account software raised financial industry output measures more after 1992 than before. The numbers are small, however. For example, own-account software in the insurance industry added $2.4 billion to the industry's output in 2000, only about 0.08 percent of its measured output.

IMPROVED EXTRAPOLATOR. A second major change was the substitution by BEA of a direct measure of banking output for the old labor extrapolation procedure. As indicated above, BEA effectively adopted a quantity index of banking transactions that had long been produced by the BLS for its banking industry labor productivity program. The new methodology raised the rate of output growth in banking over the whole period and with it, banking productivity growth. Note that this quantity extrapolator, which includes counts of loans, transactions services, and so forth, is applied to the output definition of interest earned minus interest paid—that is, to the interest rate margin.

Banking output growth also accelerated after 1992 (table 5-2). But because the methodology is consistent before 1992 and after, acceleration was not caused by the methodological change. On the other hand, the positive output and productivity growth in banking would not have been apparent without the change in output measurement methodology.

MUTUAL FUNDS. The definition of output for mutual funds and the methodology for producing real output also were changed. This is discussed in the brokerage section below.

NONDEPOSITORY FINANCIAL CHANGES. Changes in output measures for nondepository institutions were not connected to the GDP revision. By 2000, their output was no longer extrapolated by labor inputs. In addition, motor vehicle leasing was explicitly recognized in the new output measures for this industry, and that component increased rapidly in the 1990s. The mortgage banking portion of the industry also showed rapid growth in the 1990s.[6] As the result of these changes, output growth in nondepository institutions was revised

---

added to the industry's output. The industry's consumption of software is equal to the value of one year's software services from the $1 of investment, which is normally less than $1. Therefore output rises in the investment year by more than production costs of using the software. The method has the effect of spreading the cost of using the software over several years, depending on the life of the software.

6. Communication with Robert Yuskavage, October 22, 2002.

Table 5-6. *Finance Sector Value Added Growth, Old and New BEA Data*
Average annual rate of change

		1987–92		1992–97	
SIC code	*Category*	*Old*	*New*	*Old*	*New*
60	Depository institutions	−1.5	1.2	−0.8	1.0
61	Nondepository institutions	2.3	5.5	6.8	12.8
62	Security brokers	4.5	4.2	19.5	20.3

Source: Old data (1987–91), Lum and Yuskavage (1997); (1992–97), Lum and Moyer (1998); new data, Bureau of Economic Analysis, "GDP by Industry" (www.bea.doc.gov/bea/dn2/gpo.htm [October 17, 2003]).

upward, from 4.5 percent a year in the old (labor extrapolated) data to 9.5 percent in the new BEA industry data over the 1987–97 period.[7] As with the banking changes, these methodological changes were extended backward, so no break in methodology is associated with the substantial post-1992 acceleration in real output and in productivity in this industry.

Summary of Methodological Changes to Finance

In table 5-6, we compare value added growth under the new and old BEA methodologies (value added because only value added was available in the old industry data for finance). The table suggests that the implied output growth rate and therefore also the (gross output) productivity growth rates were substantially increased by the measurement changes. No breaks in methodology, however, occur in 1992. Productivity accelerations that are shown in the data for these industries (tables 5-2 and 5-4) are not caused by breaks in measurement methodologies.

It is important to note, however, that the acceleration in financial industries' output and productivity growth would not have been visible in the old data, where real output growth was extrapolated by labor input. This observation is relevant to the old contention (see Griliches 1992, 1994) that services industries' productivity looked so bad in the past because their output was measured poorly. Improved measurement does not always increase the rate of output and productivity growth, but it has done so in finance. It also is important to note that further changes to the BEA definition of output in finance are forthcoming and that even with the changes, the output measurement concept remains an

7. Communication with Robert Yuskavage, October 22, 2002.

unsettled question in finance (see chapters 6 and 7). It is likely that output is still not measured very well and possible that productivity growth is understated in these industries.

Measurement Issues in the Securities and Brokerage Industry

The securities and brokerage industry has two major components, brokers/dealers and investment bankers (SIC 6211, 75 percent of total revenue) and portfolio advice (SIC 6282, 25 percent). Portfolio advice and management for a fee is illustrated by firms such as Fidelity Investment, which charge an explicit fee for managing each account and may separate fund management from other activities of the fund, such as sales (that is, it may be in a different establishment).

BEA computes brokerage output with double deflation. A number of measures cover the range of activities that are grouped in SIC 62 (see table 5-5A). As a major part of the output measure, BEA uses an aggregate measure of the number of security trades and new issues to compute a real output index; this is supplemented by other measures, such as an implicit price deflator for security commissions (table 5-5A).

A 1999 GDP definitional change affects output in the brokerage industry. Under the old BEA methodology, the current price output of mutual funds was their net property income; output is now defined as their operating expenses. Moulton, Parker, and Seskin (1999) note that the change raised GDP in some years and lowered it in others.

This change in GDP affects mainly personal consumption expenditures but also government to a lesser degree. In personal consumption expenditures (PCE), the mutual fund charges are combined with the changes noted above in the banking industry into "services furnished without payment by financial intermediaries except life insurance." This component of PCE increased 0.8 percent in 1996 and 1.9 percent in 1997 in the old BEA data. In the new data, increases were 5.2 percent and 14.7 percent respectively, so the methodological changes contributed strongly to post-1995 growth, judging by data for the two years for which an overlap exists. But again, since the methodological change was carried back, the acceleration in output and productivity growth is not an artifact of the revision; however, without the improvements, the acceleration would not have been revealed in national accounts data.

Evaluation of the mutual fund change at the industry level is complicated. In the old SIC, mutual funds were part of SIC 672, investment offices, and were folded into SIC 67 with holding companies. Because there is no natural measure of output for holding companies, the data for SIC 67 are very problematic and are excluded from our analysis. In NAICS, mutual funds are in NAICS 525 (funds, trusts, and other financial vehicles); holding companies are elsewhere. As we understand it, the redefinition of the output of mutual funds pertains mainly to SIC 67 (and NAICS 523, the securities sector). Mutual funds may be part of a future productivity analysis of financial services after U.S. industry data have been converted to NAICS classifications, but they are not included in this one.

However, the investment management activities of mutual funds were in a different two-digit SIC from the operation of the funds themselves, namely in the securities industry (SIC 62) and specifically in SIC 6282 (investment advice). These activities remain separated in NAICS, where the management of mutual funds is in an equivalent category—the portfolio management industry (NAICS 52392), which is part of the securities sector (NAICS 523).

Other than the change to mutual funds, methodological changes in the 2000 BEA database were small for the brokerage industry. As table 5-4 shows, broker-age LP and MFP are very high—indeed, the highest for any services industry in the post-1995 period (appendix table A-1). However, table 5-6 suggests that the new BEA data record only modestly greater acceleration in brokerage than the old data did. The relevant measurement question for this industry, then, concerns not methodological changes, for there were few of empirical consequence, but possible bias in the BEA procedures.

A more refined brokerage deflator was developed by McKinsey Global Institute (MGI) for its productivity study. MGI disaggregated brokerage trades to take account of the different service levels, ranging from custom investment advice to simple online order execution. The fastest growth has taken place in brokerage trades having the smallest fees. McKinsey developed an output measure for SIC 6282 in which the growth in the real value of assets under management in different types of accounts was weighted by the average management fee. The MGI output measure suggests a growth rate very similar to that of BEA for 1987–95 but a somewhat lower rate of growth for the 1995–99 period.[8] This difference appears to be consistent with BEA's assigning a lower weight to the more rapidly growing low-fee segment of the industry. Both the BEA and MGI measures yield a very large acceleration in labor productivity. MGI also found that the acceleration in productivity growth was concentrated in the security brokers/dealers component, with a trivial contribution from investment advice.

---

8. BEA data exist only at the two-digit level. Incorporating McKinsey's new estimate for SIC 6282 into SIC 62 yields an output growth rate of 21.9 percent a year for the 1995–99 period. BEA's methodology produced an estimate of 23.4 percent a year for the same interval.

Beginning in 2000, a producer price index for the investment advice component of brokerage was published.[9] It is now used for deflation by BEA. This does not affect the measurement of brokerage output for the period we studied.

Conclusions on Finance Output Measures

Comparison of the new and old BEA database for the three finance industries can be based only on value added (GDP originating), because gross output for banks and nondepositories was not part of the database before 2000. The relevant data are in table 5-6.

Not surprisingly, the biggest changes occur in the two industries—depository and nondepository institutions (SIC 60 and 61)—that were formerly extrapolated by labor input. Output measures for these industries are substantially improved in the 2000 BEA industry database, if only because some explicit output measure was substituted for labor extrapolation. The methodological change doubled the growth of value added for nondepositories in both periods and converted a negative change (in both periods) to a positive change for banks. Small revisions also occurred in the brokerage industry that were not associated with methodology, and, for the record, the brokerage revisions increased the acceleration.

For all these industries, improvements were carried back before 1992, so the output and productivity accelerations are not an artifact of the data, as they would have been if the improvements had not been carried back. However, the accelerations are a product of the data improvements in the sense that they would not have been apparent if the data improvements had not measured the outputs of these industries more accurately.

The new output measures are no doubt improvements over labor extrapolation. But the present banking output measure in particular probably does not pick up all the changes associated with improved productivity in banking, and the complexity of measuring nondepository institution output almost ensures that gains can be made with further research.

In recent decades the nature of financial activities has changed significantly. The most notable change has been a shift away from relying on banks and similar financial intermediaries to provide loans to relying more on markets as the primary source of finance. This transformation suggests much different mechanisms for managing risk, the standardization of financial instruments, and a

---

9. Information on the PPI for the brokerage industry is contained in Irwin Gerduk's presentation to the November 2002 Brookings workshop, "Two Topics in Finance: Measuring the Output of Nonbank Financial Institutions and Alternative Measures of Corporate Profits."

move from national to global markets. These changes have complicated the quantification of financial activities in the national accounts. Financial institutions provide a more diverse range of activities as they manage large-asset portfolios and the associated risks for both customers and their own accounts. New financial products arise disproportionately in the nonbanking parts of the finance industry, but banks also have moved aggressively into providing nontraditional products (see, for example, the study of "high loan-to-value" mortgage lending in Calomiris and Mason 1999).[10]

For the brokerage industry there is no question of data consistency. The only study we know of that attempted to assess the accuracy of the BEA output data (the MGI study) found some overstatement, but it was small. Using the MGI output quantity indexes would not alter our conclusion that the brokerage industry experienced very rapid and accelerating LP after 1992.

Output Measurement: Insurance Carriers and Insurance Agents and Brokers

The insurance carriers industry (SIC 63) consists of four lines in the BEA industry accounts: life insurance, health insurance, workers' compensation insurance, and property-casualty insurance. Each line is handled separately. For example, property-casualty insurance, which is roughly half the total, also consists of multiple lines of insurance, which again are handled separately in BEA's estimation method.

The basic national accounts convention for insurance output is premiums minus claims. In the BEA application, this amounts to what A. M. Best calls "net premiums earned" (premiums net of refunds to policyholders and of payments for reinsurance) minus the sum of losses (claims) and dividends paid to policyholders. Similar definitions apply to the other insurance lines, for example, "expenses of handling life insurance." Insurance industry output is then the aggregation of the separate lines of insurance, plus own-account software and own-account construction, both of which are small.

The level of insurance industry output in the benchmark year comes from the input-output table, using the BEA output definition for insurance. Current price output for non-benchmark years is extrapolated using A. M. Best data by insurance line—for example, for property-casualty insurance, the premiums minus claims (minus dividends) definition by separate line of insurance. Deflation of property-casualty insurance in the industry file is by CPI property insurance

---

10. The Brookings workshop of November 1, 2002, "Two Topics in Finance: Measuring the Output of Nonbank Financial Institutions and Alternative Measures of Corporate Profits," considered some of these issues. Material from the workshop is reviewed in chapter 7.

indexes for auto insurance and for homeowners' insurance.[11] As table 5-5B shows, no major changes were made in the revision to the BEA industry accounts, and during the period of our study, no changes were made in the treatment of insurance in GDP.

BEA changed its treatment of insurance with its December 2003 revision. The basic premiums-minus-claims definition of insurance output is retained. A number of the changes amount to smoothing the series, for example, estimating expected losses, rather than losses during a single year or period (Chen and Fixler 2003). Smoothing has some justification, although it moves price and output further from the market transactions that are the usual starting point for economic measurement. In the future BEA will add investment earnings of insurance companies to output, treating higher investment earnings as an increase in the price of insurance. This is in accordance with the System of National Accounts (SNA) idea that investment earnings are "premium supplements"—in effect, that when insurance companies earn more on investments, they implicitly charge more for insurance policies.

A new price index for property-casualty insurance has been developed for the PPI. But in the PPI, the basic price of insurance is the premium, not the premium minus claims. The PPI also includes insurance company investment income, which it includes as an element of the price of insurance, in parallel with SNA and BEA's new treatment. BLS also publishes a PPI for insurance without the investment earnings component—that is, an index for premiums.

Thus there are several concepts for insurance output: first, insurance output depends on whether the basic concept is risk-adjusted premiums or premiums minus claims. BEA uses a premiums-minus-claims definition; BLS, in the PPI, a premiums definition. Second, insurance output depends on whether insurance company investment earnings are included and, if they are included, on whether they are treated as part of the price of insurance or part of the real output of the insurance company. Both BEA and BLS count insurance company investment earnings as part of the price of insurance, but, as mentioned, BLS also publishes another price index that uses a definition of insurance output without the investment earnings.

11. Since the CPI measures owner-occupied housing by rental equivalence (see the Brookings economic measurement workshop in May 2003, "Two Topics in Services: CPI Housing and Computer Software"), only homeowners' contents insurance is appropriate for the CPI; fire and storm damage to the dwelling are not included.

Productivity measures for the two insurance industries are problematic. First, the definition of output used by BEA is controversial and does not correspond to the output concept used for economic research on insurance. We estimate in chapter 6 that changing the output concept for insurance carriers would raise the industry's measured output and labor productivity growth rates but not by enough to eliminate its negative growth in labor productivity.

Second, better deflators are needed. During the period we study, BEA used CPI insurance indexes as output deflators for both insurance carriers and insurance agents industries. CPIs, of course, pertain to household purchases of insurance. New producer price indexes for the insurance industry were introduced late in the period we examine, but they have not yet been introduced into the BEA industry file; we presume that these indexes are the relevant ones.

For the period in which the two overlap (June 1998 to June 2003), the PPI insurance indexes show substantially lower rates of increase overall—1.4 percentage points a year less for total property-casualty (table 5-7). In chapter 6, we apply the PPI-CPI differential to the data in tables 5-2 and 5-4 of this chapter (that is, we extrapolate it back). The extrapolation causes an additional increase in insurance constant price output growth, so it is no longer negative over the 1995–2001 period. The combined effect of both concept and deflators yields a new estimate of insurance carrier labor productivity that is no longer negative, but even so, it is barely positive (see chapter 6).

Additional questions surround the available data for this industry. Insurance is not now included in the Census Bureau's Services Annual Survey (SAS) program, though we understand a budget initiative to include it has been submitted. In the absence of any public data set on insurance, BEA (and everyone else) uses proprietary data from the A. M. Best company to measure the property-casualty portion of the insurance industry.

The data from A. M. Best may be valuable, but they are neither easy to access nor easy to use. At the most basic presentational level, for example, the terms used in column headings in Best's published tables are not always intuitive, and where they are not, definitions cannot be found in Best's own glossary of insurance terms. We compared levels of Best's premiums-minus-claims data for property-casualty insurance with the level in the BEA industry file (the level is derived from the input-output table). That comparison suggests that Best covers only two-thirds to three-quarters of the industry, though we are not positive that this is the only way to interpret the difference.

Of course, input data for the insurance industry are needed, not just its receipts. The Census Bureau's SAS and economic census programs too frequently

Table 5-7. *PPI and CPI Insurance Price Indexes, and BEA Implicit Price Index for Insurance Carriers*
Average annual percent rate of change

Type of insurance	Price indexes		
Property-casualty	PPI	CPI[a]	BEA implicit price index[b]
1987–95	n.a.	n.a.	7.84
1995–2001	n.a.	n.a.	3.79
June 1998–June 2003	2.82	4.2	n.a.
1999–2001	1.77	2.73	2.72
1999–2002	2.58	4.43	n.a.
Tenant and household	*PPI*	*CPI[c]*	
1987–95	n.a.	n.a.	
1995–2001	n.a.	n.a.	
1998–2001	n.a.	2.09	
June 1998–June 2003	5.63	4.72	
1999–2001	4.13	2.39	
1999–2002	4.72	2.38	
Motor vehicle	*PPI*	*CPI*	
1987–95	n.a.	6.07	
1995–2001	n.a.	2.27	
June 1998–June 2003	3.7	4.37	
1999–2001	1.37	2.78	
1999–2002	3.13	4.74	

Sources: Bureau of Economic Analysis, "GDP by Industry" (www.bea.doc.gov/bea/dn2/gpo.htm [October 17, 2003]). Bureau of Labor Statistics, producer price index industry data; consumer price index (all urban consumers, current series).

a. Home and auto insurance weighted average. Weights (0.87 Auto, 0.13 Home) derived from Relative Importance Table (motor vehicle insurance, 2.44; tenant and household insurance, 0.37).

b. Insurance carriers total; authors' calculations based on BEA GDP by industry file.

c. Tenant and household contents insurance; does not include insurance for the dwelling.

omit collecting information on purchased inputs in services industries. Insurance is a large and important industry. A public data collection program to provide information about its outputs and inputs deserves high priority.

The insurance agent and broker industry (SIC 64) also is a large and important industry whose data seem problematic. Agents sell what the insurance carrier industry produces. It appears fruitless to review the output data for the agent industry before resolving the outstanding conceptual questions concerning insurance carriers' output. We therefore neglect this industry for the present.

Measurement Issues for Nondepository Institutions

The problem of measuring the activities of financial intermediaries that function without taking deposits (the nondepository institutions in the U.S. SIC) and the growing share of banking activities that do not depend on deposits as the source of funds have not been sufficiently studied. This is a major lacuna, since both the industry and the activity have been growing relative to the traditional deposit-taking bank that historically has been the focus of most of the attention. Paul Schreyer and Philippe Stauffer of the Organization for Economic Cooperation and Development (OECD) explored some of these issues, basing their study on the deliberations of an OECD task force on the measurement of financial services in the national accounts (Schreyer and Stauffer 2002).

Schreyer and Stauffer stress the myriad ways in which financial markets have changed: increased reliance on markets for bonds and equities; "securitization" of previously nonmarketable assets, such as mortgages; expansion of financial services in the area of portfolio management and advice; and the increased importance of intrasectoral transactions. These changes led the OECD task force to propose a broader definition of financial firms with an emphasis on the provision of financial services rather than just intermediation. These services include risk management, liquidity provision, information services, underwriting, and monitoring.

Currently, the System of National Accounts uses the concept of FISIM (financial intermediation services indirectly measured) to value financial services that are compensated by interest (FISIM is discussed in chapter 7). Under the FISIM concept, national accountants divide implicit or unpriced services between those provided to the depositor and those to the borrower. The division is done relative to an intermediate reference rate, which is taken to be the opportunity cost of the intermediary's own funds. Thus the difference between the government bond rate and the bank lending rate is taken to be unpriced services that the bank provides to borrowers (the SNA manual lists bookkeeping services and the like). However, FISIM focuses strongly on the idea of an intermediary that collects deposits and re-lends to businesses or consumers. Yet financial institutions often engage in a much broader range of activities, raising a concern that these new activities are missed or undervalued in the current system.

The OECD task force argues that the FISIM approach is consistent with the concept of the user cost of the services that are provided by the financial institution and that it can be broadened to include a wide range of different financial services. Therefore the task force has concluded that the new activities can be measured by broadening the current concepts instead of adopting a new framework. The most important changes would be to recognize that activities outside the deposit/loan framework also add value and to explicitly recognize the return from employing the firm's own capital.

In his discussion of the Schreyer and Stauffer study, Kim Zieschang emphasized the broad range of financial activities that tend to be ignored with the traditional emphasis on borrowers and lenders (Zieschang 2002). Though he concurred with the relationship between the SNA concept of output and the concept of user cost, the basic definition of user cost would be the opportunity cost of funds used to purchase an asset less the income earned, where earnings would include the expected holding gain (capital gain). Yet the national accounts traditionally have excluded all capital gains and losses. He agreed with the task force that consideration should be given to including some measure of the expected holding period gain or loss.

The general discussion of the Schreyer and Stauffer paper at the November 2002 Brookings workshop on measurement issues in nondepository institutions ("Two Topics in Finance") covered the SNA approach to interest payments and other matters. Jack Triplett argued that the FISIM concept was seriously flawed in ways that could not be easily overcome. The national accountants adopt the view that interest is not the payment for a productive service. For this reason, the accountants have problems recognizing that the provision of finance is a productive service that should be valued in the national accounts. Instead, the SNA and U.S. NIPA explain the interest rate spread as representing the value of unspecified and unobserved services that are not "directly" priced. Triplett agreed with the task force's focus on financial services rather than the interest rate spread, but he favored an explicit rejection of FISIM instead of trying to amend it in various ways.

Catherine Mann pointed to the growing volume of international lending that involved large interest rate spreads and the need to account for those spreads in terms of the value of the services provided. It is not clear that splitting the spread and allocating it backward and forward really accounts for the financial services that are being provided. Marshall Reinsdorf also raised the issue of how to treat provisions for bad loans as part of the user cost associated with making loans. This invokes the consideration of risk, which needs to be part of the discussion of financial output measurement.

Input Measurement: Capital Shares and Allocation of Self-Employment Income

In chapter 2 and in table 5-1 of this chapter, we reported MFP acceleration in the finance and brokerage industries. Multifactor productivity could be affected by measurement of inputs even if there were no output measurement questions; if capital input is mismeasured, for example, the mismeasurement will spill over into MFP.

For finance, two input problems need to be discussed—the allocation of income to the self-employed and fluctuations in the capital share because of unusual gains and losses. These problems persist throughout the services industry data. They are not unique to the finance and insurance industries, but because they loom large in this sector, we discuss them here (see also chapter 11, on data needs).

The allocation of the reported income of self-employed workers between capital and labor income creates considerable difficulty for some services industries. In the BEA industry database, all self-employment income is treated as property income. Yet some of it must be labor income.

Among securities dealers and brokers, the self-employed amounted to roughly one-seventh of employment in 2000 (table 5-8). But the property income share of brokerage industry output (measured net of indirect business taxes) in the BEA industry file is very low in that year (around 7 percent—see table 5-9). If we reallocate self-employment income to labor income based on earnings in the industry, the capital share in this industry shrinks; in some years it becomes negative. Conversely, if we assume that the self-employed earn a return on capital that is the same as that of other firms in the industry, their wage becomes implausibly low. This problem with self-employment income is well known (Christensen 1971).

The BLS productivity group resolves the problem with a parallel calculation of a normal rate of return on capital for unincorporated enterprises within the sector. They estimate the implied returns to both labor and capital within the industry—which, as we noted, yields an aggregate that exceeds self-employed income. They then reduce both incomes in proportion, to control the total to the actual self-employed income. This calculation yields the shares on the right-hand side of table 5-9. We generally used the BLS estimates of capital and labor shares for our productivity estimates and applied them to the BEA value-added estimates. We did this for security brokers/dealers, for example, and the results underlie the data on shares in table 5-3. Note that the BLS capital shares for brokerage are far more stable than the BEA shares (compare the left- and right-hand set of columns in table 5-9).

Table 5-8. *Self-Employment in the Financial Services Industries*[a]
Percent

Category	1987	1992	1997	2000
Depository institutions	0.10	0.10	0.10	0.20
Nondepository institutions	1.40	3.40	2.80	3.30
Security and commodity brokers	14.00	13.20	11.50	14.20

Source: Authors' calculations based on Bureau of Economic Analysis, "GDP by Industry" (www.bea.doc. gov/bea/dn2/gpo.htm [October 17, 2003]).
a. Self-employed as a percent of persons engaged in production.

In growth accounting models, the share of capital is taken as the output elasticity of capital, which is the weight for the contribution of capital services to production. Similarly, labor compensation is the weight for the contribution of the labor input. In principle, one wants as the share of capital the product of the quantity of capital services from a capital good ("machine hours") times the rental price of machines. In parallel, labor's share is the product of labor hours times compensation per hour. One should compute capital elasticities at the detailed level, distinguishing different kinds or classes of productive capital equipment. For example, we distinguish IT from non-IT capital, and we also distinguish among different types of IT capital. In principle, we need separate capital elasticities for each type of capital.

In practice, the capital share is either computed as a residual or by using total capital income in the industry, that is, the property income share. Implicitly, the model applies to a competitive industry, in which the level of supernormal profits (or losses) is zero in the long run. In annual data, this is not likely to hold strictly, but one usually assumes that the fluctuations are small enough to be ignored.

However, when property income fluctuates in a way that is not related to the contribution of capital equipment and structures to output, as it does with the brokerage industry (see table 5-3), these fluctuations in the capital share affect our estimates of the contribution of capital, including IT capital, to labor productivity growth. The true contribution of IT in an industry (a product of the flow of IT services and the share of IT services in production) undoubtedly does not fluctuate much in the short run. The capital share fluctuates for reasons that have little to do with IT contribution—either it fluctuates because the return to other factors fluctuates or because of fluctuations in economic rents in the industry. When fluctuating capital shares misstate the contribution of IT (or of

Table 5-9. *Alternative Labor and Capital Shares of Output at Factor Cost*[a]
Percent

Industry	Intermediate inputs	BEA shares[b]		BLS shares[c]	
		Labor	Capital	Labor	Capital
Depository institutions					
1987–88	30.87	29.82	39.31	43.61	25.52
2000–2001	25.30	22.03	52.67	46.16	28.54
Nondepository institutions					
1987–88	52.84	33.24	13.92	16.79	30.37
2000–2001	54.13	28.40	17.48	16.54	29.33
Security and commodity brokers					
1987–88	30.70	56.15	13.15	62.08	7.22
2000–2001	46.93	46.22	6.86	47.39	5.68

a. Output at factor cost is gross output excluding indirect business taxes.

b. No adjustment for the self-employed. Shares equal the compensation and property type income shares of output at factor cost, as reported in BEA, GDP by Industry.

c. The BLS capital share uses capital income data from the BLS productivity program to calculate the capital share of output at factor cost. The labor share is a residual.

any other factor), that misstatement produces a corresponding misstatement of industry MFP growth.

For some industries, including banking and insurance, the BLS and BEA capital income (or property income) levels differ substantially. If the BLS capital income is used to calculate an implied value added total, the result is not comparable with that of BEA. The BLS capital measure is the return associated with its measure of capital services, so it is the concept we need. In all cases, we used the BLS capital and labor shares but applied them to the BEA value added estimate in order to maintain consistency with the rest of the BEA database.

In the finance industries, BEA and BLS output definitions appear to result in a different level of output. For example, BLS gets an output level for banking by weighting up detailed transactions, different types of loans, and so forth (Dean and Kunze 1992). This is unlikely to coincide with BEA's interest margin definition of bank output (see the discussion of bank output concepts in chapter 7). Because BEA uses the BLS banking output measure as an extrapolator, these differences in levels probably do not affect changes in productivity.

An additional problem should be noted. The BEA industry database includes indirect business taxes (IBT) in output. For our work, we removed all IBT, so output is measured in what is sometimes referred to in the national accounts literature as "at factor cost." In its productivity estimates, BLS removes sales and excise taxes but leaves taxes on property (including motor vehicle taxes) in the total—it adds them to the cost of inputs. Either treatment is problematic, to an extent, but for most industries the difference between the two treatments is small.

Conclusions

The finance and insurance industries include some whose productivity growth ranks with the highest (brokerage, banking) and some with the lowest (insurance carriers and agents) in the services sector. Data problems affect all these industries. We have reservations about how their output is measured, high productivity or low. Except for the brokerage industry, they are all measured as margin industries, comparable to the national accounts treatment of wholesale and retail trade. In the end, though, the major omission is explicit recognition of their role in handling risk. There also are problems with the measures of their capital shares. The insurance productivity numbers look less plausible than those in the finance industries because they show negative productivity growth.

However, perspective should retained. Measurement issues affect all productivity estimates. The future of productivity measurement, like its past, lies in the search for improved measures and methods. This chapter and the ones that follow are intended to provide analyses that show where improvements can be made.

CHAPTER SIX

Price, Output, and Productivity of Insurance: Conceptual Issues

As noted in chapter 5, the insurance industries have not experienced high productivity growth rates, at least as measured by using the data in the Bureau of Economic Analysis industry accounts. Insurance carriers appear to have had negative labor productivity growth over the whole 1987–2001 period (table 5-4), and both the insurance carrier and the insurance agent industries had negative measured multifactor productivity (MFP) for most of that interval.

In April 1998, the Brookings Program on Output and Productivity Measurement in the Services Sector convened a workshop, "Measuring the Price and Output of Insurance," that included participants from both the analytic/research community and the measurement community. The latter included staff members from statistical agencies on both sides of the Atlantic and from the Pacific region as well. Although the measurement of insurance has been discussed in other forums (see, for example, Voorburg Group 1993), the all-day Brookings workshop was the most intensive and comprehensive discussion of measurement issues in the insurance sector to date.[1]

This chapter reviews the measurement of insurance output and prices in the economic measurement literature and in economic research on insurance; among other sources, we make use of the papers presented at the workshop and

1. The workshop agenda and some of its papers may be accessed at www.brookings.edu/es/research/projects/productivity/workshops/19980421.htm [February 2, 2004].

the enlightening discussion among workshop participants. However, this chapter is not intended to be a summary of the workshop, nor should it be regarded as a summary of the consensus, for no consensus emerged. Rather, it is an essay on the state of the art of measuring insurance output today. We have organized material from the Brookings workshop and elsewhere in a way that is intended to advance understanding of the issues. For example, our discussion of models of insurance company behavior makes explicit a topic that was mainly implicit in the workshop discussion; however, explicit behavioral models clarify insurance measurement issues.

In addition, we have drawn on the deliberations of a Bureau of Economic Analysis (BEA) study team that reviewed the treatment of insurance in national accounts in 1995–96. This team, known internally as the Insurance and Pensions Modernization Work Team (hereafter, "BEA work team"), ultimately split into majority and minority views on the treatment of insurance, voicing exactly the same two views that have appeared in the literature and that are reviewed in this chapter. Partly because of this split, no publicly available document was produced, but we found the materials developed by the team useful in preparing our review, particularly for the arguments favoring the national accounts view of insurance, which have not always been recorded in written or published form.[2]

A Summary of Measurement Issues

As noted in chapter 5, measuring the output of the finance and insurance industries is more difficult than measuring the output of industries that produce goods such as automobiles or computers. The finance and insurance industries produce outputs that are as heterogeneous as the outputs of the automobile and computer industries, so the quality change problem in measuring output is fully as difficult for them as for industries that produce cars or high-tech goods. But finance and insurance output is difficult to measure also because in these industries there is no agreed-on unit from which to begin. It is not just the deflated, or constant price, output measure that is controversial; in finance and insurance, controversy surrounds the measure of current price output as well.

It might seem that "number of insurance policies" is the analog to "number of computers," that "premium for a risk-adjusted insurance policy" is the analog to "price of a constant-performance computer," and that the premium revenue of an insurance company corresponds to the sales (value of shipments) of a com-

---

2. Team members were Wallace Bailey, David Kass, Ralph Kozlow, Kenneth Petrick, Mark Planting, John Sporing, Leon Taub, and Ernest Wilcox.

puter producer. However, unlike in the computer industry, where we agree on the units, the measurement issues revolve around measuring quality change. With insurance, the units are themselves at issue—which is not to say that the quality change question is less of a concern.

Speaking of services industries' output generally, Zvi Griliches remarked: "The conceptual problem arises because . . . it is not exactly clear what is being transacted, what is the output, and what services correspond to the payments made to [services industry] providers."[3] Bradford and Logue make a similar remark with respect to insurance,: "In the case of property-casualty insurance, it is not clear what one means by 'price' or 'quantity.'"[4] Insurance differs from cars and computers because there is no agreed-on unit that provides a place to start. Accordingly, most of the literature on measuring insurance output amounts to debate over the output units: to oversimplify somewhat, the two alternative output units for insurance companies are the insurance policy and the administrative services that the companies provide to their policyholders.

Two bodies of literature address insurance output measurement questions, either directly or indirectly. First, insurance is the subject of a not-insubstantial economic measurement literature—statistical agency materials, Studies in Income and Wealth volumes (for example, Ruggles 1983), and economics and statistics journals. In this first literature, measurement questions are addressed and discussed directly and explicitly—a great advantage, particularly when the strengths and weaknesses of various alternatives are compared. But in this measurement literature, the implications of alternative measurements of insurance output and of alternative concepts for measuring output are seldom tested by using them in an economic analysis or by subjecting them to a hypothesis test. The arguments tend to be abstract, divorced both from the uses of economic data and from analysis of the behaviors of buyers and sellers of insurance.

Insights on measuring insurance output also emanate from economic research on insurance, which requires price and output measures. The advantages and disadvantages of the insurance research literature are the opposite of those of the economic measurement literature. Analytic implications are tested, which is a major advantage. However, the measurement implications are often not drawn directly; one has to infer the way that the price and output of insurance should be measured, either from what the researchers do with the data they use or from their complaints about the data they need but do not have. There is no tradition of including an analytical appendix on the topic "What

3. Griliches (1992, p. 7).
4. Bradford and Logue (1998, p. 30).

data should we have had to explore this problem?" One must infer the answer from the content.

Unless otherwise indicated, the topic of this chapter is property-casualty and term life insurance. "Whole" life insurance, which has a substantial savings-investment component, is not emphasized, because true insurance is only a part of the contract. We also omit social insurance (in the United States, Social Security, unemployment compensation, and so forth), which usually is treated integrally with private insurance in the national accounts literature. However, as Lippman and McCall (1981) point out, institutions for managing risk are pervasive in a modern economy. Because such institutions are not limited to private and social insurance schemes, extending the scope of this chapter beyond the private insurance industry threatens its focus on a single class of issues.[5]

In discussing the main positions in the insurance output debate, we have tried to be evenhanded. We have, however, developed our own position, which inevitably colors what we write about others, so the reader ought to know what it is at the beginning: we favor what we describe below as the "risk-assuming" model of insurance and not the "risk-pooling" model that is incorporated into national accounts in the United States and other countries. This implies that we reject the "premiums-minus-claims" definition of insurance output that is used in national accounts. Our empirical estimates in this chapter indicate that changing the concept of insurance in national accounts—and changing the deflators—would eliminate the negative measured labor productivity growth in the insurance carrier industry in recent years, though growth would remain very low.

Models of Insurance Company Behavior

At a perhaps too superficial level, the debate on insurance output has two positions. Advocates of the "premiums" position would represent the (current value) output of the insurance industry by the total revenue from insurance premiums (plus ancillary activities of insurance companies, if any). This is also referred to as the "gross premiums" approach. The output unit is the insurance policy, so we would count output growth in the insurance industry by the increase in the number of policies sold, adjusted of course for differences in the characteristics of the policies, including, but not limited to, changes in the amount of risk assumed. Ancillary activities also may be included in the output definition.

---

5. Among the comparable arrangements that they list are those to handle uncertainty about prices (futures contracts) and uncertainty over equipment failures (warranty agreements).

Advocates of the second position contend that premiums *minus claims* is the proper measure of insurance output. Premiums minus claims equal the administrative expenses and profit of the insurance company. The insurance company is viewed as performing administrative services for policyholders, so the output unit consists of these administrative services, perhaps on a per policy or per policyholder basis.

In the North American national accounts and economic measurement literature, the premiums-minus-claims position is usually called the "net premiums" position, even though that is not the definition of net premiums employed in the U.S. insurance industry.[6] Any ancillary activities of insurance companies, typically their investment income, may or may not be incorporated in the net premiums measure of insurance output in national accounts; the U.S. National Income and Product Accounts (NIPA) and the 1993 System of National Accounts (Commission of the European Communities and others 1993) have differed in this respect in the past.

However, the gross premiums–net premiums debate is only one manifestation of two different views of how the insurance activity functions and of what insurance companies do. Each of these views leads to one side of the debate, and each also implies an integrated set of decisions on measuring the price and output of insurance.

POOLING RISK.   In the risk-pooling view of insurance, the policyholders create or pay into a pool for sharing risk. The insurance company is a facilitator and an administrator: it administers the pooling scheme, and it collects the premiums and pays the claims of the policyholders. The insurance company is essentially a cooperative, in which the members of the cooperative pay a service fee to the insurance company for performing the cooperative's business functions. As Dohm and Eggleston (1998) nicely put it: "Pooling of risk defines the insurer as an intermediary between various policyholders, where the insurer's function is to collect premiums and disperse them to claimants. The policyholders retain the risk in this model."

In the risk-pooling model of insurance, the (current price) value of the service is the insurance company's administrative expenses for operating the pool

---

6. The term *net premiums* also has different definitions in SNA93 (Commission of the European Communities and others 1993) and in the insurance industry (A. M. Best 2001). Because it is expositionally efficient to have a shorter version of "premiums minus claims" and because "net premiums" has that meaning in the North American measurement literature (see for example, Ruggles 1983; Bureau of Economic Analysis 1996; and Sherwood 1999), for this chapter we adopt the North American *measurement* usage, even though it is not ideal considering the alternative definitions of the net premiums term outside and inside the United States.

(plus profit)—premiums minus claims, or in national accounts language, net premiums. The price of insurance is the service fee charged for administering the pool on behalf of the policyholders.

ASSUMING RISK. In the alternative model of insurance, the insurance company assumes the risk. In this risk-assuming or risk-absorbing view of insurance, the policyholders buy a service—having their assets or income protected against loss. As Bradford and Logue put it: "An insurance company is a financial intermediary whose main line of business is the sale of a particular type of contingent contract, called an insurance policy."[7] In this view of insurance, the service provided by the insurance company to policyholders is the reduction of risk. Without insurance, an automobile accident implies the loss of the car; with insurance, household wealth is unaffected by the accident.

In the risk-assuming model, the service provided by the insurance company is the assumption of risk, so its (current price) output is measured by the number of policies sold times the quantity of risk assumed in each policy. The insurance premium is the price charged for assuming risk, so the price of insurance is the risk-adjusted premium. Obviously, in order to absorb risk, the company must also form and operate a risk pool, administer the policies, and pay the claims, as in the risk-pooling model of insurance. The difference in the two models is who bears the risk—the policyholders or the insurance company.

Associating the gross premiums–net premiums debate with behavioral models of insurance companies is a relatively new approach to analyzing insurance measurement issues, although it has been a part of the oral discussion of insurance measurement in North America for some time. Nearly all of the issues discussed in the insurance output measurement literature and at the Brookings workshop can be portrayed as consequences of the two different behavioral models of the insurance business.

Therefore it is not so much that contributors to the economic measurement literature and the participants at the Brookings workshop were debating the appropriate way to implement *a model* of insurance. Rather, they were debating, sometimes indirectly, *which model* of insurance company behavior—and policyholder behavior—is the relevant one. It is true that there are some side issues. For example, it was asserted in the workshop that the premiums-minus-claims rule for property insurance reduces the possibility of double counting in national accounts the output of auto repair shops paid for by insurance companies. But such pragmatic arguments are ancillary to the main conceptual issue.

---

7. Bradford and Logue (1998, p. 29).

In the following discussion, we review the arguments for and against the two behavioral views of insurance, examining national accounts, productivity, and CPI and PPI measurements separately. We later discuss a second set of issues—the treatment of insurance company investment income in output and price measures. In principle, investment income could be added to either the risk-pooling or the risk-assuming model of insurance, so clarity will be served by considering investment income questions after discussing the basic ones.

The Risk-Assuming, Gross Premiums Position

The view that an insurance company assumes risk may have entered the measurement literature (though not, to be sure, the insurance literature) with the work of Michael Denny (1980) and with Richard Ruggles's review of issues in national accounts. Ruggles states: "What households are purchasing is protection against loss, and the cost of such protection . . . consists of the full premium and not the net premium."[8] Denny is equally explicit: "The output of the insurance company is the quantity of risk shifted to the insurance company."[9] Both Ruggles and Denny were writing about, and disagreeing with, the national accounts net premiums measure of insurance. The Denny piece seems to have had relatively little impact, possibly because it was only a short comment on another article. The Ruggles view is well known in national accounting circles, but it has mostly been ignored or dismissed rather than discussed seriously.[10]

Other contributors to the measurement literature who have endorsed the gross premiums alternative include Hornstein and Prescott (1991) and Popkin (1992). In the papers prepared for the Brookings workshop, the gross premiums position was advocated by Mark Sherwood (1999), whose focus was on industry productivity measurement, and by Arlene Dohm and Deanna Eggleston (1998), who described new producer price indexes for the insurance industry. In addition, as discussed below, insurance industry researchers, including Bradford and Logue (1998) and Bernstein (1999), generally have adopted the gross premiums view of insurance price and output.

8. See his appendix on financial intermediaries (Ruggles 1983, p. 69).
9. Denny (1980, p. 151).
10. Ruggles's paper apparently was not the subject of any internal document prepared for the discussions that led to the adoption of the 1993 SNA, nor have we seen any national accounts documents from any source that either discuss Ruggles explicitly or the issues he raised for the measurement of insurance.

It is not necessary to explain at any great length the rationale for the risk-assuming view of insurance. Logically, it follows from the observation that the insurance policy is what insurance companies sell, the premium is their revenue from it, and claims are a cost to the insurance companies. Long ago, Clark Warburton (1958) remarked that a company's revenue source is a good indicator of its output, whether the company is an insurance company or a coal mine. However, various points of confusion about the gross premiums position have arisen, largely in the national accounts context. The following sections discuss some of them.

Calculation of Value Added under the Two Proposals

For countries that calculate GDP by aggregating industry value added, value added becomes a crucial statistic. National accountants have sometimes stated that the gross premiums proposal for measuring insurance output will change value added and with it, GDP (this point came up at the Brookings workshop). This is a misconception. Value added in the insurance industry is the same under both output concepts, as shown in the following paragraphs.

Under the gross premiums approach, claims are a cost of the insurance company that are treated like any other cost. This means that

$$value\ added\ (gross\ premiums\ approach) =$$
$$[premiums] - [claims + purchased\ inputs].$$

Under the net premiums approach now used in national accounts, gross output equals premiums minus claims. Value added is obtained by subtracting purchased inputs and services from net premiums. Therefore,

$$value\ added\ (net\ premiums\ approach) =$$
$$[premiums - claims] - [purchased\ inputs].$$

For value added, the two alternative definitions of insurance output imply only that claims are subtracted from premiums at different points, either as one element subtracted from gross output to get value added or in the calculation of gross output itself. The value added of insurance is invariant to the definition of insurance output.

Because insurance industry value added is the same under both proposals, the choice between gross premiums and net premiums as a measure of insurance industry output has no direct impact on the level of GDP. Sherwood (1999) makes the same point.

Treatment of Claims

Because confusion exists among national accountants, it is worthwhile indicating at this point how the accounting treatment of insurance would differ under the present net premiums definition and the gross premiums alternative, although it is not our intention to work out all the implications for the SNA. Under the present net premiums definition used in national accounts, consumers are treated as paying only the net premium for insurance. In the U.S. NIPA, insurance claim payments are treated as income to consumers, who may use the income to pay, for example, for car repairs. (Claim payments are treated as transfer payments in SNA93.)

Under the gross premiums approach, consumers would be depicted as paying more for insurance (because premiums are larger than premiums minus claims). However, claims would no longer contribute to household (transfer) income; they would instead be costs to the insurance company.

Under the gross premiums approach, the insured party is portrayed as having a shiny car both before the accident and afterward, but the accident itself and the repair of the car increase neither the insured's income nor expenditure. The loss of the property and its restitution by the insurance company are changes to be recorded in the insured's capital account, but not in the insured's income and expenditure.

Suppose that there were more car accidents and that premiums rose in step with claims. The present national accounts net premiums approach would show no increase in the cost or purchase of insurance, but the rise in automobile accidents would create a flow of income (transfer) to consumers and an increase in household expenditure on car repair. Therefore an increase in automobile accidents, with the subsequent increase in claims and repairs, results in higher real consumption, an anomalous result that surely reduces the usefulness of the national accounts for analyzing consumption behavior. Similarly, casualty insurance claims paid to nonfinancial industries for losses in a hurricane create a flow of miscellaneous receipts to those industries and extra investment expenditures by them to replace the assets lost in the storm.

Under the gross premiums approach, if automobile accidents increase, consumers pay more for insurance (because premiums go up), and one would need to consider whether the increase in premiums is an increase in price or in the quantity of insurance. The insurance companies would pay more for car repair, but consumer income and consumer expenditures on car repair would be unchanged.

In addition, changing the treatment of insurance provokes parallel changes in inter-industry accounts. Under the gross premiums approach, other industries that consume insurance are depicted as paying more for insurance than under the present net premiums approach (this is parallel to the impact on personal consumption expenditures). But claims are costs to the insurance company, not revenue and expenses to the claiming industry. None of these changes affects the level of GDP, but they do shift its allocation among sectors.

Of course, the measured volume of car repair is unchanged by the alternative treatments of insurance. However, with the gross premiums approach, the insurance company is treated as purchasing car repairs that are paid out in the form of insurance claims, although some alternative accounting treatments that involve the insurance company and the capital accounts of insured industries also are possible.

Finally, there is no inherent double counting in the gross premiums approach, although this has sometimes been alleged by national accountants. It is true that changes to the *present system* are required to avoid double counting, but competent national accountants will work out the implications of the gross premiums position, just as they worked out the implications of the net premiums approach years ago.

What Does Insurance Do to the Amount of Risk?

One argument that has been made against the gross premiums position is that it implies that the insurance company reduces the amount of risk in the economy, whereas the net premiums position does not. This seems a confusion.

When an insurance company absorbs risk, it does not reduce the quantity of risk in the economy. Insurance increases utility because individuals are not indifferent to the choice between losing a small amount with certainty (the premium) and losing a large amount with a probability *that results in an equal expected value*. This is one of the oldest results of utility theory. The nature of the gain from insurance therefore depends on the nature or form of insurance and on the consumer's utility functions defined over risky states. This problem was the subject of Erwin Diewert's (1995) paper and of George Akerlof's comments at the Brookings workshop.

A parallel often has been drawn between insurance and gambling. Both obviously involve behavior toward risk, but insurance consumers are usually thought of as avoiding risk and gamblers as cultivating it.[11] Akerlof noted in the work-

---

11. The topic also emerges in the national accounts debate on insurance because the net earnings of casinos, not the gross amount wagered, are usually entered into national accounts and other economic statistics. It is sometimes contended that the output of insurance companies should be analogous to that of casinos.

shop that insurance and gambling probably should not be considered as parallel. He suggested that gambling had entertainment value—that even though gamblers wanted to win, they normally did not play with the expectation that they would win. If casinos provide entertainment, then this is a rationale for including their margins in national accounts. This issue is not, however, a completely settled one, but we will not pursue it to any greater extent here because it is tangential to the main subject of the chapter.

The Risk-Pooling, Premiums-Minus-Claims Position

The premiums minus claims, or net premiums, approach to insurance output is endorsed in the 1993 System of National Accounts (Commission of the European Communities and others 1993); in the *Balance of Payments Manual* (International Monetary Fund 1994); and in the European Harmonized Indexes of Consumer Prices (Eurostat 1999). As Robert Parker (1998) documented in his paper for the Brookings workshop, net premiums also describes the treatment of insurance in the U.S. National Income and Product Accounts—not only the output of the insurance industry but also consumption of insurance as a final product (by consumers, for example) and exports and imports of insurance. It also has been incorporated into the European standard for collecting industry statistics on insurance (see Walton 1993 and Eurostat 1997), a standard that guides compilation of industry statistics in all the countries of the European Union.[12] The report of the Oslo meeting of the Voorburg Group (1993) recommends premiums minus claims as the international measure of insurance output for industry statistics.

Therefore premiums minus claims (net premiums) is overwhelmingly the way that insurance is portrayed in economic statistics worldwide. Notable exceptions are the new U.S. producer price indexes for the insurance industry.

The list of authors supporting the net premiums definition is long. Most are individuals who are associated with national accounts. In presentations to the Brookings workshop, Peter Hill (1998) and John Astin explained the preference for the net premiums approach in, respectively, the 1993 System of National Accounts (SNA93) and the European Harmonized Indexes of Consumer Prices

---

12. However, as noted, the term *net premiums* sometimes does not mean premiums minus claims. The SNA93 definition of net premiums depends on its special definition of insurance premiums but amounts roughly to claims adjusted for changes in reserves. The U.S. insurance industry definition of net premiums, as given by the A. M. Best company, approximates "losses" (which is the industry term for claims paid), though it uses the ordinary meaning of premiums, not the SNA definition.

(HICP). Mary Weiss, in her discussion of Mark Sherwood's Brookings workshop paper, also supported the net premiums view, with some qualifications. Others include John Walton (1993), Richard Collins (1993), and Hirshhorn and Geehan (1977, 1980).

National Accounts Rationale

As Peter Hill (1998) pointed out in his paper for the Brookings workshop, the 1968 version of the SNA used net premiums as its entire measure of insurance industry output; in so doing, it concorded with present and past U.S. practice.[13] However, as Hill also reports, dissatisfaction with the measure of insurance industry output arose because in many countries insurance output so defined is negative: in some periods and sometimes for many years, insurance companies pay out more in claims than they receive in premiums.

Profit in an inefficient or unfortunate enterprise or industry might be negative. It is even possible that value added could be negative—that is, a company or an industry might take in less than it pays out to others for the cost of purchased materials and services—although negative value added could hardly persist for very long. Output, however, can never be negative, even for short periods. Negative output makes no economic sense.

For these reasons, as Hill explains, the 1993 version of the SNA modified insurance industry output by adding insurance company investment income to the previous output definition of premiums minus claims. This change was motivated more than anything else by the need to exterminate the negative measured output that resulted from the SNA68 definition. Indeed, deliberations that led up to SNA93 contained no serious discussion of the gross premiums alternative to the SNA net premium characterization of insurance output.[14]

As Hill also pointed out in the Brookings workshop, the net premium position on insurance holds that *gross* output of insurance is measured by premiums minus claims; it does not hold that net output (another name for value added) is measured by net premiums. Net premiums equal premiums minus claims; value added equals premiums minus claims minus insurance industry purchases from

---

13. The treatment of finance and insurance played a role in the 1947 meeting between Richard Stone and U.S. national accounts experts that eventually led to the NIPA and UN systems going their separate ways (personal conversation of Jack Triplett with the late Edward Denison). However, the two systems historically have contained remarkably similar measures of finance and of insurance. The premiums-minus-claims convention for insurance output entered the U.S. National Income and Product Accounts around 1947.

14. Hill (1998) and a personal communication from Anne Harrison, of OECD, to Jack Triplett.

other industries (energy, paper, and office supplies, for example). Therefore the gross premium–net premium distinction for insurance output is not equivalent to the usual national accounts gross output–net output distinction (that is, output compared with value added). Some confusion on this point appeared during the discussion at the workshop and has undoubtedly clouded the discussion of the real issues elsewhere.

Confusion about value added under the two insurance output proposals also arose during the workshop and probably also exists in the literature on the measurement of insurance output. Whether insurance output is measured by gross premiums or net premiums, value added is the same. We made this point earlier, but because of its importance it bears repeating.

If the output concept makes no difference with respect to the national accounts' major concern, the measurement of value added and of GDP, why has so much controversy surrounded proposals to change the insurance output concept in national accounts? The following sections summarize the arguments in support of the net premiums position in the national accounts literature.

VALIDITY OF THE RISK-POOLING CONCEPT. Some national accountants and economic statisticians believe that the risk-pooling model of an insurance company depicts empirically the way the insurance business is conducted. Peter Hill explained the views of national accountants:

> How do they view the [insurance] transactions. . . ? When we talk about premiums, for the non-life insurance or accident insurance, they view it as two components. One is a payment for the service of insurance—this is essentially the net approach. The second is viewed as a transfer—this is the risk-pooling element. The household is viewed as paying a transfer into some common pool; these transfers are not regarded as themselves goods or services.[15]

This SNA view of the insurance business is buttressed by a passage in SNA93 that notes that claims are paid out of premiums: "This emphasizes the fact that the essential function of non-life insurance is to redistribute resources." Insurance claims paid are treated as transfers to the claimants.[16]

---

15. Transcript of remarks at the Brookings workshop, April 1998. In the same presentation Hill also remarked: "I don't think that those who were responsible for the final version of the SNA would be prepared to go to the stake defending the principles or methodologies which are used [for insurance]. But as in so many other areas, this is an area in which doubtless improvements can be made."

16. Commission of the European Communities and others (1993, paragraphs 8.87 and 8.88, p. 200).

The BEA work team described the SNA (and NIPA) treatment of insurance as consistent with the view that insurance companies provide pool administration services for their policyholders. It also contended that mutual insurance companies and retrospectively rated insurance plans operate explicitly like risk-pooling arrangements and offered their operations as a justification for the net premiums treatment of insurance output.

Collins states: "Insurers are engaged in the pooling of risk. . . . [Their] revenue consists of two components—a service charge for the insurance services and a transfer component to pay claims."[17] Other examples come from Eurostat regulations for the HICP and for industry statistics. The Eurostat insurance statistics manual states: "Two elements characterise the activities of insurance enterprises. At first they pool the risks of the insured. Secondly they collect funds through the insurance premiums they receive and invest these funds on the financial markets."[18] The manual also explains that the output definition for insurance industry statistics is the same as for national accounts.[19]

Of the sources cited above, only the BEA work team considered explicitly the gross premium alternative for insurance output. Alternative concepts for insurance output were also discussed by the Voorburg Group, an international statistical agency group on measuring services, in Williamsburg, Virginia, in October 1992 and in Oslo in September 1993 (the final report of the Williamsburg meeting makes reference to the fact that two alternatives exist).[20] No alternative model of insurance was mentioned in Eurostat HICP materials and papers on insurance, and apparently no alternative model was considered. As John Astin indicated in the workshop, the HICP decision on insurance was made partly because of a desire to integrate the HICP with national accounts.

The empirical validity of the risk-pooling model of insurance may not be the crucial issue for national accountants (we later suggest why it might not be). If it is, however, then empirical tests of the risk-pooling model should be crucial in determining how to measure insurance output. One might ask whether there is evidence that demanders and suppliers behave according to the risk-pooling insurance output model in the SNA or whether the alternative, risk-absorbing model is more consistent with empirical information.

17. Collins (1993, pp. 213 and 215).
18. Eurostat (1997, p. 1). On the other hand, a subsequent paragraph on the same page states: "The main economic function is to transfer risks to specialized enterprises which assure risks to a certain amount through the collection of premiums." That sentence could be interpreted as supporting the risk-assuming view of insurance, but clearly this was not the intention of the authors of the document.
19. Eurostat (1997, paragraph 5.2.4, p. 117).
20. Voorburg Group (1992, section 5).

One need not think of hypothesis testing only in terms of econometrics. In the SNA risk-pooling model of insurance, insurance company output is the fee for administering the risk pool. However, one cannot find an insurance contract that is written that way—there seems to be no price charged for a service so defined. Put another way, there is no unit in which this SNA administration service is observed. This is a strong empirical strike against the model that is embodied in the SNA (though not against the idea that policyholder services are portions of insurance output). Indeed this problem is acknowledged in some SNA materials, but only as a difficulty in implementation, not as a test of the validity of the net premiums concept of insurance:

> In the case of non-life insurance, it has always been necessary to carry into the accounts of the consuming sectors or industries a conceptual distinction between the insurance service and indemnities (transfers), a distinction which is not perceived by the consumer of the service.[21]

On the other hand, the risk-absorbing model of insurance behavior implies that the unit is the insurance policy. The price is the risk-adjusted insurance premium, which is the Bradford and Logue (1998) view as well as the Sherwood (1999) view and the view embodied in the PPI (Dohm and Eggleston 1998). As a general rule in measurement, we start with the unit in which the transaction takes place, and the insurance policy seems as natural a unit from which to begin as does a pen or a computer. We can readily observe the unit and the transaction that corresponds to the risk-absorbing model.

Other empirical evidence is provided by asking whether insurance companies that are in a formal sense organized as policyholder cooperatives (called mutual insurance companies in the United States and the United Kingdom) behave differently from other insurance companies in the same line of business. Born and others (1998) investigated the economic behavior of U.S. insurance companies that were organized as mutual companies (nominally owned by the policyholders) and stock insurance companies (nominally owned by shareholders). A third class of property-casualty insurance companies also exists in the United States— nominally stock companies that are owned by nominally mutual insurance companies. They found no significant behavioral differences:

> We do not find a discernable pattern whereby one organizational form outperforms the other, though the three types of firms are statistically

21. Walton (1993, p. 206).

different. . . . We found a notable lack of difference between stock and mutual companies. For example, neither form of organization has consistently higher underwriting profitability than the other. Our most persistent and powerful result is that stock and mutual-owned stock companies are much quicker to exit unprofitable markets and expand operations in profitable markets.[22]

This one finding might be taken as weak evidence that mutual companies act more as custodians for the policyholders, but overall the authors do not conclude that there is a difference in insurance company behavior.

However, the Born and others results show only that a single model of insurance company behavior covers both types of company organization; they do not show which model of insurance is the correct one. Mutual insurance companies may operate explicitly as managers of the risk pool, as the BEA work team suggested; if so, the empirical results of Born and others say that nominally stockholder-owned insurance companies function the same way. Alternatively, those empirical results may suggest that insurance companies that are organized as policyholder-owned mutual companies—or that began that way 100 or more years ago—function today as risk-absorbing companies, just as do stockholder-owned insurance companies. But however one interprets their results for the insurance measurement controversy, Born and others indicate that there are no major differences in insurance company behavior.

Perhaps competition forces investor-owned insurance companies to mimic mutual companies and behave as agents for their policyholders. This idea, which is consistent with economic models of agency behavior, was suggested by Brian Newson (the head of Eurostat national accounts) at the Brookings workshop. Or perhaps it is the other way around: competition forces cooperatives to behave as profit-making enterprises, a result that is well known in economics. One of the authors of this book has an automobile insurance company that carries the word "mutual" in its title. It periodically sends a small refund check when it has a favorable claims experience. We interpret that as trying to hold on to a customer, but perhaps the company's motives differ from our perceptions.

This insurance company never tries to charge an additional premium when it suffers an unfavorable claims experience, although it may use such an experience to justify increasing rates for the subsequent period. Again, that behavior probably is forced upon it by competitive conditions. The company knows that if it

22. Born and others (1998, pp. 189 and 191).

tried to bill after the fact for the company's losses, consumers would not pay because they could renew their insurance with another company. If one were in some real sense the owner of the company, one should be liable for losses. The fact that policyholders are never liable for losses of a mutual insurance company suggests that competition from stock companies prevents mutual companies from behaving as policyholders' agents in loss situations, even if, as asserted, they do so in profitable situations.

Ultimately, then, there are two pieces of relevant evidence. The first is the fact that no insurance contracts are written with a price equal to an administration fee. The second is that there seems to be little evidence that insurance companies think they are administering a pool on behalf of the policyholders. For example, one participant at the Brookings workshop remarked that when he sat on the board of directors for a major U.S. insurance company, nothing he ever heard there suggested that the company thought it was acting on behalf of the policyholders instead of the stockholders. One of us asked an executive at a major U.K. insurance company whether U.K. mutual companies behaved more like policyholder cooperatives than American ones; he chuckled and then told a story about some financial manipulation involving a mutual company. These questions are certainly worth exploring at greater length in empirical studies, but what comes out of existing studies and anecdotes does not provide much support for the view of insurance companies as policyholders' cooperatives.

Even though the risk-pooling and risk-absorbing models are very useful for thinking about insurance output, one can probably make too much of them in the context of SNA decisionmaking. At the Brookings workshop, Peter Hill remarked:

I wouldn't say, in my view, there is a recognition amongst national accountants of the intrinsic difficulties of issues that are being dealt with [at the workshop]. . . . It's my recollection that in the '93 SNA discussions, there was very little discussion at all of the specific issue being addressed [at the workshop], which is how to obtain satisfactory price and volume measures for insurance output. I suspect that from a national accounts point of view, the immediate reaction would be to be more concerned about the growth of the output than the price. But, of course, these are essentially different sides of the same coin.

He went on to suggest that the matter deserves further study: "It's extremely important to have meetings, seminars, of precisely this kind we are having today, if there is to be significant improvement. . . . I think that the [SNA] system might be improved, but only as a result of discussions of this kind."[23]

OTHER SNA CONCEPTUAL POINTS.   Some proponents of the net premiums approach for national accounts emphasize less the risk-pooling view of the insurance company and put more emphasis on the SNA conceptual view of certain financial portions of insurance transactions. Insurance, as Bradford and Logue (1998) point out, is a type of contingent contract. SNA93 contains language on the national accounts treatment of contingent contracts: "The entitlement to contingent benefits . . . cannot be treated as if it were itself some kind of asset that could be valued and recorded in the accounts. Hence, items such as [casualty-property] premiums . . . are treated in the accounts as transfers." The SNA defines a transfer payment as a "transaction in which one institutional unit provides a good, service, or asset to another unit without receiving from the latter any good, service or asset in return."[24]

The payment of an insurance claim is regarded in isolation as a payment to the policyholder without any compensating services. The BEA work team notes that the *Balance of Payments Manual* (International Monetary Fund 1994) also advocates treating insurance claims payments to policyholders as transfer payments, on the grounds that "the policyholder is receiving an economic benefit . . . without giving up anything in return."

It sometimes is not clear whether references to insurance in the SNA passages on contingent contracts and on transfer payments are simply collateral consequences of the SNA definition of insurance or whether they are separate conceptual points from which the SNA insurance definition derives. If the latter, then they are conceptual points that must be dealt with separately, and it is a valid point in the debate that only the net premiums approach to insurance is consistent with the SNA view of contingent contracts and of transfers.

But if the former case prevails, the SNA's language on contingent contracts and transfers and on insurance are not independent points at all. If so, invoking contingent contracts and transfers definitions in the gross premiums–net premiums debate is a kind of "double counting." Whichever is the case, for the sake of

23. Transcript of Brookings workshop. Hill's recollection of the SNA group's discussions agrees with that of Anne Harrison of OECD, another prominent contributor to SNA93 (personal communication to Jack Triplett).

24. Commission of the European Communities (1993, paragraphs 8.27 and 8.28, p. 188). The next paragraph (8.29) explains that life insurance premiums are not treated as transfers, but in the SNA life insurance is what is called whole life insurance in the United States. Another section of the SNA notes that the administrative expenses part of the non-life insurance premium is not a transfer but a payment by the policyholders for services that are produced by the insurance company and consumed by the policyholders.

the discussion we consider the SNA passages quoted above on their own merits—that is, as separate points that are relevant to the insurance debate and not just corollaries of the SNA position on insurance.

The statement that contingent contracts cannot be valued seems too sweeping, or perhaps it does not quite mean what it seems to mean. An insurance company can certainly sell its insurance customer base to another insurance company. For example, before the bankruptcy of the HIH insurance company in Australia, the company sold off major parts of its outstanding insurance contracts in an attempt to raise cash to forestall the bankruptcy. In that sense, an insurance contingent contract can be and is valued and exchanged as an asset. The SNA statement that contingent contracts cannot be valued is incorrect, even in the case of insurance contracts.

With respect to the argument on transfers, two points of confusion may exist. First, there is little reason to treat the payment of an insurance claim in isolation from the entire insurance contract. The purchaser of the insurance policy pays a premium to the insurance company in return for a payment that is contingent upon, for example, his or her suffering a loss of a capital asset. It is not true that, as the BEA work team quotes the *Balance of Payments Manual*, "the policyholder is receiving an economic benefit . . . without giving up anything in return" or, quoting the SNA, that the insurance company has made a payment to the insured "without receiving from the latter any good, service, or asset in return." The whole transaction has to be considered, not just the payment of an insurance claim as if there were no previous payment that created the entitlement to the claim.

Second, and more seriously, advocates of the net premiums approach have apparently misconstrued the implications of the alternative, gross premiums approach. The gross premiums approach does not imply that payment of an insurance *claim* must therefore be treated as a payment for a service, contrary to what some have apparently thought. Having property insurance means that the owner of a shiny new car has a shiny new car before an accident, after an accident, and if an accident never takes place. One can treat the insurance company as purchasing car repairs or treat the car repair in some other way. Whether one advocates gross premiums or net premiums as the output concept for the insurance company, the payment of a claim should not be treated as the provision of a service by the insurance company to the insured. The service is insurance, not the claim. Claims paid should not be treated as income to the consumer or the business that suffers a loss. Whether one wants to call the claim a transfer to the insured's capital account is a secondary matter—or one of language, not substance.

It is quite clear, however, that changing the concept of insurance output in the SNA would require collateral changes elsewhere in the SNA. National accountants have argued forcefully in other forums (though not at the Brookings workshop) that the appropriate concept of insurance output must take a back seat to other matters that are regarded as more central to national accounts. Some of these positions on insurance seem to be close to saying: "We can't change the treatment of insurance output because it would force changes elsewhere." It is true that moving away from the present net premium definition of insurance output has impacts elsewhere in the national accounts. However, that is not the issue. The issue is the appropriate way to measure the output of the insurance business.

CONSISTENCY WITH OTHER PARTS OF THE NATIONAL ACCOUNTS. Consistency is important in national accounts, so it is not surprising that it features prominently in the argument in behalf of the net premiums concept for insurance output. Therefore the majority members of the BEA work team concluded that the *primary* advantage of using net premiums as the measure of insurance output is consistency with other parts of the accounts.

Several examples of consistency arguments may be cited. The BEA work team contended that if insurance companies absorb risk, they do it with a financial instrument (insurance policies are financial instruments, within the SNA meaning of finance). First, in national accounts, the sale of a financial instrument is always treated as an exchange of assets, not as the purchase of services. Moreover, the risks involved in insurance company activities are sometimes asserted to be similar to the risks involved in stock or commodity options, hedging plans, financial derivatives, loan payment guarantees, and gambling. In none of these does the SNA take revenue as the measure of output. Casinos, as noted previously, have as output their net margins, not the total amount wagered. As another example, some national accountants have contended that the net premiums approach for insurance creates consistency between the treatment of insurance output and the treatment of banking output in the SNA.

Consistency can be a treacherous or ambiguous argument. The call for consistency with other parts of national accounts is not convincing when the other parts are themselves controversial. It is true that the treatments of insurance and of banking in national accounts have always been linked, and it is apparently also true that no one has ever criticized one of these two conventions and supported the other. But in principle, these are separate questions; there is no reason to consider them as linked logically. Precisely because banking output in national accounts has long been controversial (Triplett 1992 and the discussion of banking in chapter 7 of this book), the consistency argument in regard to insurance output and banking output will not persuade those critics of insurance who also criticize the national accounts treatment of banking.

Moreover, all consistency arguments are essentially analogies and therefore open to the criticism that the analogy is not exact. In general, analogies are useful as illustrations, less so as matters of logic.

Many contentions with respect to consistency concern finance. If an insurance policy is *defined* as a financial instrument subject to SNA rules for financial instruments and if the present definition of financial instruments creates difficulties for alternative definitions of insurance output, then one obvious "solution" is to redefine SNA financial instruments to exclude insurance policies. As noted above, some contentions on alternative treatments of insurance amount to statements that changing the concept of insurance output in the SNA would require collateral changes elsewhere in the SNA. This is not a persuasive argument for retaining the net premiums approach to insurance output; it is simply an argument against making changes.

CAPITAL ACCOUNT ISSUES. In the Brookings workshop, one participant objected that the gross premiums approach might work satisfactorily in the case of car repair (for households, that is), but it would pose difficulties if the insurance claim covered an investment good rather than an item of consumer expenditure. The example given was the destruction of a house by fire or storm. A new house is investment under all present national accounting systems.

It is not entirely clear why investment goods were deemed a problem. With the gross premiums approach, one would presumably still record the new house as investment, but it would be investment made by an insurance company, not by a household. Other accounting conventions might also be worked out.

The BEA work team proposed a capital account component of insurance representing the amount of risk transferred (measured by the claims) and a current account component representing the services provided by the insurance companies (that is, premiums minus claims). Only the second component would represent the output from current production of the insurance industry.

Barry Bosworth noted in the discussion of this point that the United States has no "other changes in assets" account. The appropriate treatment of hurricane damage to the housing stock in the SNA other changes in assets account is omitted from the present discussion and probably needs additional thought. But investment goods do not seem to present a fundamental obstacle to the use of the gross premiums approach in national accounts. And in any case, this problem of how to show the loss of a destroyed productive asset is present in both approaches to insurance output.

PARALLELS WITH RETAIL AND WHOLESALE GROSS MARGIN DEFINITIONS OF OUTPUT.   The outputs of certain industries, notably wholesale and retail trade, are defined in national accounts as their gross margins—sales minus cost of goods sold. Cost of goods sold is a generally accepted accounting term, so the data are normally recorded in retail and wholesale records. One might invoke this parallel to justify the net premiums treatment of insurance. The gross margin in trade is a measure of retail or wholesale services. A retail shoe store is not depicted in national accounts as selling shoes, but as selling the service of selling shoes. The net premiums approach to insurance output also is proposed as a measure of services provided to policyholders.[25]

In the workshop, someone asked why the textile mill was not depicted as selling the service of weaving, instead of selling, say, sheets and towels. Indeed, it is conceptually possible that almost any kind of activity could be conducted as a margin industry. Occasionally, a nominally manufacturing industry is conducted by processing clients' inputs and charging for processing (some smelting processes and historically grain mills were run this way). If the economic activity is conducted like a margin industry and if a price is set for the margin, then it makes economic sense to estimate its price and output this way. There is no "natural" way that a business has to be run and no natural analogy between insurance and some other industry that happens to be treated as a margin industry in national accounts. In addition, in Bureau of Labor Statistics productivity statistics, shoe stores are portrayed as selling shoes. Their output is not the gross margin, so obviously the choice of output measure in the trade sector is not completely settled.

"NOT GROSS PREMIUMS" ARGUMENTS.   Some participants in the debate on insurance present arguments that do not so much favor the net premiums approach as point out problems with the gross premiums approach. This is fair enough, though in the end the impact of negative arguments on each position must be totaled up, and sometimes the balance is not clear.

Peter Hill noted that insurance claims may not always be used to make repairs or to replace the item that was lost or damaged. When a consumer receives a claim payment for car damage or for a stolen television set, the consumer might not repair the car or replace the television but buy new clothes instead. In this case, the consumer does temporarily have more command over resources. He or she may behave as if the payment were equivalent to an

---

25. Certain financial industries are treated in national accounts in a somewhat parallel manner. For example, if one thinks of a bank as buying and selling finance, instead of cabbages or shoes, then the national accounts "net interest" treatment of banking has apparent, though not exact, parallels with the national accounts treatment of retail trade.

increase in income, regardless of the nature of the loss for which the claim was paid. In this example, it is not clear that one wants to treat the car insurance company as purchasing clothing.

On the other hand, the consumer's decision not to replace the car will draw down the consumer's capital account, which could be recorded, in principle, though it presents data difficulties. Spending the insurance claim on clothing is equivalent to consuming out of capital—that is, to dissaving. It was also noted that in both the United States and Europe, insurance companies are moving to a system in which they repair the car directly or directly replace the stolen television set in order to reduce insurance fraud.

DATA AVAILABILITY QUESTIONS. Under some implementations, the gross premiums approach has the insurance company, not the household, paying for car repairs. This implies that one would have to separate revenues from car repair shops to isolate those expenditures made by consumers from those made by the insurance company (this is necessary to get an accurate measure of consumer expenditure and to avoid double counting). Data might not be available to make this allocation. In addition, Eurostat materials distributed at the workshop discuss whether consumer expenditure surveys do or do not record car repairs made by insurance companies as consumer expenditures. There seems to be ambiguity on this matter.

National accountants must *now* remove all repairs made to business-owned automobiles from auto repair shop revenue, because repairs for business autos are an intermediate expense, while repairs for autos owned by households are a final product. Netting out, in addition, insurance company expenditures on car repairs is the same kind of calculation, and it is not clear that it presents more serious data problems than those encountered currently in computing consumption expenditures in national accounts.

Data problems might be even more severe for other kinds of insurance claims. As Anne Harrison noted, many insurance claims do not involve capital or repairs.[26] Examples are household goods (treated as current expenditure in all national accounting systems), including jewelry and cameras, and liability payments for pain and suffering and so forth. Whatever those insurance claims are spent on, it is not likely that one could separate out neatly consumer expenditures that are and that are not the result of insurance payments.

Obviously, data availability is not a fundamental concept. It is, rather, a matter of the relative ease of implementing two proposals. Ease of implementation is an impressive argument, but it does not clarify the concept. One might argue

26. Personal communication with the authors.

for a second-best implementation on the grounds of data availability, but one cannot claim that data availability makes net premiums conceptually preferable to gross premiums.

POSITIONS THAT MIX OUTPUT WITH VALUE ADDED. In national accounts, the word *production* frequently is employed to mean value added. Elsewhere in economics, production usually is the process that results in output (in national accounts language, *gross output*), not in value added. Terminology does not matter so much as long as meaning is clear, but sometimes meaning is not.

The BEA work team contended that the concept of current economic production is most useful if it is consistent with some measure of the economic resources used in production. The team thought that in the case of insurance, these costs are approximated by the service charge component of the insurance payment. One would certainly agree with the first statement. However, the second makes clear that the group was thinking of value added, not output. Therefore the economic resources that go into replacing items lost though accident are not being considered in the BEA statement. However, the BEA work team also seems to have overlooked the fact that value added is the same under the gross premiums and net premiums approaches to insurance industry output.

An Estimate of Productivity Measurement Bias from BEA's Inappropriate Insurance Output Definition

The choice between gross premiums and net premiums as a measure of insurance industry output affects the measure of insurance industry productivity. Premiums are far greater than premiums minus claims. For example, in 2000, A. M. Best reported that property-casualty premiums earned were $293 billion; in the same year, premiums minus claims amounted to $93 billion. By the gross premiums definition, output in this portion of the insurance industry was more than three times greater than it was under the net premiums definition. The level of labor productivity therefore is far greater under the gross premiums approach to insurance industry output. But is the change in productivity greater or lesser under the gross premiums definition of insurance output? At the Brookings workshop, some participants expressed the view that the premiums–net premiums distinction does not really matter, empirically, for productivity measurement.

In their response to Denny (1980), Hirshhorn and Geehan (1980) calculated alternative labor productivity measures for the Canadian life insurance industry over the 1955–73 period: using the gross premiums output concept, labor productivity grew 5.0 percent a year, compared with 2.8 percent a year with the net premium concept.[27] Popkin (1992) made a similar estimate for the U.S. accident/casualty industry: using the gross premium output concept instead of the net premium measure in the U.S. national accounts raised the industry labor productivity growth rate from 1.9 percent a year in the then-published BEA data to 4.4 percent over the 1980–88 interval. (In this period, BEA would have been publishing only value added in its industry database.)

Evidently in previous years the choice of output concept for insurance makes a great deal of difference in estimates of productivity growth for the insurance industry, and the national accounts output definition results in lower growth in industry productivity. These studies imply that premiums are not only larger than premiums minus claims but that premiums were growing faster than the premiums-claims margin—that is, the margin was shrinking. They also show that the measurement bias from the national accounts definition of insurance industry output is substantial.

In chapter 2 (tables 2-4A and 2-4B), we reported negative growth in labor productivity in the insurance carrier industry: –1.7 percent a year over the 1995–2001 period, estimated as a trend rate. Insurance industry MFP grew not at all (0.0 percent a year) over the same interval. Does measurement bias from the national accounts output definition account for, or contribute to, negative measured productivity in the insurance industry? To assess this issue, we constructed a measure of insurance output growth corresponding to the premiums definition, using for consistency a combination of BEA and A. M. Best data.[28] We then compared this new measure with the insurance output growth rate in the BEA data. (See chapter 5 for a description of BEA's methodology.) The results are in table 6-1.

Under the current BEA output definition (premiums minus claims), current price output of the insurance carrier industry grew at the rate of 3.1 percent a year from 1995 to 2000 and at 3.3 percent a year from 1995 to 2001 (table 6-1, panel A). We provide estimates for two end years to avoid undue influence from 2001, which was an atypical year, but as the table shows, that is not a real problem. The table also shows that current price output growth was below the growth rate of the insurance industry deflator, so that constant price output growth was negative, at –1.5 and –0.5 percent a year for 1995–2000 and 1995–2001 respectively. This negative growth rate of constant price insurance

---

27. Hirshhorn and Geehan (1980, p. 153). They removed the saving component from whole life policies. Term and group life insurance policies are "non-life" insurance in the definition of SNA93 and hence grouped in with accident insurance.

28. We appreciate the cooperation of Sherlene Lum in making the BEA file available.

Table 6-1. *Alternative Output and Labor Productivity Growth Estimates for the Insurance Carriers Industry*
Average annual rate of change

Output definition	1995–2000	1995–2001[a]
Panel A		
BEA/BLS insurance carriers industry gross output[b]		
Current price output	3.11	3.26
Constant price output	–1.53	–0.51
Price index	4.71	3.79
Labor	0.63	0.42
Output per worker	–2.14	–0.92
Panel B		
Alternative output definitions for property and casualty insurance (P&C)[c]		
P&C "premiums – losses" current price output[d]	3.01	3.22
P&C "premiums" current price output[e]	3.55	4.03
P&C "premiums + investment gains" current price output[f]	3.62	4.10
Panel C		
Insurance carrier gross output, using P&C "premiums + investment gains"[g]		
Current price output	3.39	3.65
Constant price output	–1.28	–0.14
Price index	4.71	3.79
Labor	0.63	0.42
Output per worker	–1.90	–0.55

a. P&C growth rates for 2000–01 from A. M. Best's *Aggregates and Averages* (2003).

b. From BEA industry file, computed as sum of P&C (national accounts definition), life and health insurance, P&C commodity taxes, own-account software, and own-account construction.

c. Property and casualty insurance (P&C) includes four insurance categories: health, property, auto, and workers' compensation, aggregated to match the definition used in BEA's industry file (in this definition, both the property and auto categories include auto physical damage insurance, while the health category does not include medical malpractice insurance).

d. Output defined as "net premiums earned after losses." Source: data obtained from BEA (from Sherlene Lum, 11/03/2003), derived from A. M. Best data.

e. Output defined as "net premiums earned." Source: data obtained from BEA (from Sherlene Lum, 11/03/2003), derived from A. M. Best data.

f. Output defined as "net premiums earned + investment gain on funds and other income." Authors' calculations, estimated by applying the ratio of "investment gain on funds and other income" to "net premiums earned," from A. M. Best's *Aggregates and Averages* (2003) to "net premiums earned" numbers in previous line.

g. Sum of P&C "premiums + investment gains" definition, plus other insurance components from BEA file. P&C is roughly half of insurance carrier output, but the recomputed output series uses the shares for each year.

output in the BEA database is the cause of the negative productivity rates displayed in table 6-1 and also in tables 2-4A and 2-4B of chapter 2.

BEA output for the insurance carrier industry is made up from separate lines for life insurance, health insurance, workers' compensation insurance, and property-casualty insurance, as described in the notes to table 6-1, plus own-account software and construction (both of which are quite small). Property-casualty (PC) insurance is around half of the total. We focus on the PC portion.

Using a combination of A. M. Best and BEA data (which itself is derived in part from the Best data), we estimated growth rates for alternative definitions of PC insurance (panel B of table 6-1). The first line of panel B presents the BEA output definition (premiums minus claims). As the table shows, the output growth rate we estimate for PC insurance using BEA's output definition and Best's data is approximately equal to the growth rate for the whole industry in BEA's data file. (Compare the first lines of panels A and B in table 6-1—the two differ by only about one-tenth of a point or less.)

Next, using the Best data and matching BEA procedures otherwise, we calculated current price output growth for the alternative "premiums" definition of insurance industry output.[29] This calculation also is displayed in panel B of table 6-1. Using 2000 and 2001 as alternative end points, we find that premiums grew 3.5 and 4.0 percent a year respectively since 1995—0.5 to 0.8 points faster than premiums minus claims. This clearly indicates that moving to a premiums definition of output would raise industry output growth and therefore labor productivity growth in the insurance carrier industry.

Discussion at the Brookings workshop and the analysis below suggest adding insurance company investment earnings to the insurance output measure. We followed this suggestion—that is, we treated investment income as an output of the insurance business, not as a contribution to the price of insurance (as in the SNA treatment). Again, our data source was A. M. Best. Though adding investment income increases insurance output, it does not appreciably alter the rate of change, raising it only by about one-tenth of a point a year, as panel B of table 6-1 shows. Therefore the bigger empirical effect comes from the move from premiums minus claims to premiums as a measure of insurance output. Adding investment income has a small but still positive effect on output growth.

---

29. For this, we used data from the line in the A. M. Best data labeled "net premiums earned" (that is, without deducting the losses). As explained earlier, Best's definition of net premiums earned does not employ the national accounts use of the term *net premiums*. In Best's usage, "net" is net of refunds and other adjustments to premiums, not net of losses. To avoid confusion, we retain in the text the national accounts use of net premiums to mesh with writings on national accounts.

Our final measure for PC insurance output growth is 4.1 percent a year for the 1995–2001 interval, which was used for our estimates of industry productivity growth in chapter 1. This is 0.9 points above BEA's output growth for the same portion of the industry. Our new output growth estimates in panel B of table 6-1 apply only to current-price output changes for property-casualty insurance. But labor productivity (LP) growth, for example, can be written (where all symbols are interpreted as rates of change) as

$$LP = (\textit{output} / \textit{price}) / L.$$

Therefore if current price output growth for property-casualty insurance is estimated at 4.1 percent a year instead of 3.2 percent (panel B of table 6-1) and property-casualty insurance is about half of BEA insurance industry output,[30] estimated insurance industry output growth will rise by roughly half of the difference, which feeds directly through to change our labor productivity estimate. We neglect term life insurance and other insurance for this exercise and note only that changing the insurance industry output concept in national accounts would affect other components of insurance as well. Because we make no additional adjustments to output for the other half of the insurance industry, we believe that our estimates are conservative.[31]

We restated the PC insurance output in the BEA insurance industry file by substituting, year by year, the "premiums + investment gains" output definition in panel B of table 6-1 for BEA's output definition in panel A of the table; following BEA methodology, we used our new output definition as an extrapolator for PC insurance output. The output shares for PC insurance were the yearly totals in the BEA file. From this, we obtained new output measures for the industry. We then used the existing BEA deflators and labor input to recalculate LP for this industry (note that changing the output definition would also change the shares and the deflators, but we made no adjustment for these terms).

As with the earlier Canadian and U.S. findings described above, substituting the new definition of insurance output for the one used by BEA raises measured labor productivity in the insurance carrier industry. The changes are relatively modest. For 1995–2001 LP increases by 0.4 point a year, but labor productivity still is growing at a negative rate (–0.55 average annual rate of change a year,

30. In 2000, $155 billion of a total of $297 billion.
31. On the other hand, we also should acknowledge that we may not have estimated these new PC output growth rates with as much sophistication as BEA would have brought to the same computations.

compared with –0.92 in the existing BEA data). The choice of output measure does bias labor productivity growth in insurance, but in recent years the bias does not seem as large as in the earlier estimates cited above.[32]

Therefore we conclude that a conceptually more appropriate measure of output would lead to more productivity growth in insurance than is indicated by present BEA data. However, the changes are not large, at least for recent years, and still leave the industry with negative labor productivity growth.

Should the Investment Income of Insurance Companies Be Added to Output or to the Price of Insurance?

The very essence of the insurance business requires that premiums be paid before claims. In some kinds of insurance, medical malpractice insurance for example, premiums may be paid a very long time before claims are filed. But even for casualty insurance, it is doubtful that a "spot" market for insurance could ever exist, because the incentive to buy insurance when risk of imminent loss became apparent would be too strong. This is known as "moral hazard": generally, individuals who most anticipate losses are most likely to buy insurance.

Limiting moral hazard in insurance calls for creating a fund—reserves held against future claims. Insurance companies, not unnaturally, invest those reserves. Indeed, Dennis Fixler pointed out at the Brookings workshop that investment of reserves is such an established part of the insurance business that U.S. insurance regulators typically require it. It also is well known that investment earnings lower insurance premiums because of competition among insurance companies that earn positive returns on invested reserves.

Participants at the Brookings workshop discussed whether and how insurance company investment income should be included in measures of the price of insurance and of the output of the insurance industry. There seemed to be broad agreement that the investment earnings of insurance companies should be treated as part of insurance industry output, though some disagreement also was expressed. The 1993 SNA, the PPI insurance indexes (described in Dohm and Eggleston 1998), and the papers by Sherwood (1999) and Weiss in her discussion at the workshop all contend that investment income should be included. Investment earnings are not included in the BEA insurance industry output that we used for this study, but that was changed in the 2003 benchmark revision to

32. Owing to missing data, we were unable to extend the recalculation of output to the 1987–95 interval. There is some indication that the change would have gone in the opposite direction for the early 1990s.

GDP, and, we presume, that change will be followed in subsequent revisions to the industry accounts.

The rationale for inclusion of investment income, however, differs greatly. Conceptually different rationales lead to substantial differences in how investment is treated.

One rationale has the insurance company in two lines of business—selling insurance and investing. The insurance company thus has two outputs. This rationale implies a distinction between insurance as a product and the output of the insurance industry, in which insurance companies may have multiple lines of business, only one of which is insurance. The insurance product goes into the CPI and into input flows to industries that buy insurance, in an input-output table, for example.[33] The investment output does not go into the CPI nor into the inputs of the business units that buy insurance. By analogy, a sugar beet refiner has two products—sugar and beet pulp—only one of which goes into the CPI. This "two-product" rationale implies the need to measure two insurance industry prices and two output quantities and to direct these two outputs in different directions in the input-output table.

A second, very different rationale is the one used in SNA93, under which insurance companies are assumed to act as agents or managers for their policyholders. Their investment income belongs to and therefore is imputed to the policyholders. The form of the SNA imputation is determined by the SNA convention that interest or other investment income cannot be treated as a productive service.[34] To avoid this, SNA93 assumes in an additional step that the policyholders pay the investment income back to the insurance company in the form of higher premiums (called "premium supplements" in SNA93). Thus under the SNA93 rationale, *the higher the investment income of insurance companies, the higher the cost of insurance.* Of course, it is clear that higher investment income lowers the premium paid for insurance. But the SNA price of insurance is measured inclusive of the investment earnings.[35]

On the price side, these two rationales are equivalent to asking whether the price concept of a PPI (a price index covering all of the outputs of the insurance

33. The treatment of insurance in the inputs of business units that buy insurance (that is, in what sometimes is called an "input" price index) follows the treatment in the CPI. To conserve space in the following, we discuss only the CPI. The difference between CPI treatment and treatment in the output of the insurance industry is parallel to the difference between the insurance industry output and insurance as an input to other business units.

34. This matter is discussed at length in chapter 7. Exactly the same issues arise in insurance.

35. The SNA text observes that the actual premium is in fact lower than it would be without investment earnings. But this is taken to be evidence that the observed price (the premium) is too low.

industry) differs empirically from the price concept of a CPI (a price index corresponding to consumers' consumption of insurance).[36] If insurance companies are regarded as being in two lines of business (providing insurance and engaging in investment), then the PPI and CPI concepts diverge, because the CPI concept includes only insurance products, not insurance company investment products. The PPI price for the insurance industry includes both prices. On the other hand, if the investment activity is treated as an inherent part of the insurance service itself, as in SNA93, and if that implies an unrecorded increment to the nominal price paid for an insurance policy, then the CPI and PPI concepts are similar because both include the investment activity (though perhaps not in exactly the same form).

Several positions on the treatment of investment income can be distinguished. They correspond to different positions on the rationales listed above. The different positions on investment income can also be identified with the models of insurance company behavior discussed previously. They depend also, though to a far lesser degree, on the economic measurement of interest. It is convenient to organize the discussion around the different uses for insurance statistics.

SNA and HICP

The rationale in the 1993 System of National Accounts (SNA93) for the treatment of insurance was explained in the paper by Peter Hill (1998) and in his informal remarks at the Brookings workshop. Recall first that the SNA has adopted the risk-pooling view of insurance, so the insurance company acts as an agent for policyholders; premiums minus claims is the fundamental output measure for the insurance industry, and it is the measure of the consumption of insurance by using industries and households.

As Hill's paper notes, adding insurance company investment income to the SNA net premiums output definition, which occurred with the SNA 1993 revision, eliminates the negative gross output of insurance that resulted from the old definition or at least makes the output less negative. This was part of the reason for the change, as previously explained. Note that had the SNA adopted a premiums definition of insurance in the first place, this particular reason for adding investment income to output would not have been valid, but that would not necessarily preclude adding investment to output using some other rationale, as described below.

36. The latter also corresponds to the price paid for insurance by other businesses for which insurance is an intermediate input and also determines the flow of insurance output to using industries in the input-output table.

The SNA policyholders' agent model of insurance company behavior carries over to its treatment of investment income: investment income is imputed to the policyholders as transfer income. But at the same time, the policyholders are treated as paying the entire investment income back to the insurance company in the form of what are called "supplementary premiums."

Hill explained: "In the SNA philosophy . . . it's argued that insurance companies, in fixing their premiums . . . also take into account their investment income . . . so that actual premiums are lower than what they would be in the absence of investment income." He elaborated on this point during the discussion: "I don't think that the investment income should be regarded as a component of the gross output. . . . [T]hat investment income is effectively replacing additional premiums that would have to be paid in the absence of these reserves."[37]

Another part of the SNA93 treatment of finance also influenced its treatment of insurance company investment income. In the SNA, interest is not viewed as payment for a productive service, and therefore it cannot be considered output of the firm that receives it. Indeed, in measuring industry output, the SNA (and the U.S. NIPA) normally follow the convention that output includes interest paid minus interest received; in the case of firms—such as insurance companies—that earn a substantial amount of interest or other investment income, the SNA net-interest-paid convention contributes negatively to their output (see the additional discussion of this matter in chapter 7).

Therefore, under its current conventions for interest, the SNA cannot simply recognize insurance company investment income in the accounts. Indeed, using the SNA net-interest-paid convention, if investment earnings were added to the SNA premiums-minus-claims insurance output convention, it would make insurance output even more drastically negative. Accordingly, it was necessary to provide some *non-interest* rationale for the insurance company's investment income. The SNA "premium supplement" rationale solved the problem (or most of the problem) of negative output of insurance companies.

The SNA premium supplement rationale implies that investment income is included in the current value GDP of the insurance industry, but it is treated as if it were a part of the *price* paid for insurance, not as part of the (constant price)

---

37. Collins (1993) describes the policyholders as "voluntarily" giving money to the insurance companies to hold; in exchange, they "barter" for lower premiums. It is doubtful that there is any voluntary exchange here, aside from the policyholder's decision to buy insurance. Collins ignores the reason that insurance companies acquire reserve funds in the first place, the need to limit the risk of moral hazard.

output of the insurance company. Investment income is not part of insurance real output or of real consumption of insurance; it is part of the price.

For the purpose of measuring productivity, the SNA treatment of investment earnings results in less output and a lower level of productivity in both of the alternative output approaches, and it probably also results in lower productivity growth. Under the SNA treatment, an increase in insurance company investment income leads to an increase in the price of insurance. Yet insurance companies devote resources to their investment activity, as Weiss pointed out in the Brookings workshop. It is hard to justify using a productivity measure that effectively forces the productivity of these resources to be zero.

The SNA position on insurance price and output is incorporated into the European Harmonized Indexes of Consumer Prices. Indeed, John Astin, in his remarks to the Brookings workshop, noted that the SNA position on insurance influenced the HICP position: "We are supposed to use national accounts conventions, where appropriate, and we felt that this [treatment of insurance] is in line with the ESA, the European System of Accounts." In the HICP, a premium supplement is defined as the investment income earned by insurance companies, a definition consistent with that of the SNA. The insurance service charge for the HICP includes insurance premiums plus premium supplements, and claims and changes in actuarial reserves are subtracted off (because the net approach to insurance is used, as discussed previously). This approach provides the consumption weight for insurance in the HICP. Although Astin noted that the net price was also the preferred concept for the price of insurance, for practical reasons the HICP net weight is moved by a price index for premiums—insurance companies could not provide prices for the premiums-minus-claims concept.

In summary, in both the 1993 SNA and in the HICP, the investment income of insurance is included; in both cases investment income is treated as increasing the price of insurance, not the quantity of output produced by the insurance company. In both cases, the rationale is that in the absence of investment income, insurance premiums would be higher than they actually are. Adding the investment income, or the supplementary premiums, to the price of insurance means that the SNA, and to a somewhat lesser extent the HICP, *are in effect imputing what the price of insurance would have been in the absence of insurance company investment.*

Note that both the SNA and the HICP treatments use the net approach in defining the service of insurance; they both model the insurance company as if it were a mutual company acting in the interest of the policyholders. The combination of the two procedures implies that after appropriate allocations are made across the different classes of consumers of insurance, there is no difference between the CPI and PPI concepts for insurance (consumption and industry output) and also no difference between the quantity of insurance consumed and the quantity of industry output.

As Stephen Oliner noted in the Brookings workshop discussion, the SNA treatment implies that when the stock market booms, consumers pay more for insurance. This seems an unsatisfactory depiction of the insurance market—especially for the model in which the insurance company is assumed to act on behalf of the policyholders. When an insurance company acts as its policyholders' agent (whether or not they "voluntarily" put investment funds at the insurance company's disposal), one expects the policyholders to receive rebates of the investment income but one does not expect the insurance company to then charge them more for insurance coverage.

Some national accountants have contended that the SNA insurance convention is consistent with (analogous to) the SNA imputation of services to bank deposit holders. Even if correct, the argument is not persuasive because the SNA convention for banking output also is controversial. That the two are analogous is also debatable. In the case of the bank deposit, deposits normally earn income for depositors, and everyone knows that transactions services (such as "free" checks and ATM usage) are provided to depositors in exchange for below-market interest on checking deposits. These transactions services are understandably viewed as an in-kind form of income payment. In the case of insurance, however, few believe that an accident insurance policy normally earns income for policyholders; imputing income to the policyholder is a step that is not in accord with the way transactors—either policyholders or insurance companies—normally view insurance.

Moreover, the SNA imputes the *price* of insurance, not the quantity of insurance services, so the imputation is not parallel. In the SNA banking imputation, the depositors are assumed to receive more banking services, not to pay a higher price for them. The analogy with banking services in the SNA provides little justification for the SNA treatment of insurance company investment earnings, which should be considered on its own.

The SNA insurance imputation is very complicated, and it is difficult to see that it accords with the way either policyholders or insurance companies view an insurance policy. Imputations, it is true, can always be criticized as not describing actual economic behavior. Reservations often have been expressed, for example, about the universal national accounts owner-occupied housing imputation, in which homeowners are assumed to have accounts in which they charge themselves rent and add the rent back into their incomes. But at least in the housing imputation, there is a market for rental housing and the price that is imputed to the owner-occupier is the market price. The SNA insurance imputation treats the price of insurance as if it were substantially higher than the observed premium. It is doubtful that policyholders perceive and act on this SNA price, and indeed this criticism often has been acknowledged within the SNA literature itself.

Economists would like to use data from the national accounts industry accounts to do economic analysis on industries and to use insurance data in the consumption portions of the accounts in their analyses of consumer or household behavior. The present SNA treatment of insurance makes these portions of the accounts less useful for such purposes—even if national accountants think that, on balance, the entire system of the accounting structure is improved by the insurance convention in SNA93.

A CPI or Consumption-of-Insurance Approach

The SNA and HICP adopt the risk-pooling model of insurance company behavior, so there is no difference between what the industry produces and what the consumer consumes. Because the insurance company is treated as a cooperative, all of its actions are taken on behalf of the policyholders. In the risk-assuming model of insurance company behavior, the insurance company is not acting on behalf of the policyholders, at least not explicitly. In this case, one must consider how the part of insurance company output that comes from investment activities should be treated in a consumer price index. Several positions emerged at the Brookings workshop. One position distinguishes between what Zvi Griliches called the PPI (or industry output) specification and the CPI (or cost-of-living index) specification.

For the PPI specification, one would ask what the industry produces. The CPI specification would be concerned with what the consumer consumes. The industry may have multiple products (insurance and investment management), but in the consumption of insurance by consumers (or by other producers), only insurance products matter. Therefore, in the risk-assuming model, the PPI and CPI approaches could differ in the way insurance company investment earnings are treated.

Mark Sherwood put the question another way: "Does the insurance company earn the investment return or the policyholder?" If the policyholder earns it (as would be the case in the risk-pooling model), then the CPI perspective ought to match in some manner the PPI perspective. But if the insurance company earns the investment return, then the issue is somewhat more complicated.

With respect to the CPI specification, Griliches remarked that the consumer just pays the premium; whether the insurance company has a good or a bad investment year is of no concern to the buyer of insurance. If the insurance company has a good investment year, that may be part of the industry's increased productivity, and the increased productivity may in turn lower the price of insurance to the consumer. But only the price of insurance to the household matters in the CPI; the source of the price change—whether from investment income or from some other productivity enhancement—does not matter. Griliches regarded the investment activity of insurance companies as something like a secondary product, to use the language of industry statistics.

Jack Triplett presented an analogy. He pays a disposal service to take out his trash. Suppose that the trash hauler discovers something in Triplett's trash that he can sell to someone (the analogy is the insurance company profiting from the policyholders' reserves), and suppose that competition among trash haulers results in a reduction in the price for hauling Triplett's trash. In Triplett's view, this is a reduction in the price for hauling trash, and it ought to be so treated in the CPI. He considered it wrong to add back into his trash bill the trash company's revenue from selling his trash and to treat the trash company's sale of his trash as if it were charging a higher price for hauling it away.

With respect to the idea that lower rates arise because consumers let insurance companies have their money in advance, Stephen Oliner distinguished interest forgone for paying the premium up front from the earnings of the insurance company. One could estimate interest forgone—from, for example, paying insurance monthly instead of yearly or twice yearly—and ask how much lower the semiannual premium is than the total of six monthly premiums. Some insurance companies offer a monthly option, though one also needs to reduce this estimate by paperwork costs, which are probably most of the total difference. In any event, it is very doubtful that the answer to this question gets very close to insurance company investment earnings, which is Oliner's point.

Monthly insurance payments do not eliminate the fund of reserves—nor, therefore, the problem of insurance company investment earnings. The fund arises from the nature of insurance, from the need to reduce moral hazard. It does not arise because premium payments are paid quarterly, semiannually, or annually instead of monthly or weekly.

John Astin, noting that Griliches and Triplett were approaching the matter from the theory of the cost-of-living index, asked whether there was a difference between what one would do in a CPI that was regarded as an approximation of a cost-of-living (COL) index, on one hand, and in an "inflation index" (a CPI that was not erected on a cost-of-living index) on the other. The HICP is regarded in Europe as an inflation index and not as an approximation of a COL index, as is the U.S. consumer price index. Katherine Abraham objected that that was not a meaningful question, because there were, as she put it, "many" cost-of-living indexes (though how different specifications of a COL index matter in the treatment of insurance was not spelled out).

It seems to us, too, that the distinction between a cost-of-living index and a "consumer inflation index" (on this, see Hill 1998 or Eurostat 1999) does not determine the measurement of insurance, though not for the reason Abraham gave. The essence of the cost-of-living index framework for consumer price indexes is, simply, taking the economic concept of consumption as the relevant way to think about the index (Triplett 2001). Whether a statistical agency formally adopts a cost-of-living index framework for its CPI or not, nearly everyone agrees that the concept of consumption is the relevant way to think about consumer price indexes.

Rosemary Marcuss made a similar point in her remarks: "[In] the non–cost-of-living index . . . you've still got to resort to utility and other judgments in order to try to measure quality-adjusted real output. So . . . how confident are we that there really is a clear distinction in practice between a cost-of-living index and a non–cost-of-living index in regard to insurance?"

Accordingly, for the CPI it is the distinction between the risk-pooling and risk-assuming models of insurance company behavior and the implications of those behaviors for what the consumer is consuming that matter. If one applied the risk-pooling model of insurance to consumption in the cost-of-living index framework, one would get the Eurostat approach to insurance in the HICP.

On the other hand, under the risk-assuming view of an insurance company, its investment earnings are not in the price of the insurance product bought by consumers or any other buyer of insurance. Therefore if one accepted the risk-assuming view of insurance, the COL index would use the insurance company's risk-adjusted premium as the price, and if the risk-assuming model were applied to Eurostat's "inflation index" concept, one would get the same result. The risk-adjusted price of the premium is the CPI price.

This discussion is also relevant to considering insurance as a product—for example, in an input-output table, where insurance is a cost of production for many other industries. The chosen model of insurance (risk-pooling or risk-absorbing) determines how to measure insurance as an input to using industries. Insurance also is a growing part of international trade; the United States both imports and exports insurance services, some of it direct insurance and some of it reinsurance. This distinction between industry output and the products it produces is discussed further in the following section.

The PPI Perspective

From the PPI industry output perspective, the treatment of the insurance industry's investment earnings is even more complex. Again, the two alternative models of insurance company behavior underlie the analysis. We begin with the risk-assuming model, followed by the risk-pooling model.

THE COMPANY ASSUMES THE RISK. If the company assumes the risk, premiums are the basic measure of insurance output. There are two ways to regard the investment income of insurance companies. The most straightforward view, conceptually, is to say that the insurance company is in two lines of business. The primary product is insurance. But because, as noted earlier, accounting for moral hazard results in a fund of reserves held against claims, the insurance company also is in a second line of business, investing and managing investments. Therefore one way to look at insurance is to say that the industry has two products: one is the insurance product that it sells to households and to businesses or perhaps exports; the other is investment income, which is separate from the insurance product. The output of the insurance industry (and the PPI for insurance) should include both products. We call this the two-products view.

Under the two-products view, one might regard investment or investment management activity as a secondary product, to use the language of production statistics (a secondary product is one that is primary to some industry other than the industry in which the establishment that produces it is classified). Or one might contend that the investment activity is a joint product of the insurance company, by analogy with the old example of beef and hides, both of which are inherent outcomes of the beef production process. Because of moral hazard, investment income is a joint product of the insurance production process.

As Mary Weiss noted, insurance industry investment income is part of the output of the insurance industry. One wants the output that is attributable to all of the factor inputs, and in the insurance industry there certainly are factor inputs that are associated with investment income.[38] This investment output needs to be priced in order to get a complete price index for the industry, and it also needs to be included in the output of the insurance industry in order to measure insurance industry productivity. Secondary products are found in many industries. They pose no particular conceptual difficulties. They usually are not an integral part of the production process, though they may be. When secondary products exist, their prices are routinely included in the PPI measures of

---

38. Cummins (1999, p. 85), reports the cost of investment activity at about 9 percent of total expenses for life and property-liability companies.

industry prices.[39] Data on secondary products are routinely collected through the industry statistics programs of the Census Bureau.

Joint products also are found in other industries. In industrial statistics, joint products are both primary products of the industry that produces them. Manufacturing examples include beef and hides, sugar beet sugar and beet pulp, some metal refining operations, and so forth.

One advantage of looking at insurance in this two-products way is that it is easy to reconcile the CPI-COL view of insurance with the industry output or PPI view. The industry's revenue (insurance premiums plus investment income) is not the same as the economic flow between the industry and the consumer.[40] In fact, it is generally greater than the flow between the industry and the consumer. Erwin Diewert remarked that he wanted consistency between the consumer side and the industry side; in this resolution, the two sides are not the same, but they are consistently measured.

THE "ACTIVITY" VIEW. The alternative way of looking at insurance industry output is pursued by Sherwood (1999) and indirectly by the Dohm-Eggleston (1998) paper on the PPI. Actually, neither considers CPI issues; both were working only on the concept of insurance industry output.

Sherwood (1999) makes a distinction between what he calls an "activity" that the insurance company engages in for the purpose of creating output and the output itself.[41] He puts the investment earnings of insurance companies in the category of an activity, not of an output. An analogy might be helpful: a machinery manufacturing company needs a loading dock where incoming rolls of steel are unloaded and prepared for use in the manufacturing process. We believe the loading dock illustrates Sherwood's concept of an activity: it is necessary for producing output, but it is not output itself.

The workshop did not clearly distinguish between the two-products view and the activity view. In part, the distinction was not clearly developed, and in part, it does not appear explicitly in the measurement literature on insurance. We think the two-products view is the more straightforward. The insurance company must be doing something economically besides selling insurance, and that is its investment activity. Our conclusion is embodied in our treatment of

39. Indeed, in a typical industry PPI, the BLS publishes separate price indexes for secondary products and for miscellaneous receipts.

40. In what follows, it should be understood that everything said about the consumer applies also to business purchasers of insurance services.

41. The language here may lead to misunderstanding. In international (but not U.S.) usage, "activity" means "industry." What in North America is called an "industry classification system" is elsewhere called an "activity classification system." Sherwood is not using the word *activity* in the international sense.

investment income in our recalculation of property-casualty insurance output in
panel B of table 6-1.

THE COMPANY POOLS THE RISK. Risk pooling defines the SNA view of
insurance, which is incorporated into Eurostat industry statistics. As noted
before, investment income is not treated as increasing the output of the insurance company but as increasing the price paid by policyholders for insurance.
Everything that has already been said about this convention for measuring
insurance in the national accounts applies to the PPI.

With respect to the PPI, no North American participant seemed enthusiastic
about the SNA treatment of insurance company investment earnings in industry statistics; that might represent an intercontinental difference of views. On
the other hand, industry statistics are precisely the place where alternative
approaches to insurance can most readily be displayed. The Eurostat insurance
industry guidelines suggest collecting all the relevant information that was discussed in the workshop—on premiums, claims, investment earnings, and so
forth. If all of the elements of the Eurostat industry survey are collected in individual countries, it should be easy for users to reassemble them as they wish.
The issue comes down to the price of insurance.

The Price of Insurance

Most writing on and discussion of insurance output is organized, sometimes
implicitly, around expenditures, or price (P) times quantity (Q)—that is,
around the current price measure of output. The current price output (or input)
measure is in dispute. More typically in the economic measurement literature,
debate concerns the constant price measure (Q) or the price index (P).[42]

Yet any discussion of insurance company output, or any discussion of what
the consumer buys when an insurance policy is purchased, must ultimately concern the price measure, P, because P is necessary to estimate Q. Zvi Griliches'
remark at the Brookings workshop accurately characterizes the whole insurance
output literature:

> We're spending a lot of time on the nominal, because in some ways we can
> argue about it easier. But the real problem comes in the deflation. . . . And

---

42. The SNA uses the term "volume," which is carried over from the French national accounts.
We use "quantity" here, not only because it accords better with normal English usage but also
because of the strong and long tradition in economics of speaking of prices and quantities and in
the index number literature of discussing price indexes and quantity indexes.

I think the real conundrum . . . is how you parse out of this the changes in risk. . . . Risk is a form of quantity . . . the assumption of risk is a quantity insured times the probability of loss, and to the extent that the probability changes, there is a change in the quantity of risk assumed. It doesn't matter for the nominal [output] story, but for the real [output] story it matters whether or not that's [put] on the quantity side or on the price side.

The PQ relation implies that if we know Q we know P. Any satisfactory measure for the output of the insurance industry (or of the consumption of insurance by households) must also imply a price index. Conversely, a proposed measure of the output of insurance (or of the consumption of insurance) that does not imply the specification of a price index is not an adequate measure of Q either. Deflation is not just an afterthought or just an implementation issue; the price index is an inherent part of measuring output, whether or not measures of real output are actually produced by deflating by a price index.[43] Moreover, as Griliches noted, the price index must in some manner handle the assumption of risk.

The Net Premiums Approach

John Astin (speaking of consumer expenditure) observed that a net premiums definition of the quantity of insurance implies a net premiums definition of the price index for insurance. This must certainly be correct. A great defect of the net premiums position on measuring insurance output is that it has never been combined with a net premiums specification for the price index. Astin stated at the Brookings workshop that European insurance companies told Eurostat that a net premiums price index was impractical:

> While in principle we should be measuring net premiums, you can't in practice because what you have to do is to follow the price of specific products, just as with any other item in the CPI. With insurance you have to take the premium with a particular company on a particular model of motor car for a 25-year-old civil servant in Washington, D.C., or wherever, and follow that premium through time. I just don't think that it is possible to do that on a net premium basis; it's not the way the companies operate. They couldn't do that, and in any case, in some months, you'd have a negative net price.

43. For example, if one were to construct a direct quantity index, prices come into the measure as weights.

In consequence, Eurostat (for the HICP) and BEA (for the U.S. national accounts) move a net premiums quantity concept by a price index for gross premiums. It is clear that the price of premiums times the quantity of premiums minus claims does not measure $P \cdot Q$, whether for premiums or for net premiums. A basic principle of national accounting is that the price index times the quantity index equals the change in expenditure between two periods—that is,

$$P_{1,2} \times Q_{1,2} = \text{expenditure}_2 \,/\, \text{expenditure}_1,$$

where the subscripts indicate periods 1 and 2, respectively. The HICP and BEA measures violate this basic national accounting principle.

One specification for deflating the net premiums output measure in national accounts draws an analogy with double-deflation methods for producing value added: to compute value added, outputs and inputs are deflated separately to get real value added as a residual. Analogously, to get real, or constant price, net premiums one deflates premiums by a price index for insurance premiums; claims are then deflated by, for example, a price index for auto repairs—or by the overall CPI (minus insurance)—on the grounds that too many things are bought with insurance claims and no good bill exists of what is purchased with them. Similar proposals for deflating net premiums have appeared in many places and were favorably considered by the majority in the BEA work team.

However, the double-deflation proposal appears to be an implicit repudiation of the net premiums, risk-pooling hypothesis that the consumer is buying management services from the insurance company. In the Brookings workshop, Griliches remarked: "It doesn't make sense to deflate [any part of net premiums] by automobile price [indexes] because there is nothing in the management side of the insurance transaction that should be deflated by [auto repair] price indexes." If the company is being paid for its management services, then deflation of the net premiums margin should be done by a price index for management services, as Griliches suggested.

If policyholders paid explicit fees for the net premiums part of insurance charges, the deflation problem would be simplified greatly. They don't. And because they don't, there are no explicit fees corresponding to the insurance company charges described in the SNA. To our knowledge, no proposals have been put forward in the national accounting literature for constructing an explicit price index for the insurance management services that are described in the SNA.

The net premiums position is already an imputation. To implement a deflated net premiums measure, one must impute the price of the management services. It is not satisfactory to impute the price movement of net premiums from movements of some other prices or from the price movement of gross premiums, or to impute them from the price movements of gross premiums and of repairs and other expenditures bought out of claims.[44] As already noted, these deflation proposals actually conflict with the hypothesis of insurance company behavior that underlies the net premiums view of insurance.

It sometimes has been asserted by national accountants that choosing the output measure of premiums minus claims makes the quality change problem less severe in insurance. They contend that the net premiums approach also nets out changes in risk, which is the major problem in obtaining real output of insurance under the gross premiums approach. Because of this difficulty in correcting the gross premiums price index for changes in risk (and also for changes in utilization), statistical agencies have sometimes preferred to price net premiums.

Even if this statement were correct, it is an evasion of the basic problem, not a solution to it. Changes in risk, and changes in the way that risk absorption (or pooling) is administered, must be at the heart of measuring insurance.

Moreover, it is not entirely clear that the net premiums approach reduces the importance of quality change problems. The potential for quality change problems in any price index must in some sense depend on the amount of the quality change in the product relative to the size of the transaction.

The premiums-minus-claims margin is far smaller than the total volume of premiums written by insurance companies. Even if one thought that the net premiums output definition reduced risk-related quality change, one must then consider the amount of quality change in the pool administration measure. What are the services that the insurance company performs for the policyholder? How important are they in the premiums-minus-claims margin? How subject are they to change?

For example, Carr, Cummins, and Regan reviewed efficiency studies of insurance industries, particularly results that compare insurance companies that sell through independent agents and those that have their own dedicated agents. They concluded: "Recent studies provide support for the hypothesis that the higher costs of independent agency firms are attributable to their providing more services, for which they receive additional revenues, leading to insignificant differences in profit efficiency between direct-writing and independent agency firms."[45] This passage implies that variations in the premiums-minus-

44. As Peter Hill pointed out in his discussion (Hill 1998), a claim paid for automobile damage might instead be spent on new clothing. That seems to complicate still further the price index imputation.

45. Carr, Cummins, and Regan (1999, pp. 122–23).

claims margin are substantial across insurance companies and that they are associated with different levels of service. Services to policyholders must be allowed for in either approach to measuring real insurance output. However, policyholder services are undoubtedly far larger as a proportion of net premiums than of gross premiums. In this sense, the net premiums approach may be more subject than the gross premiums approach to quality change problems, relatively speaking.

Without more studies on the measurement of insurance, one cannot know that the net premiums approach entails fewer quality measurement problems, despite frequent assertions that it does. If the unit for the insurance administration fee is the policy, then how can one tell whether the insurance company does something better for its clients? Statisticians and national accountants cannot escape the quality change problem in measuring insurance by adopting a net premiums definition of output.

The Gross Premiums Approach

Constructing a price index for gross premiums is not easy, but at least there is a clear starting point. As Griliches summarized it, the price concerns the thing that the consumer buys, which is the insurance policy: "There is no other answer." One of the strongest arguments in favor of the gross premiums position on measuring insurance output is that under this position, one can observe a transaction, and that transaction has a price, which is the premium for the insurance policy.

The major problem encountered with pricing insurance policies is adjusting for changes in risk. With the gross premiums approach, when there is a change in probability of loss, it shows up as an increase in the quantity of insurance purchased, not in its price. Weiss remarked in the Brookings workshop that the price of insurance equals the cost per dollar of expected loss, with probabilities constant. Other insurance analysts agree. For example, Born and others state:

> The ideal measure of a firm's responses to its environment would be changes in its prices and quantities. . . . For an insurance policy with a fixed set of contractual terms, it might be possible to construct a time series of prices; however, policies vary in important details, such as the deductible, or whether copayments are required, and such details are not made public. . . . Firm-level financial data on premiums and losses by year, state, and line of business [act as a proxy for what is wanted, but]

such data do not enable us to separate the price and quantity of insurance issued.[46]

There is, however, some debate on this point. Barry Bosworth put it in the context of international comparisons: if the cost of insurance is low in a city like Tokyo, which is very safe, compared with some large American city, does that mean that the American cost-of-living index is higher or not? If risk is held constant in the price index, the American consumer consumes more insurance than the Japanese consumer, so the Americans' cost-of-living index for market-purchased goods is not higher. On the other hand, one might want to hold constant aspects of the environment in a complete cost-of-living index; in this case, increased insurance costs to offset a deterioration in the environment would show up as increases in the index. Katharine Abraham remarked that this might be a substantial problem in measuring the cost of insurance to the consumer but that it was no real problem if the objective were to measure the price index for insurance companies. Although that seemingly offers a solution for the PPI view (one that is different from the CPI view), not all economists would be willing to accept an industry productivity measure in which unpriced gains to consumers are excluded.

Another problem sometimes is mentioned: suppose that the price of cars goes up and car insurance premiums rise apace, even without changes in risk or anything else. The gross premiums approach implies that this increased insurance premium is consumption of an increased quantity of insurance and that the cost of insurance has not risen. Viewed as output of the insurance industry, this formulation also seems to make sense.

Yet the CPI concept ought to be built on a price index for automobile transportation—that is, the cost per mile of constant-quality automobile transportation. In this case, then, an increase in the amount of car insurance shows up as an increased cost of using the car, whether the source of the premium increase is a change in risk, lower efficiency in the insurance company, or inflation in car prices.[47] This, again, is a topic in which there might be a wedge between the price index that is constructed for the insurance company (that is, the PPI view) and the corresponding CPI price index.

46. Born and others (1998, p. 182).
47. However, in this case, we are no longer interested in measuring the price of insurance; we want to measure the price of transportation services. If a car uses more gasoline or the price of gasoline rises, the cost of transportation goes up. Insurance contributes to the cost of transportation in a similar manner.

Conclusion on Insurance Prices

On balance, the issue seems to us to play out as follows: pricing gross premiums implies collecting a price for a direct transaction that can be observed. Changes in risk associated with the policy are quality changes. Risk creates quality change problems that are comparable to other, well-known quality change difficulties in price indexes.

The net premiums approach substitutes an imputation for direct pricing, because it implies constructing a price index for a transaction that is not normally observed and probably does not exist in a modern economy. Imputations are sometimes necessary in economic statistics, but it seems undesirable to impute when a transaction can be observed. The quality change argument sometimes made on behalf of the net premiums approach carries little weight, because the net premiums approach carries with it quality change problems that are probably as severe, relative to the size of the "price" that is measured. In any event, trying to avoid the quality change problem by imputing the price substitutes one difficulty for another, without notable gain.

The PPI now contains price indexes for the insurance carrier industry. The pricing concept is gross premiums, not net premiums. We agree with this part of the PPI pricing concept, which seems to be the right way to measure insurance output.

Some quality adjustments have been carried out in the PPI indexes for changes in risk—for example, changes in insurance risk associated with changes in the cars for which premiums are collected in the PPI auto insurance index. The PPI quality adjustment is based on the cost of insuring the vehicles, as reported by the insurance company. When changes in risk are quality-adjusted out of the PPI price index, these changes show up in deflated quantity measures as an increase in output, as we believe they should. So in that respect too, the PPI measures conform to our thinking. On the other hand, these adjustments for risk do not cover very much of the potential risk changes that insurance companies encounter.

Though it treats the premium as the unit for pricing, contrary to national accounts practice, the PPI price index for the insurance industry treats investment earnings as contributing to the price of the insurance policy, so in this respect it conforms to SNA principles. We have been told, however, that insurance industry representatives object to this treatment of investment earnings.[48]

---

48. Conversation with Irwin Gerduk.

Table 6-2. *Comparisons of Insurance Industry Concepts in Data Sources*

	Basic output concept		Inclusion of investment income	
Data source	*Premiums minus claims*	*Premiums*	*Output*	*Price*
BEA industry	X		No	Yes
PPI industry[a]		X	No	Yes
PPI product index[a]		X	No	No
Bosworth-Triplett industry		X	Yes	No

a. The producer price index (PPI) program of BLS computes both a price index for the industry and a product price index.

For this reason, the PPI also contains an alternative insurance price index that covers only premiums, not investment earnings. We believe that this PPI premiums index is a better price index for insurance than is the industry index that treats an increase in investment income as increasing the price of insurance, even though it leaves part of insurance output without a deflator. That is, we agree with the insurance industry.

Summary and New Estimate of Productivity

Table 6-2 summarizes the insurance industry output concepts in U.S. data sources and contrasts them with our preferred output concepts, as spelled out in this chapter. With respect to the basic insurance output measure, we and the PPI settle on premiums. We thus differ from the national accounts, which use premiums minus claims.

With respect to the treatment of insurance company investment earnings, we differ from both the PPI industry index and the national accounts. We favor treating investment income as a second economic activity and therefore a second output of insurance companies. This means that when investment earnings rise, output rises. In the PPI and in the national accounts, when investment earnings rise, this is treated as if policyholders pay a higher price for insurance. However, an alternative PPI is available that excludes investment earnings entirely; this has the defect of omitting the price for part of the industry's output, on our interpretation of it, but at least it does not treat the output as the price.

In the present BEA industry files, the property-casualty component of insurance industry output is deflated by insurance components of the CPI, specifically, homeowners' insurance and automobile insurance. Because the price of owner-occupied housing is measured in the CPI as rental equivalent, fire and damage insurance for the dwelling is not included in the CPI; homeowners' insurance is for contents only. Index changes for these CPI insurance components are shown in table 6-3 for various periods caused by discontinuities in the CPI series. For the 1999–2001 period, our aggregation of CPI components (2.73 percent annually) yields almost exactly the BEA industry deflator (2.72 percent a year).

The new PPI insurance industry price index is more comprehensive than the CPI. It includes fire insurance for houses and covers business, as well as household, purchasers of auto insurance. There is little reason to expect the PPI and CPI insurance indexes to agree closely, even if each is well measured. The PPI index, however, is clearly the one that is appropriate for the BEA industry file, and we presume that it will be introduced in a future revision. For the reasons discussed previously, we use the PPI for premiums, not the PPI insurance industry index, because we believe the latter treats investment earnings of insurance companies inappropriately.

For the various periods in which the two indexes overlap, the PPI rises less than the CPI, 1.4 percentage points a year less, over the four-year period for which both indexes are available (June 1998–June 2003). This seems to be the outcome of a more rapid rise in the PPI for tenant and household insurance and a less rapid rise in auto insurance (see table 6-3). Since property-casualty insurance is about half of total insurance in the BEA data, we apply one-half of the trend difference between the two indexes (that is, one-half of 1.4 points, or 0.7 points) as an adjustment to the BEA deflator. We extrapolate that difference to obtain new 1995–2001 labor productivity estimates.

In addition, we noted above that the PPI industry price index inappropriately treats an increase in insurance company investment earnings as an increase in the price of insurance. This is certainly inappropriate for an output concept, such as the one we use, that puts investment earnings into current price output, as we did in our calculations for table 6-1. We remove this from the deflator by taking the difference between the PPI insurance industry price index and its insurance premiums index. This amounts to about 0.1 percentage point a year.[49]

The results are shown in table 6-4. The top section of the table presents the data in the present BEA industry database (shown in table 6-1); the lower section presents our new estimates. In the lower section, the first line incorporates our

---

49. Perhaps coincidentally, this is about the adjustment to current price output that resulted from adding investment earnings into current price output. Adjusting both current price output and the deflator is not double counting; it is done to be consistent.

Table 6-3. *PPI, CPI, and BEA Implicit Price Index for Insurance Carriers*
Average annual percentage rate of change

Type of insurance	Price indexes		
Property and casualty	PPI	CPI[a]	BEA implicit price index[b]
1987–95	n.a.	n.a.	7.84
1995–2001	n.a.	n.a.	3.79
June 1998–June 2003	2.82	4.20	n.a.
1999–2001	1.77	2.73	2.72
1999–2002	2.58	4.43	n.a.
Tenant and household	PPI	CPI	
1987–95	n.a.	n.a.	
1995–2001	n.a.	n.a.	
1998–2001	n.a.	2.09	
June 1998–June 2003	5.63	4.72	
1999–2001	4.13	2.39	
1999–2002	4.72	2.38	
Motor vehicle	PPI	CPI	
1987–95	n.a.	6.07	
1995–2001	n.a.	2.27	
June 1998–June 2003	3.70	4.37	
1999–2001	1.37	2.78	
1999–2002	3.13	4.74	

Sources: Bureau of Economic Affairs, "GDP by Industry" (www.bea.doc.gov/bea/dn2/gpo.htm [October 17, 2003]); Bureau of Labor Statistics, Producer Price Index industry data; consumer price index (all urban consumers, current series).

a. Home and auto insurance weighted average. Weights (0.87 auto; 0.13 home) derived from Relative Importance Table (motor vehicle insurance, 2.44; tenant and household insurance, 0.37).

b. Insurance carrier total, authors' calculations based on BEA "GDP by Industry."

adjustments to current price output, from table 6-1. These adjustments add 0.4 points a year to output growth. The third line contains our adjustments to the insurance industry deflator. These adjustments add another 0.6 points to constant price output growth, so it is now estimated to grow at 0.5 percent a year (compared with BEA's estimate of –0.5 and the estimate of –0.1 in table 6-1).

The final line shows the total impact of all our adjustments on labor productivity growth: we estimate that labor productivity in insurance carriers grew at 0.1 percent a year from 1995 to 2001. This is not a high rate of growth. It is,

Table 6-4. *Alternative Productivity Estimates for the Insurance Carrier Industry*
Average annual rate of change

Output definition	1995–2001
BEA/BLS IC (total industry gross output)[a]	
Current price output	3.3
Constant price output	–0.5
Price index	3.8
Labor	0.4
Output per worker	–0.9
Total industry (this study, as adjusted)	
Current price output[b]	3.7
Constant price output	0.5
Price index (adjusted for PPI and concept—see text)	3.1
Labor	0.4
Output per worker	0.1

a. Using the output definition from panel A of table 6-1.

b. Using as the output definition "premiums + investment gains" for property-casualty insurance, from table 6-1.

however, a positive rate, rather than the negative and somewhat implausible rate produced by the present BEA insurance output estimates.

Table 6-4 is hardly the end of the story on the output of insurance carriers. Almost none of the extensive literature and discussion on measuring insurance output has dealt with quantifying and measuring the risk that insurance companies absorb and possible changes in the ways they manage risk. Largely because this chapter is a review of the issues as they stand, we have not addressed this vital question either. In some sense, the issues we have been discussing are the wrong issues: the long debate between national accountants and economists who analyze insurance has diverted attention away from a different issue, namely finding ways to incorporate measures of risk into insurance company output.

One expects that insurance companies that absorb risk would want to improve their management of risk. If they discovered better methods for doing so, then competition among insurance companies would lead to reductions in the margin of premiums over claims. This has happened. Reductions of the premiums-claims margin, other things being equal, should accompany multifactor productivity growth in insurance. It appears to us that the national accounts–SNA definition of insurance output precludes MFP growth from reduction of margins, regardless of the output deflator used. But risk poses many questions. It should be at the center of future debate on measuring insurance, not on the periphery.

Conclusion

In his study of the efficiency of insurance companies, Cummins specified three insurance company outputs:
   —risk pooling and risk bearing
   —"real" financial services relating to insured losses
   —intermediation.[50]
For property-casualty insurance, real services can include, for example, providing advice on minimizing loss probability and conducting property inspections, appraisals, and evaluations in addition to settling claims for actual losses. Settling claims promptly and fully also is an aspect of policyholder services.

   Considering insurance as involving multiple products that are partly or wholly bundled together is a useful way to think about the issue of insurance output measurement. The SNA-national accounts net premiums view essentially unbundles the policyholders' services component from the policy itself. It proposes counting these two products separately, or rather to ignore one and price the other separately. That no unbundled transactions can be found is a substantial empirical strike against this view of the insurance business. The most serious flaw in the net premiums position is the failure of its proponents to find (or actually, even to consider) a way to count, evaluate, and price the services that are crucial to its risk-pooling hypothesis. This comment applies both to the NIPA and SNA implementations.

   The gross premiums view of insurance output implicitly accepts the proposition that the risk-absorbing insurance products are bundled with their policyholder services. They are, after all, always included in one transaction. In the gross premium view of insurance, changes in risk—and also in policyholder services—become quality change problems in measuring insurance output. It must be acknowledged, however, that relatively little progress has been made in solving either of these two sets of quality change problems.

   Because policyholder services appear in both the net premiums and the gross premiums views of insurance, empirical estimates of the size, composition, and implicit prices of these services would advance either measurement. We have not found, however, a single study that quantifies policyholder services. This seems

---

50. Cummins (1999, p. 84).

very odd in view of the worldwide popularity of the net premiums position in national accounts.

Even though the national accounts literature can be interpreted as throwing a useful light on the question of policyholder services, it also has obscured the insurance measurement issues by its failure to focus on an appropriate deflator for these services. One cannot get at the management and services component of insurance by deflating separately insurance premiums and insurance claims, for the reason Griliches gave. One needs a measure of policyholder services and a way to account for changes over time in the quantities and quality of service. Because in principle the same measures should be developed for measuring insurance output by the gross premiums view, measuring policyholder services deserves a high priority for future research on insurance output.

Finally, there seems to be general agreement outside the national accounts community that insurance company investment activities (Cummins uses the term *intermediation*) represent outputs that need to be included in a comprehensive measure of insurance industry output. Investment activity is a joint product of insurance because avoiding moral hazard results in the creation of a fund of reserves that can be invested. It is most appropriate to treat the investment activity like any other joint product: both products are to be counted, and both products need a price index.

That insurance investment activity is financial output is a major problem for national accounts, but it is no problem for industry statistics or for industry analyses, including the measurement of productivity. The national accounts approach to insurance company investment activity—treating the investment activity as adding to the price of policyholder services—is hard to defend, either from the view of the insurance production process or from that of insurance purchasers.

Moreover, it should be emphasized that the national accounts treatment of insurance company financial activities undoubtedly does not stem from a conviction that insurance really works the way that the treatment suggests—that is, that insurance policyholder services increase in price when insurance companies have favorable investment experiences. It results, instead, from decisions elsewhere in national accounts, particularly about the treatment of interest, that are forced on the SNA and NIPA definition of insurance industry output.

One of the authors has attended meetings where proponents of the net premiums approach to insurance have dismissed, somewhat contemptuously, any discussion of the economic measurement of insurance and finance with the statement that "there are things in national accounts that are more important than the measurement of insurance and banking." This was not a view held or expressed by any of the participants in the Brookings workshop. Nevertheless, because it has been expressed in some parts of the national accounts community, it is appropriate to respond.

It is of course a methological bias, but we believe that national accounts have potential uses beyond those of the major aggregates, such as GDP, and should be constructed to accommodate those uses. Economists ought to be able to use industry data from national accounts in analyzing industry behaviors. They should be able to use elements of the household consumption sector of national accounts in analyzing consumer behavior. They should be able to take the inputs in the input-output table that underlies the estimation of national accounts and analyze purchaser behavior with respect to changes in input costs and so forth.

In this view of the uses of national accounts, it is problematic when decisions elsewhere in the accounting structure result in measures of industry output that are not useful for industry analysis, in measures of insurance consumption that are not appropriate for consumer demand analysis, or in measures of purchasing industry consumption of insurance that are not useful for analyzing purchaser behavior in the using industries. When this occurs, it is a strong signal that the decisions elsewhere in the accounts need to be reexamined. We think this prin-ciple applies with respect to insurance industry output measures in national accounts.

In some sense, the gross premiums–net premiums debate is the wrong debate. Insurance companies do sell insurance policies. There is no evidence that that conflicts with Griliches's statement that the insurance premium is the only place to begin to estimate the price of insurance, and there is no evidence that suggests that insurance company investment earnings raise the price of poli-cyholder services. The reason this debate has taken place is not so much that the participants have strongly held views and empirical evidence for the risk-pooling or risk-absorbing views of insurance company behavior; it has proceeded because of a long-standing national accounts convention on the measurement of insurance that originates, not in the analysis of insurance itself, but in other decisions in the accounts. The risk-pooling rationale for the national accounts treatment of insurance is a way to avoid negative measured insurance output under the old national accounts convention; it is not an empirically based methodology for measuring insurance.

Whether one looks at insurance as combining two products (risk absorption and investment activity) or three products (risk absorption, policyholder ser-vices, and investment activity) is of no consequence. Either view leads to the same result. The real issues in measuring insurance output are those familiar quality change problems that arise so frequently in the measurement of services output and productivity—in the case of insurance, measuring the values and changes in policyholder services, and measuring and valuing changes in risk. The real challenge in improving the measures of insurance output in national accounts and productivity studies and in improving producer and consumer price indexes is to make progress on estimating those policyholder services and valuing changes in risk.

CHAPTER SEVEN

Measuring Banking and Finance: Conceptual Issues

In contrast to insurance, where measured productivity growth is low, labor productivity and multifactor productivity in banking and financial institutions are relatively high—for example, using the BEA-BLS industry file, labor productivity in banking grew 3.1 percent a year after 1995, and banking MFP grew 1.5 percent a year (table 5-4). These rates exceed recent economywide productivity growth rates. The nondepository institutions industry has a bit slower labor productivity growth but faster MFP (1.9 percent and 2.1 percent, respectively). As currently measured in the BEA industry accounts, the banking and financial services industries seem to show healthy performance.

Despite the reasonable behavior of banking productivity statistics, however, serious questions surround the measures of banking and finance output in the BEA industry accounts. There are reasons for believing that output in banking and finance is poorly measured, and if so, productivity is poorly measured as well.

This chapter, like the chapter on insurance, builds on the research literature and presentations and discussion from two Brookings economic measurement workshops that covered banking and finance output and productivity— (November 20, 1998, and November 1, 2002). The first workshop brought researchers on banking production and productivity together with national accounts experts in the most exhaustive exchange of views on the topic of banking output that has taken place in any forum. In the second one, participants considered additional questions in the measurement of finance.

Overview

In several respects, the issues that arise in measuring banking output parallel those in insurance (chapter 6). Like insurance, the banking output measure that is contained in national accounts differs from the output concept and output measure that is used by economists for research on banking. We spell out these two treatments, and the rationales for them, in the following pages.

ECONOMIC DEFINITION OF BANKING OUTPUT. Economic researchers on banking have specified a banking model in which bank output is identified with balance sheet components that earn revenue for the bank, primarily loans. A loan is not something that is sold, comparable or analogous to the sale of a computer or a car, so defining loans as bank outputs oversimplifies. Rather, a loan provides a flow of finance to borrowers, which continues for the life of the loan. In the term used by some participants in the Brookings workshop on measuring banking output (November 20, 1998), when a bank makes a loan it is "renting money." Banking output, in this view, is the provision of finance to borrowers (equals revenue from lending), and the provision of finance is a flow of services. Because bank loans are not homogeneous, but vary with the type of loan and the characteristics of borrowers, the interesting and difficult questions in measuring bank output arise from the need to consider the heterogeneity of the finance that banks provide, which (as we discuss later in this chapter) is the same thing as considering the economic sources of interest rate differentials.

Additional components of banking output are bank services for which explicit fees are charged. The banking output measure should include as well any unpriced depositor services that are produced by the bank and provided to depositors in a barter arrangement in lieu of higher interest on deposits, though the banks' outputs of transactions services are often omitted from banking research.

These considerations imply that

(a)   *Output in the banking literature* $= \Sigma \, r_m L_m + \Sigma \, (f_g S_g)_{explicit} + \Sigma \, [f_g S_g]_{implicit},$

where L designates the volume of loans, with returns r; S terms are priced (explicit) services and unpriced (implicit depositor) services, as designated; and f terms are the explicit and implicit fees charged for these services.

The economists' banking output definition meets Warburton's (1958) criterion, enunciated years ago, that an output should be something that yields revenue to the bank. "The market value of the services of the banking industry, as expressed in its sales receipts, is as clear cut as in any other industry . . ." (his example was a coal mine or a laundry). However, the bank also produces *unpriced* outputs, which might not be the case for the coal mine or the laundry. "Free" checks cashed, automatic teller machine (ATM) transactions, and other transactions services are outputs of the bank, which need to be imputed in some way. This complicates the output measure of the bank, compared with Warburton's laundry but does not change his basic principle that in devising an output measure for any industry one should start with the industry's revenue sources.

NATIONAL ACCOUNTS DEFINITION OF BANKING OUTPUT. In the national accounts view of banking, interest earned from lending is not payment for the output of the bank, because lending (the provision of finance to bank borrowers) cannot be an output of an economic unit, as defined in national accounts, nor can interest be a payment for a productive service, in national accounts conventions. In national accounts, the output of the banking industry is the interest rate margin—-the difference between interest earned and interest paid. Sometimes this margin treatment is ignored or suppressed in the national accounts literature; sometimes it is explicitly acknowledged (Statistics Netherlands 1999). Revenue from fees for services, such as for returned checks, mortgage placements, and so forth, is added in (this part of output is viewed in the same way as in the economists' definition). Thus the national accounts definition is, using the same symbols as above (and adding D, the volume of deposits, with interest costs, i):

(b) *Output in national accounts* $= (\Sigma\, r_m L_m - \Sigma\, i_j D_j) + \Sigma\, (f_g S_g)_{explicit}$.

As the national accounts banking output definition was traditionally applied in the U.S. national accounts (but not in the SNA), a further definition allocates the interest rate margin to depositors:

(c) $(\Sigma\, r_m L_m - \Sigma\, i_j D_j) \equiv \Sigma\, [f_g S_g]_{implicit}$.

That is, definition (c) says that the entire interest rate margin is deemed transactions services to depositors. The interpretation of definition (c) has now been changed in the United States so that only part of the interest rate margin is allocated to depositors (Fixler, Reinsdorf, and Smith 2003), in conformance with SNA93, but the rest of the national accounts banking story remains intact. The important part of the national accounts rationale is that banking output, in definitions (b) and (c), is not the provision of finance, as definition (c) indicates; this is quite unlike the rationale behind the economists' output definition.

The alternative rationales that have been given for definitions (a) and (b) are explained later in this chapter. However, we think the simplest, most direct, and most illuminating way of reconciling definitions (a) and (b) is a new one: we point out subsequently that the banking definition in national accounts can be interpreted as a margin industry, similar to the national accounts treatment of retail and wholesale trade and parallel with insurance (see chapter 6). In trade, the margin is sales minus the cost of goods sold. In insurance, the margin is premiums minus claims. In banking, the margin is interest received less interest paid.

On this interpretation, we think the banking debate can abandon some of the rhetoric in the traditional national accounts position and most of its banking conceptual framework. Of course a bank buys and sells finance. Similarly, a shoe store buys and sells shoes. But in national accounts, the outputs of both the bank and the shoe store are recorded as their gross margins.

If one looks at the national accounts output measurement for banking as defining a margin industry—as for trade and insurance—that suggests that the real issue is whether one wants to do production analysis or compute productivity on the deflated sales revenue (receipts) or on the gross margin. In insurance and in wholesale and retail trade, the national accounts margin model of output relies on the idea that some set of services is provided that is equal to the margin—in retail trade, various retailing services that are bundled with the goods, and in insurance, the administration of the risk pool for the policyholders (see chapter 6). In both cases, improvements in the economic measurement of output as a margin require better enumerations and ways to measure those services (see chapters 8 and 6). However, the services need to be measured whether one does the analysis on the gross margin or on gross output, as Oi (1993) and others have pointed out for retail trade, so the measurement issues become largely the same.

In banking, the interest rate margin encompasses some services that are not interest—transactions services for depositors. But the major part of the story about the banking interest rate margin has to be about interest rate differentials, just as the margin story for retail trade is a story about wholesale-retail price differentials and what determines them. As we point out later, in the theory of interest rate differentials, the asset structure of interest rate differentials depends on risk, and the term structure of interest rates depends on liquidity. The theory thus suggests where to look for the services that are included in the interest rate margin and that need to be measured.

In the simplest terms, the basic difference between economists and national accountants boils down to the interest rate margin (national accounts) compared with the volume of borrowing interest (economic research). However, differences in conceptual rationales for the two approaches to banking output are also important, as is the interpretation of the output measure. Like insurance, the national accounts banking measure has been devised, not primarily from an economic analysis of the industry's production process but rather to avoid conflict with the national accounts convention for interest. The national accountants' traditional rationale proceeds from and is constrained by the national accounts treatment of interest, in a way that does not constrain researchers on bank production and productivity. The conceptual rationales determine not only the current price output measure but also the deflator and accordingly the way constant price output is measured. The conceptual framework, as well, suggests where one should search for ways to improve the measure.

A Measurement Model for Bank Production, Outputs, and Inputs

Why a model? There are many strands to the long debate over banking output, and they involve many variables. We are discussing in part the role of interest in production analysis and its treatment in national accounts. More important, we are discussing the nature, economic function, and behavior of a financial firm; for these topics, the views of national accountants and of banking production analysts differ greatly. Setting out a formal, though very simple, model of banking services and profit maximization by the bank will help interpret the variables that are crucial to the dispute in the two literatures on banking output.

The model presented in this section is derived from models of the banking firm by Baltensperger (1980) and Santomero (1984), with some modifications to highlight the measurement issues.[1] The Baltensperger-Santomero model of the banking firm underlies essentially all economic research on bank production behavior.[2] The model is manifestly not consistent with the national accounts approach to banking. Later in this chapter, we consider alternative ways that have been proposed to rationalize the national accounts approach to make it fit with the economists' model of banking. We also consider how the bank measurement model needs updating, based on insights from recent work reviewed by Allen and Santomero (1997, 2001).

Our initial model applies to the simple bank that makes commercial and consumer loans, and whose sources of funds consist only of demand deposits, time deposits (deposit certificates), and purchased funds. This simple bank earns most of its revenue from interest on loans. In addition, the bank provides some services

---

1. A more elaborate model for the financial firm is in Hancock (1991). Hancock's model incorporates some of the elements of this section, but not all, and contains others that are not considered here.

2. See the reviews of this literature in Berger and Humphrey (1997); Berger and Mester (1997).

for which an explicit fee is charged. It pays time depositors (owners of certificates of deposit) only in interest. There are no services provided to time depositors (except safekeeping). Demand depositors receive only "free" (that is, unpriced) check cashing, use of automatic teller machines (ATMs), and other transactions services; they earn no interest. This is a simplification. One could readily model accounts that both earn interest and receive unpriced services, but it complicates the model without changing the results that are important here. The bank carries deposit insurance, the cost of which is, at least in part, borne by depositors in the form of lower returns on deposits. It maintains non-income-generating reserves, whose size may or may not be constrained by regulation.

Following Baltensperger (1980) and Santomero (1984), our simple bank maximizes profit according to:

(1) $$\text{Max: } \Pi = \Sigma \, r_m L_m + \Sigma f_g S_g - \Sigma \, i_j D_j - i_G G - \Sigma \, w_h v_h$$

Subject to H (L, S, D, v) = 0

and $\Sigma \, L_i = \Sigma \, D_j \, (1 - k_j)$,

where all symbols designate vectors whose elements

L are loans (or other earning assets) of different types, with returns r, which for the moment we assume certain.

S are directly priced bank services, with fees f.[3]

D are deposits, whose *interest* costs are designated i_j (and j = 1, 2).

G are purchased funds, with interest cost i_G.

v are conventional, nonfinancial inputs (labor, materials, services of capital goods), with unit input costs w_h.

k are reserve ratios on different deposits.

Only time deposits pay interest, so (designating time deposits as j = 1), $\Sigma \, i_j D_j = i_1 D_1$ (because $i_2 D_2 = 0$). That demand deposits have no interest cost does not mean, of course, that they have no costs nor that depositors earn no return. Rather, the acquisition cost of demand deposits equals the cost of unpriced services produced by the bank and provided to depositors in lieu of explicit interest. Banks use a portion of the resources $\Sigma w_h v_h$ to produce the unpriced depositor services. Subsequently, it will be useful to assume that the portion of $\Sigma w_h v_h$ that is used to produce depositor transactions services—that is, that the cost of transactions services—can be separated from other bank costs

3. The vectors S and f do not appear in Baltensperger (1980) or Santomero (1984), and neither does G.

and that data exist to estimate the cost of those services. Data of this type are already used as weights in the banking output measure of the BLS productivity office. We designate those costs, that is, the bank's resources used to produce transactions services for depositors, as $\Sigma w_h v_{hD}$.

In the balance sheet constraint (the final equation in 1), the vector of reserve ratios, k_j, is determined by

$$k_j = R_j / D_j, \text{ if } k_j > k_j^*,$$
$$k_j = k_j^* \text{ otherwise,}$$

where R_j is the optimal reserve determined by equation 2 below, and k_j^* is the legal minimum reserve ratio for deposit type j.

Santomero (1984), in setting up the maximization model, encompasses an intertemporal maximization framework as well as making the maximization extend over an expectation, not certainty returns, as in equation set 1. We abstract from the first throughout this chapter and from the second temporarily.[4]

Several points about the model require additional comment. We begin with three relatively minor points, which clarify. We then discuss the bank production function, H (.), which portrays the bank as transforming funds it acquires from depositors and other sources into finance that it provides to borrowers.

THE BALANCE SHEET CONSTRAINT. The inclusion of a balance sheet constraint in equation 1 is unusual. All firms have balance sheets, but they do not normally appear in constrained maximization problems. The balance sheet appears in equation 1 because this is a financial firm: loans cannot legally be made or assets acquired without deposits or other sources of funds. The relation between financial inputs (deposits, or purchased funds) and the bank's acquisition of earning assets is in part a *financial* relation; it is not solely a physical production process. It is therefore expressed in (1) as financial constraint on the profit maximization process that is parallel to, and in addition to, the physical transformation function: both constraints are necessary to delimit the financial firm's production set.

The bank production function, H (.), contains the real inputs necessary for making loans—the resources required for processing forms, evaluating credit standings, and so forth—and for servicing deposits and acquiring purchased funds. These inputs are contained in the vector v. Loans can be "produced" in this sense without deposits, and the production process of servicing deposits can be executed without making loans. The function H (.) does not convey the

4. He does not include the balance sheet constraint, nor does he consider reserves.

entirety of the economic process of transforming deposits (or other sources of funds) into loans in the way that a production function for steel depicts the transformation of iron ore into steel. In this sense, both a production constraint and a financial constraint are necessary.

In most empirical work on bank production, the balance sheet constraint has been ignored, which seems an oversight.

THE TREATMENT OF RESERVES. A bank must maintain reserves. Reserves are normally placed on the asset side of a bank's balance sheet, along with its income-earning loan portfolio. A few studies have for this reason included reserves among the outputs of the bank. This is inappropriate.

Baltensperger remarked that "the first analytical models of bank behavior were models of bank reserves (liquidity) management . . . [in which] the problem to be solved [is] the optimal allocation . . . among various assets, with particular attention being paid to the choice between earning assets and reserve (liquid) assets."[5] He shows that the optimal level of bank reserves is given by:

$$(2) \qquad\qquad R = R\,(r/\rho,\ \sigma_\omega),$$

where r is the interest rate earned on loans, ρ is the cost per dollar of a reserve deficiency (examples of such costs are emergency borrowing or emergency sale of assets to cover a deficiency), and σ_ω is the standard deviation of the distribution (assumed normal, for simplicity) of the outflow of deposits (withdrawals). A bank determines its level of reserves by equating, at the margin, the revenue forgone (the opportunity cost of holding reserves) with the expected cost of a reserve deficiency, where σ_ω summarizes the probability of the bank's encountering a reserve deficiency.

This formulation makes clear the commonsense statement that reserves are a cost of the banking business. This cost is incurred not only because deposits are of shorter durations than earning assets but also because at least some of them are payable on demand, and hence their durations are unknown, except as probabilities. If withdrawals were deterministic, not probabilistic, then unregulated banks could operate by careful matching of maturities, rather than holding reserves. In any event, equation 2 makes clear that we should treat reserves as a cost of the bank, specifically as a cost incurred when financial inputs are obtained in the form of deposits payable on demand.

BANK REGULATION, RESERVES, AND UNPRICED DEPOSITOR SERVICES. It has often been predicted that with deregulation banks would no longer compensate

5. Baltensperger (1980, p. 3).

depositors with "free" transactions services, and that instead they would move to a regime that substituted explicit interest on deposits and explicit fees for transactions services. Although banks have indeed increased their revenue from fees under deregulation, this has not eliminated the system where depositors are compensated with unpriced depositor services. The fact that σ_ω (the volatility of deposit withdrawals) appears positive in equation 2 suggests why.

"Free" checks usually accrue only to depositors who maintain some *minimum* (not average) balance. If banks were simply compensating depositors for the volume of funds put at the bank's disposal, one might expect that the volume of unpriced services would depend on the average balance. However, when depositors commit to a minimum balance, this reduces σ_ω, the variability of deposit withdrawals, and accordingly will reduce the size of optimal reserves, and so reduce bank costs. For this reason, even unregulated banks may continue to compensate depositors with unpriced services, rather than paying interest on deposits and charging explicit fees for checks and ATMs. This indeed has happened. Another reason might be that the banks' costs of providing unpriced services (that is, the resources $\Sigma w_h v_{hD}$) are lower than the value placed on them by depositors, and competition has only slowly bid away the excess profit.

The significance for measuring banking output is obvious: even in a deregulated bank environment, it will still be necessary to face up to the difficult problem of valuing unpriced transactions services provided to depositors. In the model above, the *cost* of unpriced transactions services provided to depositors is included in input costs, but the value of those services does not appear explictly in the model, nor does their contribution to bank output. First, because transactions services are bartered in exchange for the use of depositors' funds, there are no explicit revenues to put into equation 1. Second, equation 1 is a model of bank profit maximization, not a (complete) model of bank production or of bank productivity. We address these matters later. However, note that inclusion of unpriced depositor services in banking output is a feature of both the national accounts and of bank researchers' views of banking; the only issue is how to value these services.

THE NATURE OF THE PRODUCTION TRANSFORMATIONS IMPLIED BY THE MODEL. The transformation process in equation 1 involves the usual (nonfinancial) capital goods, labor, and intermediate inputs that would be found in any other industry's production function (the inputs v_h). Banks also need a financial input (deposits or purchased funds) to produce the bank's financial outputs, so H (.) depicts the bank as transforming deposits and purchased funds into finance that it provides to borrowers. It is a bit hard to see why this depiction of a bank's economic function is controversial, but in the national accounts literature, it is.

In any model of banking, there must be an intuitive story for "What do banks do?" Alternatively, as Allen and Santomero (2001) put it, "What is a bank?" The banking production model in equation 1 implies an analogy with a nonfinancial firm. Indeed, the bank production function literature summarized in Berger and Humphrey (1997) and Berger and Mester (1997), as well as the national accounts literature, relies on or develops such analogies with nonfinancial firms. The question is, What is the appropriate analogy?

Several years ago, the *Economist* featured a long review of developments in banking. At the end appeared this summary:

> There is not much difference between financial firms and food suppliers. They buy and sell credit rather than cabbages, but they shift it from producer to consumer in much the same way, sometimes selling it as it is, other times canning it or pickling it or turning it into coleslaw; they sell it wholesale to other cabbage firms, or retail in the poshest emporiums and from the humblest market stalls . . . Nothing very special in that.[6]

The *Economist*'s analogy is enlightening because it cuts through many of the false notions that banks are "different." They are different in a sense because they deal in finance, so their product has unique characteristics, and they have therefore financial production processes. They are different because financial products are different from nonfinancial products—but then, so is software, and its production and distribution are different from other goods and from other services. Banks are not different in the fundamental economic sense: they are producing units that buy inputs (in their case, their inputs include financial inputs) in one market and sell in another market the product that is produced or transformed in some way from the inputs.

What are these transformation processes? The *Economist*'s summary implies several intuitive production processes for the financial firm. First, they move credit, or the provision of finance, from place to place, or from primary producers to ultimate buyers, much like the wholesale-retail distribution system does for goods. Allen and Santomero remark, "At the center, of course, financial systems perform the function of reallocating the resources of economic units with surplus finds (savers) to economic units with funding needs (borrowers)."[7]

---

6. *Economist*, April 7, 1990, p. S68.
7. Allen and Santomero (2001, p. 273).

Historically in the United States and in some other countries, loanable funds were cheap in rural areas and in small towns; the banking system moved them to large financial centers, where there was more demand and the price was higher, much as a pipeline might move natural gas from producing areas to Chicago, or a wholesaler might move cabbages from California to New York. One should be clear about this analogy: cabbages delivered in New York are not the same economic product—even if they are not otherwise transformed or processed in any way—as cabbages in California, and there is a production process in moving them from grower to final consumer.[8] Similarly, banks move finance from one location and from a set of suppliers to another location and to a set of demanders. This production process is most clearly demonstrated by purchased funds, where there is little transformation of the financial product that is shifted from one physical and institutional location to another. Such movements of finance resemble the activity of wholesale trade in nonfinancial goods.

Banks, however, seldom sell their cabbage-equivalents as is. It is the "canning" and "pickling" of credit, and "turning it into coleslaw," that defines the essence of the bank production process. The reason that loan interest rates are higher than depositor rates is only partly because the bank has moved credit, like a distribution firm, from supplier to consumer; it has also transformed that credit in the process.

Zvi Bodie and Robert Merton point out that "the redistribution of risks is a fundamental function of the financial system." Similarly, Bodie remarked that the "core function of the financial system is to provide people with ways to manage their exposure to risk."[9] The essence of the bank's transformation process involves risk, and it may also involve information. When a bank takes a deposit, it issues a relatively safe security.[10] When a bank makes a loan, the production process of financial intermediation entails procedures for the assumption of the risk that is inherent in any loan, risk that may well adhere to characteristics of the borrower or to the uses to which the borrower plans to employ the funds

8. Objections have been raised to the analogy on the grounds that finance is not the same when transported, unlike (it is asserted) cabbages. This seems an economic misunderstanding because cabbages are not the same when transported, either. As Abba Lerner (1934) remarked many years ago, "Objects having the same physical characteristics are not the same goods if they are at different places. . . . And location is not the only variant of this kind, but rather the simplest species of a large genus." The analogy cannot be faulted because of some supposed, but mistaken, objection that cabbages are homogeneous commodities.

9. Bodie and Merton (2000, p. 255); Bodie (1999, p. 372).

10. Relatively safe but not riskless. Negative interest rates appeared on Japanese government bonds, because investors shunned bank deposits out of fear for the safety of Japanese banks.

made available by the bank.[11] It is thus difficult or impossible to analyze banking without taking risk bearing into account.[12] It is equally difficult without considering the accumulation of information about borrowers and their activities that is crucial to operating successfully as a banker.

The asset structure of interest rates involves risk. The term structure of interest rates involves liquidity. Banks also operate on the liquidity margin, transforming liquid assets into illiquid ones of higher value.

BANK OUTPUTS. Our simple bank has as explicit outputs the provision of finance through loans (we distinguish commercial loans and consumer loans—together, $\Sigma \, r_m L_m$) and financial services for which fees are charged ($\Sigma \, [f_g S_g]_{explicit}$). However, the bank also produces unpriced outputs, in the form of transactions services to depositors.[13] They provide the transactions services to demand depositors, without explicit charges, but depositors do pay for these services, in the form of interest that depositors forgo.[14] Banks accordingly earn *implicit* revenue from these depositor services, in the form of forgone interest payments to depositors. At the same time, banks produce these services, and they incur costs for producing them, in the form of the resources employed in check clearing, ATM operations, and other transactions services provided to holders of demand deposits.

Because transactions services are sold in a barter transaction, no explicitly priced entries appear in the accounts of the bank or of the depositors. The barter is netted out of the profit statement in equation 1; if transactions services were sold as explicitly priced services, then $\Sigma \, (f_g S_g)_{explicit}$ would of course be larger, but so would $\Sigma \, i_j D_j$, because banks would now pay for demand deposits with explicit interest, rather than with unpriced services. The cost of providing the services remains as a part of $\Sigma \, w_h v_h$, the bank's use of real resources.

There is, incidentally, no reason that the cost of transactions services should necessarily equal the interest forgone. Probably the cost is less than the interest forgone, for reasons noted earlier, and for other reasons. It may be profitable for

11. Mortgages on very expensive houses have higher rates, not because their wealthy owners are poorer credit risks but because there is a thin market for these houses if foreclosure occurs.

12. The same point is obviously true for the output of insurance. Sherwood (1999) defines insurance output as the assumption of a certain quantity of risk.

13. Safekeeping services may also be an unpriced output, in the case where safekeeping takes place in time or demand deposits.

14. As an approximation, this forgone revenue of the banks is $i_1 D_2$—the interest cost of *time* deposits applied to the quantity of *demand* deposits. This specification assumes that the closest substitute for a bank demand deposit is another deposit with the bank. In response to presentations of some of this material elsewhere, some economists have contended that the closest substitute for a bank demand deposit is a government bond or other security.

the banks to provide transactions services on an unpriced basis, instead of paying market interest on demand deposits. It is presumably partly for this reason that bankers speak of "deposit products," which is otherwise strange jargon to use for a necessary input that costs the bank.

The output of the bank is understated by the omission of bartered depositor services from equation set 1. For productivity measurement, these unpriced services need to be counted. The services—"free" checks, ATM transactions, and other transactions services—can in principle be enumerated, and their quantities can be observed. Their prices, however, must be imputed, for valuing bank output and to provide the price measures for banking.

However, the cost of producing these depositor services is correctly accounted for in the bank's profit function, so there is no need for an additional entry there. This has been the source of some confusion.

It is not true, as has sometimes been stated, that in this model demand *deposits* are simultaneously an input and an output of the bank. Because the bank produces unpriced outputs that are bartered in compensation for the banks' use of depositors' funds, this does not imply that the deposits themselves are bank outputs. Deposits are financial inputs in equation 1; the unpriced services are (unobserved) outputs.

SUMMARY: BANK OUTPUT. Using the above, we add to the bank's output in equation 1 an imputation for the value of unpriced bank services. A parallel imputation must be made to bank payments to depositors. We accordingly modify the banking model of equation 1 by redefining the services outputs, S_g and the bank's costs of acquiring deposits:

$$(3) \qquad \Sigma f_g S_g = \Sigma (f_g S_g)_{explicit} + \Sigma [f_g S_g]_{implicit}$$
$$\Sigma i_j D_j = i_1 D_1 + [i_2 D_2],$$

where the square brackets designate imputations (and recalling that demand deposits were designated D_2).

If banks minimize the costs of acquiring deposits, they will provide implicit services up to the point where the cost of acquiring demand deposits equals the cost of acquiring other sources of funds. This implies that in the last line in equation set 3, $i_1 = i_2$, and suggests an implementation strategy for estimating depositor services.

The imputations raise *measured* bank output and *measured* bank outlays to depositors. The imputations also raise *measured* bank productivity and measured bank deposits costs. But the output and productivity measures that include the imputations are the correct ones.

The imputations do not affect bank profit (which was correctly measured before).[15] They do not change bank value added, because the resources employed in generating "free" checks (a portion of v_h) were counted all along.

Parenthetically (for present purposes), because the imputations measure the correct costs and revenues from banking operations, they also yield correct marginal conditions for profit maximization for the bank, and thus they are the correct measures for analyzing bank behavior. However, a regime of explicitly priced services would likely change the quantity of services demanded or supplied, compared with a regime of implicitly priced services. That is not the subject of this paper.

BANK INPUTS. The simple bank has as inputs the usual capital (that is, capital goods, buildings, and equipment), labor, and materials. But because it is a financial firm, it must obtain financial inputs, among which are demand deposits and time deposits.

The treatment of deposits is controversial, because in national accounts no interest-bearing deposit can be a productive input to the bank. In the production function literature, the treatment of demand deposits has been controversial because of neglect of unpriced depositor services in these studies. The treatment of demand deposits in the production literature has been discussed elsewhere and will not be addressed here.[16]

OUTPUT AND PRODUCTIVITY OF THE SIMPLE BANK. With the amendments above, the simple bank's output consists of

$$(4) \qquad \text{Output} = \Sigma\, r_m L_m + \Sigma\, f_g S_g$$
$$= \Sigma\, r_m L_m + \Sigma\, (f_g S_g)_{explicit} + \Sigma\, [f_g S_g]_{implicit},$$

where the brackets indicate imputations. Its current-price level of labor productivity is then

$$(5) \qquad \text{Labor productivity} = \text{Output} / \text{Labor input}$$
$$= \{\{\Sigma\, r_m L_m + \Sigma\, (f_g S_g)_{explicit} + \Sigma\, [f_g S_g]_{implicit}\} / \text{L}\}.$$

Suppose that loan outputs were omitted from equation 5. Omitting loan outputs understates banks' output and productivity. The national accounts approach omits consideration of bank loan output. Similarly, omitting the

---

15. This was one reason why Allen Berger proposed in the November 1998 workshop that the whole set of issues surrounding unpriced services could be skirted by estimating bank profit-function productivity, instead of the usual production function or cost function approaches.

16. See Hancock (1991) and the discussion of demand deposits in Triplett (1992).

imputations for in-kind services provided to depositors also understates output and productivity. The production function approach always counts bank lending activity but generally omits consideration of unpriced bank services, not so much for conceptual reasons, but more for lack of data.[17] Humphrey and Lozano (2002) consider the effects of omitted output variables on banking productivity studies.

MODIFYING THE BANKING MODEL TO TAKE RISK AND LIQUIDITY INTO ACCOUNT. The model of banking presented so far is derived, as noted, from the work of Baltensperger and of Santomero in the early 1980s. Allen and Santomero (1997, 2001) review more recent thinking among banking economists on the question "What do financial intermediaries do?"

Allen and Santomero point out that in the models of the 1980s and earlier, economists viewed banks as institutions whose contributions to economic activity stemmed from their reductions of transactions costs to investors and their role in processing asymmetric information (banks know more about borrowers' creditworthiness than individual investors can know). More recent research has emphasized, in their view, banks as managers of risk. Of course, banks have always functioned to reduce the risk exposures of fund providers, so this is not a new function of banks, but it has received more attention recently. Allen and Santomero also contend that the way the banks manage risk has changed, and that some of the changes are connected with nondepository activities, which have become relatively more important even for banks that accept deposits.

These risk-managing, information-managing, and liquidity-providing roles of banks (and other financial institutions) must be taken into account in future measurement models of banking and in future research on improving bank output measures. At the moment, we are not aware that these newer developments in the theory of the banking, or the financial intermediary, firm have been considered in the banking measurement literature, with the exception of Schreyer and Stauffer (2002). Most of the discussion still concerns the "simple bank," not the financial intermediary of the twenty-first century. That extension is yet to come.

National Accountants' Critique of Economists' Measure of Banking Output

Richard Ruggles (1983 and elsewhere) was not the first to criticize the national accountants' approach to banking and to offer an alternative that—actually—corresponds to the output concept that economists have used for banking

17. See the review in Berger and Humphrey (1997).

research during the past two decades.[18] But despite Ruggles's position in developing the SNA, other national accountants seem never to have responded to his proposals, at least in publication. As far as we can determine, Ruggles's position was never reviewed in the deliberations that led to the 1993 System of National Accounts, nor was there a position paper or internal review memo that explored the issues he raised. Though one presentation of the alternative approach to banking output was made to the "expert committee" that met to develop SNA93, the expert committee only considered a revision to the standard national accounts approach to banking and did not seriously consider any alternative approaches. Regrettably, this national accounts tradition of ignoring the alternatives is preserved in recent BEA publications.[19]

Because of other national accountants' silence, Peter Hill's presentation to the November 1998 Brookings workshop on banking output measurement is extremely valuable. Hill, who was a major author of SNA93, presented a national accountant's response to the economists' model of banking production. In the following paragraphs, based on the workshop transcript, we summarize Hill's remarks.

Two themes dominate this national accountants' critique. The first concerns the treatment of interest in national accounts and the necessity for treating interest in the output of the banking industry in a way that is consistent with the way it is treated elsewhere in the accounts. This first theme is intertwined with the second, which is a view of the banking process itself—the production transformation process and the definitions of inputs and outputs. This view differs from the economists' model.

Hill noted that terminology sometimes creates semantic difficulties that get in the way of discussion of the real issues, and he explained that the term "production" in national accounts is sometimes used more narrowly than is generally the case in economic analysis. He also expressed "problems with viewing deposits and loans as inputs and outputs."

In Hill's view, loans and deposits are stocks, not flows. We think this point touches on a problem with empirical research on banking. The stock of loans outstanding is intended to represent the flows of finance that loans provide to

---

18. Clark Warburton (1958), a prominent monetary economist in the 1950s and 1960s who was cited earlier, suggested a similar proposal for measuring banking, and there were others (Hodgman, 1969; Sunga, 1984). There is, incidentally, no evidence that critics of the national accounts, such as Ruggles or Warburton, influenced modern research on banking production and productivity; rather, the idea that banks buy finance, transform it, and sell it to borrowers is just a natural way for an economist who models production to portray the output and production processes of banks.

19. Fixler, Reinsdorf, and Smith (2003).

borrowers, but the characteristics of the finance are not well represented by the count of the number of loans. Deposits might be more or less homogeneous and separated into a relatively small number of types, but bank loans can hardly just be counted. If we say that the bank is selling "finance" to borrowers, this surely cannot adequately be represented simply as the number of loans on the bank's books.

In response to Hill's point, David Humphrey noted that production economists really wanted flows. Their use of loans and deposits as proxies for the flows of finance was dictated by data considerations and did not represent the concept that they wish to use. Humphrey's response opens the question of how one represents the heterogeneity in the flow of finance that banks are providing to borrowers (and undoubtedly, to a lesser extent, that depositors are providing to banks). These issues are present in both approaches to banking. For example, in the revised 1999 BEA output measure for banking (which was adopted subsequent to the discussion in the Brookings 1998 workshop), the numbers of deposits and loans appear as indicator variables for moving bank constant price output. BEA presumably regards them as proxies for some underlying measures of the flows of financial services. Similar approaches have been adopted in some European countries. Hill's point thus applies to the BEA measures of banking output as well as to those of economic researchers.

Hill then turned to the banking production process:

> I have some difficulty when people say that deposits are in some sense being transformed into loans. I don't see that this is analogous to the way intermediate inputs are transformed into outputs in most processes of production that take place in the economy. . . . These two claims continue to exist after the process of intermediation has taken place. It's not that one is consumed or transformed into the other. Clearly, the deposit is not consumed in the way in which intermediate inputs are consumed in physical processes of production.

This last point seems to hearken back to the objection that deposits and loans are stocks and not flows. The proper analogy is to the treatment of durable goods in production analyis—use of capital services from durable capital equipment does not imply they are used up in the sense that coal is burned in a boiler.[20] Similarly, deposits could be thought of as providing financial flows to

---

20. This is an old matter from production analysis. The "used up" analogy for capital goods, which was once prominent in national accounts thinking about capital, was refuted in Haavelmo

the banking production process as long as the deposit remains in the bank, analogously with durable goods in other production processes, which contribute capital services as long as they remain employed.

The essence of the national accountants' position on banking output is shown in the following passage from Hill's remarks:

> For while there is no argument about intermediation being an extremely important function, I find it difficult to view this as a process of production in the way that this is generally defined [in the SNA]. Lending, in itself, is not viewed as a process of production [in the SNA]. [This means that the flow of interest payments, both by the banks to their depositors, and by the borrowers to the banks, are not defined in the SNA as payments for productive services. On the other hand,] . . . financial institutions do have operating expenses as distinct from the interest cost and those operating expenses do have to be covered by some sort of output [in the SNA]. National accountants now view this [by] saying that the sales receipts which cover these operating expenses are, in fact, a component of the interest flows and should be separated out from them, leaving the pure interest flows as pure lending and borrowing.

As noted earlier, Hill's other point is the consistency of the treatment of banking output and value added with the rest of the SNA. "Banking is a particularly difficult and also a particularly important industry, but it's not possible, within this overall [SNA] framework, to treat it in some way which is different from the way other industries are [treated]." He emphasized that interest, in the SNA, is not deemed a payment for performing a service, which means that lending is not in itself the production of a service and that interest received in the accounts of nonfinancial enterprises is not treated as if it were a secondary activity that increases the output of nonfinancial enterprises. When a nonfinancial enterprise finances its activities by debt, rather than equity capital, the value added of this firm in the SNA is invariant to its debt-equity position. Hill pointed out that the treatment of interest in financial firms is exactly parallel to its treatment in nonfinancial firms.

(1960), who credited Frank Knight for the insight. For the treatment of capital services in production and productivity analysis, see also Jorgenson (1989); Hulten (1990); Diewert (1980); and Schreyer (2001). The issue was discussed in the context of the national accounts in Tripett (1996).

The National Accounts Approach to Banking Output

In contrast to the bank production function approach, the national accounts approach to banking does not count as banking output the financial service for which interest, as interest, is paid. Putting it another way, national accountants do not count the provision of finance to bank borrowers as an output of the banking industry, if by provision of finance we mean lending, or the supply of credit, or the use of loanable funds, or what has sometimes been called the "renting of money."

There are two ways to look at the national accounts approach to banking. Historically, it came out of the view that interest could not be the output of banks.[21] To obtain some output measure, a convention was adopted that the interest rate spread between loan and depositor rates could be used in national accounts as the output of banks, as long as it was interpreted as something that was not interest (as Hill said, "sales receipts which cover . . . operating expenses"). An alternative view, not fully articulated or fully accepted as far as we can tell, is just to say that of course the interest rate spread is interest. However, banking is treated in national accounts as a margin industry, comparable to wholesale and retail trade and insurance.

The rationale matters for interpretation of the banking measure. It matters more in determining where measurement improvements will be sought, particularly for price measures (deflation) and therefore for the measures of constant price output of finance.

Rationale: The Treatment of Interest in National Accounts

As Hill (1996) explains in his paper for the Brookings November 1998 workshop, the national accounts approach to banking is really a consequence of the national accountants' view of interest. Interest, in national accounts, is primarily a transfer, or a receipt of property income, involving owners of financial claims and others. Interest is not regarded as a payment for a productive service.[22] If interest is not a payment for a productive service, it cannot be payment for an output of banks.

---

21. As Warburton (1958) noted, this national accounts view of interest descends directly from Alfred Marshall's list of what were then called "factors of production": land, labor, capital, and entrepreneurship. The idea that finance could be part of economics arose only in the latter half of the twentieth century.

22. Hill (1998, p. 3) makes the useful point that "productive" is descriptive, here, not pejorative. "Productive" means a process that "generates value added and factor incomes," as those terms are defined in the SNA.

"The concept of production used in the SNA requires some activity, or process, to take place involving labor and capital assets in which inputs are transformed into outputs and in which factor incomes are generated. Lending is not an activity of this kind."[23] This, of course, is a definition. But as a consequence of the definition, the provision of finance is not an output of banks in the SNA. On the same reasoning, deposits do not *themselves* provide "productive" inputs to banks in the SNA view, again contrary to the treatment of bank financial inputs in banking production function studies.

Because the SNA definitions of value added and factor incomes might be seen as somewhat arbitrary, the following example might be useful. Consider accounts for a nonfinancial firm (a coal mine or a laundry). In national accounts, intermediate purchases of productive services are deducted from gross output to get value added. Value added is the compensation of labor and capital inputs employed in the industry (factor costs, in national accounts language). Because interest is not regarded as a payment for a productive service, interest paid is not deducted in the calculation of value added, which means that (net) interest *paid* remains in value added. For a nonfinancial firm, the effect is to make its payment for the use of capital invariant to the firm's debt-equity ratio (the convention is thus consistent with the Modigliani-Miller theorem in finance).[24] Another way to view it is to say that any interest *earned* by a coal mining company is removed from the output of the coal industry; but interest *paid* is included in the coal industry's value added, because it is part of the industry's cost of capital.

When this *net interest paid* rule is applied to financial firms, however, it excludes the major source of bank revenue (income from lending activity) from banking output and leads to negative banking value added.[25]

(6) $$VA = \{(\Sigma\ i_j D_j - \Sigma\ r_m L_m) - \Sigma\ w_h v_h\} < 0,$$

23. Hill (1996, p. 2).

24. "Operating surplus [an SNA term that is approximately the capital share, in normal economics language] . . . is a measure of the surplus accruing from processes of production *before* deducting any explicit or implicit interest charges, rents or other property incomes payable on the financial assets, land or other tangible non-produced assets required to carry on the production. It is, therefore, invariant as to whether . . . the inventories, fixed assets, land or other non-produced assets owned by the enterprise and used in production are financed out of own funds (or equity capital) or out of borrowed funds (or loan capital)." (SNA93, para. 7.82).

25. We omit from the equation and from the following discussion bank services for which explicit fees are charged. The treatment of these is not controversial.

where, as before, D terms are bank deposits; L terms are loans; i and r are deposit and loan interest rates, respectively; and v_h are ordinary purchased inputs, with prices w_h. The first term itself is normally negative, so gross output is negative, and value added more so. Gorman colorfully remarks that the national accounts treatment of interest flows—unless adjusted—leaves the "commercial bank . . . portrayed as a leech on the income stream."[26]

To avoid portraying the bank as a leech on the income stream (VA < 0), banks are assumed to provide services equal to the entire net proceeds from banks' lending operations. Algebraically,

$$(7) \qquad \Sigma f_u S_u \equiv -(\Sigma\, i_j D_j - \Sigma\, r_m L_m),$$

where S_u is a vector of unpriced services with implicit prices f_u. In the historical BEA interpretation (Gorman, 1969), these unpriced services were identified with depositor transactions services, so on this interpretation, the $\Sigma f_u S_u$ term in equation 7 equals the term $[\Sigma f_g S_g]_{implicit}$ in equation 3. However, equation 3 also shows that $\Sigma f_u S_u > \Sigma\, [f_g S_g]_{implicit}$.

Note the negative sign inserted on the right-hand side of the equation: equation 7 does *not* say that loans are an output of the bank, as algebraic manipulation would suggest. Rather, the minus sign incorporates the "adjustment" that avoids Gorman's leech on the income stream portrayal.

Hill remarked that this "negative value added" view was very old-fashioned, and that it did not represent the modern view of national accountants.[27] The point is well taken. Nevertheless, the history of the banking imputation in national accounts is important in understanding the tenacity with which national accountants hold to a view of banking production and output that does not represent the mainstream views of economists and to an output measure that would not be used in economic research on banking production and productivity. Moreover, in the most recent statement of the rationale for the national accounts treatment, Fixler, Reinsdorf, and Smith write, "Applied to banks, the usual treatment of interest flows would yield a negative contribution to national income."[28] The negative value added rationale remains relevant to understanding the national accounts treatment of banking.

As the result of the foregoing logic, national accounts have historically focused almost exclusively on payment services and other similar services provided

26. Gorman (1969, p. 156).
27. Transcript of the November 1998 Brookings workshop on banking output.
28. Fixler, Reinsdorf, and Smith (2003, p. 33).

by banks. "The SNA's resolution of the paradox [that banking absorbs resources, even though lending is defined as nonproductive] is to treat the bank as providing services which are separate from, and additional to, the actual borrowing and lending."[29] As this statement suggests, the national accountants' logic points them in the direction of finding nonfinancial services that are equal to the interest rate margin.

It is well established that some services are often compensated implicitly in the form of interest rate spreads (for example, when depositors accept lower interest on deposits that yield "free" payment services). Though these services might be "financial" in some sense, they do not represent the provision of finance. The question is, Does the whole of the interest rate margin consist of such services? The financial services that are included in banks' output in national accounts do not include any activity (such as the provision of finance or the renting of money) that is compensated with "pure" interest, if there is such a thing.

The basic national accounts approach to banking was introduced by Yntema (1947) and Stone (1947). Historically, there have been several variants, differing mainly in the sectors to which the imputed services, $\Sigma f_u S_u$, are allocated and in the differentials that are used to calculate the imputed services.

Treatment in SNA93

As Hill (1996) explains, the 1993 System of National Accounts (SNA93), the world manual for compilation of internationally comparable national accounts, provides a more complicated treatment of banking, which is known as "financial intermediation services indirectly measured," or FISIM. In FISIM, the value added of banks is still defined as in equations 6 and 7. However, this output is imputed, in the new treatment, to borrowers as well as to depositors. The allocation mechanism involves adding a "reference" rate (η) that lies between the borrower and depositor rates, so (using equations 6 and 7)

$$(8) \qquad \Sigma f_u S_u \equiv -[\Sigma\ i_j D_j - \Sigma\ r_m L_m]$$
$$= -[\Sigma\ (\eta - i_j)D_j - \Sigma\ (r_m - \eta)L_m]$$

so that

$$(9) \qquad \Sigma f_{uD}\ S_{uD} = \Sigma\ (\eta - i_j)\ D_j$$
$$\Sigma f_{uB}\ S_{uB} = \Sigma\ (r_m - \eta)\ L_m.$$

---

29. Hill (1996, p. 2).

In equation set 9, the "free" services provided to depositors (S_{uD}) are measured by the extent that depositor interest rates fall below the reference rate, η. Services provided to borrowers (S_{uB}) are measured by the extent that the loan rate lies above the reference rate, η.[30]

The reference rate has not been well defined. It has variously been set at the midpoint between borrower and depositor rates or might also be specified as the rate at which banks buy and sell purchased funds. More recently, it has been specified as the government bond rate.

DISCUSSION. The national accounts definition of bank output remains quite different, at least at first inspection, from what is implied by the profit maximization model of equation 1 or the production and productivity model in equations 4 and 5. In equation 1, the revenue from bank lending contributes to profit (normal for an output), and the cost of deposits subtracts from profit (normal for an input). Implicit services are part of output, but hardly the only part, and probably not nearly the largest part.

In the national accounts view, interest rate spreads are not interest, they are something else—free checks, ATM usage, and other transactions services for depositors, and record-keeping, credit ratings, and advice and so forth for the borrowers. Certainly, some kinds of deposits have traditionally been compensated, in whole or in part, with "free" services, which makes the nominal interest rate spread larger than it would otherwise be. Whether transactions services and some similar services to borrowers can account for the entire interest rate spread seems doubtful, for several reasons.

It is hard to see that the cost of free transactions services provided to depositors could be greater than the spread between demand deposit interest and interest paid on time deposits or certificates of deposit, since the latter receive no transactions services at all. It is true that depositors could invest in government bonds and earn the government bond rate, but most do not. It is thus difficult to justify the national accounts view that the difference between time deposit rates and interbank loan rates or government bond rates could be unpriced services to time depositors, who receive no depositor services. In any event, sometimes certificate of deposit rates in the United States are above the government bond rate for comparable maturities, and sometimes below.

It is even more difficult to accept that very much of the borrower rate is accounted for by free services of various kinds that have figured in national

---

30. For further discussion, see Hill (1996) and Fixler, Reinsdorf, and Smith (2003).

accounts discussions.[31] The national accounts approach to banking makes it tautologically true that various payment and other like services (other than the provision of finance) exhaust the interest rate spread between depositor and borrower rates. A more plausible hypothesis is that *some* of the spread (an amount to be estimated) is accounted for by free services.

In the past, the idea that banks' lending (the provision of finance) might be an output of banks has met very strong opposition in the national accounts community. In some sense, this distinction between the provision of finance and "other" unpriced services might be more semantic than real. Some SNA language seems to accommodate a more conventional finance view of the borrower-depositor interest rate spread: "Some financial intermediaries raise most of their funds by taking deposits; others do so by issuing bills, bonds, or other securities. The pattern of their financial assets is different from that of their liabilities *and in this way they transform the funds they receive in ways more suited to the requirements of borrowers.*"[32]

If the interest rate spread is caused by the transformation of credit, then there is little that is really different in the SNA view of banking, it is just expressed differently. On this interpretation, the traditional national accounts antipathy to "interest" as the income of banks may be an anomaly from the past.

In summary, the national accounts approach to banking output in effect accommodates interest rate *differentials* as part of bank output, because differentials are interpreted as payments for services *other than the provision of finance*. However, these interest rate differentials are regarded as *not* interest, to fit the national accountants' view that interest cannot be a payment for a productive service.

A Proposed Reconciliation:
Banking as a National Accounts Margin Industry

We propose to reinterpret the SNA's FISIM approach to banking: it is an interest rate margin. Its use in national accounts can be interpreted as creating in

31. In any case, the true interest rate on business loans is typically higher than the rate quoted in the contract, because of requirements to keep compensating balances. Compensating balances mean that the true interest rate spread is larger than the nominal spread, so taking account of compensating balances requires an imputation that widens the observed interest rate spread. The national accounts model, if extended to encompass compensating balances, would depict the borrower who was compelled to hold compensating balances as receiving more services than the borrower who was not compelled. Allen and Santomero (1996) explain why banks require compensating balances.

32. Commission of the European Communities and others (1993, para. 6.122). Emphasis added.

banking another national accounts *margin* industry, like wholesale and retail trade, and insurance.

On our reconciliation, FISIM (the interest rate margin) becomes the difference between banks' selling prices for renting money (the borrowing rate) and something like the "cost of goods sold" (actually, of course, banks sell services). The cost to the banks of acquiring the finance that they resell is the total cost of deposits and other sources of funds, including interest costs and an imputation for the cost of transactions services.

On our reinterpretation, the national accounts approach and the economic research approach both come out of the same model of banking, the one that is summarized earlier. The difference between them is—solely—that the economists prefer to work with gross receipts, the national accountants with the interest rate gross margin. The difference between the two approaches to banking is parallel with retail trade, where most researchers (and the BLS productivity office) use gross receipts as their output measure, but where national accountants use the gross margin.

OUR PROPOSED RECONCILIATION. We begin from the specification of banking output that is in the economic research on banking and show how FISIM relates to it. Return to equation 4. We disregard the direct fees portion of banking output, because the treatment of fees is not in dispute. The nonfee portion of banking output is

(4a) $$\text{Nonfee output} = \Sigma \, r_m L_m + \Sigma \, [f_g S_g]_{implicit} \,.$$

Part of revenue is implicit owing to the banks' barter arrangements for transactions services. The interest margin (analogous to the gross margin in trade) is the difference between revenue and the cost of acquiring what the bank sells, namely, the cost of acquiring finance. From equations 1 and 3, this cost is simply

(3) $$\text{Cost of acquiring finance} = \Sigma \, i_j D_j \, (= i_1 D_1 + [i_2 D_2]) + i_G G \,,$$

which consists of actual deposit interest, imputed deposit interest, and interest on purchased funds. Alternatively, where $\Sigma w_h v_{hD}$ are the resources the bank uses to produce transactions services that are bartered to depositors (these costs were defined in the explanatory paragraph to equation 1),

(3a) $$\text{Cost of acquiring finance} = i_1 D_1 + \Sigma w_h v_{hD} + i_G G \,.$$

Equation 3a consists of actual deposit interest, purchased funds interest, and the cost of producing transactions services that are used to pay for deposits. Equation 3a is only useful if the cost of producing transactions services equals the value of them to the recipients.

Now consider the bank's profit function in equation 1, but add to the equation the components that are netted out, namely, the unpriced or implicit services provided to borrowers on the output side and the implicit interest forgone on the cost side:

$$(1a) \quad \Pi = \Sigma \, r_m L_m + \Sigma \, (f_g S_g)_{explicit} + \Sigma \, [f_g S_g]_{implicit} - \Sigma \, i_1 D_1 - [i_2 D_2] - i_G G - \Sigma \, w_h v_h.$$

As Allen Berger remarked in the Brookings 1998 workshop, banks' profit is unaffected by the addition of the imputed terms, but of course the normal labor productivity measure is not.[33]

Ignoring the explictly priced fee output because its treatment is not in dispute, banking interest gross margin in equation 1a is

$$(10) \quad gross \; margin = \Sigma \, r_m L_m + \Sigma \, [f_g S_g]_{implicit} - \Sigma \, i_1 D_1 - [i_2 D_2] - i_G G \, .$$

This is nearly the SNA's FISIM, though the discussion of FISIM does not pay much attention to banks' purchased funds ($i_G G$), but it is not quite FISIM. The FISIM calculation is:

$$FISIM = \Sigma \, r_m L_m - \Sigma \, i_1 D_1 - i_G G \equiv \Sigma \, [f_g S_g]_{implicit}.$$

Bearing in mind that $\Sigma \, [f_g S_g]_{implicit}$ are only depositor transactions services in the model discussed earlier, FISIM clearly overstates those, because (see equation 10), the term $[i_2 D_2]$ is omitted from the margin. It should be added back in. National accountants now recognize a problem but propose as their solution to redefine the implicit services to make them equal to the way they calculate the interest rate margin. This has then led to the "reference rate" proposal to split the redefined implicit services and the subsequent searches for a suitable reference rate.

We would largely dispense with the SNA idea of the reference rate (though there is a small role in certain situations for something that has some similarities). We would abandon completely the SNA idea that one can find borrower

---

33. The interest forgone to receive implicitly priced services is equal to their value, even though the cost of providing them may be less.

services (bookkeeping services and so forth) that have some parallel with depositor transactions services and that account for any perceptible portion of the interest rate spread.

The national accountants seem to have gotten into this search for a reference rate by drawing a parallel that in fact lacks parallelism. It is clear that a barter arrangement exists on the depositor side and that this barter arrangement demands an output imputation. That imputation appears in the bank profit function in equation 1a and in the gross margin expression in equation 10. From this imputation on the depositor side, national accountants have concluded that some comparable barter arrangement exists on the borrower side, which also demands a parallel borrower side imputation. That seems doubtful. It also seems to rest on some questionable assumptions about opportunity cost.

Banks' services to borrowers are the provision of finance, as the banking research literature makes clear. To measure banking output, one does not need much (if any) role for supposed services that are not finance (the SNA's bookkeeping). And an independent "story" about borrower services is no longer necessary, because with our reconciliation it is no longer necessary for national accountants to hold onto a rationale that interest is not the payment for the service of providing finance.

The reference rate discussion has focused on the wrong direction in looking for services and on an inappropriate model. In their use of the reference rate, the national accountants seem to be arguing that depositors and borrowers could go into the banking business, if they liked, so the opportunity cost of funds to the banker is the same as the opportunity costs to demanders and depositors. The SNA reference rate (equals government bond rate in BEA's implementation) is a rate that bankers could earn on funds they receive from depositors or from purchased funds, so it is the bank's opportunity cost of doing something else with the funds they have available, if they choose not to make loans (the purchased funds market is another alternative, so the purchased funds rate is also an opportunity cost measure).

In the SNA and BEA implementations, the difference between the government bond rate and the rates banks pay to depositors is taken as the measure of unpriced services to suppliers of funds to the bank, including certificate of deposit holders. But when the interest on certificates of deposit exceeds the government bond rate for the same maturity, we doubt if banks are providing negative services to certificate holders, as the reference rate hypothesis suggests, or that when the certificate rate–government bond rate changes sign that the amount of services the banks provide changes sign also. Moreover, in countries where banks have more market power, or where deposit rates are regulated so deposit rates are lower (and loan rates higher), the reference rate idea explains the market power margin by asserting that the banks provide more services to depositors and to borrowers. That is not sensible.

The reference rate discussion hides, rather than illuminates, the measurement of services provided by banks. Of course, it is tautologically true that once depositor implicit services are estimated and once the margin is calculated correctly, the difference between the price the bank charges for funds and the bank's costs of acquiring the funds must represent services of some kind that are produced by the bank. That the gross interest margin (correctly measured, as just described) measures services, tautologically, does not provide insight into what the services are. The first step in economic measurement is a taxonomy. That has not so far come out of the national accountants' discussions of the reference rate.

Our reconciliation points the way to where efforts to improve banking output measurement should focus attention. Inside banks' interest rate margin is the spread in interest rates, so we need to know what causes those interest rate spreads. The research that is germane to improving the measure of the margin is research on interest rate spreads. An extensive research history exists on that topic. The asset structure of interest rates is a function of risk. The term structure is a function of liquidity. To get a better measure of the banks' interest rate margin, national accountants should focus attention on risk and liquidity, which is where the relevant economic research has focused.

Banking produces risk management and liquidity services, and the question is how to measure them. This is necessary, actually, whether the output measure starts from the national accountants' gross margin or from the economists' banking receipts. Our reconciliation suggests that it is misguided to look for nonfinancial services provided to borrowers, on some parallel with bartered depositor services, and to justify splitting the interest spread on arguments of this sort, as the SNA reference rate has tried to do.

The banker, like the cabbage seller, has advantages from being a banker. Allen and Santomero (1996) and many others have discussed why bankers exist. In the end, therefore, the bank has functions. When the banks perform their economic functions, they are simply producing.

None of the arcane and disputatious arguments in the national accounts approach to banking would be necessary if the national accountants just said: of course banks buy and sell finance, and of course the payments for finance are interest, but we are treating the bank as another margin industry. We think that is the way—not to resolve the debate between the present national accounts treatment of banking output and the treatment of banks in the research literature on banking production, regulation, and productivity—but to turn it in a more fruitful direction.

Thus the debate on banking output can be viewed as exactly parallel to the ongoing debate on insurance output. Our reconciliation proposal does not so much solve the banking output problem as convert it into a debate that is already ongoing in insurance and in retail and wholesale trade.

In insurance, two approaches exist. The national accounts approach to insurance output defines it as net premiums (premiums minus claims). An alternative takes gross premiums as the output of the insurance company.[34] In chapter 6, we show that the difference in approach results in differences in productivity estimates for insurance. In retail trade, gross receipts and gross output give similar measures, though perhaps partly because BEA's implementation of the gross margin approach has a good deal of gross receipts in it (chapter 8). Many empirical estimates of banking productivity exist, but the empirical bias (if any) from using the national accountants' gross interest rate margin is not clear (see the reviews cited earlier).

The debate on insurance is still unsettled, so it provides no direct guidance for banking. But if the debate on banking becomes structured so that it is parallel with insurance, then measurement research on both these major segments of finance can proceed more nearly in parallel than has been the case in the past, because—though both may be unsettled—they both await similar resolutions.

We think this is an enlightening way to view the issues. Retail and wholesale trade and insurance are all margin industries in national accounts, and banking can be added to the list. The issues are, Does treating gross interest margins as the output make sense for measuring productivity? Does it lead to a better framework for discussing improvements to the measurement?

Banking and Cabbage Sellers—Again

Earlier we used the *Economist*'s cabbage-seller analogy to illustrate and provide insight on the issues in measuring banking. Analogies are never exact and cannot "prove" anything. But they can be instructive, so we use the cabbage analogy again to illustrate parallels between the national accounts approach to banking output and its treatment of the gross margin in wholesale and retail trade.

---

34. In Sherwood (1999) and also in chapter 6, this debate on the appropriate measurement concept for insurance is identified with differing hypotheses about the behavior of insurance companies. In the gross margin approach (premiums minus claims), the insurance company acts as an agent for the policyholders and receives a fee (the gross margin) in compensation for its actions. In the gross premiums approach, an insurance company acts to absorb risk for the policyholders, and so it acts in its own behalf.

Our (integrated) cabbage seller buys cabbages from the farmer and sells them at retail. The bank buys finance from depositors and sells it to borrowers. In each case, the margin between buying and selling prices (times the quantity) is the national accounts measure of the output of the industry. The main difference between the two situations is the bank's supplemental production, and bartering, of transactions services to pay depositors.

To make the cabbage analogy more nearly fit the banking problem, suppose that the cabbage firm compensates the cabbage farmer partly in cash and partly by bartering wheat. It operates a wheat farm to produce the wheat that it barters to obtain cabbages (as the bank has a transactions services unit that produces transactions services to barter to the depositors). The banking productivity economist, confronted with these facts, would say that the cabbage firm's output is measured by its revenue from selling cabbages, plus its output of wheat, that is, equation 4—less the explicit fees part, which does not apply to this example.

What about the gross margin view of the cabbage seller's output in this extension? One cannot estimate the cabbage gross margin from the difference between monetary buying and selling prices for cabbages, because the cost of acquiring cabbages would be understated. One must instead add into the monetary payments for cabbages the cost of the wheat that is paid out to the cabbage farmers.[35] The difference between these total payments to the farmers for cabbages and the revenue from selling cabbages is the firm's true margin. The true margin, plus the value of wheat that is produced, is the cabbage firm's output in national accounts.[36] The result looks like equation 4, except that there are no explicit fees in this problem.

The BLS productivity office publishes labor productivity measures for retail trade. BLS uses sales receipts as the output measures for its retail trade labor productivity measures, so it would count as output the cabbage firm's sale of cabbages, plus presumably its output of wheat. In the BEA industry file, the output of the cabbage-selling firm is its gross margin (cabbages are netted out), plus its output of wheat for bartering. The BEA-BLS difference in modeling the output of retail trade for the cabbage seller amounts to the same difference that exists in treatments of banking output in bank production and productivity analysis, on the one hand, and in national accounts, on the other.

There is also a role in the cabbage analogy for something that is roughly similar to the SNA "reference rate." By selling its cabbages retail, our integrated

---

35. An accountant would no doubt object to this definition of the "cost of goods sold," but it makes a good economic definition.

36. If there is no profit on wheat, its cost and its value are the same (the cost of wheat is a component of the firm's cost of buying cabbages; the value of wheat is a component of the firm's output).

cabbage seller forgoes the wholesale price of cabbages, which it could obtain by buying them from the farmer and selling them to some other retailer. Alternatively, a cabbage retailer could forgo dealing with farmers by buying its cabbages at wholesale. Think of the wholesale price as the reference rate (η) for cabbages: the wholesale price therefore provides the basis for splitting the total gross margin for the integrated cabbage seller into a wholesale margin component (η – the farm price) and a retail margin component (retail price – η). Compare these expressions with the parallel banking ones in equation 9:

—For deposits (bank purchase of finance from depositors): ($\eta - i_j$)

—For loans (bank sales of finance to borrowers): ($r_m - \eta$)

—For purchases of cabbages from farmers, the wholesale margin: (η – the farm price)

—For sale of cabbages at retail, or the retail margin: (retail price – η).

The present SNA logic is not similar, that is, the reference rate for cabbages has nothing to do with any "pure" cabbage price (as the SNA rationale for the banking reference rate rests on "pure" interest). It could be similar if the SNA reference rate for banking were not the elusive pure interest rate, but simply the wholesale interest rate, the rate at which banks buy and sell purchased funds. Indeed, we think that is a sensible interpretation for the SNA reference rate, one that evades a host of difficulties with the present SNA interpretation.[37]

The farmer could always sell to retail buyers, or the buyer could go to the farm. Either, in other words, could assume the functions of a cabbage retailer/ wholesaler. The cabbage-selling firm exists because it is more efficient at distribution than the farmer or the retail buyer.

Similarly, the national accountants seem to be arguing that depositors and borrowers could go into the banking business, if they liked. But the banker, like the cabbage seller, has advantages from being a banker.[38] In the end, therefore, the cabbage retailer and the bank have functions. When the banks and the cabbage sellers perform their economic functions, they are simply producing.

The "User Cost of Money," Fixler-Zieschang's Reference Rate, and the SNA Reference Rate

Fixler and Zieschang (1997) proposed an alternative, though problematic, reconciliation of the SNA approach to banking output and their own version of the production function approach. In our view, the only common element

---

37. A participant in the 1998 Brookings workshop on banking remarked that the search for "pure" interest (the riskless return to waiting), had a 200-year history. A modern view has risk at the center of interest, not at the periphery.

38. Allen and Santomero (1997) and many others have discussed why bankers exist.

between the two is that they both use the term "reference rate." But they use it in very different ways and for different purposes. The SNA approach to banking output is inconsistent with the model used by Fixler-Zieschang, and no logical link between the two has been provided.

Fixler-Zieschang make use of the idea of "user cost of money" associated with Barnett (1980) and Hancock (1991). Though its expression may appear a bit complicated, at its root the user cost of money is a way of expressing the bank's opportunity cost of the funds that it makes available to borrowers. Fixler, Reinsdorf, and Smith introduce the term "user-cost price" to express the difference between the loan rate of interest and the bank's user cost of money; this has a more intuitive algebraic expression, and we use it in the following without changing the language.[39]

As originally employed by Barnett and Hancock, the user cost of money idea was advanced to settle empirically some former disputes in the banking production and cost function literature. If a bank earned a rate of interest that was higher than the user cost, this component of the bank's portfolio could be viewed as an output of the bank. Using the simple analogy with the cabbage business, if the sale price of cabbages exceeds their opportunity cost to the cabbage firm of acquiring them, then the business must be a retail seller of cabbages. The opportunity cost parallel in this case is essentially the price the firm forgoes when it decides against wholesaling cabbages to another grocery store in order to stay in the retail cabbages business.

If the government bond rate is the reference rate, then the "user-cost price" becomes the amount the bank forgoes by making loans to borrowers instead of investing its funds by buying government bonds.

Fixler-Zieschang note that a reference rate appears in the Barnett-Hancock user cost of money and in FISIM (see the reference rate, η, in equation 9, earlier in this chapter). By identifying the FISIM reference rate, η, with the Barnett-Hancock user cost of money, they suggest that the SNA banking imputation, FISIM, is consistent with the user-cost approach in the bank production function literature. This has been put forward as the rationale for the revised BEA banking output measure (Fixler, Reinsdorf, and Smith, 2003).

DISCUSSION. There is some sense in which if two equations are algebraically identical, they must represent the same measurement, even if the underlying logic from which each is derived differs. There is also some sense that arguing about whether an interest spread is or is not "interest" is not very "interesting." Nevertheless, there are three points about the Fixler-Zieschang proposal.

39. Fixer, Reinsdorf, and Smith (2003, p. 36).

First, the Fixler-Zieschang proposal comes from a model in which lending, or the provision of finance, is an output of the bank. No recent contribution to the production function approach to banking disputes this point, including the views of economists who use the Barnett user cost framework for research on banking, particularly the work of Hancock (1991) and Fixler-Zieschang. Most of the history of the national accounts approach to banking has been characterized by very firm opposition to the idea that lending is the output of the bank (see our discussion earlier in the chapter). Thus, algebraically equivalent or not, the Fixler-Zieschang reconciliation incorporates a rationale, or model of banking behavior, into the national accounts approach that is inconsistent with the national accounts approach.

Second, the Barnett-Donovan user cost of money, which is relied on for the Fixler-Zieschang reconciliation, is employed for a very different purpose than the reference rate in FISIM. In Hancock (1991), the user cost of money serves to determine empirically whether a bank asset or liability is an output or an input. If the bank earns interest r_m on loan L_m, and $r_m > \eta$, the bank must be selling finance, and loan L_m is an output of the bank. If a bank liability (such as a deposit) costs the bank interest i_j, the liability is a financial input to the bank if $i_j < \eta$.

The reference rate in the Barnett-Hancock-Fixler-Zieschang tradition is not used to split the interest rate spread into one portion of output that is imputed to the borrowers and another portion of output that is consumed by the depositors. The reference rate is used to determine which assets are bank financial outputs and which liabilities are bank financial inputs. Its use in banking research, including research by Fixler and Zieschang, is inconsistent with the SNA model of banking.

The user cost of money literature in banking research and the SNA banking output measure both refer to a "reference rate." But it is not the same reference rate, there is no connection between them other than the name, and the two models of banking behavior that use the term "reference rate" are inconsistent in their views of banking output. Nothing in the user cost of money literature suggests that the reference rate is the "pure" rate of interest or that the difference between the reference rate and actual interest charged and paid by banks is a measure of their nonfinance services. Quite the contrary. For these reasons, the Fixler-Zieschang reconciliation does not reconcile.

There is only one condition under which the Fixler-Zieschang reconciliation will work, and it is the one that we present earlier: if national accountants agree that FISIM is just the banking interest gross margin, then the national accounts output measure can be reconciled with the banking research output measure—under this condition, both stem from the same model of banking output, only national accountants prefer to use the gross interest rate margin in national accounts. But for this reconciliation, the reference rate is neither central nor necessary, as we pointed out earlier.

Conclusions

We think the future debate on measuring the output of banks should be parallel to the discussion for insurance and wholesale and retail trade. Does it make more sense to analyze the productivity of the gross margin than of sales receipts? If so, why? Is analysis at the level of the gross margin more likely to suggest how to improve the measurement of output?

We are not sure whether the gross margin/sales debate is parallel with the gross output and value added choice that has long faced productivity researchers. The shoe store gross margin can be thought of as shoe store sales less a purchased input (shoes for resale), just as value added equals shoe store sales less all purchased inputs. There is a clear preference among researchers for the gross output view. For example, Basu and Fernald (1995) show that empirically the choice matters for the analysis they do (they examine whether there are spillovers across industries in productivity changes). We know of no comparable studies on the usefulness of the gross margin/sales view, but we think that this is an appropriate research topic for future industry productivity research.

Finally, whatever concept—gross margin or sales—improved measures of banking output (and of insurance output and retail/wholesale output) will demand more explicit listing and enumeration of the services that are inside the margin.[40] They matter for either concept, after all. When the national accountants' discussion moves away from bookkeeping and record-keeping as services to borrowers and toward measuring the banks' risk-absorbing, risk-management, and liquidity services, that would be a great step forward.

---

40. For retail trade services, see Oi (1992) and Betancourt and Gautschi (1993).

Discussion of Banking Output

The current methodology the Bureau of Economic Analysis uses to approximate the value of banking output provides a testable hypothesis, which is outlined here. Independent of any test results, BEA would be well advised to try to determine the robustness of alternative indicators of the value of banking output. One possibility would be to use the Bureau of Labor Statistics transactions-based banking quantity index of loan, deposit, and trust services and multiply that output quantity indicator by a corresponding price-cost index of the same banking services.

To illustrate the usefulness of the suggested transactions-based output quantity approach, I briefly note the results of applying payment transactions and service delivery measures to Europe. This example illustrates what should also be taking place within the U.S. banking sector regarding reduced operating costs and measured productivity change.

BEA Banking Methodology

Of the three main services provided by banks (deposit, loan, and trust services), banks do not price—or do not price at a market rate—many of those that they offer to depositors. The two-stage production process that characterizes banking effectively involves trading "unpriced" deposit output services to raise funds (the first stage) needed as an intermediate input to finance loan and security holdings (second stage). Demand deposits are paid in kind with compensating output services (transaction processing, safekeeping, access to cash), while savings deposits are paid with a combination of compensating services plus a below-market rate of interest. Certificates of deposit, which are mostly insured, are paid at close to a market rate, while overnight federal funds purchases (which are not insured) are paid at a market rate. In contrast, some services provided by banks are directly priced and thus earn fee income. This arrangement evolved from the Depression-era regulatory prohibition against paying interest on demand deposits, implemented to reduce the incentive to seek out riskier asset returns thought to be needed to pay competitive interest rates on deposits.

Current BEA methodology determines the value of banking output as the sum of the value of these unpriced (mostly depositor) services plus the value of the fee income. The value of unpriced services equals the value of interest received (which covers the priced component of loan and risk-absorbing services supplied but not any associated compensating balance requirement) minus the value of interest paid (which mostly covers the priced component of deposit services). Since interest received equals total revenue minus fee income, and interest paid equals total cost minus labor, materials, and physical capital operating expenses, we have the following:

Value of unpriced output = interest received − interest paid
= total revenue − total cost + operating cost − fee income
= profits + labor, materials, and capital costs − fee income
= value added − fee income.

The implicit assumption here, which forms a testable hypothesis, is that changes in input prices in value added would equal changes in output prices if unpriced output were priced. While it is not possible to determine the direct correlation between changes in the input prices that form value added and the resulting change in the prices or returns of all banking services, it is possible to determine the extent to which changes in input prices are reflected in the revenues of banking services that are directly priced. This involves estimating a Panzar-Rosse H-statistic in a revenue function framework (Panzar and Rosse 1987).

In simple terms, the equation to be estimated can be expressed as

$$TR = f(R_i; \text{output; balance sheet composition variables}),$$

where TR is log total revenues; R_i is log input prices (labor, physical capital, materials, and funding); and output is the log of the BLS index of bank transactions or a bank-specific output measure. The H-statistic is equal to 3 MTR/MR$_i$. If this value equals 1.0, then the percent change in input prices (R_i) is fully reflected in the percent change in total revenues (TR), holding output and balance sheet composition constant. If the H-statistic is not significantly different from 1.0, then the maintained hypothesis underlying the BEA methodology would be supported since changes in input prices would be reflected in similar changes in the value of banking output.[41]

Even if this test is passed, the BEA procedure could benefit from considering if the avoidance of a tax on demand deposits—the 10 percent reserve requirement—should properly be measured as a rise in the value of banking output. It clearly is a reduction in costs, but this cost is not included in the BEA analysis. Instead, the value of interest received will rise.

In order to avoid reserve requirements, banks instituted business (and later consumer) sweep account arrangements that "sweep" excess daylight demand balances into a nonreservable liability account at the end of the day and pass back the interest earned from the corresponding assets held to the business demand deposit account holder (but not to the consumer account holder). The bank saves the 10 percent reserve requirement cost by this reclassification, loses the interest earned on the swept business demand balances, but retains the interest earned from swept consumer demand balances. The value of reserves held by the Federal Reserve fell from $37 billion in 1990 to only $11 billion in 2002, freeing up this amount for additional loans or security purchases.[42] This raises the value of interest received even with constant interest rates and, according to the equality (value of unpriced output = interest received − interest paid), has correspondingly raised the value of unpriced output computed by the BEA. One could interpret this as a rise in "productivity" since the cost of a government input—reserve requirements—has been reduced. However, since swept demand deposits—which pay no interest but incur reserve requirements—will be invested in earning assets, the value of interest received by the bank from this source will rise, but a portion also is recorded as a rise in interest paid to business sweep account holders. Thus the "productivity" change resulting from sweep accounts will be a net, not gross, figure.

41. The H-statistic also is used as an indicator of the degree of market competition, where a value of 1.0 suggests perfect competition and values significantly less than 1.0 indicate oligopoly.

42. Almost all of this remaining $11 billion earns a return for banks because it is used as a compensating balance to pay for use of Federal Reserve payment services.

Alternative Methodology:
Direct Measures of Output Quantities and Prices

An alternative methodology that is more direct but also more difficult to implement would be to use the existing BLS index of banking deposit and loan transactions and trust services—a direct quantity measure of banking output—and combine it with a price index of banking services (prices where they exist and unit costs where they do not). One improvement to this index would be to include the service delivery aspect of ATMs and branch offices. These delivery vehicles are costly to provide and, in order to lower delivery expenses, the former are replacing the latter in terms of the number of depositors and borrowers served. The BLS quantity index of banking output is composed of

— number of checks written
— number of electronic payments
— number of time account deposits and withdrawals
— number of new and existing loans
— trust activities.[43]

Unfortunately, this quantity index is available only nationally. If it were available by bank, academics would prefer such a measure of banking output to what they now use, which is the dollar value of various loans, security holdings, and (sometimes) deposits listed in publicly available bank balance sheet data.

A more difficult but doable task involves the development of a price index of banking service outputs. Loan pricing data exist in the Federal Reserve's Survey of Terms of Business Lending and from the Loan Pricing Corporation, which collects even more detailed loan pricing information. The Federal Reserve also collects deposit rate and required minimum balance data, which, along with ATM fees and other deposit charges, can be used as well. The bottom line is that the current BEA approach to determining the level and change in banking output would benefit by seeing whether this methodology would reasonably duplicate the results of a more comprehensive and standard approach with a set of quantity and price indexes similar to those used in other sectors of the economy.

---

43. This index has certain limitations that would need to be addressed. One is that time-series data on the number of checks written and processed—which in 2000 was believed to be around 68 billion—is now revised to only 42 billion but no corresponding adjustment has been made to earlier published times-series data. A second issue is that the source of the cost accounting weights for many banking services in the BLS index—the Federal Reserve's *Functional Cost Analysis* survey—no longer exists and, when it did exist, the weights referred to smaller banks and savings institutions, not to the largest banks.

Figure 7-1. *Payment Shares in Europe, 1987–99*

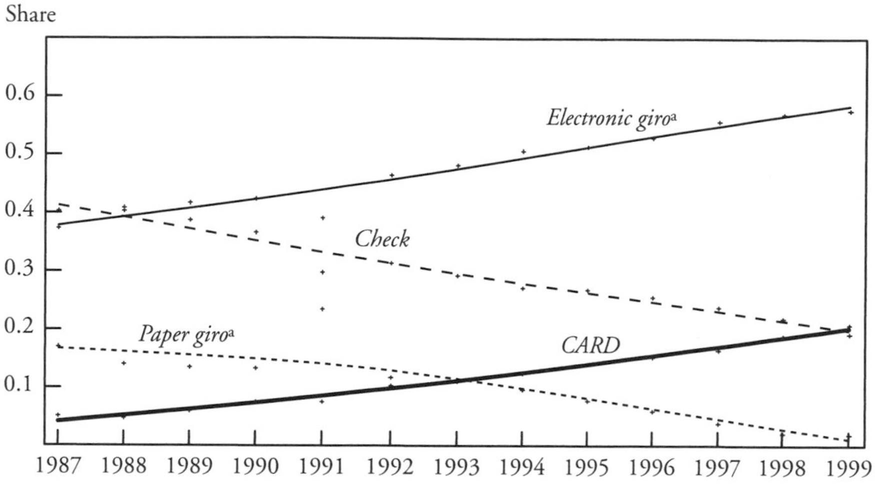

Share

Source: Humphrey and others (2003).
a. Refers to transfer of funds among financial institutions.

Output Indicators Generate Costs: Support for a Banking Service Quantity Index

A study using cross-country panel data on the number of payment transactions—checks, paper giro (direct debits, credit transfers), electronic giro, and cards—and the number of service delivery vehicles (ATMs and branch offices) explained almost all of the observed 24 percent reduction in the ratio of bank operating cost to assets across twelve European countries over 1987–1999. The cost function used regressed bank operating cost (OC) on six output characteristics in

$$OC = f(\text{four types of payment instruments};$$
$$\text{two service delivery methods; input prices}),$$

rather than the usual cost function formulation relating total interest and operating cost (TC) in

$$TC = f(\text{value of loans, securities, deposits; input prices; time dummy}).$$

The goal was to identify the specific sources of bank output variation, scale economies, and technical change or productivity as opposed to assuming that the flow of banking service output is proportional to the stock of loans, securities, or

Figure 7-2. *Predicted Unit Operating Cost for Europe by Log of Asset Value, 1987, 1993, and 1999*[a]

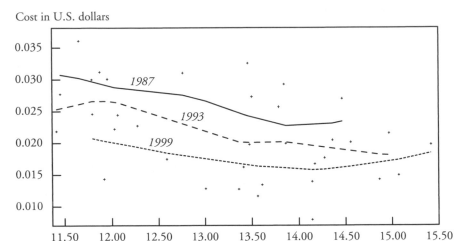

Cost in U.S. dollars

Source: Humphrey and others (2003).
a. Composite function—input prices held constant at their mean values.

deposits held on the balance sheet and that "time" locally identifies aggregate technical change (Humphrey and others 2003).

Europe has shifted more rapidly from paper-based payments (checks and paper giro transactions) to electronic payment instruments (electronic giro and cards) that cost only one-third to one-half as much to process. Figure 7-1 shows how the transaction shares of these four types of payment instruments have evolved over time. The shift to markedly cheaper payment instruments raised the share of electronic payments in Europe from .43 in 1987 to .79 in 1999. During the same period, the number of ATMs expanded from 49,000 to 205,000 while the number of branch offices rose by only 0.3 percent (from 172,400 to 172,900, or only 500 net new offices). These two changes were associated with a predicted savings in bank operating costs of $32 billion, or almost 0.4 percent of the twelve countries' GDP. Changes in these predicted unit operating costs are illustrated in figure 7-2. The downward shift in the curves from the switch to cheaper electronic payments and ATMs directly indicate the technical changes under way in the banking industry and identify the specific source of these changes (which are service quantity measures). Although less dramatic, similar changes are occurring in the United States.

Discussion of Output Measurement in the Insurance and the Banking and Finance Industries

These chapters provide a comprehensive discussion of the Brookings workshops on measuring financial service output, in particular the output of the insurance industry and the banking industry. Jack Triplett should be commended for providing the detail of the discussion. I also want to thank Jack for the opportunity to comment on the chapters. The output of each of the two industries is among the most difficult to measure and certainly the subject of much debate. I will comment on each industry separately.

Chapter 6: Price, Output, and Productivity of Insurance

Though the chapter raises many issues regarding the measurement of the output of the insurance industry, I will address only two of them: premiums versus premiums-minus-claims and the inclusion of investment income.

Premiums versus Premiums-minus-Claims

The chapter attributes the difference between these two methods of output measurement to the different activities associated with risk assumption and risk pooling. In my view, there is no real distinction between these two activities in terms of the service output of an insurer; an insurer does not engage in one without the other. To put it differently, an insurer's profit derives from the heterogeneity of the distribution of risk of its policyholders; there would be no profit to be made if the insurer provided the exact same coverage to a homogeneous set of policyholders. The assumption of risk is profitable only if the insurer can exploit the benefits of risk pooling.

These two measures of output measurement are the most commonly cited and certainly in terms of national income accounting they are the two main contenders. The premiums-minus-claims view is the one employed by the Bureau of Economic Analysis and the System of National Accounts (SNA). However, over the years, most recently in BEA during the 1990s, there has been considerable debate about adopting the premiums approach. As with any measure, there are benefits and costs. Also, as is well understood, the selection of a measure depends on its use. In the case of the national accounts, there is a need to meet the requirements of a variety of users.

For studies of productivity one is interested in output measures that reflect the relationship between input and output at the firm level and that can be aggregated to measure the productivity of the industry to which the firms belong. In contrast, the main objective of the national accounts is to provide comprehensive overall measures of economic activity. Perhaps a useful way to think of the difference is to consider the differences between partial and general equilibrium analysis. Both make simplifying assumptions, but for different measurement objectives. More important perhaps is that it follows that one cannot really evaluate the correctness a partial equilibrium–oriented measure relative to a general equilibrium–oriented measure. On the other hand, there should be a consistency between the general and partial equilibrium views; if there is an inconsistency, then the value of both is called into question.

Regarding the output measure of the insurance industry, the difference between the premiums and premiums-minus-claims views of output measurement concerns the importance of the disposition of claims. In an industry analysis of insurance providers, there is no reason to be concerned with the disposition of claims. The payment of claims erodes profits, and there is a set of inputs involved in the activities that underlie the payment of claims. The former does not affect productivity; the latter does. In contrast, from a national accounts perspective, the disposition of claims and their impact on the other sectors of the economy are crucial, because the payment of claims triggers a set of transactions by the claimants that also must be recorded in the accounts. That the treatment of claims is crucial is indicated by the fact that it has its own section in the chapter and is referred to often in other sections.

Because the implication of different treatments of claims often is a source of confusion, it is useful to consider a simple example. Consider the case of auto insurance. Suppose a claim is submitted by policyholder for C dollars and the

Table 7-1. *Production Accounts, Premiums-minus-Claims Approach*

Insurer		Auto repair	
Use	Source	Use	Source
Profit (P – C)	Output (P – C)	Inputs and profit (C)	Sales (C)
P – C	P – C	C	C

National account		Appropriation (household)	
Income	Expenditure	Use	Source
Insurance profit (P – C)	Insurance service (P – C)	Insurance purchase (P – C)	
Auto repair (C)	Auto repair (C)	Auto repair (C)	
		Saving (–P)	
P	P	0	0

insurer pays that amount. Further suppose that the policyholder repairs the auto at a cost of C and that all transactions take place in the same time period. A useful way to illustrate the difference between the two approaches is to consider a simple representation of the T-accounts that represent some of the sectors of the economy.

Under the premiums (P) minus claims (C) approach, the output and profit are the same in the account for the insurer (table 7-1). The policyholder receives the claim and purchases auto repair services, which is recorded in the account for the auto repair firm. Note that to keep the example simple, the policyholder pays the premium out of saving. It should also be noted that the value of the purchase of the insurance service by the household is equal to the value of the output of the insurer. The national account aggregates the insurer and auto repair firm to come up with aggregate economic activity as measured by either aggregate income or expenditure. Finally observe that in the aggregate the measure of the value of output for the economy is the premium.

In the following accounts, I present one method of recording the disposition of claims under the premiums approach (table 7-2). This method is different from the one suggested in the chapter, about which more will be said below. The output of the insurer is recorded as premiums, and note that the policyholder's purchase of insurance is now recorded as premiums. There is no change

Table 7-2. *Production Accounts, Premiums Approach*

Insurer		Auto repair	
Use	Source	Use	Source
Claims (C)	Output (P)	Inputs and profit	Sales (C)
Profit (P – C)		(C)	
P	P	C	C

National account		Appropriation (household)	
Income	Expenditure	Use	Source
Insurance profit	Insurance service	Insurance purchase	Claim (C)
(P – C)	(P)	(P)	
Auto repair (C)	Auto repair (C)	Auto repair (C)	
		Saving (–P)	
P + C	P + C	C	C

in the account for the auto repair firm. With no other change, one can see in the aggregate that the output rises to premiums plus claims. This value derives from the double counting of claims that is evident on the income side of the national account.

It is important to note that the above illustration follows from the assumptions about the policyholder receiving the claims and using them to pay for the auto repair. But those are not the only possibilities. Alternatively, the insurer could contract for the auto repair. Indeed, as the chapter states, "However, with the gross premiums approach, the insurance company is treated as purchasing car repairs that are paid out in the form of insurance claims, although some alternative accounting treatments that involve the insurance company and the capital accounts of insured industries also are possible." The problem of deciding on a treatment of claims is complicated by the fact that within a given type of insurance, the behavior of policyholders toward claims varies, and this variation is increased when one considers different types of insurance. In other words, assumptions regarding the disposition of claims for auto repair may not be appropriate for claims under fire insurance or workers' compensation. If the one-size-fits-all model is not going to work, then the question becomes "What type of approach allows for maximum applicability?" Since the premiums-minus-claims approach does not require any assumptions about whether policyholders save or spend the claims, it covers more contingencies than does the premiums approach.[44]

Some might look at the addition to the policyholder's (household) income and say that the premiums-minus-claims approach is incorrect because it effectively treats the purchase of the auto repair services as consumption. However, this has more to do with the treatment of autos than the treatment of insurance. For example, if a home burns down, then the expenditure attending the rebuilding of the house with claim money is considered investment, not consumption. Furthermore, in the case of workers' compensation insurance, the claim payment is income—preservation of income is the point of the insurance—and the policyholder decides whether the funds will be spent or saved.

The chapter claims that such "pragmatic arguments are ancillary to the main conceptual issue," but they are not if the national accounts are to achieve their objective of providing overall measures of economic activity. There is an obvious tension between the demands of economic theory and the demands of constructing national account measures. Ideally, one would want to be able to easily use the national accounts measures to obtain the measures demanded by theory. One's ability to do so depends on the transparency of the method and the availability of underlying detail. BEA has striven to provide both.

Furthermore, BEA has sought to improve the premiums-minus-claims approach to more accurately capture the behavior of insurers. In December 2003, BEA introduced some major changes in the treatment of insurance that are described in Moulton and Seskin (2003) and Chen and Fixler (2003). Briefly, BEA now employs a measure of normal claims or expected claims, with an adjustment for catastrophes, instead of actual claims when computing insurance output. In addition, BEA now expands the measure of policyholder payments to include a premium supplement that derives from the investment income earned by the insurer on unearned premiums.

Inclusion of Investment Income

Models of insurance firm behavior generally recognize that investment income is an important component of the pricing of insurance. Investment income serves as a substitute for premium income; thus in years when investment

44. This is not to suggest that the premiums-minus-claims approach is the only way to overcome many of the complications of accounting for the disposition of claims. The point is that such problems have to be fully addressed. Also, the position that the premiums-minus-claims approach is flexible enough to cover a variety of contingencies is different from the consistency in the national accounts argument that is presented in the section entitled "Consistency with other parts of the national accounts" as a rationale for the premiums-minus-claims approach.

income is relatively great the prices for insurance may stay the same or even fall. Furthermore, investment income reflects the value of the financial intermediation services that a policyholder simultaneously purchases with insurance protection. The BEA measure of the premium supplements uses a measure of expected investment income that captures the return to the insurer from all sources of investment income, including capital gains and losses. As pointed out in the chapter, the 1993 SNA measure of insurance output contains a premium supplement, which is based on actual investment income rather than expected income.

Though the chapter in the end supports the notion that investment income should be added to the output measure of the insurer, it states that this should be achieved in the "two-products" view. Since this view is described as treating investment income as a secondary product or as a joint product, it is not clear which is preferred. If financial intermediation services are treated as a distinct product, as would be the case in a secondary market, then it would not be appropriate to include the value of these services in the price of insurance. But because in general there is an inverse relationship between premiums and investment income, it would seem that the joint product approach is the one to be preferred.

In sum, the new BEA measure of insurance output is premiums plus premium supplements minus normal claims, and both the premium supplements and normal claims depend on a model of expected outcomes. These changes affected only the nominal measure of insurance output; the method of computing real output did not change with the comprehensive revision. Current BEA procedures use components of the CPI and the PPI; selection of components is determined by line of insurance to be deflated. Future research will examine the double-deflation procedure by line of insurance. It is hoped that the BLS PPI for property and casualty insurance can be used to deflate premiums earned and investment income. To complete the double deflation, a claims index would be constructed that would use components of the CPI and the PPI. The full impact of the change in the BEA measure has not yet been fully studied, and it remains to be seen whether the productivity results described in the chapter will stand.

Chapter 7: Measuring Banking and Finance

This chapter also addresses many issues, but I will restrict my attention to three of them: the view of production, measuring bank output, and the relationship between FISIM (financial intermediation services indirectly measured) and the user cost approach.

View of Production

The chapter describes a production process in which a bank's output is labeled provision of finance and one of the inputs is labeled purchase of finance, the other inputs being the usual productive inputs, labor, capital, and so on. This notion appeals to the intermediary role of banks, which is one of the models of banking that can be found in the literature. In this view, the measure of bank output centers on earning assets and deposits are taken as inputs.

The terms *provision of finance* and *purchase of finance* are not clearly defined. First, these terms seem to focus on the funds rather than on the financial services provided. Second, the purchase of finance is not the same as the purchase of an input in the usual sense. The borrower is purchasing finance, and we do not generally consider finance in the production function. Also, though the purchase of finance can be associated with acquisition of deposits from customers, the notion does not fit well with banks issuing equity or bonds to raise funds that they can loan. More important, this view completely ignores the fact that deposit products can be ends in themselves. Indeed, Allen and Santomero (2001), who are cited in the chapter, describe how banks are losing out to mutual funds in selling savings products. But it is not just for investment-type products that banks compete with mutual funds; both institutions offer insured deposits, but having an account at a bank allows for more flexibility in terms of using the funds for transaction purposes. Finally, if deposits are primarily a purchase of finance, which is treated as an input, then it would seem that both the interest paid and the implicit value of the financial services would have to be considered as the purchase price.

Calling loans a provision of finance captures the funds actually lent but does not seem to capture the financial services involved in making loans. These services have to do with overcoming the problems of asymmetric information, a view that is widely accepted in the financial economics literature. A firm that has a reputation as a good credit risk need not go to a bank—commercial paper is one alternative. The role of banks as a lender arises out of the private nature of the lending transaction—the bank acquires information about the borrower through the loan process and thereby reduces the problem of adverse selection and is in a position to monitor how the money is spent, thereby reducing the problem of moral hazard. These are the financial services that Fama (1985) and others identified when they argued that banks were special.

It is for these reasons that the chapter's analogy between banks and cabbage producers is limited, if not incorrect. First, it implies that only earning assets are output. Second, the services associated with deposit products are payment for an input, funds. Third, the focus is on the products and not on financial services, which is where it should be.

Measuring Bank Output

In the economics and finance literature one can find a variety of models of a banking firm, each with a focus on a particular aspect of the role banks play in an economy. One model focuses on the role of banks as intermediaries channeling funds from savers to investors and their attendant role in the endogenous money supply process. Gurley and Shaw (1960) supply an early example of this genre. Another model focuses on formulating a measure of bank output that fits into the national income and product accounts. Gorman (1969), for example, examined this issue in terms of the problem associated with banks under the standard measure of value added. Because a major source of bank income is the difference between interest received and interest paid, there is likely to be a huge negative component of value added.[45] As Gorman pointed out, if value added were negative then the nonsensical implication would be that banks are a drag on the economy.

Fixler and Zieschang (1991) provides an examination of different national income accounting treatments and discusses them within the context of the user cost of money approach.[46] One of those methods is the gross output approach in Ruggles and Ruggles (1982) and Sunga (1984) that is advocated in the chapter. The gross output measure is consistent with the financial firm/user cost approach in the sense that the economic price of a financial product is a function of the interest rate. In the gross output treatment the value of sales to business consumers and final consumers—households, government, and foreigners—is computed as the sum of service fees and interest received by banks from these entities. Both Ruggles and Ruggles and Sunga accommodate their views to the national accounts by creating ways for treating the interest received by households and government. For example, Sunga creates an additional production

---

45. Value added typically is measured as wages + profit + interest paid − interest received.

46. Because the purpose of Fixler, Reinsdorf, and Smith (2003) was to describe the BEA implementation of the user cost approach, it did not discuss the body of literature on the merits of the user cost approach relative to other approaches. There was an implicit reliance on sources like Fixler and Zieschang (1991), which is included in the references for Fixler, Reinsdorf, and Smith, and it was assumed that researchers interested in a more in-depth analysis would examine those references.

sector for households and government so that their interest receipts are not mixed with those of banks. The gross output approach is, however, different from the financial firm/user cost approach. Implicit in the gross output approach is the identification of liabilities as inputs and assets as outputs of banks. When one looks at specific products, this assignment may not correspond to the designation under the user cost approach.[47]

The approach represented by either equation (1) in the chapter modified by equation (3) or by equation (4) is a variant of the gross output approach in that it adds an imputation for uncharged-for services. Since the gross output approach assumes that the interest paid on loans captures the value of services, the uncharged-for services must derive from deposits. However, the treatment of deposits is confusing. The chapter states, "Deposits are financial inputs in equation 1; the unpriced services are (unobserved) outputs." Banks receive deposits in the context of financial products that combine the receipt of deposits with a host of financial services, some explicitly paid for and some implicitly paid for. So deposits and their attending financial services are inextricably linked. If deposits are an input (productive?), then how does one draw the line between the implicit payments for deposits as an input and the implicit revenue generated from transactions services related to deposits?

As explained in Fixler, Reinsdorf, and Smith (2003), the user cost approach provides a model of bank behavior that treats financial services as the output of banks and yields a valuation of the unpriced services provided to both borrowers and depositors. Avoiding negative value added was not the motive for adopting the user cost approach.[48] The user cost approach relies on a reference rate that represents an opportunity cost of money that is free of credit risk. This rate is used by banks as a guide to allocating resources. Because the model seeks to cover all of the financial services produced by banks, the included set of asset and liability products contains more than loan and deposit products. Deposits are not considered to be a production input but rather a type of financial product that is a package of financial services. Depending on the user cost price, the product can play different roles in the financial operations of a bank. Similarly, loans are not considered to be a production output but a package of borrower-

47. The user cost approach is based on an optimization problem regarding bank profit. The first-order conditions yield user costs of money, and as noted in Hancock (1985), these can be used to designate products as financial inputs or outputs. But it should be noted that such designations are subsidiary to the user cost approach.

48. The problem of negative value added is mentioned in Fixler, Reinsdorf, and Smith in the introduction section as part of an explanation of why the standard treatment of value does not work for banks. This point was also made in Gorman (1969) as mentioned above.

related financial services. This view allows for the large variety of deposit and loan products offered by banks.

The general form of user cost prices, ignoring explicit fees is, for assets, price = interest rate on asset minus reference rate; for liabilities, it is price = reference rate minus interest rate on liability. Observe that the imputed price of implicit services is based on an interest rate margin. For example, in the user cost price of loan (asset), the positive difference between the loan interest rate and the reference rate provides a measure of the value of the implicit services related to assuming the credit risk associated with the borrower. There are two aspects of the user cost approach that need some further explanation. One is the selection of the reference rate and how it affects the role products play in the financial operations of a bank. The other is the margin nature of the user cost price.

The reference rate in principle represents the opportunity cost of money to a bank. There are many candidates for this rate: overnight interbank rates, private financial instrument rates (commercial paper or bonds), government bond rates. Because U.S. Treasury securities are default risk free, they are most often used as the reference rate. Though in principle, one could have for each bank a reference rate based on its portfolio of Treasury securities, the data requirements of such a computation are large and an industry approach is usually adopted. Therefore for the recently released comprehensive revision in the U.S. national accounts, the implementation of the user cost approach was based on the computation of a Treasury rate derived from all bank interest revenue on Treasury securities, which implicitly captured the aggregate portfolio of Treasury securities.

One can see in the expressions for the user cost prices above that the selection of the reference rate affects the magnitude and perhaps the sign of the user cost price. It is possible that for some deposit products, the user cost price will be negative, indicating that the bank treats the product as a financial input in its financial operations. One can think of the bank as providing the financial services associated with such a product as a loss leader. In other words, to be competitive (and to secure deposits) banks must offer a variety of deposit products, some of which will be less profitable than others depending on the structure of interest rates at the time.

The chapter asserts that treating banks as a margin industry is a way to reconcile economic views of banking with national account treatments. Despite the margin embedded in the user cost price of financial services, banking is not viewed as a margin industry in the user cost approach. A margin industry in the national accounts is intended to capture the services associated with reselling a particular good. In the case of retail trade, the retailer acquires the property right to a specific good and then resells it, making the cost of goods sold a crucial component in valuing the services of the retailer.[49] Banks (and other financial intermediaries) do not act in this way. The assertion in the chapter rests on the view that deposits are inputs. Banks receive deposits from individuals for a variety of reasons, but in no case is the property right to deposits altered—deposits are always a liability to the bank. In a fractional reserve banking system, banks create money from the lending of excess reserves, which creates a new commitment for the bank—it must provide the funds promised to the borrower. The objective of bank liquidity management is to prevent a situation in which depositors' withdrawal demands cannot be met. If the reserve requirement were set to 100 percent, then the loan constraint in equation (1) disappears and the funding for loans would come from borrowings from other banks or from the issuing of bonds or equity. None of the latter activities could be described as purchasing a good for which the cost of goods sold is a relevant measure. Furthermore, money is fungible and any particular loan may have several sources of funding, so computing the cost of a loan by the sources of funds is difficult. In terms of the user cost approach, the user cost price reflects an accounting of an opportunity cost as represented by a reference rate. In other words, the user cost price does not reflect an actual transaction between a seller and a supplier. The BEA implementation of the user cost approach in the national income and product accounts does not change the definition of gross output. (Gross output includes imputed output and output for which explicit fees are charged.) Banks' purchases of intermediate inputs are unaffected.

Relationship between FISIM and the User Cost Approach

In the chapter it is argued that the perceived link between FISIM and the user cost approach is incorrect because the former focuses on the decomposition of financial services to borrower services and to depositor services and that this decomposition is not part of the user cost approach. On a pedagogical note, the chapter incorrectly states that Fixler and Zieschang (1999) proposed a reconciliation between FISIM and the production function approach. That paper does not propose a reconciliation but rather sets out to show how a user cost approach can be used to impute prices of financial services that are not explicitly charged for. It thereby enables the creation of price and quantity indexes and the attending real output and productivity measures. The output measure focuses on all financial services and thus entails measures of depositor and borrower

49. Ignore the existence of consignment contracts between retailers and manufacturers.

services. One can therefore obtain measures of the borrower and depositor services produced in the economy—a measure that is proper for the national accounts, as explained in Fixler, Reinsdorf, and Smith (2003).

Although tracing original intent is important in a history of ideas, at the end of the day both FISIM and the user cost approach to banking decompose aggregate bank net interest income into borrower services and depositor services. The user cost of money concept is consistent with the SNA FISIM concept and its Eurostat implementation in the sense that they both use a reference rate to impute the value of unpriced financial services—this point is recognized in the chapter. FISIM, unlike the user cost approach, is not based on a microeconomic theory of a financial firm. As stated in the SNA, "The reference rate to be used represents the pure cost of borrowing funds—that is, a rate from which the risk premium has been eliminated to the greatest extent possible and which does not include any intermediation services."[50] In the user cost approach, as described above, the reference rate represents a credit risk free opportunity cost of money that is used to impute the value of unpriced financial services for both depositors and borrowers. More important, this approach is not limited to deposits and loans but includes many other assets and liabilities and thereby seeks to measure the entire financial service output of banks. Whether the two approaches provide equal measures of borrower and depositor services depends on the selection of the reference rate and the set of admissible assets and liabilities.

Finally, the main point of the chapter is that a margin approach as exhibited by equation (10) is the proper measure of bank output as opposed to the user cost approach. That equation is easily transformed into a user cost–type equation using the assumptions in the chapter. First, from the discussion of equation (3) it is clear that the imputed interest on deposits is an interest rate that represents the depositor's opportunity cost of acquiring unpriced services from the bank. That rate may be considered a reference rate, and let it be defined by R. Second, since the imputations do not affect bank profit (see the discussion in the text), the rate for imputing the dollar value of deposit services also is equal to R. To simplify the example, assume only a single deposit product with deposits D and a single loan of L. The expression for the gross margin (GM) in equation (10) can thus be written as

$$GM = rL + RD - iD - RD.$$

50. Commission of the European Communities and others (1993, paragraph 6.128).

Using the loan constraint in equation (1), $L = (1 - k)D$, the above expression for the gross margin becomes

$$GM = r(1 - k)D + RD - iD - RD$$
$$= [r(1 - k) - R]D + (R - i)D.$$

The second equality is a user cost–like expression for the gross margin. The bracketed component of the first term represents the imputed value of loan services, and the parenthetical component of the second term represents the imputed value of deposit services.

Reply to Dennis Fixler

There are only a few differences between our position and Fixler's, though there are miscommunications and misunderstandings. As only one example of the latter, we did not say that "a margin approach . . . is the proper measure of bank output"; we said that an appropriate subject for debate is whether gross margin or output is the proper measure for productivity analysis in banking as well as in insurance and wholesale/retail trade. We can only concede that in a number of places our writing apparently was not clear enough.

The main issue, as we see it, is determining which approach to banking—gross interest rate margin or gross output—offers the most useful approach to improving the measure of banking output. Like Fixler, we think that improving the measure of banking output requires better measures of what banks do. On the loan output side, that implies addressing banks' risk-bearing, liquidity-generating, and information advantages, for which they charge varying interest rates. On the deposit side, it requires better information on the nature and value of transactions services that banks render to depositors in a barter arrangement for the use of depositors' funds. On both loan and deposit sides, we need an enumeration of the services, not just an aggregation of them, because the elements in bank outputs provided to borrowers and to depositors can change. Whether one decides to measure bank output by the gross margin approach (FISIM) or the output approach (bank production and regulation literature), both approaches need the same information.

We applaud Fixler's statement clarifying that there is no logical or economic connection between his user cost of money model of banking and the SNA FISIM model. This is also the point we were attempting to make, so we are in apparent agreement.

Our main difference with Fixler, then, concerns the utility of his user cost of money approach as a tool for improving the measure of bank output. Merely subtracting some reference rate from the loan rate (the user cost mechanism for the lending side) does not tell us much about how to improve the measure, because the issue is how to model the diversity in bank lending rates—that is, the interest rate structure. For demand deposits, one needs to enumerate and value the transactions services bartered to depositors in partial payment for the financial inputs they provide to banks. Subtracting the deposit rate from some reference rate (the user cost approach for the depositor side) tells us nothing about the composition and valuation of the separate transactions services provided to borrowers, so after applying the user cost approach to deposits, we are right back to where we started, needing explicit measures of the services. The user cost approach, elegant and appealing as it is, has not yielded any breakthroughs in measuring banking output.

On insurance, Fixler apparently rejects our attempt to use alternative models of insurance company behavior to sort out the issues (the insurance company as operating the risk pool, on one hand, or absorbing the risk, on the other). He does so on the grounds that "the assumption of risk is profitable only if the insurer can exploit the benefits of risk pooling."

Apparently, we were unclear. The risk-pooling (SNA) model is a model in which the insurance company *only* administers the pool. In the risk-absorbing model (economics insurance literature and U.S. PPI insurance index), the company both absorbs the risk and, of course, operates the pool. In the former model, the firm acts as the agent of the policyholders (this is explicit in passages in the SNA); in the latter, it acts for itself.

There is no inherent or logical double counting in treating insurance one way or the other. National accountants will work out the implications of either alternative, which is our understanding of what Fixler is saying in his discussion of double counting. There is no disagreement between us on this point. Data availability questions intrude, as they always do, and Fixler emphasizes them.

Ours may not be a persuasive framework for considering the two positions on insurance, and apparently it did not persuade one reader. If there is no model behind the two approaches to insurance, then both approaches are arbitrary. How then does one choose between them, and how does one sort out the

arguments that have been presented over many years for one or the other of the two positions? For example, the SNA view that the insurance company administers the risk pool on behalf of the policyholders is crucial to the SNA's treatment of investment income as if it were an increase in the price of insurance. Fixler presents a "general equilibrium/partial equilibrium" proposal, but we doubt that it will prove enlightening or instructive in dealing with the contentious issues that have long inhibited the measurement of insurance output.

CHAPTER EIGHT

Output and Productivity in Retail Trade

The retail trade sector has been the largest single contributor to the post-1995 resurgence of growth in productivity. This is a surprise to many—particularly those who identify productivity growth with the emergence of the newer, more glamorous high-tech economy. Retail trade is among the oldest of industries, and, at least in the United States, it has concentrated increasingly on employing the least-educated and least-skilled workers. Between 1975 and 2000, average hourly earnings in retail trade declined from 88 to 78 percent of the private sector average, while retail trade's share of total employment fluctuated in the range of 16 to 19 percent. On the other hand, retailing has been affected greatly by many of the most significant technological changes of the last few decades. The development of computers, scanners, and the Internet all have contributed to the rapid pace of innovation in the industry.

Our data (see chapter 2) indicate that the growth of labor productivity in retail trade has been strong and that it has accelerated in recent years. One objective of this chapter is simply to determine whether productivity growth in retail trade has in fact accelerated or whether it has only appeared to, an illusion caused by faulty data or concepts. The discussion that follows summarizes the trends in retail output and productivity as reported in the BEA industry data set and by the industry productivity program of BLS, which (like our estimates using the BEA industry database) also shows strong labor productivity growth in retail trade. However, there are questions about the appropriate measure of the output of the retail sector, gross sales or the gross margin (sales minus cost of goods purchased for resale).

We review the methodology of the consumer price index program with respect to the use of the price indexes to compute real output at the level of subgroups of retail stores, and we look at some recent research on the sources of productivity in the general merchandise segment of retail trade, where innovations seem most evident. We conclude with an examination of the implications for productivity growth in electronic shopping and e-commerce.

Overview

Information on productivity trends in the retail sector is available from both BLS and BEA. The strength of the BLS program lies primarily in the detail that it provides for individual segments of the retail trade sector. With its latest release, BLS has shifted over to the North American Industry Classification System (NAICS) and published measures of output, employment, and output per hour for the total retail sector and twelve subsectors below the aggregate. BLS also publishes data for twenty-four industries below the subsector level. The information extends over the period 1987–2001. The primary limitation of the BLS data is that the analytical measures stop with labor productivity. The BLS program defines output as the real value of sales, using CPI indexes as price deflators. The labor inputs are measured in terms of hours, not employees—an important adjustment for retail trade—but no information is available on inputs of purchased materials or capital.

BEA includes total retail within its industry data set, but information on underlying industry trends is very limited. However, as discussed in chapter 2, the BEA data can be extended with information on inputs of capital services from BLS to provide estimates of the change in multifactor productivity as well as labor productivity. The BEA data are still reported on the Standard Industrial Classification (SIC) system. The primary results of the shift from SIC to NAICS by BLS were to separate eating and drinking establishments from retailing and to change the boundary between wholesale and retail trade so that some establishments that sell at retail to both households and business were moved from wholesale to retail trade. The latter change is important for products such as building materials and office supplies.

Both BEA and BLS rely on the Census Bureau's annual survey of retail trade and the CPI for their basic data for constructing estimates of output. The most important distinction between the BLS and BEA data for the retail trade sector is that BEA relies on a gross margin concept—sales minus the cost of goods purchased for resale—to define output and BLS uses a sales measure. As discussed in chapters 6 and 7, this notion of a margin as the definition of output also arises in insurance and banking. The implications of focusing on margins instead of sales is discussed more fully later.

A brief overview of the industry is provided in table 8-1. Columns 1 and 2 show the distribution of sales and employment in 2001 among the twelve major subsectors. Aggregate retail sales were $3.1 trillion, and employment totaled 16.1 million. Motor vehicle dealers and electronic shopping retailers stand out with the highest volume of sales per employee, while sporting goods and miscellaneous retailers have the lowest. There also is a wide variation in gross margins, ranging from a high of 43 percent for furniture stores to a low of 17 percent for motor vehicle dealers. Gasoline dealers and other general merchandise have particularly low margins. The general merchandise category is divided between department stores and other general merchandise because it has emerged as an area of intense competition, with Wal-Mart and similar large-format stores being classified within other general merchandise.[1] Additional detail is also shown for nonstore retailers in order to highlight the growth of electronic shopping.

The BLS data show a sharp acceleration of growth in the real value of retail sales and labor productivity after 1995. Electronic stores, other general merchandise, and electronic shopping exhibit double-digit rates of growth in both output and labor productivity. Productivity growth rates are lowest for food stores, gasoline stations, and department stores. However, only gasoline and miscellaneous retailing fail to record an acceleration of growth in productivity in the post-1995 period.

A comparison of BEA and BLS total retail data is provided in table 8-2. The two sources yield nearly identical measures of the growth in real gross output, despite the inclusion of eating and drinking establishments in the BEA data. Under the old SIC classification, the BLS methodology yielded a slightly lower rate of overall output growth. However, the alternative output measure, real value added from BEA, has a significantly higher rate of growth after 1995, which can be traced both to an increase in the nominal share of value added in the gross margin and to a lower rate of price increase. The labor productivity measures also are very similar in indicating a strong post-1995 acceleration of growth. Again, the largest difference results from the inclusion of eating and drinking establishments in the BEA data because they have a below-average rate of improvement in productivity.

1. The classification system hides much of the economics of Wal-Mart since its smaller stores are in NAICS 452112 (discount department stores) and the larger stores, plus Sam's Club, are in NAICS 4529. In addition, the distribution centers, which some believe are the source of much of Wal-Mart's advantage, are in NAICS 493 (warehousing).

Table 8-1. *Growth of Output and Labor Productivity by Major Subsector of Retail Trade, 1987–2001*
Annual percent change

Category	Percent of sales 2001	Percent of employment 2001	Gross margin (percent of sales) 2001	Output		Output per hour	
				1987–95	1995–2001	1987–95	1995–2001
Retail trade	100.0	100.0	26.7	3.0	4.8	2.0	3.6
Motor vehicle and parts dealers	26.8	13.3	16.8	2.5	3.9	1.6	1.9
Furniture and home furnishings stores	2.9	4.1	43.5	3.3	5.6	2.7	3.6
Electronics and appliance stores	2.7	3.9	26.2	13.3	18.8	11.5	14.7
Building material and garden supply stores	9.2	8.4	29.2	3.5	6.5	2.3	3.5
Food and beverage stores	15.3	19.5	28.3	–0.0	1.0	–0.9	0.7
Health and personal care stores	5.3	5.9	29.5	2.2	5.7	1.0	3.2
Gasoline stations	7.8	6.0	19.8	1.6	1.0	1.8	1.3
Clothing and clothing accessories stores	5.3	7.5	41.6	3.5	5.7	3.9	5.1
Sporting goods, hobby, book, and music stores	2.5	4.2	37.7	5.6	5.7	3.2	5.0
General merchandise stores	13.7	15.5	25.2	4.9	6.2	2.9	5.1
Department stores	7.3	9.0	30.3	4.2	2.7	1.0	1.6
Other general merchandise stores	6.4	6.5	19.4	6.6	11.9	6.1	10.9
Miscellaneous store retailers	3.3	7.4	39.8	6.4	4.7	4.5	3.1
Nonstore retailers	5.1	4.2	40.4	6.8	12.9	5.6	12.4
Electronic shopping and mail-order houses	3.5	1.8	37.7	13.8	21.6	8.9	16.3
Total	$3.1 trillion	16.1 million	$841.1 billion				

Source: Industry Productivity Program of the U.S. Bureau of Labor Statistics and the U.S. Bureau of the Census, *Annual Benchmark Report for Retail Trade and Food Services: 2003.*

Table 8-2. *Alternative Measures of Output and Productivity Growth in Retail Trade, 1987–2001*[a]

Average annual percent change

Measure	1987–95	1995–2001
Output		
BEA output	2.9	4.9
BEA value added	2.9	6.8
BLS output	3.0	4.8
Employment		
BEA	1.7	1.7
BLS	1.1	1.3
Labor productivity		
BEA	1.2	3.2
BEA value added	1.1	5.0
BLS	2.0	3.6
Contribution of		
Intermediate inputs	0.5	−0.1
Capital	0.3	0.3
IT capital	0.1	0.3
Multifactor productivity		
BEA output	0.4	3.0
BEA value added	0.6	4.5

Source: BEA industry data set, BLS industry productivity program, and authors' calculations.
a. The BEA data are on an SIC basis; the BLS estimates are reported using the 2002 NAICS.

The BEA data on purchased inputs and capital services can be used to extend the calculations to estimate the role of increased capital per worker, purchased inputs other than goods for resale, and MFP. Those calculations are shown in the lower part of table 8-2. It is interesting to note that the contribution of purchased inputs is actually negative after 1995 and that there is a positive but small acceleration of growth in IT capital. As a result, all of the acceleration in labor productivity growth is attributed to a greater rate of improvement in MFP.

Interesting insights into the source of the productivity gains are provided by recent studies based on examination of microeconomic data from government surveys of individual establishments. A recent study by Foster, Haltiwanger, and Krizan (2002) emphasized the importance of the turnover of establishments and the changing mix of store formats. Using an establishment-level data set of retail firms, they concluded that virtually all of the productivity growth in the sector had resulted from more-productive stores replacing less-productive exiting establishments. In an extension of that work, Doms, Jarmin, and Klimek (2003) show that the growth in productivity can be related to investments in IT and other new technologies by the large retailing firms, who are growing at the expense of smaller, less-sophisticated firms.

Measuring Output: Gross Margin versus Sales

The above discussion of the BEA and BLS measures of retail trade output noted the close correspondence of their estimates of the growth in output and productivity. Yet the two agencies use much different conceptual definitions of output. The BLS productivity program employs a consistent methodology for all of its estimates of industry output, focusing on a concept of gross output that is equivalent to total shipments (adjusted for inventory change) or sales. Their basis for emphasizing the gross output concept is that it is most consistent with the notion of an underlying production function that relates output to inputs and allows a full consideration of substitution between purchased inputs, capital, and labor.

In contrast, the BEA focuses on the concept of a gross margin, sales less cost of goods sold, as its primary measure of output. While a much narrower concept than total sales, the gross margin is more inclusive than value added because it includes the cost of a broad range of purchased inputs—such as rent, electricity, and advertising—to the production process. In its use of the gross margin, BEA is following a standard national income accounting practice. As shown in table 8-1, the gross margin averages only about one-fourth the value of retail sales.

Yet the striking feature of the comparison of the BEA and BLS estimates is that they yield nearly identical measures of the growth in real output—because, lacking a means of adjusting its measure of the gross margin for price changes, BEA extrapolates the real value of the gross margin with an estimate of the real value of retail sales. It begins by computing the gross margin in both current and constant values for thirty-four industry groupings within the retail sector. In nominal terms, information on the gross margin is readily available from retailers, and it is reported as part of the Census Bureau annual survey. However, BEA constructs the constant value measure by assuming that it is a fixed proportion of the deflated value of sales at the lowest level of detail. Thus the constant dollar value of the margin, R, in industry i and year t is given by

$$R_i^t = r_i^{base} \cdot Q_i^t,$$

where r^{base} is the ratio of the nominal value of the gross margin to nominal sales in the base year and Q is the constant dollar value of sales. The gross margin is simply a proportionate rescaling of output at the lower level of detail; with aggregation, it differs from an aggregate measure of sales only in reflecting changes in the distribution of sales among stores with different margin rates. The BEA procedures for estimating real sales are virtually identical to those of BLS: deflation of merchandise line sales with corresponding components of the CPI.[2]

Despite the common result, the issue raised by the choice between sales and the gross margin is an important one. What is the output of a retail establishment? Should productivity be calculated on the basis of gross receipts or the gross margin? How is output best measured? Are there reasons to believe that one output concept facilitates making improvements in the data better than the other one?

The approach of the BLS productivity program is to maintain that the deflated value of sales is the natural unit for measuring output. Therefore they simply apply their standard framework, used in other industries, to the retail trade sector. In considering a production process with substitution between capital, labor, and purchased inputs, they would argue that there is no particular justification for distinguishing between purchased goods for resale and other purchased goods and services that go into the delivery of a final product.

In a technical sense, deducting the cost of goods sold in order to focus on the gross margin requires assuming separability in the overall production function. A simple example where this assumption does not hold is provided by the sale of bicycles, which once were delivered to the retailer fully assembled. Now they typically arrive in a box, and customers can choose between having the store arrange for assembly or doing it themselves. The shift to delivery in a box reflects a trade-off between wages at the factory plus delivery costs compared with the costs of labor at the store or the opportunity costs of the consumer. Furthermore, it is often argued that one of the keys to Wal-Mart's success has been its efforts to get suppliers to do more of the work of delivering the product to the store shelf (Oi 2000). This implies the potential for substitution between cost of goods sold and in-store labor.

The use of sales as a measure of output, however, can have the effect of rendering largely meaningless the BLS focus on the growth in labor productivity.

---

2. The growth in the BEA output measure will also differ from that of BLS, because BEA adjusts its estimate to benchmark values every five years.

This is evident in table 8-1, where output per hour is reported as rising at a phenomenal 15 percent a year in electronics stores but at an average of 3.6 percent in retailing as a whole. Despite the fact that the nominal sales of electronics stores grew more slowly than total retail, the prices of the products they sold, dominated by computers, declined at a 12 percent annual rate. As a result, real sales grew 19 percent a year, and, with a relatively modest 3.5 percent gain in labor, reported labor productivity soared.

Electronics stores are in the business of selling boxes (filled with computers) that they obtain from the manufacturer. The fact that the machine inside has experienced dramatic technical improvement should have few implications for efforts to measure the productivity of the workers in the retail establishment. An index that combines the improvements within the box with changes in the number of boxes bears little relationship to the actual activities of the retail store. A similar, though less dramatic, problem arises for electronic shopping, which includes Dell's Internet sales of computers.

Use of the retail gross margin as an output measure for retail trade can be seen as an effort to focus more narrowly on activities within the retail establishment. The BEA largely defeats the value of this concept, however, when it assumes that the margin is a fixed proportion of sales in real terms. If BEA published its measure of labor productivity at the level of electronics stores, for example, the measure would behave the same as the BLS measure.

Developing a meaningful measure of the real value of the gross margin is a challenging task. One approach would be to follow the double-deflation approach the BEA employs elsewhere to obtain real measures of value added. That is, purchased goods for resale would be deflated by an index of producer prices plus transportation, paralleling the use of the CPI to deflate the sales. The real value of the margin would be the difference between two deflated values. However, many analysts doubt that indexes of sufficient accuracy could be developed to obtain, in effect, the real value of the margin as the residual of changes in two large numbers.

An alternative, currently being implemented by BLS in the producer price index, seeks to price the margin directly by asking stores to report the difference between the vendor price and the selling price of specific items. Furthermore, it may be possible to identify those characteristics of store formats that account for variation in the gross margins and to construct an index that controls for changes in those characteristics or their prices. As part of its current program to directly price the margin, the BLS is collecting information on store characteristics—such as square footage, storage area, and the number of stock-keeping units (SKUs)—and identifying stores as discount, gourmet, warehouse, or combination outlets. This effort will provide a data set that allows analysts to explore the sources of variation in retail margins.

Walter Oi has stressed that the output of a retail firm should be viewed as a composite bundle of services that surround the product that it sells (Oi 1992, 2000). Betancourt and Gautschi (1993) suggested classifying those services into five broad categories: convenience of location, assortment, assurance of delivery in the desired form and at the desired time, information, and ambience. Since the returns on many of these services are embedded in the price of the product, it is difficult to decompose the retail sale into its constituent elements. Ratchford (2003) demonstrated the importance of changes in the associated services for measuring output and productivity trends in retail food stores.

The notion of embedded services led Oi (2000) to conclude that the gross margin is not a particularly useful concept of the output of a retail firm. The margin, as a simple measure of the difference between retail and wholesale prices, is likely to be strongly influenced by economies of scale and volume discounts. Margins also can change in response to variations in monopoly power.

In the 1998 Brookings workshop "Measuring the Output of Retail Trade," Roger Betancourt argued along similar lines: the quantity of goods sold and the quality of the distributional services are inextricably linked (Betancourt 1998). He also agreed with Oi in arguing that retail trade is subject to economies of scale that arise from several different sources.[3] While both of these issues can be accommodated within a gross margin framework, they result in a much more complex view of the production process. The important conclusion that emerges from the Oi and Betancourt research is that the analysis of retailing should begin with a focus on sales and the bundle of services that retailers provide. Both favor the BLS emphasis on the real value of sales as the point of departure.

However, the same issues that complicate the use of the gross margin as the measure of output also arise in any effort to undertake a full-scale growth accounting exercise to measure the contribution of all of the inputs. Even if output is defined as the real value of sales, we still need a measure of the real value of purchased inputs. If the production relationship is viewed as having two categories of purchased inputs, goods purchased for resale (I_1) and purchased inputs that are included in the gross margin (I_2), together with capital (K), labor (L), and changes in technology (A), the production function can be represented as:

---

3. Betancourt identified three: fixed costs, demand uncertainty about the flow of customers, and the association between store size, variety, and the average size of a transaction. He also summarized several empirical studies that found significant evidence of increasing returns to scale.

(1) $Q = F(I_1, I_2, K, L, A)$.

Cost shares, v_i, can then be used to decompose the overall growth in output into the contribution of the growth in each of the inputs and the residual of multifactor productivity:

(2) $\Delta \ln Q = \bar{v}_1 \Delta \ln I_1 + \bar{v}_2 \Delta \ln I_2 + \bar{v}_k \ln K + \bar{v}_l \ln L + \Delta \ln A$.

Cost shares also can be employed in a situation of increasing returns to scale, but the magnitude of the returns to scale must be independently imposed. Furthermore, by carrying out the decomposition with chain superlative indexes, the empirical importance of any misspecification of the true production function is minimized. However, the calculations require physical measures of the growth in each input. In the process of computing MFP, deducting the contribution of the first input, I_1, is equivalent to obtaining a measure of the real value of the gross margin.

While the gross margin data from BEA allowed us to compute the full decomposition of labor productivity in table 8-2 and report an estimate of MFP, it required a huge simplifying assumption that growth in the real value of the margin parallels growth in sales. The BEA treatment, just like that of the BLS, leads us to attribute to retail trade developments that more rightly should be associated with the supplying industries. In some categories, such as electronics stores, the BEA and BLS output measures both overstate the role of the retailer and undervalue the contribution of the manufacturer. In other cases, such as general merchandising, the contribution of the retailer may be undervalued.

Retail Price Indexes

In constructing their measures of real output, both BEA and BLS rely on matching sales data by merchandise line with price measures from the CPI. The store is one of the characteristics that BLS holds constant in selecting a specific product for price. Since BLS gradually rotates the sample of retail outlets from which it collects prices, the procedure will gradually capture the changing mix of outlets that customers patronize. By pricing a fixed set of products within a fixed store format, the CPI should correctly adjust for price change, leaving other sources of change in nominal sales to be reflected in the measures of real output. However, retailing has been a highly competitive sector in which rapid innovation has taken the form of new stores replacing old. In many cases this process of change involves the introduction of new store formats that combine the above-mentioned composite bundle of services in new ways. Some of these new store formats may involve a quality improvement, but just as often they combine reduced services with lower prices. Examples of the latter are the large warehouse clubs and superstores.

There is a concern therefore about the ability of the pricing programs to capture the effects of the shifts of sales among store formats. When a new store enters the sample, all of the difference in the price of an item between the new and old outlets is assumed to reflect a difference in quality or in the associated services that are provided. None of it is recorded as a price change. This procedure will capture most of the implications of changes in store formats. However, the procedure may introduce a bias if the opening of new stores in an area and the shift of consumers toward those stores reflect a reduction in the quality-adjusted price. The problem is lessened if competition forces the stores that are still in the sample to match the pricing of the new entrant before they are rotated out. But it appears that the shift to new outlet types is an ongoing, incomplete process. Therefore the potential for bias is closely related to the problems raised by the introduction of new products in the CPI.

The issue of outlet substitution in the CPI and potential bias was examined by Reinsdorf (1993), who compared average prices of stores that were being rotated into the sample with those that were leaving. He found a price differential of about 1.25 percent. Given a sample rotation of five years, the difference in affected categories of retail would be about 0.25 percent a year. We do not know how to divide the price difference at two outlets between quality and a pure price component, but the continual shift of consumers toward the new discount stores suggests that some of it is related to price. Other authors adjusted the outlet price differences reported by Reinsdorf for the subset of items that are affected by outlet bias, further lowering the estimated effect.[4]

On balance, most studies suggest that the outlet bias is relatively small, and the CPI does capture a large portion of the change in prices that accompanied the structural evolution of the retail sector. The problems are the same as those that have been raised before with respect to the adequacy of the CPI to measure overall price changes. The CPI is the primary basis for adjusting personal consumption expenditures in the national accounts, and it should be no less appropriate for valuing retail store output.

Instead, the more basic problem arises with the effort to develop input price indexes for retail trade. Such indexes are needed if we wish to move beyond simple measures of output per labor hour to examine the sources of productivity

---

4. The issue is discussed more thoroughly in National Research Council (2002).

gains in retailing. As mentioned above, the PPI program of BLS has introduced a new initiative to focus on the gross margin as the appropriate measure of output in the retail trade sector. The margin price is defined as the difference between the retail price of an item and its acquisition cost. An effort is made to include any discounts offered by the vendor or the retailer to consumers. In the case of establishments that also provide a range of directly priced services, such as the service shops of auto dealerships, the combined price index incorporates both a margin measure and the price of the services. However, any changes in retailing services within the establishment are not measured in the PPI program. The presumption is that month-to-month changes in these services are held constant by holding constant the outlet in the PPI sample.

Data are available only since the beginning of 2000, and currently only for a portion of retailing (food, automotive, gasoline, drug, and miscellaneous retailing). For those few situations in which a match can be made with the CPI price indexes that are used to deflate retail sales in the BLS productivity program, it is evident that the margin prices are quite different. For example, the margin price for food stores in 2001 averaged 10 percent above the December 1999 initial value. In contrast, the sales price deflator for food stores rose by only 2 percent between 1999 and 2001. A similar result is obtained for auto dealerships: the margin prices rise faster than the final goods prices.

If the margin prices were used to compute output and productivity, this limited sample suggests that there would be a significantly lower rate of productivity growth in the retail portion of the production chain. However, the data are still too limited to provide an assessment of the usefulness of the margin price indexes. The PPI program has yet to release price indexes for electronics stores and nonstore retailers, categories in which we would anticipate large differences between the margin and final goods price indexes.

Productivity Growth in General Merchandise

As reported in table 8-1, general merchandise constitutes both a large portion of overall retail trade and a category of particularly rapid growth in labor productivity. It has generated a lot of interest from a productivity perspective both because of the format innovations introduced by Wal-Mart and other warehouse or superstore operations and because of the suggestion that innovations in IT technologies played a major role in their success. Retail trade, however, is not a large overall user of IT capital. IT capital income was only 2.5 percent of value added over the 1987–2001 period, compared with a 5.5 percent average for nonfarm business as a whole and 33 percent for telecommunications. The contribution of IT to labor productivity growth in retailing has risen recently (table 8-2), but IT still has contributed only 0.3 percentage point to the industry's growth in labor productivity of 3.2 percent a year since 1995, a contribution that is overwhelmed by the MFP contribution (3.0 points a year).

The influence of Wal-Mart is difficult to isolate in the industry data because its operations are spread across several SIC and NAICS groupings. However, the McKinsey Global Institute (2001) used internal corporate data to estimate the source of gain in Wal-Mart's labor productivity and its contribution to the general merchandise segment. They argue that Wal-Mart has maintained a substantial productivity advantage over its competitors of 40 to 50 percent. The productivity advantage is attributed in turn to managerial innovations, intensive use of IT applications (including scanners using UPCs, computer systems to track inventory and facilitate communication, and the early adoption of electronic data interchange), and economies of scale. The McKinsey Global Insitute authors also argue that Wal-Mart has achieved significant efficiency gains in its use of capital, though they do not present a formal analysis. The productivity advantage fueled rapid growth in Wal-Mart's share of the market—and more recently, emulation by other retailers. Their analysis suggests that rapid productivity gains can be sustained in future years as Wal-Mart's competitors adopt its business model. This is a story in which IT applications are an important, though not the only, source of increased productivity.

E-Commerce

The development of the Internet has opened up a wide range of new commercial activities. The sudden emergence of new Internet-based businesses in the latter half of the 1990s created a lot of confusion about how to measure e-commerce, and there were wide disparities among estimates of its projected growth. In addition, there has been very active discussion and research on the implications of e-commerce for the structure of markets and its impact on productivity growth in the overall economy.

Considerable progress has been made on the issue of measuring the volume of e-commerce and its growth. Beginning in 1999, the Census Bureau began to publish quarterly estimates of e-commerce transactions at the retail level, and it has incorporated questions about e-commerce sales in its annual surveys of manufacturing, wholesale trade, retail, and selected services (Mesenbourg 2001). The results for 2001 are reproduced in table 8-3. It is evident that business-to-business (B-to-B) sales, at 93 percent of the total, are the dominant source of e-commerce. This reflects a pre-Internet practice of exchanging data

Table 8-3. *U.S. Shipments, Sales, Revenues, and E-Commerce, 2001 and 2000*

Description	Value of shipments, sales, or revenue[a]				Year-over-year percent change		Percent distribution of E-commerce	
	2001		2000					
	Total	*E-commerce*	*Total*	*E-commerce*	*Total*	*E-commerce*	*2001*	*2000*
Total	14,577	1,066	14,658	1,062	−0.6	0.4	100	100
Business-to-business	6,676	995	6,950	997	−3.9	−0.2	93.3	93.9
Manufacturing	3,971	725	4,209	756	−5.7	−4.1	68	71.2
Merchant wholesale	2,705	270	2,741	241	−1.3	12.1	25.3	22.7
Business-to-consumer	7,901	71	7,708	65	2.5	9.2	6.7	6.1
Retail	3,141	34	3,059	28	2.7	22.1	3.2	2.6
Selected services	4,760	37	4,649	37	2.4	−0.1	3.5	3.5

Source: U.S. Department of Commerce, *E-Stats*, March 2003.
a. Shipments, sales, and revenues are in billions of dollars. The allocation between business-to-business and business-to-consumer e-commerce is based on several simplifying assumptions: manufacturing and wholesale e-commerce is entirely business-to-business, and retail and service e-commerce is entirely business-to-consumer. Definitional differences among shipments, sales, and revenues are ignored

Figure 8-1. *Retail E-Commerce Sales Annual Growth, 2000–02*[a]

Percent change

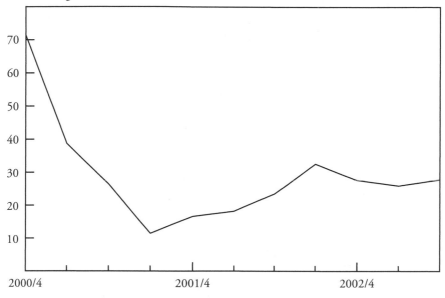

Source: U.S. Bureau of the Census.
a. Growth rates are relative to same quarter of prior year.

over private electronic exchanges. Within business, e-commerce sales have become a standard mature practice and are now a slowly growing share (15 percent in 2001) of the total.

At the retail level, e-commerce was only about 3 percent of total sales, or $70 billion, in 2001; but as shown in figure 8-1, it is growing at about 30 percent annually. However, this rate is far below the projections of a few years ago (Bakos 2001). Among fixed-location retailers, automotive dealers make significant use of e-commerce, but nonstore retailers (electronic shopping and mail-order companies) like Amazon are responsible for most of the remaining e-commerce transactions. In services, e-commerce is a major factor only for making travel reservations, where it claimed about one-quarter of the market in 2001. The rapidity with which the Census Bureau developed its e-commerce reports suggests that e-commerce will not pose a major measurement problem for the statistical agencies.

The effects of e-commerce on the economy and on productivity in particular are more uncertain. The nonstore retail component shows an extraordinary 12 percent annual rate of productivity growth in the BLS data provided in table 8-1, and electronic shopping (combined with catalog sales) shows a rate of 16 percent. But as previously discussed, the BLS measures do not provide an estimate of productivity growth within the retail component of the supply chain, particularly when sales are dominated by high-technology items whose prices are falling rapidly. Dell Computer, for example, is part of the nonstore segment. Instead, a more complete picture of the efficiency of e-commerce requires more detailed information on its costs. Furthermore, the nonstore segment's share of retail sales is too small to have accounted for a significant portion of the reported acceleration of labor productivity in total retail. At present, the surveys of the Census Bureau do not collect detailed cost information for these segments of the retail industry, and a more informed picture may need to await release of information from the 2002 Economic Census.

At its heart, the Internet is a system for transferring information, and it can do so at vastly reduced cost, but it is not so evident how that increased flow of information will affect commerce. Buyers could use the information to improve their evaluation of their options, leading to an intensification of competition, and sellers could use information about buyers to promote greater price discrimination or to tailor the product to the buyer. For some types of goods, electronic sales will reduce delivery charges, but in other cases the electronic sale is going against a long trend of substituting the customer's time for in-store labor and delivery. Just as some buyers will go to a conventional store to check out their options before purchasing over the Internet, others will use the Internet to inform themselves before purchasing at an off-line store. The information services of the Internet offer dramatic economies of scale, but it is not at all evident how those rents can be captured by a specific vendor, since buyers can easily separate the decision of what to buy from where to buy.

In an early assessment of the role of the Internet, Smith, Bailey, and Brynjolfsson (1999) suggested that the low search costs of Internet-based transactions should intensify competitive pressures and improve market efficiency in producing lower prices, reduce the cost of changing prices, and lead to less price dispersion. In their summary of the empirical research, however, the most surprising finding was the relatively high dispersion of prices on the Internet. Later studies also have found substantial price dispersion, implying that the gains in market efficiency have not been that substantial.[5]

Lucking-Reiley and Spulber (2001) suggest that the most significant economic aspects of e-commerce are likely to lie within the area of business-to-

5. For examples and additional citations, see Clemons, Hann, and Hitt (2001), and Pan, Ratchford, and Shankar (2001).

business transactions and that they can be divided into four areas: efficiencies in automated transactions; new market intermediaries; consolidation of demand and supply through organized exchanges; and changes in the extent of vertical integration of companies. In particular, the Internet enables companies to coordinate geographically dispersed production processes. It should enable them to exploit differences in prices over much greater distances (for example, through the development of call centers in the Philippines). Many of these changes will lower costs, without necessarily improving productivity. Firms will substitute purchased inputs for their own capital and labor.

Moreover, as mentioned earlier, recent growth in the B-to-B component has been quite modest, suggesting that additional economic benefits may be limited. One explanation is that electronic transactions among businesses (the use of private electronic data interchanges, for example) are an older technology than the current infatuation with the Internet would suggest, and many of the largest gains have been realized. Certainly, earlier forecasts of the growth of B-to-B e-commerce have been wildly off target.[6]

Other authors have conjectured that e-commerce will ultimately be more important for various types of digital services (video and audio) that can be delivered over the Internet, rather than for goods that must be physically delivered, which are the focus of current transactions. These sales are currently limited by the availability of bandwidth for residential users and concerns about the protection of intellectual property rights. The delivery of products over the Internet as well as their sales will increase the possibilities of substitution between Internet stores and traditional distribution channels (Haltiwanger and Jarmin 2002).

Conclusion

Retail trade has often been identified as a significant source of the post-1995 resurgence in productivity growth. However, as discussed above, part of that conclusion may be the product of a measurement system—both in the BEA industry database and BLS productivity program—that credits to retailing the benefits of improvement that should more properly be assigned to other parts of the economy.

One fundamental shortcoming of the statistics results from the lack of price measures of the cost of goods sold by retailers that would allow us to distinguish their contribution to the final product. The producer price index program of

6. Lucking-Reiley and Spulber (2001, p. 55).

BLS has moved to address this problem with a new effort to collect information on retail margins. However, the data are still too limited in coverage and available time periods to enable evaluation of their usefulness for separating the contribution of retailing from the rest of the production and distribution process.

However, the PPI program does not confront directly the question of retailing services, which are central to the measurement issues raised by Oi (2000), Betancourt and Gautschi (1993), and Ratchford (2003). The index of the gross margin of gasoline stations declined by 50 percent between its introduction in June 2003 and December 2003; anecdotes and observations suggest that part of this decline is a decline in services that were once provided with the sale of gasoline, though others have contended that time saving from the installation of credit card "swipers" at the pump should also be taken into account. None of the present retailing measurement programs deals with these changes.

Focusing on the gross margin clearly emphasizes the role of retailing services, for they are the margin. But it is not at all clear that the margin provides a better framework for measuring retailing services. What seems to be required is a better taxonomy of the services and a program for measuring them. This is required, actually, whether the output concept is the gross margin or gross receipts.

There can be no doubt that retailing has been an area of dramatic change and technological innovation that may have improved productivity substantially. Certainly, the data do suggest that the superstores and warehouse clubs have been an important market innovation since large changes in the pattern of consumer expenditures can be observed, and the example of Wal-Mart suggests that there have been large cost reductions in supply-chain management.

In addition, e-commerce is a small but rapidly growing segment of retailing, although we have little direct information on its influence on productivity. Substantial progress has been made by the Census Bureau in providing data on e-commerce sales, but little is known about the segment's cost structure. Also it seems evident that the Internet and other aspects of the electronic transfer of information will lead to many changes in the structure of conventional retailing that may be more important than the development of e-commerce alone.

Discussion of Output and Productivity in Retail Trade

Triplett and Bosworth provide an overview of major issues affecting productivity and its measurement in retail trade and e-commerce, paying special attention to answering the following question: Are the measured productivity gains in these areas real or an artifact of the method used to measure them? The chapter provides an excellent summary of the key issues affecting the measurement of retail productivity; it also provides a survey of what is known about productivity change in specific retail sectors and about the impact of information technology and e-commerce on retail productivity. I concentrate here on issues related to the measurement of retail productivity and touch only briefly on the impact of information technology and e-commerce.

Measuring Output

The proper measurement of output is a key issue in discussions of retail productivity and a difficult one to address given available data. The output of retail trade is really a set of services that reduce full price (Oi 1992, 2000; Betancourt and Gautschi 1993). Usually these services are not separately priced; the consumer pays for them indirectly through the margin that the retailer obtains. This margin, in turn, allows the retailer to cover the cost of providing the services. Though I will discuss some promising approaches below, currently it is not feasible to directly measure these services on a large scale. Therefore the practical question of

251

output measurement for the official productivity measures is whether (deflated) margin or sales adequately measures these services better.

The answer to the question of which measure is preferable ultimately depends on which tracks services better. If service per (deflated) dollar sold is constant, then there will be a one-to-one correspondence between sales and service. This might be a reasonable approximation for stable formats such as auto dealers. But service as a proportion of output undoubtedly declined for electronics stores, leading to the overstated productivity change noted by Triplett and Bosworth. Conversely, an increase in service as a proportion of output may explain the anomalous behavior of gas stations—one would think that the option of using a credit card at the pump was a service-enhancing change for consumers, so productivity may have increased more than measured. If (deflated) margins increase (decrease) with increases (decreases) in service so that there is a one-to-one correspondence between margins and services per unit sold, then margin would be an appropriate measure. However Triplett and Bosworth highlight the difficulty of measuring margins in real terms and also note that the relation between services and margins is tenuous—margins also are determined by scale economies and monopoly power as well as services.

What Are the Services?

Basically anything that reduces shopping costs (Oi 1992, 2000), provides information about better buys (Wernerfelt 1994), makes shopping more pleasant (Betancourt and Gautschi 1993), or lowers transportation costs for consumers (Messinger and Narasimhan 1997) is a retail service. As Triplett and Bosworth note, Betancourt and Gautschi (1993) suggest a grouping of the services into five broad categories. Retail services are valuable to consumers because they help consumers to make better decisions, reduce search and transaction costs, or make shopping more enjoyable. Many services can be provided by either the manufacturer or retailer (assembly of bicycles, packaging of foods, advertising). The services often substitute for consumer labor; obviously they are very difficult to measure.

Several studies have attempted to quantify retail services. Betancourt and Gautschi derive a relation between margin and services and estimate it by using proxies such as number of establishments, number with a product line, inventory, advertising, and payroll per establishment across forty-nine industries. Using a household production model, Messinger and Narasimhan develop an equilibrium model of supermarket breadth of assortment. Their empirical estimates indicate that one-stop shopping gives a positive net return to consumers despite increasing margins by 1.56 percent. Using 1982 data on demand, price, services, and market conditions of a sample of 430 supermarkets, Betancourt and Malinoski (1999) estimated demand and supply models incorporating services. The latter were measured as an index of the number of services offered by a given store. Adding one service category was found to have a value of approximately 3 percent of sales.

In a recent paper (Ratchford 2003) I studied the anomalous behavior of the BLS Index of Labor Productivity for retail food stores. This index declines from 1972–95 despite the adoption of scanners and substitution of capital and purchased services for labor. During this period there was a large increase in the number of stores offering services such as Sunday hours, pharmacy, deli, service meat, and film processing. There also was a large increase in items per store. Incorporating indexes of services and breadth of assortment into a cost function showed that these services were associated with increases in costs. Adjusting for changes in services and breadth of assortment indicated a rate of total factor productivity growth for retail food stores of about 1 percent a year from 1959–89 and a slightly lower rate for 1990–95 (end of the study). Therefore the evidence indicates that the measured decline in labor productivity in this industry can be explained by the rapid increase in services provided.

In sum, the output of retailing is a number of services that are difficult to quantify. If those services do not change much per (deflated) dollar sold, the deflated sales measure should be a satisfactory measure of output. But retail formats keep changing, and one suspects that services have changed quite a bit in a number of retail industries. The empirical attempts to incorporate services mentioned above tend to suggest this. More work is needed to explore the direct measurement of retail services, to explore how sales and margin measures coincide with direct measures of retail services, and to explore how much retail services change over time.

Price Indexes

The discussion of price indexes by Triplett and Bosworth is straightforward and informative. I just have a comment and some questions. My comment is that indexes of wholesale prices and margin prices will have uses in areas other than productivity—for example, in studying relationships between manufacturers and retailers.

One of my questions is why the CPI prices and margin prices diverge so much. The two areas of divergence between CPI prices and margin prices cited by the authors, in food stores and auto dealerships, would seem to be areas in which margins would be particularly difficult to measure. Popular items sold in retail food stores are subject to frequent trade promotions in which retailers are asked to provide feature advertising or displays, which are additional services that are valuable to manufacturers and consumers. Food retailers often forward buy to take advantage of the promotional price, and they often pocket the promotional allowance without lowering prices or performing the feature and display activity associated with the promotion. Moreover the promotional allowances often come in a separate budget, and they may not be reflected directly in wholesale prices. One wonders how these complexities are captured in the BLS margin indexes.

Similarly, margins on automobile sales are determined by negotiation and are affected by inventories and the availability of manufacturer rebates (Ratchford and Srinivasan 1993). They also are determined by volume incentives provided by manufacturers that are not directly reflected in manufacturer invoices. Again one wonders how these complexities are captured in the BLS margin indexes.

My other question is about scanner data. For the grocery, drug, and mass merchandise categories, huge amounts of detailed price and quantity data are available in scanner data. These data are not especially difficult to process, and they are routinely used by the retailers and manufacturers that supply these categories. My (possibly naïve) question: To what extent are these data used in price and output measurement? They would seem like a logical source.

Information Technology

Just because investments in IT do not seem to be comparatively large, that does not mean that IT could not have a substantial impact, and one wonders how well its contribution has been measured in the data summarized in table 8-2. That there appears to be only one detailed source of information on the relation between IT and retail productivity, McKinsey Global Institute (2001)—which uses data that cannot be checked—indicates a need for more study of the impact of IT on retail productivity.

E-Commerce

The authors' discussion of the Internet as a system for transferring information is an excellent summary of the role of the Internet. In retail markets its main role may be to make a consumer's search for information more efficient by providing easy (cheap) access to information. Therefore an evaluation of the impact of e-commerce on productivity requires measuring changes in consumer productivity—reductions in the cost to a consumer of making a purchase that yields a given amount of utility. There is now some evidence on the impact of the Internet on consumer productivity from the auto market. The Internet leads to saving in search time and substitutes for time with other sources, especially the dealer (Ratchford, Lee, and Talukdar 2003). Internet auto buying services and Internet use in general do lead to lower prices (Scott Morton, Zettelmeyer, and Silva-Risso 2001, 2003). Though cars are not sold over the Internet, these changes are having an impact on the structure of automobile retailing, which is likely to accelerate in the future. Dealers are not required to spend as much time demonstrating cars and negotiating prices, but they are losing their ability to price discriminate because price-conscious consumers come to the dealership better informed. The result should be lower dealer costs, reduced dealer services, increased price competition among dealers, and downward pressure on margins. While the ultimate impact of these changes on dealer productivity alone is unclear, the benefit to consumers appears to be substantial. In general, a complete evaluation of the impact of the Internet must include consumers as well as traditional retailers.

Conclusions

In their concluding section, Triplett and Bosworth emphasize that the link between output measures and services needs more research. I could not agree more. I have tried to help in developing that link by noting some approaches to the measurement of retail services that appear in the literature. Despite their shortcomings, the existing measures of retail productivity have the advantage of being based on relatively transparent measurement procedures that have changed relatively little over time. A reasonable strategy for identifying the impact of changes in retail services on productivity would be to begin with the existing indexes in order to see how much of the variation in them can be explained by changes in measures of services.

CHAPTER NINE

Output and Productivity in Other Services

Measurement problems in the services industries are not exhausted by the ones we treated in previous chapters. We singled out certain industries for extended discussion partly because the research literature deals with them more extensively and partly because in a number of them (finance, insurance, and retail trade) perplexing conceptual problems need to be addressed in order to improve productivity measures and our understanding of productivity change.

Business services, medical care, and education are three services industries that also were covered in the Brookings economic measurement workshops, and they too are large industries that present severe problems for measuring output and productivity—indeed, efforts to do so often result in negative productivity growth rates. But, as we learned in the workshops, the output measures are not yet of sufficient quality to yield a reliable evaluation of productivity developments. By summarizing the state of knowledge about them, which in some cases is meager, we may stimulate additional research.

Business Services

Business services include a diverse set of activities, such as professional and consulting services (other than legal and financial), advertising, data processing, and building maintenance. The range of activities and revenues reported in the 1997 Economic Census is shown in table 9-1. About 80 percent of the outputs of the

Table 9-1. *SIC Codes and Descriptions for Business and Professional Services*

SIC code	Category	1997 revenues	PPI price index
73	Business services	528.5	
731	Advertising services	28.2	Yes
732	Credit reporting and collection	9.8	No
733	Mailing, reproduction, stenographic	29.2	No
734	Building services	25.8	Yes
735	Equipment rental and leasing	31.7	Yes
736	Personnel supply services	91	Yes
737	Computer and data processing	224.1	Yes
738	Miscellaneous business services	88.5	No
87	Engineering and management services	317.4	
871	Engineering and architectural services	108.6	Yes
872	Accounting, auditing, and bookkeeping	54.6	Yes
873	Research and testing services	51.6	No
874	Management services	102.5	No

Source: U.S. Bureau of the Census, *1997 Economic Census: Comparative Statistics for United States, 1987 SIC Basis* (www.census.gov).

business services industries are purchased by other domestic firms; the 20 percent that goes to final demand is sold to government or sold overseas. OECD (1999) reports that the United States was the largest exporter of what it called "strategic business services" and that sales by foreign affiliates of U.S. business services firms also were growing rapidly (foreign affiliate sales were larger than direct exports). In each case, Europe is the major foreign market for U.S. business services firms.

The GDP originating (value added) of the business and professional services industry (SIC 73 and 87) has more than doubled as a share of GDP over the past quarter-century, to about 8 percent.[1] It also is one of the fastest-growing export sectors. Yet until recently we had no measures of real output of the industry or of real exports, and GDP originating was projected on the basis of employment data (Yuskavage 1996).

1. In the BEA industry data set, professional services (SIC 87) are included with museums (SIC 84) and services NEC (not elsewhere classified) (SIC 89), but the latter two groups are small. Furthermore, the change in SIC classification in 1987 resulted in a significant realignment of these industries, requiring a combination of SICs 73, 84, 87, and 89 for comparison with earlier years.

Business services is one of several industries in which the lack of physical indicators of output or output price indexes has often led statistical agencies to project output growth on the basis of changes in the inputs. The OECD notes that "productivity performance in strategic business services . . . has been poorly researched to date and is more difficult to measure."[2] In the OECD's report on the availability of country data on business services, only France was listed as having a deflator for business services output at the time data were gathered.

In the absence of deflators or direct quantity measures of business services, the two most common methods for estimating output are to project the output on the basis of employment changes or to use wage rate changes as a proxy for changes in the output price deflator. In both cases, the implied labor productivity growth is zero.

The use of labor input alone as a proxy for output change translates into a negative rate of change in multifactor productivity for industries, such as business services, that have experienced a large increase in capital intensity with their increased reliance on computers and other high-tech inputs. Sustained negative rates of change in multifactor productivity seem implausible to many researchers. In the absence of other information, it might be better to base the projection of output on a combination of all of the inputs; that would make the default assumption one of constant multifactor productivity rather than constant labor productivity.

To the extent that business services are an intermediate input to other industries, the assumption of zero productivity growth has no implication for the measurement of economywide productivity, only for its distribution. In effect, any productivity gains are attributed to the using industries. On the other hand, understanding why the economy is making more use of business services—and why they contribute so strongly to U.S. export performance—demands better measures of output. Improving the measurement of business services therefore is important for other reasons, even if not for measuring aggregate productivity growth.

Some progress has been made in recent years (Yuskavage 1999). With the expansion of the industry accounts to include measures of gross output for business services in 2000, BEA moved away from relying solely on input price indexes. Some components of business gross output, such as advertising, computer software, and equipment rental, are deflated with price indexes from a variety of sources (Lum, Moyer, and Yuskavage 2000) instead of with wage rates.

2. OECD (1999, p. 15).

Since 1995, the BLS also has expanded the producer price index to measure the prices or fees of some components of business and professional services; table 9-1 shows the industries that are covered by the new indexes. In most cases, these new indexes exist for only a few years, and their use to construct measures of real output creates methodological breaks in the BEA industry data. In some cases, such as professional services, the BLS asks respondents to reprice at periodic intervals a particular bundle of services. This is an application of what is known internationally as "model" pricing, a methodology that was first developed by Statistics Canada, Canada's national statistics agency, for pricing construction. Some of the BLS methods and results were described at a May 1999 Brookings workshop, "Measuring the Output of Business Services," and the application of the PPI and BEA computer software indexes to developing a measure of labor productivity was presented at "Two Topics in Services: CPI Housing and Computer Software," a workshop held in May 2003.[3]

Model pricing amounts to collecting a hypothetical price for a defined bundle of services. The BLS does ask respondents to take market conditions into account, and they make some adjustments for quality change. However, respondents may simply mark up the individual inputs that go into the bundle of services. There are insufficient observations at present to evaluate the resulting price indexes fully, but the rates of change have been less than those implied by the previous reliance on wage rates.

The challenges are even greater in other areas, such as business consultant services, because it is difficult to define a unit of their output. A few attempts have been made to collect information from business services providers about what they contribute to the output of their customers. Examples are Nachum (1999), who surveyed a group of European management consulting firms, and Gordon (1999), who collected information from U.S. consultants. The results are interesting, but so far they have not yielded any breakthroughs on the most difficult of the problems. Even if the use of consultants improves the productivity of the purchasing firm, extracting an estimate of the consultant's effect from surveys—either of the seller or the buyer of the service—is not a promising approach.

At the workshop on business services, Robert Gordon argued that improvements in the output measures for management consultants should rank relatively low among the priorities of the statistical agencies because the measurement problems are severe and because, since management consultants are an

---

3. Gerduk (1999), Swick (1999), and Kunze (2003). Also, see Abel, Berndt, and White (2003) and Prud'homme and Yu (2002) for computer software prices.

intermediate product producer, improvements would not affect the estimates of productivity growth in the aggregate economy. Furthermore, he argued that much of the work of consultants was redistributional in nature, beating down the prices of suppliers rather than enhancing productivity. Separating those tasks in a statistical measure would be a daunting undertaking; Gordon therefore favored measuring their output with a price index of their inputs, explicitly ruling out an effort to measure productivity.

Martin Baily disagreed with the characterization of the activities of management consultants in the Gordon paper, arguing that most of their activities focused on internal management and other aspects that directly related to productivity. However, he agreed that the most appropriate treatment of management consultants might be to integrate them back into the industries that use their services rather than attempt an independent valuation of their services. This would raise measurement problems only for the portion of the services that are sold to government or as exports.

Because business services are so diverse, measuring them requires an industry-by-industry approach and the painstaking resolution of problems that are unique to individual industries. Some evidence of recent progress is evident in the number of industries in table 9-1 for which BLS has initiated price indexes. These indexes exist for only the most recent years; therefore their introduction into the industry data set of BLS may raise problems of continuity of data. However, for computer services and equipment rental, the sectors where the output price is most likely to differ substantially from a wage rate measure, the price indexes have been extended back to the 1970s. The most significant gaps are in research and management services.

The current estimates of output and productivity growth in business services reflect the variability in the quality of the available data. At present, the BEA data do not include engineering and management services (SIC 87) as a separate industry, so we have limited the analysis, shown in table 9-2, to business services (SIC 73).

The rapid expansion of the industry is readily apparent in the double-digit rates of growth in nominal output. It also is clear that the new price indexes are capturing some of the productivity in individual segments of the industry, because the average rate of price increase is much less than the rate of wage increase. The rate of increase of labor productivity consequently is now reported at above 3 percent a year over the 1987–2001 period when it is measured using gross output.

Most of the gains in labor productivity are attributed to rapid growth in purchased intermediate inputs and in capital inputs. Consequently, the residual

Table 9-2. *Ouput and Productivity Growth in the Business Services Industry,*
1987–2001
Average annual percent change

Measure	1987–95	1995–2001
Nominal output	11.0	11.6
Price deflator	2.2	1.9
Wage	4.2	6.8
Output		
BEA output	8.6	9.5
BEA value added	6.7	6.6
Employment		
BEA	5.4	5.6
Labor productivity		
BEA output	3.0	3.7
BEA value added	1.2	0.9
Contributions of		
Capital per worker	0.0	0.9
IT capital per worker	0.2	1.0
Intermediate inputs	2.2	3.2
Multifactor productivity		
BEA output	0.7	−0.4
BEA value added	1.1	−0.5

Source: Authors' calculations based on BEA industry data file.

measure of MFP increases slowly. In fact, the change in MFP is estimated to be
negative over the 1995–2001 period. From what we know about the complexity
of measuring output and from the fact that important business services still are
not covered by the PPI, we suspect that output, and therefore productivity
growth, is probably understated.

Medical Care

It has become commonplace knowledge that inflation in the cost of medical
care outstrips the overall inflation rate. For example, between 1985 and 1995,
the medical care component of the CPI rose 6.5 percent a year, although the
overall CPI rose only 3.6 percent. Until fairly recently, deflators for medical care
output have been based almost exclusively on the medical care components of

the CPI. Many economists believe that the CPI medical price indexes overstated inflation in medical care.[4] If so, output growth in medical care is understated and so is productivity growth.

Beginning in 1993 and 1994, BLS introduced in its producer price index program new price indexes for hospitals and for physicians' services industries. These new indexes reflected a new methodology for measuring the price of medical care. In the historical CPI, the unit of pricing was the cost of a day in the hospital. For the PPI, the BLS draws a probability sample of treatments for medical conditions. For example, for the PPI price index for "mental health care treatment in a hospital," the probability selection might be "major depression." The BLS then collects the monthly change in costs for treating that condition (see Catron and Murphy 1996 for more information on BLS procedures). The new medical care PPI indexes are a great improvement on the previously available CPI medical price information; see, for example, the assessment in Berndt and others (2000).

Overall, the new PPI indexes present a picture of lower medical care price inflation than that presented by the CPI for the period in which the two overlap (Catron and Murphy 1996). BLS subsequently introduced similar methodology into the CPI (Cardenas 1996).

The PPI medical care indexes are now used as deflators in the BEA industry file that we used for our study. The change in the deflator is one reason that our labor productivity estimates for medical care grow more rapidly after 1995, the year we use as a break point for all of our industry analyses. Indeed, as shown in table 9-3, medical care had negative measured growth in labor productivity before 1995 (–0.5 percent a year), when deflation was done mostly with the CPI; after 1995, it turned positive (0.9 percent a year). A portion of that acceleration is caused by changing the price deflator.

The CPI medical care components continue to rise more rapidly than the PPI (table 9-4), even though CPI methodology has moved in the direction of the PPI (Cardenas 1996). The difference amounts to 1.5 percentage points a year in recent years, more or less, depending on the component (table 9-4). One reason presumably is that the CPI includes only households' out-of-pocket expenses. The PPI includes all charges for medical care, so it measures what is needed to deflate medical care output. The deflators may have improved after 1995, but productivity data for the medical care industry still appear anom-

---

4. A comprehensive discussion of price indexes for medical care is found in Berndt and others (2000). See also Triplett (1999a) and Cutler and Berndt (2001).

Table 9-3. *Output and Productivity Growth in the Health Services Industry, 1987–2001*

Average annual rate of change

Measure	1987–95	1995–2001
Nominal output	8.7	5.6
Price deflator	5.4	2.6
Real output	3.2	2.9
Employment	3.6	2.0
Labor productivity	–0.5	0.9
Contributions of		
Capital per worker	0.2	0.4
Non-IT capital per worker	0.0	0.1
IT capital per worker	0.2	0.3
Intermediate inputs	0.9	0.9
Multifactor productivity	–1.5	–0.4

Source: Authors' calculations based on BEA industry data file.

alous. As table 9-3 shows, MFP growth in this industry remains negative, though it is less negative than before.

Another anomaly is the negligible contribution to labor productivity growth from non-IT capital, which in this case includes medical equipment. We note in chapter 10 numerous problems with the data on medical equipment—they appear to be both undercounted and misclassified in current prices, they may be misallocated in the BEA capital flow tables (so creating a greater undercount to the medical care industries that are their primary users), and the allowance for quality change in their deflation is doubtful. Because so many innovations in medical treatments involve medical equipment, one would certainly expect that non-IT capital would be prominent among the sources of labor productivity growth in this industry.

Note that improvements in the measures of medical care equipment would almost certainly lower the industry's MFP—that is, we would expect that a full accounting of the medical care industry's capital inputs would increase their share and their contribution. When capital is undercounted in the growth accounting framework we use, MFP is overstated. Yet in this industry, MFP growth is negative as currently measured. The realization that measured MFP would likely be more strongly negative if medical equipment were better measured calls for more examination of the output measure and its deflator.

Table 9-4. *Medical Care Price Indexes from the PPI and CPI, 1995–2001*

Index	2001 index[a] value	Annual rate of change
Producer price index		
Offices of physicians	111.5	1.83
General medical and surgical hospitals	112.3	1.95
Consumer price index		
Medical care	123.8	3.62
Medical care services	120.3	3.13

Source: Authors' calculation from the producer price index (series codes PCU8011 and PCU8062) and the consumer price index (series codes CUUROOOSAM and CUUROOOSAM2).
a. 1995 = 100.

Even with the improved PPI methodology it has been difficult for BLS to find data to adjust for changes in the efficacy of treatments. Although there is some controversy on how far statistical agencies should go in building measures of treatment efficacy into price and output measures, we doubt if anyone seriously disagrees that the price index should be adjusted or corrected *in some fashion* to account for improvements in medical efficacy. Because medical economists generally believe that progress has been made in medical technology—better prognoses, less time spent in the hospital for any given condition, less painful and onerous procedures during treatment, and so forth—they believe that inadequate adjustment for changes in medical technology creates an upward bias in price indexes for medical care.

There is less universal agreement, however, on the basis for adjustment. In the PPI, the BLS looks for information on the changes in costs associated with improvements in medical efficacy. Some economists would go considerably further, asking for information about the medical outcome and the value to the patient of changes in medical outcomes. Research on cataract surgery by Shapiro and Wilcox (1996) serves to illustrate the issues.

At one time, cataract surgery involved a lengthy hospital stay, a week or ten days in intensive care. Now, it is mostly an outpatient procedure, often performed in a doctor's office or clinic. Put another way, the number of days in the hospital has dropped from ten or more to zero. If the price index were based, as the CPI was formerly, on the cost of a day in the hospital, there is no reasonable way to "adjust" the price index for the value of an improvement that reduced the number of days to zero. If one were to ask a hospital, in the usual BLS "cost-based" formulation, how much more costly the improved procedure was, the answer would be negative. Making a negative quality adjustment for an improved procedure makes no sense—and BLS would not do that. The point is that traditional price index procedures for handling product or service improvements do not work for most medical improvements.

From the patient's point of view, the modern operation surely is better. The operation once required the patient to be immobilized for a lengthy period. Not only is it now less costly in terms of what is paid for (hospital care, for example), it also is far less unpleasant for the patient. The operation has fewer adverse side effects, does not require wearing thick corrective lenses, and in many other ways has improved from the patient's point of view. Given the choice between immobilization and the far less unpleasant recovery period associated with the modern operation, patients would undoubtedly be willing to pay more for the modern operation.

A medical outcome measure would take into account all the ways in which the improvement in cataract surgery was beneficial to the patient. (See Gold and others 1996 for a discussion of medical outcome measures.) Some of these improvements, however, go outside the traditional "market boundary" of national accounts and of the CPI and PPI. The patient might well be *willing* to pay for the improved technology, but in fact the technology comes to him (or to his insurance company) for less monetary cost or expenditure of market resources than the old treatment did. There are no market prices to determine the value of the improved procedure.

Should these improvements be credited in national accounts to the productivity of the medical care industry or to its output? Or should improvements that are not explicitly paid for—and for which the value of a transaction cannot be directly inferred—be ruled out of national accounts (or out of national health accounts) on the grounds that they fall outside the traditional market boundary for measuring GDP? For example, the time spent in recovery from cataract surgery is part of the cost to the patient—even leaving aside the disutility of immobilization—but the value of this time cost is not traditionally considered in national accounts, nor do they value the reduced disutility of less time spent immobilized. The time cost of the patient, the greater utility to the patient of less unpleasant treatment, and the value to the patient of a reduction in unwanted side effects are all elements that would go into a measure of medical outcomes (see Gold and others 1996). But should they go into an economic accounting of medical care? That question remains somewhat controversial among economists.[5] Some of these issues were discussed in the conference papers contained in Triplett (1999a) and also in Cutler and Berndt (2001).

Stating the problem this way underscores the difficulties that statistical agencies face in producing price indexes for medical care. Calculating the change in costs for treating an episode of illness requires not only the traditional statistical skills in gathering prices, but also a great deal of medical knowledge about changes in the efficacy of medical treatments—knowledge that in many cases is scientifically uncertain or whose validity is contended. It also requires knowledge about patient valuations of changes in treatments—particularly when changes involve the patient's time and tolerance for pain—and valuation of the disutility of side effects or of the onerous implications of frequent treatments.

In addition, some changes in medical treatment may increase expenditures in some PPI index categories while reducing them in others; however, the PPI methodology contains no obvious way to take these cost savings into account. As an example, consider the increased use of drugs that permit treatment of patients with mental conditions on an outpatient basis, rather than in a mental hospital. Substitution of drugs (and clinical visits) for hospital care will reduce the cost of treatment for a specified diagnosis, but the cost reduction will be reflected inadequately in the PPI because the PPI holds the weights for the various expenditure categories (hospitals, doctors' offices, pharmaceuticals, and so forth) constant. The PPI collects the costs of treatment by disease category, which is a great improvement over previous methods, but it still collects the cost of treating a specified disease *in the hospital.* Costs in the hospital will not measure the cost change of treating the disease when cost savings occur because the treatment shifts across institutional categories that are identified in the national health accounts—hospitals, doctors' offices, and so forth.

New research price indexes for medical treatments that adjust for changes in the effectiveness of medical treatments include Cutler and others (1996); Cutler, McClellan, and Newhouse (1999); Berndt, Busch, and Frank (2001); Shapiro and Wilcox (1996), as already noted; and other contributions in Berndt and Cutler (2001). These new price indexes confirm that the historical CPI medical care component was biased upward as a deflator for medical care industry output, as does comparison of the new PPI indexes with movements of the CPI. How much did medical care productivity measures that used the historical CPI as output deflators understate the amount of productivity growth in medical care?

---

5. We leave aside here problems with measuring medical outcomes, which are formidable. The question is what one wants to do with medical outcome measures, if perfected or improved.

A complete estimate has not been prepared. To provide an evaluation of the bias in existing measures, Triplett "backcasts" an estimate for a mental health care price index (Triplett 1999b). One part of the backcast is an estimate formed by matching, for the period following 1992, PPI and CPI components and using the differences in trends as an adjustment factor for the CPI for the earlier period. He weights these indexes according to costs for mental health treatment and makes an additional correction based on the research of Berndt, Busch, and Frank (2001). The adjusted mental health care price index shows essentially no medical inflation during the 1985–95 interval.

He then uses the adjusted price index to estimate the growth in the quantity of per capita mental health care services (or real expenditure growth).[6] Adjusted, real output growth is substantially positive, at about 6.6 percent for 1985–95. For the same period, the unadjusted real output growth rate in mental health care is negative, at about –1.5 percent per year. The adjusted real output growth is thus nearly 8 percentage points higher than the unadjusted estimates. The implications for medical care productivity are obvious.

Mental health services may not be representative of the rest of medical care. Improved price indexes for other diseases might not make as much of a difference in output trends as they apparently do in the case of mental health care. Yet the negative real output growth in mental health services in the unadjusted data is roughly consistent with the negative productivity trends for total health care shown in other data. Table 9-3, for example, shows labor productivity growth for the entire medical care sector of –0.5 percent annually for 1987–1995. In addition, the heart attack price index of Cutler and others (1996) and the cataract surgery price index in Shapiro and Wilcox (1996) suggest that revisions to real expenditure trends for these disease categories might be similar to—and that they certainly go in the same direction as—Triplett's revisions for mental health.

It is unlikely that this backcast is exactly valid, but neither is the historical CPI as a deflator for medical care. One should also not infer that the exercise estimates the bias in current medical care productivity figures, for many things have changed. However, improvement of MFP in medical care seems more likely than the deterioration that present measures of medical care output show. We think that the data in table 9-3 suggest that medical care output is still understated in available data, particularly so since the contribution of medical equipment to medical advances also seems understated.

---

6. Treatment for mental disorders accounts for more than 8 percent of total U.S. health care expenditures, about one-tenth (9.5 percent) of all allocable U.S. personal health care expenditures, and just over 1 percent of GDP.

Education

Education is crucial to any discussion of the sources of productivity growth. Yet while many studies have documented the contribution that improvements in education and job skills have made to overall productivity growth, a surprisingly limited amount of work has been devoted to measuring the output and productivity of the education industry—particularly within the growth accounting framework that we have applied to other industries.[7] Part of the difficulty is that many educational institutions are in the government sector, where the lack of competitive market pricing has made it difficult to measure output or to assume that the payments to capital and labor reflect productivity. In addition, education is an area in which progress has been stymied by long-running debates over perceived changes in the quality of the output.

In April 2000, Brookings sponsored a workshop entitled "Measuring the Output of the Education Sector" as part of its program on output and productivity measurement in services. The participants generally agreed with the perception that the productivity of the education industry, measured in the standard context of output per unit of input, had not increased significantly and may in fact have declined. But there was very little agreement on how to develop strong quantifiable measures of either output or productivity. Concerns were expressed about how to adjust for the influence of nonschool factors on student performance, about the importance of taking account of multiple outputs (such as the various missions assigned to the public school system and the combination of education and research in higher education), and about the long lags between education and economic returns in the form of higher earnings. Particular concerns were expressed about how to adjust for variations in education quality.[8]

Despite the limitations, we have constructed some illustrative measures of labor productivity in education. As shown in figure 9-1, enrollment in the U.S. education system has grown considerably since the mid-1960s, but nearly all of that growth has been in higher education. Enrollment of the baby-boom generation produced a peak in the number of students in elementary and secondary education in 1971 that was not to be exceeded until 1996. Enrollment in higher education, however, nearly tripled between 1965 and 2000.

7. Jorgenson and Fraumeni (1992a), Denison (1985), and Bishop (1994).
8. Many of these difficulties are highlighted in a paper prepared for the program by Steven Rivkin of Amherst College. A draft is available at www.brookings.edu/es/research/projects/productivity/workshops.htm.

Figure 9-1. *Enrollment in Educational Institutions by Level, 1965–2003*

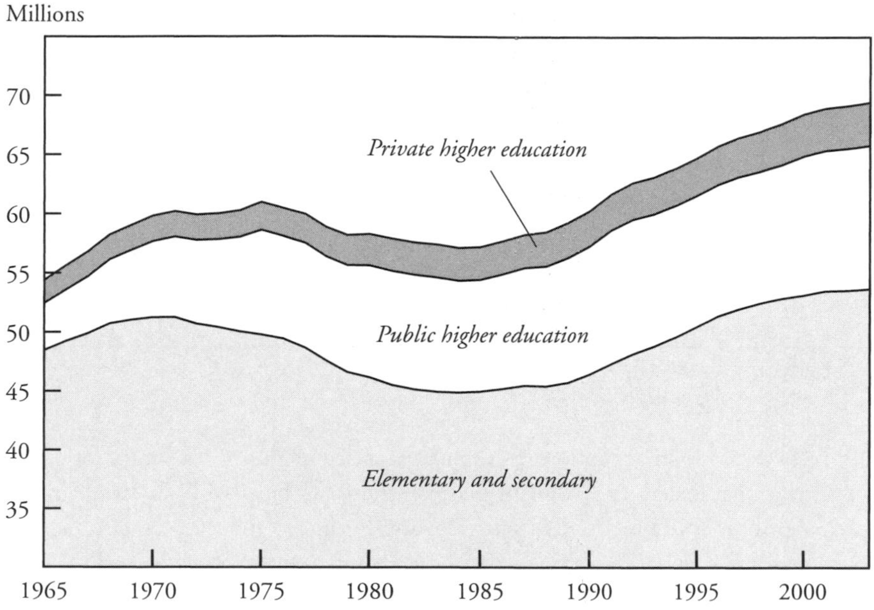

Millions

Source: *Digest of Education Statistics*, various years.

Summary measures of productivity trends in elementary and secondary education are reported in table 9-5. Several points are notable. First, there has been a substantial increase in real expenditures per student. Since we have no direct measure of the price of educational output, expenditures are simply deflated by the GDP price deflator as a measure of general inflation. Second, labor productivity as measured by students per teacher or per staff member has been steadily declining. That should not be a surprise; most of the increases in staffing supposedly were undertaken to raise the quality of education, a factor that our calculation so far ignores, or to expand the school's focus on students with special needs.

Comparable measures are constructed for higher education in table 9-6. Again, productivity is declining if measured by enrollment per instructor, and it is rising if measured by real expenditures per instructor. However, universities are a classic example of a multiple output firm in which output consists of research, housing, and entertainment (sports) in addition to education. All of these ancillary activities are reflected in the measure of expenditures, but no measure of prices is available.

Table 9-5. *Output and Productivity of Elementary and Secondary Education, 1970–2000*
Average annual percent growth

Growth in	1970–80	1980–90	1990–2000
Enrollment	−1.0	0.1	1.4
Nominal expenditure	8.8	8.3	5.6
Real expenditure[a]	1.7	3.9	3.4
Instructors	0.8	1.0	2.0
Total staff	2.2	0.8	2.5
Enrollment per instructor	−1.8	−1.0	−0.6
Enrollment per staff	−3.1	−0.7	−1.1

Source: National Center for Education Statistics (2003).
a. Computed with the GDP price deflator.

Tuition is not an accurate measure of the price of the education component of educational institutions' output because there has been wide variation in the proportion of education costs that it covers. Recently, government support for public colleges and universities has been declining, and many institutions now use tuition charges to fund their scholarship programs. In effect, price discrimination has become a major tool of education policy as schools use it to extract consumer surplus and to attract the most desirable students. In addition, most of the efforts to construct price deflators for the R&D component, which represents about 10 percent of total expenditures, are based on composite input prices with no attempt to adjust for productivity.[9]

Our productivity measures ignore the issue of quality, yet quality is at the center of the education debate. However, many of the available tests indicate very little change in the quality of elementary and secondary education at the national level in recent decades. The results of the National Assessment of Educational Progress (NAEP), for example, indicate that test scores for seventeen-year-olds have changed very little over the past three decades (table 9-7).[10] Alternatively, we might focus on the change in test scores between nine and seventeen years of age as a measure of the value added by the school system, but that also shows little difference. Other tests imply a somewhat more significant decline that began in the mid-1960s and extended throughout the 1970s.[11]

9. See the discussion in Fraumeni and Okuba (2002).
10. National Center for Education Statistics (2003).
11. Some of these different measures were cited by John Bishop at the Brookings workshop.

Table 9-6. *Productivity in Higher Education, 1970–2000*

Average annual percent growth

Characteristic	1970–80	1980–90	1990–2000
Enrollment	3.5	1.3	1.0
Public	3.9	1.4	0.8
Private	2.1	1.2	1.8
Real expenditure[a]	2.7	4.3	3.4
Instructional staff			
Public	4.7	1.5	2.6
Private	1.8	2.5	2.8
Enrollment per instructor			
Public	–0.7	–0.1	–1.7
Private	0.3	–1.2	–1.0

Source: National Center for Education Statistics (2003).

a. The adjustment for price inflation is based on the GDP price deflator.

Similarly, if we use scores on the Graduate Record Exam (GRE) to measure the quality of university graduates, we find that the quantitative scores have increased and the verbal scores have gone down (figure 9-2). Overall, it is difficult to conclude that quality changes have been a significant factor at the national level and most of the debate may be more relevant to distinctions among schools or for judging the results of various "reform" programs.

The issue of quality change generated considerable controversy at the workshop. Some participants emphasized the long lags in the process by which changes in education affect the quality of the overall workforce and noted what they perceived to be considerable quality improvements over the past century; others placed greater weight on the relevance of more recent changes in judging the industry's performance.

One concludes from this that there are all kinds of measurement problems in computing the productivity of the educational sector, including the definition of current price output, the price deflator, and the measure of labor input. Jorgenson and Fraumeni (1992b) estimate the output of education by assessing its contribution to human capital and therefore to lifetime earnings streams of graduates. Their estimates are far larger than the output that is currently recorded in national accounts, a result that is consistent with the hypothesis that educational productivity is biased downward because of mismeasurement of educational output. However, outcomes also may reflect the role of education as

Table 9-7. *Literacy Test Index Scores of Seventeen-Year-Olds, 1971 and 1999*

	1971	1999	Change	Standard deviation
Total	285.2	287.8	2.6	1.3
Male	278.9	281.5	2.6	1.6
Female	291.3	294.6	3.3	1.4
Parents' education				
Not high school graduate	261.3	264.8	3.5	3.6
High school graduate	283	273.9	−9.1	2.1
Post high school	302.2	297.5	−4.7	1.2
Literacy of nine-year-olds	207.6	211.7	4.1	1.3

Source: National Center for Education Statistics (2003). Test scores are from the National Assessment of Educational Progress (NAEP).

a sorting device to distinguish people of differing abilities, potentially overstating the contribution of education alone.

Recently, the topic of education output has become a more significant research issue as national statistical agencies have explored means of measuring the output of government and other nonmarket activities as part of an expansion of the national accounts.[12] A major objective is to move away from input-based valuations to direct estimation of the value of output. In the area of education that has led to considerable work to extend the estimates of Jorgenson and Fraumeni on educational outcomes to other countries, using earnings to value education.

A recent paper by O'Mahony and Stevens (2003) examines the output of the education system in the United Kingdom from two different perspectives. The first adjusts the student enrollment numbers for changes in an index of test scores as a measure of quality change. It encounters the difficulty of assigning a weight, or value, to the change in test scores. The second approach uses a regression of the relationship between earnings and education to value schooling over an individual's working life. This yields a set of relative income weights that can be used to value years of schooling. However, the earnings-based outcomes measure cannot be related back to a specific year of education output without additional assumptions.

12. See, for example, Panel to Study the Design of Nonmarket Accounts (2003), Australian Bureau of Statistics (2003), and Pritchard (2003).

Figure 9-2. *Graduate Record Exam Scores, 1965–2000*

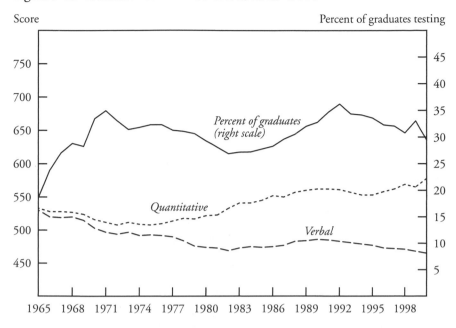

Source: *Digest of Education Statistics* (2002).

Improvements in the measures of educational output should be an issue of substantial importance to the United States. Higher education has emerged as an area of significant comparative advantage, at least as measured by the desire of students in other countries to enroll in U.S. colleges and universities. It is a growing and significant U.S. service-producing industry. On the other hand, reductions in public funding and in hours of faculty teaching have intensified the debate over quality. Education also is likely to be strongly affected in future years by the ongoing revolution in the information processing industry.

CHAPTER TEN

High-Tech Capital Equipment: Inputs to Services Industries

We estimate that services industry labor productivity advanced at the trend rate of 2.41 percent a year since 1995. We also estimate that roughly a quarter of the services industry labor productivity growth (0.59 percentage point) came from investment in information and communications technology capital (table 10-1: these estimates were taken from tables 2-1 through 2-7 of chapter 2 and appendix table A-1). In some services industries, the IT contribution was much larger—for example, in communications IT contributed 1.3 percentage points, but out of a very rapid 6.7 labor productivity advance (see appendix table A-1).

Estimating sources of labor productivity growth requires accurate and comprehensive measures of high-tech inputs. This is true of our study, as well as of previous aggregate-level studies that have estimated IT contributions, such as Oliner and Sichel (2000) and Jorgenson and Stiroh (2000). In this chapter, we address several issues concerning the measurement of IT and other high-tech capital inputs:[1]

---

1. For this chapter, we use information developed in the following five Brookings output and productivity measurement workshops: "Two Topics in Services: CPI Housing and Computer Software" (May 23, 2003); "Hedonic Price Indexes: Too Fast, Too Slow, or Just Right?" (February 1, 2002); "The Adequacy of Data for Analyzing and Forecasting the High-Tech Sector" (October 12, 2001); "Communications Output and Productivity" (February 23, 2001); and "Measuring Health Care" (December 17, 1999).

Table 10-1. *Labor Productivity in the Services Sector, 1995–2001*
Average annual rates of change

LP growth and contributions	1995–2001
LP growth	2.41
IT contribution	0.59
MFP growth	0.88
Other	0.93

Source: See tables 2-1 through 2-7; and table A-1.

Methodology. Many U.S. high-tech deflators are constructed with hedonic indexes, but not all of them are. How much difference does price index methodology make, and if it does make a difference, why? Do hedonic indexes fall too fast, as sometimes alleged? Are there defects to the methodology that justify restricting further expansion of their use, as has also been proposed?

Conversely, are we understating the contribution of high-tech capital because some components of high-tech equipment and software are not now well measured? Questions have been raised about the apparently small declines in communications equipment price measures, for example. Even in computer and peripheral equipment, the increased performance of some components may not be accounted for, and the rate of introductions of new and improved products makes it hard for statistical agencies to keep up.

Software. This is a special problem. Software is acquired by users in three ways, purchases of prepackaged standard software, purchases of custom software, and "own account" software that is designed and built by users. For all three, estimating a quality-adjusted price index is a difficulty that has not been resolved. Moreover, the estimate of the implicit expenditures on "own-account" software, which makes up a large fraction of U.S. software investment, is also controversial.

Allocation of high-tech (and other capital) among using industries. The major sources of information on the industrial distribution and use of high-tech capital are the "capital flow" tables that are periodically estimated by BEA. Through the IT investment boom of the late 1990s, the most recent data pertained to the 1992 table (Bonds and Aylor 1998). If the IT capital equipment went to different industries after 1992 than it did before, then our IT capital is mismeasured at the industry level. We assess this possibility, using the 1997 capital flow table that has just recently become available.

Coverage and special problems. We consider as special examples communications equipment (as just noted), software prices and expenditures, and the production of medical care equipment. For medical equipment, the problem is not only the deflators. Very little data exist on investment (expenditures and quantities) in medical equipment by type of equipment. The medical care industry accounts for 7 percent of total value added (appendix table A-7), so the lack of data on its own high-tech inputs is a serious gap that undoubtedly biases its MFP measures (though data deficiencies in the output of medical care loom even larger—see chapter 9).

Depreciation of capital equipment. This is another major empirical problem that affects our measures of capital inputs. We do not discuss this matter here.[2]

Hedonic Price Indexes for High-Tech Equipment: What Are the Issues?

Two conflicting beliefs—neither strictly consistent with the empirical evidence—color much of the discussion of hedonic indexes.[3] Some economists believe that hedonic indexes always fall more rapidly than price indexes constructed with traditional statistical agency methods, which are often referred to as "matched model" indexes. Others hold that matched model and hedonic indexes will coincide, provided the matched model indexes are based on samples that are frequently replenished and reweighted.

Many comparisons of matched model and hedonic indexes have been carried out in the more than forty years since Griliches's (1961) influential article. Reviews of some of these comparisons are in Triplett (1989) and Gordon (1990). In these research studies, seldom do matched model and hedonic indexes coincide.

However, much of the early evidence on matched model and hedonic indexes is inconclusive. Early comparisons of hedonic and matched model indexes were not computed on the same database so that in the absence of such controlled experiments, the indexes differ in a number of ways and not just in their techniques for dealing with quality change.

Table 10-2 presents the results of some empirical studies that have computed matched model and hedonic indexes from the same database. The table is based on chapter 4 in Triplett (forthcoming), which also describes the studies.

---

2. See, among many other possible references, Fraumeni (1997).

3. Besides the Brookings workshop on this topic, this section draws on chapter 4 of Triplett (forthcoming).

Table 10-2. *Comparison of Hedonic and Matched Model Indexes Estimated from the Same Database*

Study	Product	Date	Difference: MM minus hedonic (percentage points, average annual rate of change)
Dulberger (1989)	U.S. computer processors	1972–84	−9.8 to −11.0
Lim and McKenzie (2002)	Australian PCs	2000–01	−10 to −20
Okamoto and Sato (2001)	Japanese PCs	1995–99	−10 to −20
	Japanese TVs	1995–99	+8.0 to +8.4
	Japanese cameras	2000–01	+5.9
Evans (2002)	French PCs	2000–01	−28
Van Mulligan (2003)	Dutch PCs	1999–02	−4.3
	Dutch notebooks	1999–02	−2.8
	Dutch servers	1999–02	−3.5
Silver and Heravi (2002)	U.K. TVs	Jan.–Dec. 1998	+2.2 to +2.6
	U.K. washing machines	Jan.–Dec. 1998	+1.7 to 1.9

Most of these studies concern electronics in some form; a majority cover computer equipment, such as PCs. In the table, the empirical findings are tabulated as percentage point differences in annual rates of change—for example, in the Okamoto and Sato (2001) study of Japanese cameras, the difference of +5.9 percentage points in table 10-2 is the difference between their matched model index that declined by 27.8 percent per year and their hedonic index that fell only 21.9 percent during the same interval. In this case, the difference is entered with a positive sign, indicating that the hedonic index lies above the matched model index at the end of the period. Negative signs in table 10-2 correspond to the cases where the hedonic index declines more rapidly. The range of differences shown in the righthand column of table 10-2 corresponds to the authors' computing alternative hedonic indexes, alternative matched model indexes, or both.

As table 10-2 shows, matched model and hedonic indexes never seem to agree exactly, so the view that hedonic and matched model indexes agree is overwhelmingly refuted by the empirical evidence. However, some of the differences are small. For example, when Okamoto and Sato (2001) found a difference of −2.4 to −3.0 percentage points for Japanese PC prices, this difference is less than 10 percent of the 42–45 percent per year average decline in PC prices in Japan.

Others are substantially larger. Even small differences, however, appear to be showing statistically significant differences from methodology.[4]

Table 10-2 also shows clearly that hedonic indexes do not always decline more than matched model indexes. The usual presumption about hedonic indexes (that they decline faster) is confirmed by the computer studies, but not by those for appliances, where the opposite is usually the case.

What determines whether (and when) hedonic indexes differ from matched model indexes? What determines the sign of the difference? When, and why, do hedonic indexes rise more slowly (fall more rapidly) than matched model indexes? Triplett (forthcoming, chapter 4) lists four determining conditions:

—Frequency of resampling and reweighting in the matched model index. It has long been known that fixed samples cause serious problems for price indexes for high-tech products. Price changes of newer varieties of a product frequently differ from those of older varieties. If the price index samples are not kept up to date, significant amounts of price change are not recorded. This understanding entered the price index literature with the work of Berndt, Griliches, and Rosset (1993) on pharmaceuticals and Dulberger (1993) on semiconductors. Both studies pointed to price index errors (in both cases, missed price declines) because of fixed producer price index (PPI) samples that had gotten out of date. These results have influenced PPI sampling procedures but continue to present difficulties for measures of high-tech products. See, for example, the discussion of communications equipment in the PPI, in the following sections, where out-of-date samples appear to have missed part of the price decline from newer communications equipment products. This finding, by Dulberger, and by Berndt, Griliches, and Rosset, is periodically rediscovered, sometimes in the research literature and sometimes in statistical agency literature, but it is neither new nor in doubt. It implies, of course, that frequently replenished and frequently reweighted samples will do a better job at measuring price indexes for high-tech products than samples whose composition is held fixed over some interval. It does not, however, in itself, ensure that hedonic indexes will agree with matched model indexes.

—Weight of entering and exiting products. It seems reasonable that the lower the shares of new and disappearing products, the less sensitive the index to

---

4. Triplett (forthcoming) reasoned as follows. Most of the authors of the studies cited in table 10-2 produced alternative matched model indexes and alternative hedonic indexes, using different implementations of the two methodologies. Differences in the indexes in each study can be arrayed as within group (for example, within hedonic or within matched model) or between group. One can then ask: Are the between-group differences larger than the within-group differences? The answer is always yes, whether the between-group estimate is large or small.

the sample composition effects discussed in the previous paragraph. Additionally, as explained in Triplett (forthcoming), a hedonic index makes an explicit price imputation for entering (in some formulations, exiting) products; thus it also seems reasonable that the smaller the shares of such products, the less need for hedonic indexes. That is, the technical superiority of the hedonic over the matched model index is the capability of the hedonic index to take explicitly into account price changes that occur with the introduction of new product varieties; thus, the lower the incidence of those new introductions, the less need for the hedonic index, and the more satisfactory the matched model index. This seems a major part of the contention of Aizcorbe, Corrado, and Doms (1999). It is correct, as far as it goes.[5]

—Amount of price change that occurs at new product introduction, rather than after. In high-tech goods, a stylized fact—dating at least to Dulberger (1989) and Fisher, McGowan, and Greenwood (1983)—is that new varieties are frequently introduced at lower quality-corrected prices than those of the old varieties that remain on the market. Prices of the older varieties react, with shorter or longer lags, or the older varieties exit from the market. But whether this scenario describes a market for a given product obviously depends on the conditions of that market. If manufacturers take new product introductions as an opportunity to also introduce price increases, then quality-adjusted prices for new product varieties will be higher than for continuing varieties. For example, in the appliance market studies in table 10-2, the newer varieties were apparently being used by their sellers to mask some price increases.

—Speed with which prices of older products adjust. If new product varieties are introduced at quality-adjusted prices that are above or below those of the old regime, little price change will be missed if older product varieties adjust rapidly. The price changes associated with the newer varieties will, at worst, enter the index with a lag.

The difference between matched model and hedonic indexes will be smaller the greater are the first and last factors (for example, if older products adjust rapidly to prices of new entrants, the difference between matched model FR&R

5. Aizcorbe, Corrado, and Doms emphasize that their frequently reweighted system means that entries and exits from their sample get low weights. Price changes that are associated with entries and exits, they contend, will therefore have a small impact on their indexes, even when the FR&R procedures miss these price changes. At some degree of frequency, their contention must be correct. On the other hand, Van Mulligen (2003) (also FR&R) found that entries and exits corresponded to around 20 percent of the expenditure weight, *monthly*. Silver and Heravi (2002) also emphasize that weights of entrants and exits in their samples of appliances are not low. Too little information has been presented on this matter in other studies; it is an important factor that influences whether matched model and hedonic indexes differ.

indexes and hedonic indexes should be small). The difference will be greater when the second and third factors are larger (for example, the larger the price change at introduction, the greater will be the difference between FR&R indexes, which miss such price changes, and hedonic indexes, which measure them).

Data on the same four factors can be used to answer another question that is often asked: if hedonic indexes differ from matched model indexes, which is right? Since Denison (1989), some economists have judged that hedonic indexes, particularly for computers, fall "too fast."

Some authors of studies in table 10-2 have carried out analyses of the four factors just described. For example, Okamoto and Sato (2001) examined the implied price changes for entering PCs and TVs in their data and compared them with movements of continuing varieties. The price changes differed. Even though Okamoto and Sato used a monthly replenished and reweighted sample, price changes from new entrants were substantial. No matched model method will pick up those changes, and their omission biases the matched model indexes. Okamoto and Sato's analysis shows conclusively why their hedonic index differs from their matched model index, and we can infer that the hedonic is better. Other authors have carried out similar analyses, with corresponding results; for example, Dulberger (1989) and Silver and Heravi (2002). But overall, too few studies have done so.

It is important to bear in mind that the matched model method is actually a group of methods, for quality change is handled in different ways in different situations, and the methods employed differ somewhat in different countries.[6] The popular view that nonhedonic price indexes have no quality adjustments is incorrect. Rather, all indexes are quality adjusted, explicitly or implicitly (but it is often the latter, which makes the analysis of them difficult).

For the dominant procedure used in the U.S. CPI and in many other indexes, the bias from matching is a complex interaction between the method used by the agency and the economics of the market. Price changes—up or down—that accompany the introduction of a new product variety will tend to be "linked out" of the index. Thus the index will fail to pick up all price declines when, as is true for computers, prices are falling. Symmetrically, it misses some inflation when prices are rising. The quantitative importance of this failure has been established in a study by Moulton and Moses (1997).

In comparing hedonic indexes and matched model indexes, the salient points are as follows:

---

6. See the presentation to the Brookings measurement workshop by Jorgen Dalen, summarized on the Brookings website (www.brookings.edu).

—The matched model index tends to link out too much price change when price changes and quality changes occur simultaneously. The bias is upward when prices are falling, but downward when prices are rising.

—The hedonic index, no matter how it is implemented, implies a quality-adjusted price change for new and disappearing models. They are not ignored, or "linked out" but incorporated into the price index when they are introduced.

—Taking these two points together, one can see the symmetry of the studies in table 10-2. Where price declines are particularly rapid, the hedonic index records more price change, because the matched model index tends to link out some of the downward price movement of new varieties, where the hedonic index incorporates them. However, when the new varieties are introduced at higher prices, the matched model index symmetrically misses price increases, when the hedonic index includes them. The analysis in Silver and Heravi (2002) indicates that this latter situation applies to their results, even though their appliance indexes are falling.

In summary, the analysis of differences in hedonic and matched model indexes goes a long way toward resolving some of the debates that have long surrounded them. We understand that new methods are sometimes mistrusted, and that statistical agencies need to be conservative, to an extent. But the introduction of hedonic indexes for high-tech products marks effective measurement of their price changes, which would not have been done adequately with older methods. No real evidence exists that hedonic indexes for IT products have overstated their price decline. The debate on "whether hedonic indexes?" is over. The debate now concerns how to improve them.[7]

Price Trends for Communications Equipment and Semiconductors

U.S. investment in information technology (IT) accelerated after 1995. Investment surged in all major components of IT (computer equipment, communications equipment, and software). The data—particularly the price data—for the two hardware components differ in ways that are perplexing.

Between 1990 and 1995, domestic computer equipment prices (computers plus peripherals) fell about 14 percent a year, as measured in the national accounts; after 1995, the rate of decline stepped up, to 22 percent a year (table 10-3). The drop in computer prices has been fueled by astonishing declines in

7. We judge "how to improve them" to be the thrust of the Committee on National Statistics Report's chapter on hedonic indexes and quality change (Schultze and Mackie, 2002, chap. 4), though some readers have interpreted the chapter differently.

Table 10-3. *BLS and BEA High-Tech Price Indexes, 1990–2000*
Average annual rates of change

SIC	Industry	1990–95	1995–2000	1995–2001
Computers				
	BEA computers and peripheral equipment	–13.7	–21.6	–21.0
	BEA domestic computers and peripheral equipment total	–14.2	–23.9	–23.3
357	PPI office, computing, and accounting machines	n.a.	–10.1	–9.4
3571	PPI electronic computers	–11.8[a]	–16.8	–15.9
Communications equipment				
	BEA communications equipment	–1.2	–3.4[b]	–3.5
366	PPI communications equipment	1.2	–0.6	–0.8
3661	PPI telephone and telegraph apparatus	1.1	–0.9	–1.4
Semiconductors				
3674	PPI semiconductors	–2.7	–7.1	–6.7
3674#1A1	PPI MOS and related devices	–6.9	–18.4	–20.9
3674#1A1201	PPI microprocessors	–8.1	–52.9	–53.4
	BEA memory chips[b,c]	–13.8	n.a.[d]	. . .
	BEA microprocessors[b,c]	–39.6	n.a.[d]	. . .
365	PPI radio and TV receiving equipment, except communication types	–0.6	–1.3	–1.5

Source: BEA, NIPA, table 5.5.4 (Price Indexes for Private Fixed Investment in Equipment and Software by Type, last revised January 16, 2004), www.bea.gov (May 2004); and BLS, producer price index industry data.
  n.a. Not available.
  a. 1991–95.
  b. Worldwide prices.
  c. Grimm (1998, pp. 8–24).
  d. Discontinued series (BEA uses PPI indexes now).

the prices of semiconductors, particularly microprocessor chips—more than 50 percent a year between 1995 and 2000 (PPI series; table 10-3).[8]

Communications equipment manufacturing is also a heavy consumer of semiconductors. But in contrast to the dramatic story for computer equipment

8. Technological change has also been very rapid in some components of computer equipment where semiconductors are not the source of the improvement. For example, the manufacture of hard drives does not rely on technological change in semiconductors. However, technological change in hard drives is the product of the same miniaturization technology that fuels technological change in the manufacture of semiconductors.

prices, the PPI index for the communications equipment industry (old SIC366) rose between 1990 and 1995 and fell modestly after 1995 (table 10-3). The BEA price deflator for communications equipment investment in the national accounts shows declines throughout the 1990s, but at a very modest rate nowhere nearly comparable to the deflator for computer equipment.

Jorgenson and Stiroh (2000) and Jorgenson (2001) have suggested that because of their semiconductor content the price indexes for communications equipment should more nearly resemble computer equipment price indexes. Additionally, Doms and Forman (2001) note that more patents have been issued in communications than in semiconductors, so clearly much innovation has occurred in communications equipment. What can account for differences in the price indexes for these two major IT-producing industries? The question is particularly intriguing because the computer equipment indexes published by the statistical agencies are mostly hedonic price indexes, whereas the PPI communications equipment indexes are not.

The communications industry is the most IT-intensive industry in our data, but communications equipment is used widely. This equipment is a high-tech input to many industries, not only to the communications industry. Most local area network (LAN) equipment, for example, is located in industries other than communications. Capital inputs from communications equipment influence productivity in most of our services industries.

Interpreting Government Price Indexes and Research Studies

In interpreting research on semiconductor and communications equipment prices and the relevant government price indexes, it is important to bear in mind the diversity in technologies employed in these products and in their price movements. Many types of semiconductors exist, and there are many types of computer equipment and communications equipment.

Within each of these categories, price trends are not homogeneous in government data. For example, the PPI index for the semiconductor *industry* (SIC 3674) fell about 7 percent annually in the late 1990s, but this figure was far less than the PPI for microprocessors (50 percent a year; see table 10-3).

Similar differences exist within computer equipment. For the broader aggregate computers and peripherals (old SIC 357), the PPI declined only about 10 percent a year. The PPI for the computer industry (old SIC 3571) fell faster, about 17 percent annually for 1995–2000 (tables 10-3 and 10-4). But within that 17 percent aggregate computer industry price decline, PC computer prices declined more than 30 percent a year in the PPI data, while large mainframe computer prices declined about 12 percent a year (table 10-4). In the aggregate

Table 10-4. *Detailed BLS and BEA Computer Equipment Price Indexes,*
1990–2000

Average annual rates of change

SIC	Industry	1990–95	1995–2000	1995–2001
Computers				
3571	PPI electronic computers	−11.8[a]	−16.8	−15.9
	BEA domestic computers and peripheral equipment total	−14.2	−23.9	−23.3
3571#11	PPI large-scale	−9.7[a]	−11.8	−13.3
3571#12	PPI mid-range	−4.3[b]	−20.5	−22.1
	BEA domestic mainframes	−14.1	−26.5	−26.5
3571#15	PPI portable computers	−19.8[b]	−34.1	−33.9
3571#14	PPI PCs and workstations	−15.6[b]	−31.9	−31.5
	BEA domestic PCs	−19.0	−32.4	−32.0
Peripherals				
3575	PPI terminals	−1.8[c]	−1.5	−1.3
	BEA computer terminals	−10.2	−9.0	−8.6
3571	PPI storage devices	−12.7[b]	−11.8	−11.2
	BEA computer storage devices[d,e]	−8.8	−14.9	−14.3
3577	PPI peripherals, n.e.c.[f]	−2.1[c]	−3.8	−3.3
	BEA computer peripheral equipment, n.e.c.[d,e,f]	−11.4	−13.4	−11.7
	BEA domestic and foreign computers	−13.6	−22.2	. . .

Source: BEA, NIPA, table 5.5.4 (Price Indexes for Private Fixed Investment in Equipment and Software by Type, last revised January 16, 2004), www.bea.gov (May 2004); and BLS, producer price index industry data.
  a. 1991–95.
  b. 1993–95.
  c. 1994–95.
  d. Includes imports.
  e. Data from BEA, National Economic Accounts (Additional Table).
  f. Printers are located in this component.

index, the price declines for computers were diluted with those for peripheral equipment, such as terminals, which declined only about 1.5 percent a year (see table 10-4).

Comparisons among research studies or among different government computer equipment indexes are very sensitive to the level of aggregation at which the comparisons are made. The same point undoubtedly applies to communications equipment: from what we know about the manufacturing technologies, we should not expect that price change for the rest of telecommunications equipment necessarily looks like the price declines for LAN equipment.

Semiconductor Input Costs to Computer and Communications Industries

Computer equipment and communications equipment production both use semiconductors, but the similarity ends there. Many types of semiconductors exist. To explain the impact of chip prices on the two using industries, Aizcorbe, Flamm, and Khurshid (2002) first explore whether the mix of semiconductors used in the manufacture of computer equipment differs from the mix used to make communications equipment. Their "computer equipment" end-user category is approximately SIC 357 (computer and peripheral manufacturing) and "communications equipment" approximates SIC 3661 (telephone apparatus manufacturing).

More than half of the chip inputs to computer manufacturing are microprocessor and memory chips. For communications equipment, far more of the semiconductor inputs are the older technologies. Thus the mix of semiconductor inputs differs.

The mix question only becomes interesting if the prices for different types of semiconductors diverge. Using detailed data that distinguish twelve classes of semiconductors, Aizcorbe, Flamm, and Khurshid (2002—hereafter, AFK) confirm the dispersion of price movements in the PPI shown in table 10-3 (though not necessarily the rates of change). Newer-technology semiconductors that are used more intensively in computer manufacturing have prices that fall more rapidly than the older types that account for a larger share of semiconductor inputs to communications equipment.[9]

AFK estimate that costs of semiconductor inputs contribute about 16 percentage points of decline annually to computer manufacturing costs. But semiconductor inputs contribute only about 4 percentage points of decline annually to communications equipment manufacturing costs.[10] Taken by itself, differences in their semiconductor costs should lead to differences in the two industries' output price indexes of about 12 percentage points annually.

Table 10-3 shows that price indexes for computer and communications equipment industries differ, but that the difference depends on the level of detail and also on which agency's data are examined. The PPI indexes for electronic

9. Because they use worldwide weights, these calculations may understate the inter-industry difference. U.S. production of computer equipment is heavily skewed toward high-end technologies, so domestic production probably uses a larger share of high-end chips than does worldwide computer equipment production.

10. These are rough estimates because purchases of semiconductors are not recorded very well in government data on either industry. This is an old problem that plagues the analysis of the U.S. high-tech sector. See Triplett (1996).

computers (SIC 3571) and telecommunications equipment (SIC 3661) differ by about 14 points a year; in recent years (that is, for 1995–2001, the two indexes decline by 15.9 and 1.4 percent a year), which is similar to AFK's 12-point semiconductor cost differential. The BEA deflators suggest a far larger difference, approaching 20 points a year, mainly because the BEA computer indexes fall so much more than the PPI, even though they are derived from PPI indexes (see table 10-3).[11] BEA communications equipment deflators are close to the corresponding PPI indexes.[12]

Several qualifications apply. AFK believe that the newer, more technologically dynamic chips (for which price indexes drop the fastest) are better measured than the price indexes for the older kinds of chips, which have received less research attention. Perhaps the differences among *recorded* price movements for different kinds of chips reflect partly measurement differences. If so, their semiconductor indexes understate the price decline.

Second, one would like ideally to explore the relation between input cost and output price measures for IT at a very detailed commodity level, distinguishing the mix of inputs to detailed items of equipment. Prices of PCs fall more rapidly than, say, prices of terminals, probably because PCs use more of the most rapidly falling semiconductor chips. Similarly, the semiconductor mix for the switches and routers studied by Doms and Foreman, which are probably technologically similar to computer processors, undoubtedly differs from the mix of semiconductors used for telephone handsets (which are analogous in their function to computer terminals). Thus to use differential semiconductor costs to explain the differences in price movements between the communications equipment and computer equipment industries, one should start by trying to account for the differences in price movements among products within the industries, using their differences in semiconductor inputs. Data limitations, however, prevent work at this level of detail.

A third issue is relevant but has not been explored. Substitution among different items of computer and communications equipment may shift the mix of

---

11. BEA investment deflators include imported equipment, while the PPI covers only domestic production. A separate BEA index for domestic computer equipment falls a bit more rapidly than the overall investment deflator, though in some cases imports have declined in price more rapidly (terminals, for example). Additionally, BEA and PPI computer equipment indexes may differ because of weighting effects; the BEA Fisher index for peripherals (which includes printers, monitors, and scanners) differs from the PPI fixed-weight Laspeyres index for the same products.

12. The choice between three-digit (366) and four-digit (3661) PPIs is not a factor in these comparisons because they record similar price changes. See table 10-3.

semiconductors inputs into the two industries. Throughout the long history of computer equipment, the products with the smallest rates of price decline systematically exhibit shrinking market shares. Tape drives were supplanted by disk drives for auxiliary storage, for example, and PCs have eroded mainframe computer market shares; both are classic textbook cases of commodity substitution by users in response to relative price change. These shifts in relative prices may reflect differences in semiconductor uses and cost trends attributable to semiconductor technology. But in turn, at the level of aggregate computer equipment production, end-user commodity substitution alters the mix of semiconductors by increasing the shares of semiconductor inputs with the most rapidly falling prices. In other words, the whole question of semiconductor input shares is endogenous.

Substitution among different types of communications equipment might be less possible and therefore have less effect on the semiconductor mix used in production of communications equipment. Again, few data exist to explore this question in the detail that one might desire.

Leaving these qualifications aside, if the BEA computer equipment deflators are measured correctly, that leaves roughly 8 percentage points of annual change (that is, the 20-point differential between the computer and communications equipment price indexes, less the 12-point predicted difference from semiconductor costs) to be explained by factors other than semiconductors. Those factors include measurement error in the price indexes for communications equipment. This is the problem that Doms and Forman (2003) and Doms (2003) address.

Communications Equipment Prices

Doms and Forman (2003) estimated price indexes for four types of LAN, or local area network equipment—switches, routers, hubs, and interface cards. This equipment carries out switching and traffic control functions, mainly for data communications, and mostly for users within the same LAN. They found a range of price declines for the equipment they studied, from 14 percent annually for all sizes of routers to 22 percent annually for LAN switches (table 10-5). All of the Doms-Forman indexes declined considerably faster than the PPI index for telecommunications equipment (SIC 3661).[13] In consequence of these

13. In their paper, they apparently compared their indexes with the PPI for industry SIC 3667, "other communications equipment," a miscellaneous grouping that includes fire and burglar alarms and traffic signals. However, as this PPI index does not differ that much from the PPI index for telecommunications equipment, this does not have much of a bearing on the interpretation of their study.

Table 10-5. *Research Price Indexes for Communication Equipment*
Various periods, average annual percentage rates of change

Component/aggregate	Change (percent)
Components	
Routers (1995–99)[1a]	–13.6
Switches (1996–2000)[1b]	–21.9
Hubs (1996–2000)[1b]	–30.1
LAN cards (1995–2000)[1c]	–18.3
Modems (1994–2000)[2a]	–23.3
PBX/KTS (1995–2000)[2b]	–4.8
Total fiber-optics equipment (1994–2000)[2a]	–10.1
Aggregates	
PPI communications equipment, SIC 366 (1994–2000)[3]	–0.4
PPI telephone apparatus, SIC 3661 (1995–2000)[3]	–0.6
BEA communications equipment (1995–2000)[4]	–3.3
Doms communications equipment, "conservative" (1994–2000)[2c]	–5.4
Doms communications equipment, "moderate" (1994–2000)[2c]	–8.3
Doms communications equipment, "aggressive" (1994–2000)[2c]	–10.6

Sources:
1. Doms and Forman (2003).
  a. Table 6; b. figure 3; c. table 9.
2. Doms (2003).
  a. Table 14; b. table 5; c. table 17.
3. BLS PPI industry data.
4. BEA NIPA table 5.5.4.

great price declines, and also of the growth of data communications (which may itself be a consequence of the price declines for data communications equipment), investment in LAN equipment has expanded very rapidly. They note that it accounted for $3 billion of U.S. investment in 1992 but expanded to $16 billion in 1999. Data in Sichel (2001) suggest that LAN equipment accounts for about 17 percent of communication investment in 1999.[14]

14. Sichel (2001, table 2).

In subsequent work, Doms (2003) reports new price indexes for modems, PBX/KTS (internal telephone network switching equipment), and price indexes (less precisely estimated) for equipment that process communications in fiber-optic technology. Price indexes for these three components drop at rates from 5 percent annually to 23 percent per year (table 10-5). Again, all decline more rapidly than the PPI index for the communications equipment industry.

Doms (2003) aggregates the components index estimates from table 10-5 into an estimated price index for the whole communications equipment category. He makes the "conservative" assumption that all PPI price indexes for categories of equipment that are presently unstudied are correct and combines those components with research prices indexes from the ones discussed in preceding paragraphs and others. This gives a PPI-like deflator for communications equipment that falls by 5.4 percent a year from 1994 through 2000, when the published PPI showed only −0.4 percent annual price decline. Doms also makes "moderate" and "aggressive" assumption estimates, which decline more (table 10-5).

A Proposed Reconciliation

PPI product indexes and census industry and product detail do not provide adequate or obvious matches for the LAN equipment products studied by Doms and Forman. We thus proceed another way.

Current PPI indexes for industry 3661 are the product of a communications equipment industry sample that was introduced in December 2000 (*PPI Detailed Report*, January 2001). The last PPI sample initiation before that was about 1993. Investment in LAN equipment grew very rapidly in the second half of the 1990s. We speculate that LAN equipment was underrepresented substantially in the telecommunications equipment PPI in the second half of the 1990s because it was less important when the last sample was drawn and because the PPI uses a fixed-weight index number system.

To put a bound on the estimates, suppose that LAN equipment and the modems, internal switching gear, and fiber optic equipment studied by Doms, were missing entirely from the 1993 PPI sample used for the last half of the 1990s. On this assumption, we can combine Doms and Forman's roughly 18–20 percent a year decline for LAN equipment with the rest of the PPI to produce an "adjusted PPI," provided we know the weight of LAN equipment in industry 3661. Using Sichel's weight (17 percent, which may be an understatement), the PPI 3661 industry index would have dropped by 4–5 percent a year, rather than the published 0.9 percent.

An alternative estimate comes from Doms (2003), who estimates the aggregated price decline of all products for which research indexes exist: he gets −14.0 percent annually, for 1994–2000.[15] On his "conservative" assumption (no bias for any product that has not yet been studied), the PPI would decline by 5.4 percent a year during the same period, an estimate that is in the same range.

AFK suggested that semiconductor inputs contribute about 4 percentage points of decline annually to costs of communications equipment. This is similar to the average rate of decline in the "adjusted PPI" above and in the conservative estimate by Doms. That is, if all of the other items of communications equipment in the PPI were measured correctly, but the PPI missed the rapidly growing components of LAN equipment and other new equipment in the second half of the 1990s, or included them with insufficient weight, this would account for all of the 4 percentage point contribution of semiconductor inputs suggested by AFK, or even a bit more.

However, note that AFK estimated that computer industry costs declined 16 percentage points annually because of price declines in its weighted semiconductor input mix. The BEA deflator for domestic computers and peripherals declined 24 percent a year (table 10-3), over 50 percent more than "predicted" from its semiconductor costs.[16] How can that be? Three possibilities exist.

First, BEA computer price indexes may have declined too fast. We do not put much weight on this alternative, though we recognize that others may find it appealing.

Second, AFK use worldwide prices and worldwide weights. It is likely that U.S. computer equipment production uses more of the highest-technology semiconductors, whose prices are falling most rapidly. If so, AFK's end-user semiconductor indexes might understate the fall in semiconductor prices to the U.S. computer industry.

Finally, as already noted, AFK are more confident in their price indexes for the more advanced semiconductors and less confident in the measurement for some of the other classes. If those other semiconductors were falling in price more rapidly than their data indicate (as AFK suggest), that might also contribute to understatement of the cost declines experienced by computer manufacturers—and understate communications equipment semiconductor costs, as well.

---

15. Doms (2003, table 14).

16. As noted, the PPI counterpart declined only 10 percent a year during the same period, for reasons that are not entirely clear, but are probably connected with the following: (1) in a few cases, BEA maintained its own indexes into this period, and (2) differences in the aggregates are created by Fisher index and Laspeyres index formulas.

Those less advanced semiconductors are used more intensively in communications equipment manufacturing. If the price declines for those semiconductors are understated in the AFK study, then the true contribution of semiconductors to cost decline in communications equipment was greater than the 4 percentage points a year that they estimate. In this case, then, there is additional room for potential mismeasurement in the output of the communications equipment industry beyond the products examined by Doms and Forman, so the "conservative" estimate by Doms, as well as our reconciliation estimate, understates bias in communications equipment price indexes.

Issues for Further Research

Obviously, more studies on communications equipment are needed to improve our estimates of these products. The potential of fiber optics and the adequacy of statistical methods are also subjects for further investigation.

Fiber Optics

The potential of fiber optics has received great attention in the press and elsewhere. Fiber-optic technology increases the size of bandwidth, that is, the number of communications that can go through the system, and not primarily (as with LAN equipment and other switchgear) the speed of connections or data transmission. Preliminary price indexes for switching and connecting equipment for fiber-optic data transmissions, comparable to the LAN equipment studied by Doms and Forman, are in Doms (2003).

Much of the investment spending on fiber optics goes into communications structures investment—digging the holes to lay the fiber-optic lines is a major part of the expenditure on them. Even if fiber-optics *equipment* is declining in price, the total cost of fiber-optics investment may not be declining rapidly (because digging does not seem to be among the economy's technologically advancing sectors—see our estimates of negative construction industry productivity growth in chapter 2). Moreover, from an economywide perspective the total cost of fiber optics is probably understated because municipalities, caught up in the new economy hype, failed to ensure that companies laying the fiber optics restored streets to their previous condition.

Investment in fiber optics is clearly directed toward building capacity for the future. Because capital stock intended for future use will not be used to capacity currently, our capital service estimates will overstate the contribution of communications equipment IT to industry productivity. As a consequence, it will show up as a drag on the current measure of MFP in services and other industries that use communications equipment. Proper accounting for fiber optics awaits further research and data development, which deserves priority.

PPI Resampling

We speculated that the PPI for communications equipment might have missed price decreases because of its relatively long interval between resamplings. Previous research for other products, including Dulberger (1993) on semiconductors, and Berndt, Griliches, and Rosett (1993) on pharmaceuticals, shows the same thing. In technologically dynamic products, most of the "action" is in the new varieties. When the product samples are not kept up to date, much of the price change will be missed. Similar findings for nontechnological products in Silver and Heravi (2002) indicate that this problem may be widespread (they studied household appliances).

The PPI has been expanded rapidly into services industries in recent years. The professional staff of the PPI has done an extraordinary job on filling out price information for services industries, work that is impressively innovative and essential for understanding the U.S. economy in the twenty-first century.

However, it has sometimes not been recognized that the services industry work has been done on a shoestring. The PPI services initiative was financed in part by stealing resources away from the PPIs for industries producing high-tech goods.[17] Understanding the modern U.S. economy requires data on services, it is true, but not at the expense of data that help us understand our industries that produce high-tech goods. The high-tech goods-producing portions of the PPI require up-to-date, rapidly replenished samples and attention to improved methods for quality adjustment, even if that implies more resources.

This problem, summarized above, was discussed in a Brookings workshop, "Communications Output and Productivity" (February 23, 2001). In response, Irwin Gerduk of the Bureau of Labor Statistics (BLS) at another workshop, "The Adequacy of Data for Analyzing and Forecasting the High-Tech Sector" (October 12, 2001), presented an initiative for revising PPI samples more frequently to achieve adequate coverage of new products in high-tech sectors. These new PPI plans are intended to reduce the new item bias in its measures of price changes for technological equipment that arose from holding the PPI sam-

---

17. The widely acknowledged "Boskin Statistics Initiative" (Survey of Current Business, February 1990) contained funds for a substantial expansion of BLS average hourly earnings for services industries (even though comprehensive industry earnings measures had been available for years in quarterly or annual form). But it contained nearly nothing for the far more important statistical lacuna of price indexes for these industries. That budgetary imbalance has not been fully corrected in the intervening decade.

ples fixed for too long a period. The BLS explained that, owing to previous budget stringency, reinitiations of PPI samples were curtailed, but the BLS has applied recent expansions of resources to what it agreed had become a serious problem. As just suggested, static PPI samples, initiated around 1993, seemed to have missed many of the new products that dominated investment in communications equipment in the late 1990s.

Workshop participants agreed that the BLS initiatives should provide substantial improvement in the measures of communications equipment investment but stressed that much of the sector is not yet covered adequately in the research and price statistics. A wide range of communications equipment is undergoing rapid quality change. Concern was also expressed about the adequacy of current methods for measuring the depreciation of high-tech capital.

The Brookings workshop (October 2001) brought forth considerable discussion of the advisability of using statistical methods for high tech, including hedonic price adjustment, that differed from the methods used for other sectors. Some participants thought it was a positive example of tailoring the methodology to the industry, while others worried about comparability of the results for producing a coherent view of the aggregate economy. We believe that comparability, though always desirable, should not be made the enemy of improvements.

Software

Expenditures on software in the U.S. national accounts are as large as investment in computer hardware. Prud'homme and Yu (2002) report that in the Canadian national accounts software expenditures exceeded computer equipment expenditures by 38 percent in 2001. Measuring software is fraught with difficulties, and far less progress has been made than on measuring capital investment in hardware components of IT.

To begin, it is usual in national accounts and elsewhere to group software investment into three categories—standardized (or prepackaged), custom software, and own-account software. The latter two categories are both custom software; they differ by who does it. Custom software is purchased by the user from another firm. Own-account software is constructed by the using firm. In Canada investment in prepackaged software has grown at 20 percent a year; its share, only 18 percent of software investment in 1981, it has more than doubled, to 45 percent in 2001. During the same period, the share of own-account software has declined from 60 percent to 25 percent of the total (Prud'homme and Yu, 2002). Trends in the United States are similar.

However, at the Brookings economic measurement workshop on software and housing (May 2003), IBM economists Ellen Dulberger and Patrick McMahon disputed the usefulness of this basic three-way classification. They observed that most custom software includes installation of prepackaged elements of software and that the three-way grouping ignored integration and support costs of software that were relevant to costs of using software. As Dulberger put it, "In actually purchasing a package . . . there are a number of associated costs such as implementing the package, doing the integration with other software accounts and then providing ongoing support and management of that application, in whatever environment it has been implemented in. Those are all relevant to the cost of implementing and using application packages."

Ana Aizcorbe also emphasized the point made by Dulberger: there are many ways that firms acquire software, "and sometimes they acquire it in a way that feels more like a service." In those cases, it is difficult to disentangle the part of the price that is for software and the part that corresponds to services that the vendor provides to the purchaser. In this way of looking at it, software consulting and support (generally placed by government statistics in other SIC industries) is integral with the use of software. It is not possible to consider software statistics for the three categories by themselves.

This point seems to be most relevant to the question of what should be capitalized in national accounts. The 1993 System of National Accounts (Commission of the European Communities, 1993) recommended that software expenditures be capitalized in national accounts. This step was followed by the Bureau of Economic Analysis (BEA) in 1999, as Brent Moulton's presentation to the Brookings workshop (May 2003) brought out. The IBM objection can be interpreted as saying that if one only capitalized expenditures on the three categories (prepackaged, custom, and own account) as if they were individual industry outputs that were purchased separately as investment, not all of the costs of software investment were capitalized. Presumably, when software consultants recommend a packaged application software, this is unambiguously counted in the output of the prepackaged software industry; on the other hand, possibly it is not. The "computers and office machines" Current Industrial Reports (CIR) includes "non-manufacturing revenue" of roughly $250 million, which comes from extra revenue from loading software onto hardware. Of course, sales of secondary products are included in all industrial statistics. But perhaps, as the IBM economists suggested, data are not cleanly separated between the three basic software categories in national accounts. Note the connection, here, with the often-stated proposition that "reengineering" and "coinvestment" costs of implementing IT may be as large as the IT purchases (Brynjolfsson, Hitt, and Yang 2002).

Without minimizing the potential inadequacies of the three-way classification for software, we believe it is still useful for discussing the measurement problems that software poses. For any product, measurement issues include obtaining revenue or expenditures on the product, measuring price indexes for deflation, and defining taxonomy to guide what is measured.

Expenditure

On the expenditure side, the situation is not as good as one might like it to be. The trend of output for the prepackaged software industry is clouded by some industry and product classification issues, in common with similar problems in some other services and high-tech industries.

Expenditures on prepackaged software for business investment and for consumption exist, but interpretation of those expenditures must take into account that much software is bundled with some other expenditure, either with software consulting and support, as the IBM economists suggested, or with purchases of hardware. Abel, Berndt, and White (2003) report that "volume licensing sales have largely replaced the shrink-wrapped full packaged product sales" that dominated Microsoft sales in the early 1990s. Most of these license sales were to computer manufacturers and other hardware producers, so the end product reached the consumer through a purchase of a bundle of computer hardware and software.

At the other end of the scale, expenditures on own-account software must be estimated from a variety of sources. As Brent Moulton's presentation to the Brookings workshop (May 2003) indicated, country practices for estimating expenditures on own-account software differ greatly. An OECD taskforce noted that the share of own-account software in total software investment ranged from more than 40 percent in Denmark and France to half that, or less, in Sweden and Israel (Lequiller and others, 2003). Other OECD studies have noted that the proportion of software investment, especially own-account software investment, to computer equipment investment was twice as high in the United States as in the United Kingdom. Francois Lequiller and others (2003) concluded that the estimates differed by more than the actual volumes of investment differed.

We concur that the share of software in IT investment and in total investment is not a very firm number. We are not sure whether the available evidence suggests that the estimated share is too small (which would mean that we understate the contribution of IT in table 10-1) or too large. If it is too large, then we overstate the contribution of IT in our work and in consequence understate the improvement in MFP in IT-using industries.

Price Indexes for Prepackaged Software

Though no one thinks that the price of the packaged software is measured very well, it seems paradoxical but true that this might be the best piece of information on software that is currently available. Two relatively recent papers are Prud'homme and Yu (2002) and Abel, Berndt, and White (2003).

Both papers present nearly identical tables that summarize previous price index research on software.[18] The earlier studies cover mostly spreadsheets, word processing, and database software in various periods from 1986 to the present, and in two countries, the United States and Germany. These previous studies estimate price declines at rates from 2.5 percent to 16 percent a year. The U.S. PPI also contains a price index for software since 1997. It has been declining about 6 percent a year. The BEA software deflator was originally built on some of the earlier research studies; when it subsequently incorporated the PPI software index in 1997, BEA made a "bias adjustment" based on the earlier studies.

Though their price index procedures are very similar (both use frequently weighted, traditional matched model methods), the coverage of the Prud'homme and Yu (hereafter PY) and Abel, Berndt, and White (hereafter ABW) studies could not be more different. PY estimate price indexes for some thirty-five different categories of products, using data from retail stores sales provided by AC Nielsen Company. They thus have a very wide range of products but cover only sales through retail outlets. They include no software provided through the vehicle of bundling with hardware or by license.

ABW cover the products of only one company, Microsoft, grouped into four categories. But their data cover all distribution channels—for example, Excel sold as a stand-alone package, Excel within a suite of software (such as Microsoft Office), and Excel provided, usually within a suite, as bundled software on a new computer. Their data also distinguish maintenance agreements and license arrangements, primarily for business users. Though they note in their text that different forms of delivery imply different prices for the software, they do not actually present price indexes for different distribution channels— stand-alone "shrink wrapped" software, for example, compared with prices paid by original equipment computer manufacturers for the same products. For the period 1993–2001, their "all Microsoft products" index declines at an

18. Prud'homme and Yu (2002, table 8); Abel, Berndt, and White (2003, table 4).

average of 4.3 percent a year, and it declines more since 1997 than the PPI index for software.

Prud'homme and Yu emphasize the tremendous variation in price behavior for different categories of software. Over their 1996–2000 interval, combined business applications dropped at 4.4 percent per year. But within the total business category, networking software increased 18 percent a year, while electronic forms software fell more than 18 percent a year. Yu emphasized in his Brookings presentation (May 2003 workshop) that selecting a small number of software packages for pricing, as is commonly done, can produce very misleading results. For example, BEA uses early studies on spreadsheets and word processor programs to make a "bias adjustment" in the PPI software index. Yu described this as "quite dangerous" because the price movements for one or two categories may not be representative of what is happening in software prices for other categories.

Ana Aizcorbe, in her Brookings discussion, emphasized the same point as Yu: software consists of "a broad array of different products, and this makes it difficult for someone trying to measure prices to go and pluck a few representative goods with which to represent the whole industry."

Both papers, reflecting the concentration in the price index number literature on index number formulas, presented Paasche, Laspeyres, and Fisher index numbers and spent considerable space on comparing their movements. In the Canadian study, the Laspeyres index of software prices rose 18 percent annually, but a Paasche price index for the same software declined nearly 25 percent a year. Yu remarked in the Brookings workshop (May 2003) that "those two indexes don't make much sense." Following the prescriptions in the index number literature, PY therefore computed a Fisher index, which is a geometric mean of the Paasche and Laspeyres.

Jack Triplett wondered whether the geometric mean of two measures that don't make sense itself makes sense. Roger Betancourt responded in a similar way, as he called attention to studies that suggest serious problems with doing chain indexes at monthly frequencies. Though PY certainly had a point that monthly weights were better than no weights at all (Yu compared an index without weights to adding a Volvo and a submarine), there seemed to be index number problems at this level that are not satisfactorily resolved by the theoretical framework that lies behind the "superlative" index (the Fisher index is a superlative index). The appropriate economic model for handling high-frequency indexes has not yet been developed.[19]

19. See the introduction to Feenstra and Shapiro (2003).

ABW, however, found a different Paasche-Laspeyres problem: in their data, the Paasche index rises more rapidly than the Laspeyres index. With their interpretation of index number theory, this is an anomaly. It is not clear why they say this, however: the theory of the output price index predicts that a Paasche index will rise more rapidly than will a Laspeyres, because sellers want to shift their sales toward products whose prices increase (Fisher and Shell 1972). ABW have constructed a price index for the output of one company, so it seems ideally to fit the framework of the output price index theory.[20]

Though PY and ABW focused on the index number problems, the discussion of the papers brought out other measurement difficulties. The retail part of the market that was covered in the PY data is only a very small part of the present distribution of software. One would like to know whether prices in different channels are moving differently. Perhaps the levels are different, but the rates of change are similar.

Another point has to do with constructing what PY call "maximum overlap" indexes with monthly chaining. The maximum overlap method brings new products into the index as soon as possible. There is little question that bringing new products in quickly is greatly superior to holding the price index sample fixed over a long period. If the price change occurs after the product is introduced and the product is picked up quickly, and the weight is adjusted as the weight changes, then the price index should pick up all of the true change in price.

But still, price change may be introduced, not after the new product appears, but at the point at which it appears. If a new version of the software is introduced at a quality-corrected price that is higher or lower than the one it replaces, the instantaneous price change that accompanies the introduction of that new software will not be picked up in a matched model index, frequently reweighted or not (as noted earlier in this chapter). Many of the changes in software, especially upgrades and new versions of existing software, raise serious questions on that score.

One also wants a methodology to correct the price index for any new features that one gets from Microsoft Word 10, or whatever, and possibly also to adjust for the features one liked in version 9 (the ease of doing something simple, for example) that have been deleted in version 10. This is a price measurement issue for all high-tech products, not just for software. There is little evidence in favor

20. Ernst Berndt noted that the theory of the output price index applies to a competitive industry, not to one where there is a dominant seller. Even a monopolist who sold two products, however, might shift output toward the product whose price rose more rapidly, if that occurred because demand elasticities for that product were rising.

of the notion that no price index changes are missed if one just computes a monthly, chained index with monthly weights, especially in a market where producers are introducing new products in order to find and exploit market niches.

Custom Software and Own-Account Software

One can debate the merits of price indexes that have been estimated by government agencies and by researchers for prepackaged software. But no price indexes exist for custom software or for own-account software.

In the national accounts, BEA assumed that labor productivity in custom software was unchanged, so output was extrapolated by labor input. Software production makes extensive use of IT equipment, especially of computers, and the amount of IT capital employed in producing software has increased greatly, as it has in most service industries. BEA's assumption of zero labor productivity growth in the production of custom software thus amounts to an assumption that multifactor productivity in custom software has been declining. That does not seem a reasonable assumption.

Kent Kunze's (2003) paper for the Brookings workshop (May 2003) discussed a new BLS measure of labor productivity for the software industry. Though the BLS measure covered prepackaged software, not custom software, part of the interest in this new measure concerned the light it might shed on the BEA zero productivity assumption, as evidenced by Brent Moulton's comments on it.

To estimate real output for its labor productivity measure, BLS simply deflated software industry receipts from the Census Bureau by the PPI price index for software, linked to the BEA software deflator for the years before 1997. That is, of course, standard procedure. However, it raises all of the questions about the price index for software that were discussed in the previous section. With this output measure, BLS estimates that labor productivity in prepackaged software has advanced 20 percent a year over the entire 1987–2000 interval for which the measures have been produced.[21] Labor productivity actually decelerated in this industry after 1995, to 8.6 percent a year.

It is not clear that the BLS productivity measure for prepackaged software is instructive for measuring labor productivity in own-account and custom software. For the latter two types of software, better output measures are needed. Much interest exists in trying to model the performance of software, in ways that are parallel with models of the performance of computers and other electronic equipment. In the hardware components, the performance measures used

21. Kunze (2003, table 2).

by economists and in hedonic price indexes originated in research by computer scientists on the improved performance of computers (Triplett, 2003).

Some have proposed measuring software with what are called "function points." Function points have been explored in some software technical and engineering literature, and considered by a number of statistical agencies, including BEA and the Australian Bureau of Statistics. They were recommended in a widely circulated report by McKinsey Global Institute (2001).

Patrick McMahon of IBM remarked in the Brookings workshop (May 2003) that he was in the business of outsourcing and application management services for software. He and his colleagues often talked about how one can "measure the output of the work that we're doing and how to quantify that output." He indicated that the discussions were "very interesting," but they did not have an answer to the economists' problem of measuring software. Ellen Dulberger indicated that the general consensus of the computer software industry is quite critical of the function point approach. Thus, at present, finding a productivity measure for the production of software and using that to generate estimates for the output of software (and implicitly the price) does not seem very close to an operational solution.

Finally, there is the problem of own-account software. Here, there is no price index. There is also dispute about the size of the implied expenditure. As Moulton described in his presentation to the Brookings workshop, different countries have taken very different approaches to measuring own-account software.[22] As a result, the size of this component of investment differs greatly among OECD countries.

An OECD report remarks that "the UK, with a software producing industry 50 percent larger than Denmark's as a percent of GDP, has software investment levels less than one-third the size of Denmark's" (Lequiller and others 2003). The authors of the report calculated the ratio of capitalized software investment to total expenditures on computer services (computer services were apparently intended to be inclusive of software but not to incorporate all of software). This ratio went from a little over a tenth for the United Kingdom to 50 percent in the United States and more than 85 percent in Japan.

The report also contains a simple chart that shows software price indexes from 1992 onward for a sample of eleven OECD countries (figure 10-1). The chart resembles a fan: in Sweden, software prices were reported to have risen nearly 30 percent over the five-year 1995–2000 interval, in Australia they fell nearly 30 percent, and other countries were arrayed in between. The United

22. See also Moylan (2001).

Figure 10-1. *Investment in Software, Price Indexes from 1992 Onward*[a]

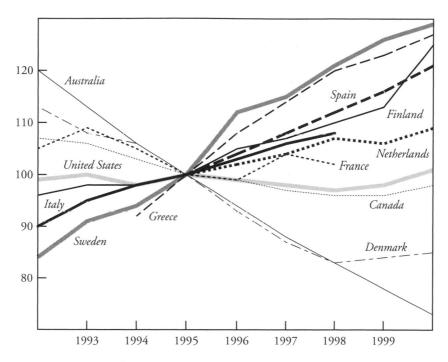

Source: Lequiller and others (2003).
a. 1995 = 100.

States and Canada had price trends that were lower than all of the European countries. This chart resembles one produced more than ten years ago by Andrew Wyckoff (1995), who plotted international price indexes for computers, with the same implausible result (it also resembled a fan). Much work remains to be done on improving measures of software, especially considering the importance of software in measures of IT.

Measurement difficulties in software may have overstated the contribution of IT to productivity growth: for example, the very large share of own-account software estimated for the United States by BEA may be too large (as some international comparisons might suggest). If so, BEA data (and our IT capital input for the work in chapter 2) have too much growth in IT, and the contribution of IT to labor productivity is overstated. However, perhaps the prices of software have been declining more rapidly than the deflators now used by BEA suggest. Then, the real growth in software investment is greater than is measured in the present numbers. In this case, the U.S. data show too little growth in IT investment, and as a result we have understated the contribution of IT to labor productivity growth. In the first case (overstatement of IT's contribution), the effect would be to reduce the level of MFP growth in the IT-using sectors; in the second case (understatement of IT contribution to labor productivity), the effect is to overstate the contribution of MFP to labor productivity growth. There is not enough information to take a stand on this matter.

However, it is true that our results in chapter 2 indicate a strong acceleration in MFP growth in many IT-using industries. If the growth of IT were overstated in our data because of overstatement of real software investment, then MFP acceleration in service industries would be even stronger than our estimates show. One should not let inadequacies in the present state of the data on software obscure the good news: ten years ago, we had no capitalized data on software to put into a measure of IT.

Allocation of High-Tech Capital among Using Industries: The Capital Flow Tables

We estimate the contribution of IT (and other capital) to industry labor productivity growth (see table 10-1 of this chapter, table 2-7 of chapter 2, and appendix table A-1). For this purpose, we use the estimates of capital services, by industry and by type of equipment (and structures), that are prepared by the BLS productivity program. It is important to ask how we get estimates of IT capital, by using industry.

The BEA periodically estimates capital flow tables. The capital flow table is an adjunct to the preparation of the input-output table. It basically flows investment spending through the rest of the table to the using industries. This investment spending is turned into capital stock data through the perpetual inventory method (Hermann and Katz 1997), which we will not explore here. In turn, BLS relies on BEA capital stocks, by industry and type of equipment, to produce the capital services estimates that we use to estimate productivity in our fifty-four industries.

Data on production of high-tech equipment (IT and medical equipment) are available, as are imports and exports required to get domestic investment. But in industry statistics, such as the Census Bureau's Economic Census and Industry Annual Surveys, the output of high-tech sector industries is much better measured than the high-tech inputs purchased by using industries. The Census Bureau also conducts a survey of investment spending, but the detail is fairly sparse from the standpoint of information by industry on investment in IT or different types of IT.

In the absence of good, detailed, survey information, the allocation of U.S. investment by equipment type to using industries rests, in many cases, on indirect extrapolators. For example, computer and software production is allocated among using industries in the BEA capital flow table in part by estimated employment of computer programmers. But this number rests on the BLS industry-occupation employment matrix, which is a product of somewhat shaky data combined with assumptions.

Sometimes, the allocations appear puzzling. For example, one would think that medical equipment goes mostly to the medical care industries. Yet 35 percent of electromedical and electrotherapeutic apparatus investment goes to nonmedical industries, including agriculture, retail trade, and business services. The size of nonmedical uses of this medical equipment is surprising and suggests problems with the industry classification or with the methods for allocating the equipment across using industries. As a result of such anomalies, one lacks confidence in the statistical allocations of computers, communications equipment, and software and other high-tech inputs among the industries that use them. If allocations are problematic, it is difficult to be sure that estimates of the productivity impact of IT and other high-tech equipment on using industries are valid.

Sumiye Okubo of BEA made a presentation on the difficulties of constructing the BEA capital flow table to the Brookings workshop on high tech data (October 12, 2001). The presentation was illuminating because it revealed the paucity of data available to carry out these vital estimates. At the same workshop, John Gates discussed the information collected by the Census Bureau on the inputs and outputs of the information technology sector. Goals for expanding the detail in the 2002 Economic Census were outlined.

Even if accurate when compiled, the BEA capital flow table presents an estimate of investment at a point in time. It does not track, for example, the medical sector's investment in medical equipment through time. For the period of our study, the latest available capital flow table pertained to 1992 (Bonds and Aylor 1998). The capital flow table does not allocate the capital stock, it allocates the investment flows. Consequently the stock depends on past capital flow tables as well as the latest one. However, especially for capital goods with short service lives such as computers, out-of-date allocations can be serious. One can extrapolate the capital flow table with Census Bureau production statistics by assuming that the composition of equipment investment by industry remains the same as it was in 1992. But if IT capital flowed to different industries in the last half of the 1990s, our industry IT intensity and IT capital services variables are mismeasured.

The 1997 capital flow table is now available. We can use this to assess probable errors of allocations in our IT allocations; table 10-6 contains the comparisons. As presented in table 10-6, the capital flow table shows the disposition of IT investment across using industries. For example, it shows that 28 percent of 1992 nonsoftware IT investment went to the communications industry, about the same as the 1997 share. In contrast, the share of the group of professional services that were in old SIC 87 went from 2 percent of the total to more than 6 percent. These shares are the product of the industry's IT intensity and its size, so changes in the shares reflect both changes in intensity and size.

We are concerned mainly with IT intensity. In Triplett and Bosworth (2002), we documented the most IT-intensive U.S. industries, measured as the share of IT in value added, using alternative definitions of IT. We also computed alternative measures of intensity, for example, IT with respect to total capital and to total costs (our output elasticity for the contribution of IT capital services), so the calculations were done nine ways, altogether. The list of IT-intensive industries was not appreciably different. Most of them were in services. We have marked the most IT-intensive industries (using the value added share) with an asterisk in table 10-6.

We are unable to recompute intensity at this time. Dividing changes in IT shares shown in table 10-6 by the rate of growth of output (appendix table A-1) suggests where the largest revisions to IT intensity are likely to occur.

Medical Equipment

High-tech capital inputs into services industries are not exclusively IT. The industries producing medical equipment are prominent users of semiconductors, and indeed of embedded computer-like components, but they also benefit from nonelectronic miniaturization and other technological advances that are breathtaking.[23]

Moreover, like IT, technical change in medical equipment is transforming the output in the industries that use the equipment. Fuchs and Sox (2001) report the results of a survey of physicians on the importance of medical innovations: MRI and CT scanners are at the top of the list, and diagnostic medical equip-

---

23. This section is condensed from Triplett and Gunter (2001).

ment innovations, including mammography, ultrasound scanning, and endoscopic devices, also appear high on the list of significant innovations. Other medical equipment examples are implanted devices for patient treatment and monitoring. One could compile a very long list of technological marvels for which innovations in medical equipment were sources or facilitators of improved medical procedures.

However, a huge difference exists between data for high-tech IT equipment data and high-tech medical equipment. In IT equipment, data on price indexes and output are fairly well measured, even though many questions remain, and the Bureau of Economic Analysis has integrated the data into its national accounts and its industry and I-O (input-output) accounts.

No such luxury exists for medical equipment. It is natural to look for medical equipment data in the national health accounts (NHA), because the NHA are intended to bring together all expenditures on medical care in the U.S. economy. The NHA contain no data on medical equipment. "Investment" in the NHA includes only buildings (structures) plus R&D, not medical equipment. The 1999 Census Bureau Annual Capital Expenditures Survey reports that half of the $51 billion of capital expenditures made by the health and social assistance sector was equipment, so $25.4 billion in equipment investment were missing in the NHA for that one year alone.

In chapter 2, we reported that the medical care industry had a small positive labor productivity growth after 1995, but that its MFP growth was still negative, as it was before 1995 (see chapter 2, tables 2-4A and 2-4B). One serious reservation about those productivity estimates concerns the accuracy of the output measures, which provides the major part of the agenda for improving health care data (see chapter 9). The medical care output measure was the subject of a Brookings workshop ("Measuring Health Care," December 1999) and is also the concern of various contributions on measuring the prices of medical treatment in Triplett (1999), Cutler and Berndt (2001), the review of medical care price indexes in Berndt and others (2000), and—for the framework for improving the measurement of medical services in the NHA—Triplett (2001).

Medical Equipment in the Health Care Sector

The other part of the story concerns measures of investment and capital stock for the high-tech capital inputs into the medical care sector. We emphasize that medical technology is by no means restricted to medical equipment. The successful development of a new operation may owe much more to advances in human capital than to advances in physical capital. Technological advances in

Table 10-6. *Industry Rank by Share of Total ICT, 1992 and 1997 Capital Flow Tables*[a]

	1992			1997			
Industry	SIC	Share of ICT (without software) (percent)	Industry (SIC)	NAICS code	Share of ICT (without software) (percent)	Share of ICT (with software) (percent)
Communications services	48	28.37	Communication services, sum	5133, 5132, 5131	29.20	21.49
			Telecommunications*	5133	22.08	16.53
			Cable networks and program distribution	5132	5.61	3.82
			Radio and television broadcasting*	5131	1.51	1.14
Financial services	60, 61, 62, 67	10.44	Financial services, sum	521, 522, 55, 533, 523	9.47	9.83
			Monetary authorities, credit intermediation and related activities (60, 61)*	521, 522	6.02	6.38
			Management of companies and enterprises (67)	55	1.26	1.51
			Lessors of non-financial intangible assets (679)	533	0.05	0.07
			Securities, commodity contracts, investments (60, 62, 67)	523	2.13	1.87
Wholesale trade	50, 51, 52	6.87	Wholesale trade (50, 51)*	4200	3.56	3.69
Retail trade, excluding eating and drinking	53, 54, 55, 56, 57, 59	3.06	Retail trade, sum (50, 52, 53, 54, 55, 56, 57, 59, 7699, 7622, 7623, 7629, 7378)	44, 45	4.59	3.64

	SIC		Description	NAICS		
Business services, excluding miscellaneous	731, 732, 733, 734, 736, 738, 737 except 7377	5.63	Business services, sum*	5418, 5611, 5612, 5614, 5616, 5617, 5418, 5619, 5141, 5112, 5613, 5142	4.29	4.83
Engineering, accounting, research, management, and related services	87	2.09	Engineering, accounting, research, management, and related services, sum	5412, 5413, 5414, 5415, 5416, 5417, 5419	6.01	9.40
Transportation by air	45	5.42	Air transportation	4810	6.87	5.14
Insurance services	63, 64	3.15	Insurance carriers and related activities (63, 64)*	5240	2.61	3.32
Miscellaneous equipment rental and leasing	735	3.41	Consumer goods and general rental centers (735)	5322, 5323	0.43	0.34
Computer rental and leasing (NAICS: 53242)	7377	0.46	Machinery and equipment rental and leasing	5324	0.22	0.20
			Automotive equipment rental and leasing (751)	5321	0.66	0.48
Construction	15, 16, 17	2.72	New and maintenance and repair construction (15,16,17)	2300	2.31	2.76
Chemicals and allied products	28	2.47	Chemicals and allied products, sum*	3251, 3252, 3253, 3254, 3255, 3256, 3259	2.06	2.91

(continued)

Table 10-6. *Industry Rank by Share of Total ICT, 1992 and 1997 Capital Flow Tables*[a] *(Continued)*

	1992			1997		
Industry	*SIC*	*Share of ICT (without software) (percent)*	*Industry (SIC)*	*NAICS code*	*Share of ICT (without software) (percent)*	*Share of ICT (with software) (percent)*
Electronic and other electric equipment	36	2.19	Electronic and other electric equipment, sum (36)*	3342, 3343, 3344, 3346, 3351, 3352, 3353, 3359	1.28	2.22
Industrial machinery and equipment	35	1.97	Industrial machinery and equipment, sum*	3323, 3324, 33299, 3325, 3326, 3327, 3328, 33291, 3331, 3332, 3333, 3334, 3335, 3336, 3339, 3341	1.68	2.68
Instruments and related products	38	1.95	Instruments and related products, sum	3345, 3391	0.60	1.03
Electric services	491, 493	1.92	Power generation and supply	2211	1.09	1.71
Printing and publishing	27	1.86	Printing and publishing, sum*	5111, 3230	1.09	1.08
Gas production and distribution	492	1.40	Gas production and distribution, sum	2212, 4860	1.35	1.25
Real estate	65	0.33	Real estate (and owner-occupied dwellings)	5310	1.40	1.21
Water transportation	44	0.03	Water transportation	4830	1.29	0.89

Railroad transportation	40	0.03	Rail transportation	4820	0.30	0.31
Trucking and warehousing	42	0.25	Trucking, warehousing, couriers and messengers	4840, 4930, 4920	1.34	1.33
Local and interurban passenger transportation	41	0.07	Local and interurban passenger, sum	4850, 487, 488	0.62	0.58
Other transportation equipment	372, 373, 374, 375, 376, 379	1.02	Other transportation equipment, sum	3364, 3365, 3366, 3369	0.83	0.32
Hotels and other lodging places	70	0.13	Accommodation	7210	0.26	0.24
Eating and drinking places	58	0.25	Food services and drinking places	7220	0.43	0.41
Health services, excluding hospitals	801, 802, 803, 804, 805, 807, 808, 809	0.28	Ambulatory health care services	6210	1.41	1.28
Hospitals	806	0.75	Hospitals, sum	6230, 6220	2.61	2.48
Personal services	72	0.71	Personal and laundry services	8121, 8122, 8123, 8129	0.56	0.43
Oil and gas extraction	13	0.34	Oil and gas extraction	2110	0.40	0.55
All other		10.45			9.18	11.97

Source: BEA, capital flow tables.

* Among most IT-intensive industries.

a. ICT = Computers and peripheral equipment, communication equipment, and photocopy and related equipment.

Table 10-7. *Distribution of Capital Investment to the Health Sector, 1992,*
BEA Capital Flow Table
Producer's prices, millions of dollars

Line no.	I-O commodity group (commodity number in parentheses)	Health services, excluding hospitals		Hospitals	
		Amount	Percent of total	Amount	Percent of total
	Construction	3,500	37.8	10,408	50.9
	Nonmedical capital equipment	726	7.8	1,594	7.8
	Medical capital equipment	5,035	54.4	8,438	41.3
139	(3821) Laboratory apparatus and furniture	83	0.9	270	1.3
140	(3823) Process control instruments	0	a	34	0.2
141	(3824) Fluid meters and counting devices	0	a	3	a
142	(3825) Instruments to measure electricity	0	a	7	a
143	(3826) Analytical instruments	12	0.1	49	0.2
144	(3827) Optical instruments and lenses	4	a	21	0.1
145	(3829) Measuring and controlling devices, n.e.c.	1	a	6	a
146	(3841) Surgical and medical instruments	2,487	26.9	4,043	19.8
147	(3842) Surgical appliances and supplies	48	0.5	1,498	7.3
148	(3843) Dental equipment and supplies	585	6.3	18	0.1
149	(3844) X-ray apparatus and tubes	1,193	12.9	622	3.0
150	(3845) Electromedical equipment	622	6.7	1,867	9.1
	Total	9,261	100.0	20,440	100.0

Source: Bonds and Aylor (1998).
a. Less than 0.1 percent.

pharmaceuticals are as impressive as technical advances in medical equipment. Our focus is not on medical technology, however, but on high-tech equipment.

A great amount of medical equipment is not high tech. Of the investment categories distinguished in the BEA capital flow table (table 10-7), high-tech medical equipment is located mainly in the following categories: surgical and medical instruments (20 percent of hospitals' equipment investment, 27 percent for nonhospitals); X-ray apparatus and tubes (only 3 percent of hospitals' capital investment, but 13 percent for nonhospitals); and, especially, electromedical equipment (9 percent of hospitals' investment, a bit less than 7 percent for non-hospitals). We focus on the X-ray apparatus and electromedical equipment categories (codes 149 and 150 of table 10-7), because these industry classifications account for a large share of the equipment that is associated with advanced technology in the medical sector.[24]

Three primary sources of production data on medical equipment exist.[25] The Economic Censuses, taken every five years, provide information on medical equipment, classified by industry. The Census Bureau's annual surveys of manufactures (ASM), which are also classified by industry, provide annual data comparable to those from the Economic Census. The third major data source is the Census Bureau's Current Industrial Reports (CIR), which cover some manufacturing industries, including the medical equipment industries. The CIR are product oriented, which means they report products wherever produced—for example, all electromedical equipment, and not just the outputs of establishments that are primarily electromedical equipment manufacturers. The CIR also report data for product class 3345101, which is the NAICS electromedical industry (334510), omitting hearing aids and ionizing radiation equipment products. For our purposes, the CIR is most relevant because of its product detail and demand-side product groupings, which are the classifications that are appropriate for grouping investment data.

Production Trends for Medical Equipment

Several classification and presentation problems limit the usefulness of CIR data on medical equipment. These problems force users to estimate trends for a number of medical equipment product categories for which census information is collected but not published in a way that can be used in analyses.[26] Details of the estimates are contained in Triplett and Gunter (2001). The results are presented in table 10-8, with the data arrayed by the use-oriented classifications of the Current Industrial Reports (CIR). The table covers the period since 1995, which of course is also the period of the investment boom in high-tech equipment in the United States.

Overall, production of medical equipment has grown by about 8.5 percent a year, led by growth in medical diagnostic equipment, in medical therapy

24. The category "surgical and medical instruments" includes some high-tech equipment but also a great amount of low-tech equipment, including surgical knives, clamps, and forceps.

25. Other data on medical equipment investment and production also exist. The Federal Reserve Board's industrial production index and the Census Bureau's manufacturing orders and shipments program (M-3 reports) contain fairly aggregated information on medical equipment. Donahoe (2000) discusses regulatory filings for hospitals that contain data for investment in equipment but are not currently tabulated in usable form. Data on medical equipment investment were also formerly compiled by the American Hospital Association.

26. David Gunter's assistance was invaluable in solving a great many difficult problems.

Table 10-8. *CIR Value of Shipments, Electromedical and Medical Irradiation Equipment, Classified by Use*
Millions of dollars

Equipment	2000	1999	1998	1997	1996	1995
Medical diagnostic	5,338	4,822	4,808	4,380	4,075	3,581
Patient monitoring	1,243	1,316	1,371	1,301	1,307	1,151
Medical therapy	4,834	4,776	4,089	3,715	3,162	2,849
Surgical systems	1,352	1,252	1,234	1,174	1,059	937
Other	1,044	958	894	854	866	685
Total	13,810	13,124	12,396	11,424	10,470	9,203

Source: U.S. Department of Commerce, Current Industrial Reports, table 2 (electromedical and irradiation equipment); and estimates by Triplett and Gunter (2001).

equipment (and in "other"). As table 10-8 also shows, the largest components of medical equipment—medical diagnostic and medical therapy equipment—have rapid growth. They are also the components where many of the data gaps (suppression for nondisclosure) occur in CIR.

The rapid growth in medical diagnostic equipment is led by the various types of scanners and related imaging devices, including digital radiography equipment, CT scanners, ultrasound scanners, and MRI scanners, all of which have been expanding between 7 and 12 percent a year. The actual growth rates for MRI scanners cannot be extracted from the CIR data because data are collapsed to avoic disclosure. After 1997, MRI scanners combined with EEG (electroencephalograph—brain scanner) and EMG (electromyograph—muscle imager) have expanded about 13 percent annually (Triplett and Gunter 2001).

Production of medical therapy equipment has grown even more rapidly than medical diagnostic equipment. The leaders are pacemakers (12.5 percent a year), defibrillators (15 percent a year), and the ubiquitous "all other" (14.4 percent a year).

Each of the CIR's use-oriented groupings contains large and growing "other" categories of products. Combined, the "other" and "all other" product categories of medical equipment account for 23 percent of the total medical equipment reported in the CIR in 2000, and the combined "all other" categories have been growing at 11 percent a year. Additionally, CIR contains an "other electromedical equipment, nec" (not elsewhere classified) component. Expenditure on this group of products has been growing at a spectacular 46 percent a year, post-1995. "Other" groupings are never meaningful product categories. When a large proportion of an industry's output, and a large proportion of its growth, is in the "other" classifications, it is a sure indication that the classification system is seriously out of date. The CIR product classifications, though established on sound principles, as far as they go, are obscuring information on the growth of high-tech medical equipment. Further discussion is in Triplett and Gunter (2001).

Price Indexes and Constant Price Value of Shipments for Medical Equipment

Estimating constant price measures of U.S. medical equipment production requires deflators. The PPI contains price indexes for the electromedical equipment and the irradiation equipment industries. As is true generally for the PPI program, the PPI medical equipment industry indexes also contain component price indexes for products produced within the industry. Most deflation, whether in national accounts or elsewhere, takes place at the product level. Thus, in many ways the most useful part of the PPI's output is its often neglected product detail. Happily in this case, the product nomenclature used for the PPI is consistent with the CIR product classifications (this has not always been true for other industries in the past).

The major problem we encounter in producing constant price production measures for medical equipment arises from insufficient detail in the PPI product information, combined with disclosure or perhaps nonreporting problems. The latter involve some of the same cases discussed above in the CIR—in particular, MRI, EEG, EMG, and endoscopic equipment.

In table 10-9, we have reaggregated PPI product indexes to match the product-oriented grouping system in the CIR and calculated annual average rates of change to cover the 1995–2000 interval. As noted earlier, diagnostic medical equipment appears in both the irradiation equipment industry and the electromedical equipment industry. The CIR re-aggregates the detailed commodities to obtain a diagnostic medical equipment category. The PPI does not. Diagnostic equipment from the two industries is thus tabulated separately in the first two lines of table 10-9.

Generally, more detail exists in CIR. For example, electromedical diagnostic equipment corresponds to six lines in CIR; PPIs exist only for ultrasound, electrocardiograph (EKG), and "all other" (table 10-9). Electrocardiograph production is

Table 10-9. *Annual Growth Rates, Producer Price Indexes*

CIR product code		Average annual growth rate, 1995–2000	Annual percent changes				
			2000	1999	1998	1997	1996
Medical diagnostic equipment							
	Medical and dental diagnostic irradiation equipment	0.22	-0.1	-0.7	0.5	1.5	-0.1
	Diagnostic electromedical equipment	-2.31	-6.6	-2.4	-1.0	-1.1	-0.3
3345101106	Ultrasound scanning devices	-1.52[a]	n.a.	-3.4	1.2	-2.6	-1.2
3345101109	Electrocardiograph (EKG)	-4.48	-0.3	-3.3	-15.4	-1.6	-0.9
Several	All other medical diagnostic (including MRI 1998–2000)	0.72	0.8	-0.2	1.5	0.7	0.8
3345101103	MRI		n.a.	n.a.	n.a.	-0.1	-0.5
Patient monitoring equipment		-5.38	-6.3	-5.9	-0.1	-8.7	-5.7
3345101227	Intensive care/coronary care units, including component modules such as temperature, blood pressure, and pulse	-3.05	-0.6	0.0	-1.5	-4.7	-8.2
Several	Prenatal, respiratory, and all other patient monitoring	-8.33	-13.5	-12.8	1.4	-13.2	-2.5

Therapeutic equipment

Electromedical therapy equipment		-3.00	-2.3	-2.7	-2.7	-4.0	-3.3
Several	Ultrasound therapy, Dialyzers, and all other medical therapy equipment	-0.73[b]	0	-0.9	-1.3	n.a.	n.a.
3345101244	Pacemakers	-3.32[a]	-5.2	-4.4	-3.3	-0.3	n.a.
3345101247	Defibrillators	-5.20[b]	-5.1	-5.8	-4.7	n.a.	n.a.
3345101254	Medical laser equipment[c]	-1.93	-1.93	-1.93	-1.93	n.a.	n.a.
Radiation therapy		n.a.					
Surgical systems							
3345101361	Electrosurgical equipment	0.17	0.0	-0.3	0.8	n.a.	n.a.
Several	Heart-lung machines, blood flow systems, and all other surgical support systems	n.a.	-0.2	-0.6	1.6	n.a.	n.a.
Parts, accessories, and all other electromedical equipment		-1.81	0.5	-2.0	-3.8	-2.5	-1.2

Source: Producer Price Index.

n.a. PPI not available.

a. Average annual growth rate, 1995–99.

b. Average annual growth rate, 1997–2000.

c. Percent changes assume average annual PPI growth is constant between 1997 and 2000. The PPI only reports data for those two years.

a small (around 4 percent) part of the production of electromedical diagnostic equipment, so the "all other" grouping in the PPI amounts to more than half of electromedical diagnostic equipment, which repeats the "other" grouping problem in the CIR.

Similar, though somewhat less severe, problems arise in the remaining categories of medical equipment. MRIs call for a special note. Before 1997, the PPI contained a separate price index for MRI equipment. It fell by 20.1 percent (total) between 1990 and 1997 when the price index was discontinued. Note also that CT scanners are not separately identified in the PPI product detail, nor are EEG, EMG, and endoscopic equipment.

Triplett and Gunter (2001) use available PPI detail to deflate CIR production growth for items of medical equipment. Table 10-10 summarizes average annual growth rates for current-price CIR, PPI indexes, and deflated, constant-price CIR. The cells marked "X" in the table indicate where no matching detail is available. The "Y" cells designate components where a single PPI component index corresponds to a group of CIR components. In both cases, deflation by necessity combines components that may have dissimilar characteristics, technologies, or price movements.

The main picture that emerges from table 10-10 is that we cannot get nearly far enough. The PPI contains some useful product detail on medical equipment but not nearly enough. Sample size, responses to government surveys, and disclosure problems are all no doubt factors. Details are already largely familiar from the previous discussion.

For the irradiation diagnostic equipment category, we have no detail at all (cells marked "X"). The aggregate-level PPI indicates very little inflation, so that the current-price and constant-price CIR are nearly the same.

For electromedical diagnostic equipment, nearly all the detail available, as well as the aggregate index for the category, indicates falling prices. Thus very strong current-price rates of growth in CIR (9 percent a year) correspond to even stronger constant-price rates of growth (11.5 percent a year). But for the categories of diagnostic equipment for which we think technical change has been the most rapid (for example, MRI), we cannot tell very much about growth, either current price or constant price. We presume that the medical sector is investing heavily in scanners and imaging equipment, but government data do not tell us much about it.

The rest of table 10-10 shows a similar story. When we can learn something about it, prices for high-tech medical equipment are falling, as measured by the PPI. In some of them (for example, pacemakers, defibrillators) expenditures are rising. But we need more data and more detail.

Accuracy of PPI Indexes

Problems posed by quality change in price indexes are well known, dating even before the famous article by Griliches (1961). We have been able to locate only one piece of economic research on medical equipment, the study of CT scanners by Trajtenberg (1990). This study is now quite old. Its price indexes extend only to 1982. Trajtenberg showed that CT scanners declined at an average rate of 13.6 percent a year for the period that he studied. But the U.S. government does not publish a price index for CT scanners, even though they remain a large component of medical investment (table 10-10).

In the earlier discussion on communications equipment we used information on semiconductor inputs to review the plausibility of price indexes for industries that were heavy users of them. We cannot follow the same course in medical equipment, partly because the input measures are not available.

The 1997 Economic Census shows that the share of semiconductors and related electronic components in the electromedical equipment industry is substantial. But surprisingly, less detail on electronic components is published for this industry (a major user of them) than for the irradiation industry, which is a smaller consumer of electronic components and semiconductors.[27]

For the irradiation equipment industry, the Economic Census also collected purchases of computers that were intended to be embedded into the final product. Regrettably, no information on embedded computers was collected for the electromedical industry, where scanning and imaging equipment is produced. A scanner is basically a device for making images coupled with a computer to convert those images into three-dimensional portrayals of organs so that they can be studied by medical professionals. One would expect that the manufacture of a piece of medical equipment that uses an embedded computer would benefit from the great expansion of computing power and consequent decline in the price of computers.

This fragmentary information on technological inputs is suggestive. We can be sure that the contribution of technological inputs lowers the cost of medical equipment and increases its performance, but we lack sufficient information to determine the magnitudes. Beyond semiconductors and computers themselves, miniaturization technology has contributed greatly to the effectiveness of medical equipment. It might not be possible to associate any of this with a high-tech input. But, clearly, we have too little information on the technological inputs into the medical equipment industries.

27. The data are presented in Triplett and Gunter (2001, table 10-7).

Table 10-10.　*Summary of PPI and CIR Growth Rates*

CIR product code		Average annual percent change (1995–2000)		
		PPI	Constant price CIR	Current price CIR
Medical diagnostic equipment				8.3
Medical and dental diagnostic irradiation equipment		0.22	7.27	7.5
3345170103	Digital radiography equipment	X	X	7.2
3345170106	Computerized axial tomography (CT or CAT SCAN)	X	X	7.1
3345170109	Dental and conventional X-ray	X	X	4.4
3345170112	All other medical diagnostic X-ray equipment	X	X	12.3
3345170115	Nuclear medicine equipment (all equipment used for nuclear in vivo studies)	X	X	7.2
Electromedical diagnostic equipment		−2.31	11.60	9.02
3345101106	Ultrasound scanning devices	−1.52[a]	16.62[a]	12.0
3345101109	Electrocardiograph (EKG)	−4.48	0.13	−4.4
3345101115	Audiological equipment	0.72[b]	8.15[b]	−1.3
3345101121	Respiratory analysis equipment	Y	Y	−5.1
3345101112 + 3345101124	EEG, EMG, and all other medical diagnostic equipment			
3345101103 + 345101112	MRI and EEG, EMG	Y	Y	8.9[c]
3345101103 + 3345101118	MRI and endoscopic equipment			
3345101118 + 3345101124	Endoscopic equipment and all other medical diagnostic	Y	Y	−6.9[c]
Patient monitoring equipment		−5.38	7.32	1.5
3345101227	Intensive care/coronary care units, including component modules such as temperature, blood pressure, and pulse	−3.05	2.48	−0.6
3345101233	Prenatal and respiratory monitoring	−8.33	12.69	−2.9
3345101237	All other patient monitoring	Y	Y	4.4

(continued)

Table 10-10. *Summary of PPI and CIR Growth Rates (Continued)*

CIR product code		PPI	Constant price CIR	Current price CIR
			Average annual percent change (1995–2000)	
Medical therapy equipment				11.2
Electromedical therapy		−3.00	15.43	11.96
3345101244	Pacemakers	−3.32[a]	19.60[a]	12.5
3345101247	Defibrillators	−5.20[c]	21.52[c]	15.0
3345101254	Medical laser equipment[d]	−1.93[c]	−2.46[c]	3.7
3345101241	Ultrasound therapy	−.73[c]	12.11[c]	19.6
3345101251	Dialyzers, including machines and equipment	Y	Y	11.4
3345101257	All other medical therapy equipment	Y	Y	14.4
Radiation therapy		X	X	5.0
Surgical systems		0.17[c]	4.62[c]	7.6
3345101361	Electrosurgical equipment	X	X	5.1
3345101364 + 3345101367	Heart-lung machines, excluding iron lungs and blood flow systems	0.26[c]	3.50[c]	12.9
3345101371	All other surgical support systems	Y	Y	4.5
Other		−1.81	10.78	
3345101374	Other electromedical equipment (except diagnostic and therapeutic), n.e.c.	X	X	46.1
3345101477	Electromedical parts and accessories, (including diagnostic and therapeutic), n.e.c.	X	X	4.5

Source: *1997 Economic Census*, table 7.

a. Average annual growth rate, 1995–99.

b. These two figures aggregate data that correspond to the lines below for which data are not reported separately.

c. Average annual growth rate, 1997–2000.

d. Percent changes assume average annual PPI growth is constant between 1997 and 2000. The PPI only reports data for those two years.

X = No matching detail available for these cells.

Y = Values for these cells are combined into the value for the previous cell.

Conclusion

We believe that gathering additional information on high-tech medical equipment is important for analyzing its contribution to improved health care. It is no doubt true that improving the database for medical equipment will not, by itself, answer all of the questions that have been posed about the contribution of medical technology to health care costs. But it is hard to see how one can address many of those questions without better information on the flows of medical equipment into the medical care sector.

CHAPTER ELEVEN

Data Needs

The U.S. statistical system has made vast strides in recent years in improving the data available for the analysis of productivity and particularly for estimating productivity in the services industries. These improvements have not been widely noticed. The title of this chapter shows that we have no doubt that measurement problems remain, and we use our research to demonstrate where resources for improvement can be allocated. But we do not want our list of improvements to obscure the fact that the situation today is far better than it was when Baily and Gordon (1988) reviewed consistency of industry data for productivity analysis or when Griliches (1992) reviewed the state of data on output and productivity measurement in the services industries. A tremendous amount has been accomplished.

Plaudits go to most of the government agencies, which have acted on data needs expressed in earlier work. First in importance, for our purposes, are the improvements in the BEA GDP by industry accounts (Yuskavage 2001). These accounts now include a full reporting of inputs and outputs, which imposes the discipline of a check that was not present when the accounts focused only on value added. Adding gross output to the industry data file not only added information, it also improved the consistency of the whole file.

Second, the Bureau of Labor Statistics, in its producer price index (PPI) program, moved aggressively in the 1990s into constructing output prices for services industries. This valuable work was carried out without a comparable expansion of funds to conduct the work. A number of these initiatives have been discussed in the series of Brookings workshops on economic measurement—for example, Gerduk and Holdway (2001). Not all the problems of services sector deflation have been solved, and for some services industries the difficulty of specifying the concept of output limits the validity of deflators. But the remaining problems should not obscure the progress that has been made. Tremendous improvement has occurred since Griliches (1994) discussed measurement problems in the services industries.

Third, the Census Bureau, in its Economic Census and its expansion of its annual surveys of services, has generated more information about services industries and collected more penetrating information on purchased services than was the case with earlier economic statistics for the United States. Information on purchased inputs at the industry level is still a problem for productivity analysis, but the state of the statistics is much improved.

Fourth, the continuing work on deflators for high-tech capital deserves strong praise. Beginning with the IBM-BEA work on computer equipment deflators in the mid-1980s (Cole and others 1986), recent substantial contributions to improving these deflators have been made by BLS (in the PPI and CPI), by BEA, and by the industrial production unit of the Federal Reserve Board. This work is of inestimable importance for all analytic purposes, not just for productivity analysis. The United States is a services economy, but it is also a technological economy, and measuring technological inputs is vitally important.

Fifth, BEA revised and extended its measures of the capital stock by industry and asset type to include updated estimates of depreciation, and the productivity program of BLS used those measures to develop detailed estimates of capital services by industry. Therefore we now have measures of capital inputs for industries, including services, that distinguish, in considerable useful detail, between types of information technology equipment and other types of capital.

All of these improvements have enabled us to construct detailed growth accounts for fifty-four industries with a separate accounting in each for the contribution of information capital. We know of no other country that has a comparable database.

At the same time, the expanded usefulness of the data has provided insight into some of the remaining problems and highlighted their importance. For example, when only an estimate of value added was available at the industry level, the integration problems in the industry accounts that were discussed by Yuskavage (2001) were simply unknown to researchers, unless they dug deeply beneath the veneer of the published statistics.

In what follows, we address data issues and suggestions for improvements that arose at the various workshops on measurement issues that the Brookings Institution has sponsored since 1998. Our recommendations are based on the workshops and on our own research, as reported in previous chapters of this book.

Inconsistent Data Sources

At present, BEA constructs the industry measures of value added and its components from sources that correspond to those used to measure the income side of the national accounts—that is, the IRS for profits and BLS for wages and salaries. Data that are derived from company reports must be converted to an establishment basis. In contrast, the measures of gross output are constructed from the sources used to construct the input-output accounts, primarily the Census Bureau business censuses and surveys, which focus directly on establishments. Intermediate purchases are then estimated residually as gross output minus value added. This contrasts with the I-O accounts, which provide direct estimates of both gross output and purchased inputs, with value added being the residual.

As shown in table 11-1, the industry estimates of value added (GDP originating) can differ substantially from those of the I-O accounts. Columns 1 and 2 show the estimates of value added from the industry accounts and the 1992 I-O table. The differences and percent differences are shown in columns 3 and 4. A time dimension is provided by including the percent differences in the measures of gross output from the 1996 annual I-O table. As noted by Yuskavage (2000), the differences are largest at the industry level, with some offset within industry groups. Somewhat surprising, the percent differences are larger and more volatile for the goods-producing industries, but that is partially a reflection of the more detailed division of the goods-producing industries.

The quantity (constant price) measures of gross output are computed at the four-digit SIC level largely by using price indexes from the BLS price programs and aggregated as chained indexes to the two-digit industry level. Information about the composition of purchased inputs is taken from the I-O accounts, but it must be interpolated for non–I-O years; therefore purchased inputs lack the compositional detail needed to compute high-quality chain indexes. The volume measure of value added is effectively computed as the difference between the quantity values of gross output and purchased inputs.

The concerns about measurement error are most evident in our measures of labor productivity. While we expect measures of labor productivity growth to vary between gross output and value added, the magnitudes often are very large and volatile over time. For our group of fifty-four industries, the standard deviation of the difference between the two growth rates is 3.6 percentage points, even though average growth is 2 percent in each case. It is unlikely that the

Table 11-1. *Comparison of Gross Domestic Product by Industry and Input-Output Table Value Added, 1992 and 1996*

Industry	1992 Value added comparison				1996 Gross output	
	Gross product	I-O table	Difference	Percent difference	Percent difference	Change 1992–96
Private industries total	5,369.8	5,354.7	−15.1	−0.3	1.9	2.2
Goods-producing industries	1,504.2	1,572.2	68.0	4.5	7.2	2.6
Agriculture, forestry, and fishing	111.6	99.2	−12.4	−11.1	7.7	18.8
Farms	80.5	74.1	−6.4	−8.0	8.6	16.6
Agricultural services, forestry, and fishing	31.2	25.1	−6.1	−19.6	4.1	23.7
Mining	87.4	91.9	4.5	5.1	4.8	−0.3
Metal mining	5.6	4.5	−1.1	−19.6	2.4	22.0
Coal mining	12.0	15.9	3.9	32.5	−15.1	−47.6
Oil and gas extraction	62.0	63.2	1.2	1.9	10.2	8.3
Nonmetallic minerals, except fuels	7.7	8.3	0.6	7.8	−1.8	−9.6
Construction	234.4	220.9	−13.5	−5.8	52.5	58.2
Manufacturing	1,070.8	1,160.2	89.4	8.3	0.4	−8.0
Durable goods	587.1	618.5	31.4	5.3	0.4	−5.0
Lumber and wood products	32.2	32.3	0.1	0.3	6.2	5.8
Furniture and fixtures	16.5	19.9	3.4	20.6	0.9	−19.7
Stone, clay, and glass	25.9	29.8	3.9	15.1	0.2	−14.8
Primary metal industries	39.3	42.9	3.6	9.2	−1.0	−10.2
Fabricated metal products	69.2	71.5	2.3	3.3	0.2	−3.1
Industrial machinery and equipment	111.5	108.9	−2.6	−2.3	0.2	2.5
Electronic and other electric	106.3	99.0	−7.3	−6.9	−0.8	6.1
Motor vehicles and equipment	58.5	51.6	−6.9	−11.8	0.4	12.2
Other transportation equipment	57.2	68.3	11.1	19.4	1.2	−18.2
Instruments and related products	51.0	76.7	25.7	50.4	−0.6	−51.0
Miscellaneous manufacturing industries	19.5	17.8	−1.7	−8.7	2.6	11.4

(continued)

Table 11-1. *Comparison of Gross Domestic Product by Industry and Input-Output Table Value Added, 1992 and 1996 (Continued)*

Industry	1992 Value added comparison				1996 Gross output	
	Gross product	I-O table	Difference	Percent difference	Percent difference	Change 1992–96
Nondurable goods	483.8	541.7	57.9	12.0	0.4	–11.6
Food and kindred products	105.2	122.9	17.7	16.8	0.6	–16.3
Tobacco manufactures	13.8	25.7	11.9	86.2	–0.3	–86.5
Textile mill products	25.6	23.8	–1.8	–7.0	–0.4	6.7
Apparel and other	27.3	25.4	–1.9	–7.0	0.3	7.2
Paper and allied products	45.3	51.3	6.0	13.2	–0.6	–13.9
Printing and publishing	77.8	93.4	15.6	20.1	0.7	–19.4
Chemicals and allied products	118.0	125.1	7.1	6.0	1.1	–5.0
Petroleum and coal products	27.8	20.3	–7.5	–27.0	–0.1	26.9
Rubber and miscellaneous plastics	38.2	50.0	11.8	30.9	0.2	–30.7
Leather and leather products	4.9	3.7	–1.2	–24.5	0.0	24.5
Service-producing industries	3,821.9	3,790.4	–31.5	–0.8	–1.2	–0.4
Transportation	192.9	193.3	0.4	0.2	–0.6	–0.8
Railroad transportation	21.6	22.1	0.5	2.3	–5.2	–7.5
Local and interurban passenger transit	10.9	12.4	1.5	13.8	15.7	1.9
Trucking and warehousing	74.5	82.4	7.9	10.6	–1.2	–11.8
Water transportation	10.6	13.3	2.7	25.5	–2.7	–28.2
Transportation by air	50.0	42.1	–7.9	–15.8	0.7	16.5
Pipelines, except natural gas	5.5	5.3	–0.2	–3.6	1.3	4.9
Transportation services	19.8	15.7	–4.1	–20.7	–4.8	15.9
Communications	162.8	142.1	–20.7	–12.7	–2.8	9.9
Telephone and telegraph	127.8	116.5	–11.3	–8.8	–3.7	5.1
Radio and television	34.9	25.5	–9.4	–26.9	0.4	27.3
Electric, gas, and sanitary	179.5	160.6	–18.9	–10.5	–2.0	8.5
Wholesale trade	406.4	405.6	–0.8	–0.2	1.4	1.6
Retail trade	547.1	510.1	–37.0	–6.8	–1.4	5.3
Finance, insurance, and real estate	1,126.3	1,175.1	48.8	4.3	–4.3	–8.6
Depository institutions	198.9	165.7	–33.2	–16.7	–3.9	12.8

(continued)

Table 11-1. *Comparison of Gross Domestic Product by Industry and Input-Output Table Value Added, 1992 and 1996 (Continued)*

Industry	1992 Value added comparison				1996 Gross output	
	Gross product	I-O table	Difference	Percent difference	Percent difference	Change 1992–96
Nondepository institutions	24.8	24.9	0.1	0.4	–33.6	–34.0
Security and commodity brokers	54.2	52.6	–1.6	–3.0	–1.7	1.3
Insurance carriers	77.8	63.4	–14.4	–18.5	–15.2	3.3
Insurance agents, and brokers	39.2	40.5	1.3	3.3	10.1	6.8
Real estate	724.7	820.9	96.2	13.3	–1.9	–15.2
Holding and other investment	6.7	7.1	0.4	6.0	58.4	52.5
Services	1,206.9	1,203.6	–3.3	–0.3	0.9	1.2
Hotels and other lodging	50.3	52.2	1.9	3.8	–1.6	–5.4
Personal services	40.6	37.8	–2.8	–6.9	0.6	7.5
Business services	222.0	229.0	7.0	3.2	8.2	5.0
Auto repair, services, and parking	51.3	48.0	–3.3	–6.4	–0.1	6.4
Miscellaneous repair services	17.5	24.4	6.9	39.4	–1.9	–41.4
Motion pictures	18.0	18.8	0.8	4.4	0.7	–3.7
Amusement and recreation services	45.1	43.9	–1.2	–2.7	1.8	4.5
Health services	376.7	371.8	–4.9	–1.3	–1.2	0.1
Legal services	92.1	84.2	–7.9	–8.6	–0.4	8.2
Educational services	46.4	44.0	–2.4	–5.2	–1.7	3.4
Social services	37.3	40.1	2.8	7.5	–6.8	–14.3
Membership organizations	39.9	40.8	0.9	2.3	–1.5	–3.7
Other services	159.5	158.6	–0.9	–0.6	0.1	0.6
Private households	10.1	10.1	0.0	0.0	2.5	2.5
Statistical discrepancy + inventory valuation adjustment	43.7	–8.0	–51.7			

Source: Yuskavage (2000) and authors' calculations. The 1992 comparison refers to value added from the industry accounts relative to the I-O table. The 1996 comparison is for gross output from the industry accounts and the annual I-O table.

volatility could result solely from changing patterns of outsourcing. Instead, all of the inconsistencies between the income and I-O data sources are concentrated in the residual calculations of each industry's intermediate purchases. Purchased inputs matter less for MFP, since the computation of MFP using either gross output or value added yields essentially the same estimates of its contribution to aggregate (value added) MFP.

In the long run, the objective is to fully integrate the GDP by industry and the I-O accounts. The integration is currently incomplete because of insufficient source information, and the problem is particularly severe for services. Census Bureau sources cover about 90 percent of gross output but only 30 percent of purchased inputs. The business surveys of the Census Bureau are being expanded to provide more detail, and BEA is planning to achieve a partial integration of its GDP by industry and the annual I-O accounts over the next several years.[1]

Alternative Data Sets

The BEA is not the only source of industry-level data. Two different programs of the BLS—its productivity program and its employment projections program—also produce industry data that can be used for productivity analysis.

Previously we discussed the BLS measures of output and productivity for durable and nondurable manufacturing, but the BLS productivity office also produces more detailed estimates within manufacturing. The manufacturing output series of BLS and BEA both are gross output, and both rely on Census Bureau shipment data. However, BLS constructs its own measures of output and excludes an estimate of intramanufacturing shipments. For two-digit SIC industries the difference in output growth can be quite substantial, ranging from –0.8 percent to +1.0 percent a year over the 1995–2000 period. The differences seem too large to explain by changes in the amount of intramanufacturing shipments, but we do not know the sources.

More relevant for our focus on services, the employment projections program of BLS produces detailed industry measures of output and employment over the period 1972–2000, covering both goods-producing and services-producing industries. This is a basic data source for the productivity studies of Dale Jorgenson and his colleagues. The data set includes output measures for a considerable number of the services-producing industries that we have used in our analysis. Table 11-2

---

1. The BEA plans are discussed in Moyer and others (2004).

Table 11-2. *Differences in Growth Rates of Industry Output, BEA Industry Accounts and BLS Office of Employment Projections, 1987–2000*

Average annual rate of change

Industry	1987–1995			1995–2000			Change		
	BEA	*BLS*	*Difference*	*BEA*	*BLS*	*Difference*	*BEA*	*BLS*	*Difference*
Railroad transportation	3.6	1.0	-2.5	0.7	-0.6	-1.3	-2.9	-1.6	1.2
Local and interurban passenger transit	1.5	1.6	0.2	2.4	1.2	-1.1	0.9	-0.4	-1.3
Trucking and warehousing	5.7	4.0	-1.7	4.1	4.6	0.6	-1.7	0.6	2.2
Water transportation	2.7	1.4	-1.3	4.7	-0.5	-5.2	2.0	-1.9	-3.9
Transportation by air	3.6	4.8	1.3	5.4	1.5	-3.9	1.8	-3.3	-5.2
Pipelines, except natural gas	-1.6	-0.4	1.2	0.1	-3.0	-3.2	1.7	-2.6	-4.3
Transportation services	6.2	5.7	-0.5	6.2	5.7	-0.5	-0.0	0.0	0.1
Telephone and telegraph	5.4	4.5	-0.9	13.4	7.6	-5.8	8.0	3.1	-4.9
Radio and television	2.3	1.9	-0.4	4.7	2.7	-2.0	2.4	0.7	-1.6
Electric, gas, and sanitary services	2.5	0.4	-2.1	1.5	1.6	0.1	-1.0	1.2	2.2
Wholesale trade	4.4	4.0	-0.3	6.0	4.3	-1.8	1.7	0.2	-1.5
Retail trade	2.9	1.9	-1.1	5.5	4.3	-1.3	2.6	2.4	-0.2
Depository institutions	1.5	3.4	1.9	2.9	6.4	3.5	1.4	3.1	1.6

Nondepository institutions[a]	8.2	1.0	-7.2	12.3	9.5	-2.8	4.1	8.4	4.4
Security and commodity brokers	9.5	7.2	-2.3	23.4	22.0	-1.3	13.8	14.8	1.0
Insurance carriers	0.7	1.3	0.6	-1.5	0.6	2.2	-2.3	-0.7	1.6
Insurance agents, brokers, and service	-1.8	1.2	3.0	4.1	4.0	-0.1	5.9	2.8	-3.0
Real estate	4.0	2.1	-1.8	3.5	2.1	-1.3	-0.5	0.0	0.5
Hotels and other lodging places	2.4	2.0	-0.4	3.2	2.7	-0.5	0.8	0.7	-0.1
Personal services	3.2	2.8	-0.4	2.7	3.9	1.2	-0.5	1.1	1.6
Business services	8.6	6.8	-1.8	11.1	9.5	-1.6	2.5	2.7	0.2
Auto repair, services, and parking	3.2	3.8	0.6	4.1	5.2	1.1	0.9	1.4	0.5
Miscellaneous repair services	3.7	2.3	-1.4	1.0	1.7	0.8	-2.7	-0.6	2.2
Motion pictures	4.4	5.7	1.3	3.0	6.6	3.6	-1.5	0.8	2.3
Amusement and recreation services	7.4	5.6	-1.8	3.9	6.7	2.8	-3.5	1.1	4.6
Health services	3.2	3.0	-0.1	2.6	2.8	0.2	-0.6	-0.3	0.3
Legal services	1.4	1.4	-0.0	2.9	2.0	-0.9	1.5	0.6	-0.9
Educational services	3.3	2.2	-1.1	2.7	2.9	0.2	-0.6	0.7	1.3
Value added weighted sum	2.5	2.1	-0.5	3.5	3.0	-0.5	1.0	1.0	-0.0

Source: Gross output measures from the BEA industry data set and the employment projections program of BLS (www.bls.gov/emp/home.htm).
a. The BLS measure includes SIC 67 (holding and other investment offices).

provides a comparison of the output growth rates over the 1987–2000 period for twenty-eight of our twenty-nine industries for which it appears that the coverage by SIC codes is the same.

It is evident from the table that growth rates for individual industries calculated by using the BEA and BLS projections data sets often differ substantially. The differences are large even for industries, such as transportation, communications, and utilities, whose source data we believe to be of quite high quality. For example, the BLS reports a substantial slowdown in airline output growth (comparing 1995–2000 with the previous period), whereas the BEA data indicate acceleration. The BLS measures also report less growth in the large retail and wholesale trade sectors, whereas we previously found a large acceleration of growth in both labor productivity and MFP. On the other hand, the BLS data show more output growth acceleration in depository banking, insurance, and the amusement and recreation industry; the latter is one of our negative productivity industries.

Using value-added weights, we find that the BEA data imply slightly faster growth of output in the services-producing industries as a whole in both 1987–95 and 1995–2000, but the magnitude of overall post-1995 acceleration is the same. Thus, despite the large differences at the level of individual industries, the two data sets are in surprisingly close agreement about the overall acceleration of output growth in the services-producing sector. Since it has been our experience that the two agencies produce very similar employment estimates at the industry level, the BLS output measures seem to offer strong support for the finding in the BEA industry data of a large improvement in productivity growth in overall services, even though they conflict greatly at the detailed level.

We have been surprised by the degree of overlap between the industry programs of BEA and BLS; yet it appears that there has been very little effort to compare and contrast their sources and methods. It seems evident that there would be substantial benefit to tracing down the sources of difference in the alternative output measures. It is confusing for the statistical agencies to publish such contradictory measures, particularly when the sources of variation are not documented. They clearly incorporate different source data or methods. While we are unlikely to see movement toward an integrated U.S. statistical system (where such redundancies would be eliminated by consolidating these statistical programs and thereby melding resources to improve the data), this is one area where there would be significant gains from greater coordination of research efforts between the two agencies.

Negative Productivity Growth Industries

Negative productivity growth always attracts skepticism, as well it should. In our estimates, the following industries had negative labor productivity growth over the 1995–2001 interval: education (–0.95 percent); amusement and recreation (–0.41 percent); hotels (–0.57 percent); insurance carriers (–1.66 percent); local transit (–0.61 percent); and construction (–1.12 percent). Negative MFP trends are evident in some services industries, particularly health and educational services.

Analyses of the negative productivity issue include Corrado and Slifman (1999) and Gullickson and Harper (2002). Both studies set the negative productivity industries (a larger number in their studies than in our results) equal to zero; they then recompute aggregate productivity growth. There is no doubt some value to this procedure as a "what if?" exercise. However, we see little reason for supposing that cutting off the left tail of the distribution of productivity changes improves the estimate of the mean.

Instead of mechanical "lopping off the tail" exercises, we believe that the statistical agencies should take negative productivity growth as an indicator of the areas in which they need to allocate resources to improve measurement. An exercise to trace down the source of the negative changes in productivity could offer considerable insight into sources of some of the measurement errors. Because the sources can include errors in price deflators, in current price output measures, in inputs—both capital and intermediate inputs—and also in labor hours, identifying the sources inevitably is a multiagency task, and we believe it should be undertaken as such.

Labor Hours and Input by Industry

The labor input in our study is persons engaged in production, not hours, which is the labor input in the BLS productivity reports and in Jorgenson, Ho, and Stiroh (2002); in addition, we do not apply a labor quality adjustment. Neither of these aspects is included in the BEA industry data set, and we lacked the resources to estimate an index of labor quality at the industry level.

The reliance on employment rather than hours is a serious shortcoming of our analysis. We have, however, little confidence in the estimates of hours across industries. The major source of industry hours is the BLS monthly establishment survey known as the Current Employment Survey. The objective of this survey can only be described as archaic, for it persists in collecting hours and earnings information *only* for what it calls "production workers" in manufacturing and "nonsupervisory workers" in the rest of the economy. The BLS productivity program estimates the hours of "nonproduction" and "supervisory" workers, using whatever information it can find. Hours of self-employed and salaried workers are obtained from the BLS-Census Bureau monthly household survey, the Current Population Survey (CPS).

With the huge changes in workplace organization and management in recent years, the boundary between "production" and "nonproduction" workers has lost its meaning. The same statement applies to "supervisory" and "nonsupervisory" workers outside manufacturing, except there the distinction has always been unclear. There is a documentable need for BLS to collect information on the hours of all workers. We understand that planning is under way within BLS for this expansion, which deserves accelerated attention.

In addition, estimates of the change in labor quality are of increased importance at the industry level. Relative earnings of workers in some industries, such as retail trade, have changed substantially. It would be of considerable value to know the extent to which those changes in wage rates can be associated with changes in the average education and skill level of the workforce.

IT Capital

In a February 2001 Brookings workshop on the communications industry, "Communications Output and Productivity," several participants expressed concern with the price indexes for communications capital equipment. This matter was discusssed in detail in our high-tech chapter, which also covered the problems of measuring software and medical equipment. But we would not want to understate the importance of additional improvements in the high-tech area by omitting these topics from this chapter.

The discussants at the Brookings workshops argued for more detail on high-tech products and more information on the extent to which semiconductors are embedded in other products. A recommendation was also made for BEA to provide a more detailed inventory of the methods used to obtain price deflators for specific categories of high-tech products in the national accounts, over what time period. There was some concern about the historical comparability of the national accounts data, given the pace of introducing new price indexes, but of course, that should not be interpreted as a call for holding back the improvements now being made.

Furthermore, the product classification system used within the communications industry and employed in Doms and Forman (2003) cannot be easily related to the product classification used by the government agencies. Similar problems appear in other industries that were covered in the workshops, for example, it appears that the Economic Census is still collecting information on Morris Plan banks, even though apparently none of these banks survive. The problems of classifying medical equipment are discussed in chapter 10.

Work on improving product codes is now under way within the Census Bureau and Statistics Canada. We suggest that in this work the product codes for telecommunications equipment and other high-tech components be given a high priority, in addition to the service product codes that are the current focus of attention. The agencies need to develop a product classification for telecommunications and other high-tech equipment that reflects modern uses of this equipment and its technology.

We also found that collapsing patterns (for nondisclosure) in the Current Industrial Reports and even in the Economic Census created gaps and breaks in time series. Moreover, the collapsing patterns sometimes create inconsistency with the PPI product categories that are themselves collapsed because of disclosure problems. More attention needs to be paid to the presentation of the data in these cases, and more cooperation and coordination is needed between BLS and the Census Bureau on collapsing patterns, though we are aware that disclosure is a difficult problem in industries where there may be only a few dominant producers.

Capital Flow Table

The BEA capital flow table (which allocates investment to using industries) is at the root of all analysis of capital and IT contributions by industry. That we and others have found that IT is a major contributor to the post-1995 advance in productivity in the United States underscores the importance of the capital flow tables.

At present, the tables are produced for each five-year benchmark of the national accounts, but they are based on extremely sketchy information on the distribution of investment by purchasing industry (purchases of computers, for example, are allocated among industries by somewhat questionable data on employment of computer professionals, and the proportions of computer professionals may no longer describe which industries are buying computers). More resources need to be put into that activity and better data are needed for these allocations.

NAICS and SIC Bridge Tables and Comparability of Time Series

The divergent time schedules for implementing NAICS across the statistical agencies—particularly with regard to BLS employment—has greatly weakened the U.S. industry database. A second cross-tabulation, or bridge table, between the NAICS and SIC classifications of the data is needed. Such a table has been prepared for 1997. A second match for the 1992 Economic Census is, we understand, being undertaken as a research activity within the Center for Economic Studies of the Census Bureau; constructing this bridge table deserves more support, perhaps as a production activity. It would expand the capability to create longer time series of consistent industry data. As matters now stand, the BEA industry data prior to 1987 are on the 1972 SIC; after 1987 they are on the 1987 SIC; and data after some year yet to be determined will be on NAICS.

With improvements in data quality, comprehensiveness, and relevance, researchers are sometimes confronted with breaks in time series that frustrate analysis. The SIC-NAICS changeover is but one example. Progress sometimes requires breaks in series, and if so, researchers must live with them. But sometimes statistical agencies can provide estimates for research purposes that extrapolate data improvements backward. For some changes in national accounts, such changes are fairly routine. We note in the chapters on finance and insurance, for example, that nearly all of the changes BEA has made to data for those industries recently were carried back to avoid breaks in series, which assures us that the acceleration of productivity in those industries in recent years is not just a statistical mirage. The BLS now makes available a research CPI series that estimates the effects on the past CPI of measurement improvements made to the index in the 1990s.

We also recognize that extrapolations may introduce estimation errors that are more severe than those that exist in current data, since often the exact database used for current data is not available in the past. What is the basis, for example, for extrapolating the Census Bureau's Service Annual Survey for years before data were collected? Service data for those years are lost forever. Nevertheless, backward extrapolations of improvements, where feasible, deserve higher priority than they have sometimes been given.

Medical Care

The medical care sector raises serious measurement problems along many dimensions. The national health accounts contain no information on the purchase and stock of medical equipment, and there are few price indexes that could be used to convert from nominal to real values. This leaves us largely ignorant of the contribution of investment in medical equipment to output of the medical care sector. Yet some of the most dramatic medical advances have been embedded in new equipment. Part of the problem lies with product groupings of the statistical collection programs that lack sufficient detail to identify many types of medical equipment, but the one used in the Census Bureau Current Industrial Reports (CIR) provides a useful "demand side" starting point for development.

In addition, there is the well-known problem of measuring medical care output. A hospital price index from the PPI now spans roughly ten years, and it is clearly a substantial improvement (it also raised the rate of growth of medical productivity, which is suggestive). But more work needs to be done, as the December 1999 Brookings workshop "Measuring Health Care" made clear. These issues are addressed in volumes edited by Berndt and Cutler (2001) and by Triplett (1999a), so we do not consider the issues at great length in this book. But many problems remain.

In particular, proper allowance for improvements in medical treatments requires scientific data on medical outcomes. Not only is the basic information difficult to obtain, but there is also some controversy on whether it crosses over the traditional "production boundary" in national accounts. For example, does the increased value to the patient of improvements in surgery that make it less onerous and unpleasant and reduce recuperation time belong in national accounts if no additional charges are made for the less-invasive surgery? It is difficult to see how an effective measurement can ignore these improvements, yet other similar "nonmarket" changes are not included in the concept of GDP or in the CPI. This creates resistance to changing methods.

In addition, the concept of medical care in the national health accounts and even their basic structure impede development of more effective measures of health care for analytic purposes (Centers for Medicare and Medicaid Services 2004). These problems were discussed in Triplett's paper on accounting for mental health care, presented to the Brookings workshop on medical care productivity (Triplett 1999b).

Business Services

This is a large, diverse, and rapidly growing sector of activity that raises severe measurement problems. One dimension of the problem is the lack of an agreed-upon definition of the industry's output—particularly for business consulting. Without a clear definition of the unit of output, it is difficult to provide guidance on the objective of a price measurement program. In related areas, the PPI program has had some success in trying to price a standard engineering or architecture job. One of the Brookings workshops was devoted to measuring the output of business services, but we were not successful in finding much research on these topics, nor were comprehensive solutions suggested. The conceptual and practical measurement issues remain unresolved.

As suggested in chapter 9, we think that a project within BEA to integrate forward the *inputs* of business services into the inputs of their using industries would be useful. This proposal is not easy to carry out, as it no doubt requires tracing some input and output flows at a lower level than now exists in the I-O tables. It is similar to Denison's suggestion for estimating productivity at the final demand level rather than the industry level, though we would not propose going nearly so far (Denison 1989).

National Accounting Concepts and Productivity Data

The national accounts serve many purposes; one of these is productivity analysis. It is conceivable that BEA may face choices between national accounting concepts, as expressed for example in the SNA, and concepts that are useful for productivity analysis. If so, both analytical purposes must be kept in mind in making decisions about the national accounts.

In the Brookings workshops on insurance and finance (in April 1998 and November 2002, respectively), we were impressed by presentations that indicated that the System of National Accounts adopted concepts for the output of these two important sectors without considering productivity concepts and indeed without engaging in the kinds of conceptual discussions that took place in the Brookings workshops. No doubt some researchers will not agree with our conclusions in chapters 6 and 7; participants in the Brookings workshops expressed a number of different and conflicting positions. Yet it seems inconceivable that adequate measures of output can be developed without considering the positions that were expressed there and that are summarized in chapters 6 and 7.

In most countries, national accounts do not provide adequate industry databases to permit industry-level productivity analyses, so in most countries productivity needs for national accounts data simply are not expressed and are not a factor in decisionmaking about national accounts. The United States is different. It has such a database and use of the national accounts industry database for productivity analysis will only grow more common in the future. For this reason, BEA must take the lead in developing national accounting in the directions required for productivity analysis.

We are impressed with the quality of the 1993 SNA overall, and we agree with BEA's decision to improve the international comparability of U.S. national accounts by making them accord more closely with the SNA. But the SNA, too, can be improved. These remarks are directed toward aspects of the SNA—its production accounts and the measurement concepts for them—that have not been developed fully and are currently under review.

Research and Data Development in Margin Industries

On a related point, we explained in chapters 6, 7, and 8 that in four large industries—wholesale trade, retail trade, insurance, and banking and finance—national accounts incorporate a concept of output that is based on gross margins, or something analogous, while researchers prefer an output concept that begins with industry sales receipts. There are productivity issues here and also output and price measurement issues. In neither case are the issues well developed.

Why do productivity researchers prefer receipts to the gross margin? On what basis is productivity measured better when the output concept is receipts rather than the margin? One can pose the same question for national accountants: SNA 1993 does not explain why national accounts use the gross margin as the output concept for retail and wholesale trade; the document just says "Do it."[2]

For data development, the issue is as follows: Is the gross margin easier to measure than an output concept that begins from receipts? This has been asserted for insurance (because the margin, it is claimed, sidesteps the need to adjust the policy for changes in risk), but we are not fully convinced, as we spell out in chapter 6.

We point out (in chapters 6, 7, and 8) that in each case in which national accounts measure industry output with the gross margin, part of the logic is that the margin consists of services that are bundled with the part of receipts that is outside the margin. For example, in retail trade, retailing services are bundled with the goods retailers sell, and in insurance, the premiums-minus-claims margin consists of administrative and policyholder services. What exactly are those services? How have they changed? How can anyone measure the real, or constant price, output of the margin without enumerating and measuring the services that are in the margin?

As Zvi Griliches pointed out in the Brookings workshop on insurance, "double deflation" of insurance policies and claims has nothing to do with the policyholder services that the margin supposedly measures. If the insurance margin is intended to measure policyholder services, then it seems obvious that Griliches

---

2. We do not know the history of the trade gross margin in national accounts. Stone (1947) does not mention treating retail and wholesale trade differently from other industries, nor does Jaszi (1958), though both devote considerable space to banking and insurance.

was right: we need to measure the services and deflate them, not deflate what is outside the margin. The same point applies to retail trade: deflating retail sales and the goods purchased for resale has little to do with the retailing services that are the focus of the gross margin view. Yet little work has been done on the services that are incorporated into the margin, nor to our knowledge have statistical agencies even tried to enumerate them.

Moreover, measuring the services that are bundled with the sale is essential whether or not one wants to do productivity analysis at the gross margin—they also are needed for measuring an output concept that uses gross receipts, as Walter Oi and others have pointed out for retail trade. Without better enumeration and measurement of retailing services, our output and productivity estimates are flawed, whether for studies carried out on gross margins or on deflated gross receipts.

More conceptual work is needed on the appropriate output basis for productivity studies in services industries that are now measured in national accounts by gross margins, and possibly some work is needed on whether there is a real reason why national accountants prefer the gross margin (value added is the same whether the industry output is gross margin or gross receipts, so GDP is invariant to this choice at the industry level). Needed also is attention to the services that are included in the gross margin and survey work to enumerate and measure them.

BEA should take the lead in these studies. Since the four margin industries are large and since the issue comes up only because of national accounting practices, BEA can, first, show why the gross margin output measure is superior for national accounting purposes, if it is. In the current BEA deflation for these four industries, the national accounts gross margin concept often is combined with a deflator or with other data that are erected on a different output concept—as, for example, with the use of CPI sales price indexes to deflate the gross margin concept in retail trade (however, PPI retail price indexes will measure the price of the gross margin). Better enumeration and measurement of the services that are in the margin will create more compatibility in BEA's measures, assuming it sticks with the gross margin concept; in any case, it will also improve output measures that are based on gross receipts.

Industry-Specific Issues

Some of the statistical concerns specific to individual industries are raised and discussed more thoroughly in other chapters.

Industry Productivity Accounts, 1987–2001

Table A-1. *Sources of Change in Output per Worker, 1987–2001, Least Squares Trend Growth*

SIC code	Industry	Growth in output per worker		Capital	
		1987–95	1995–2001	1987–95	1995–2001
	Private nonfarm business	1.31	2.14	0.23	0.53
	Goods-producing industries	2.14	2.09	0.23	0.38
	Agricultural services, forestry, and fishing	0.10	1.18	0.29	0.60
10-14	Mining	3.54	1.61	0.68	0.72
10	Metal mining	5.82	5.64	−0.50	1.13
12	Coal mining	7.37	5.54	0.21	0.96
13	Oil and gas extraction	2.72	0.16	0.84	0.20
14	Nonmetallic minerals, except fuels	1.48	1.35	0.52	0.92
15-17	Construction	−0.37	−1.12	−0.08	0.49
	Manufacturing	2.77	3.64	0.26	0.37
	Durable goods	3.88	4.79	0.29	0.49
24	Lumber and wood products	−0.63	0.80	−0.10	0.13
25	Furniture and fixtures	1.77	1.84	0.12	0.23
32	Stone, clay, and glass products	1.02	0.88	−0.01	0.54
33	Primary metal industries	2.82	0.52	0.04	0.12
34	Fabricated metal products	1.45	1.44	0.12	0.32
35	Industrial machinery and equipment	6.20	6.92	0.40	0.64
37	Motor vehicles and other transportation equipment	3.15	3.23	0.13	0.28
36,38	Electronic equipment and instruments	7.61	10.04	0.81	0.91
39	Miscellaneous manufacturing industries	0.87	2.44	0.14	0.44
	Nondurable goods	1.41	2.39	0.32	0.55
20	Food and kindred products	1.25	1.21	0.15	0.28
21	Tobacco products	2.81	0.16	0.60	0.18
22	Textile mill products	2.83	2.91	0.15	0.47
23	Apparel and other textile products	2.31	7.35	0.26	0.82
26	Paper and allied products	1.44	1.04	0.30	0.39
27	Printing and publishing	−0.61	0.58	0.37	0.55
28	Chemicals and allied products	1.42	1.68	0.58	0.68
29	Petroleum and coal products	1.47	3.09	0.30	0.14
30	Rubber and miscellaneous plastics products	2.99	3.09	0.16	0.53
31	Leather and leather products	1.63	4.72	0.99	0.66

Contribution of Intermediate inputs		MFP		Contribution of IT capital		Non-IT capital	
1987–95	*1995–2001*	*1987–95*	*1995–2001*	*1987–95*	*1995–2001*	*1987–95*	*1995–2001*
0.81	0.85	0.28	0.76	0.18	0.44	0.04	0.09
1.43	1.19	0.48	0.53	0.12	0.19	0.11	0.19
0.68	0.19	−0.86	0.40	0.10	0.13	0.19	0.46
1.75	1.89	1.11	−1.00	0.09	0.24	0.58	0.47
2.40	−2.68	3.92	7.19	0.31	0.26	−0.80	0.88
3.37	1.97	3.79	2.60	0.12	0.19	0.10	0.77
1.53	2.72	0.35	−2.76	0.07	0.25	0.77	−0.04
0.82	−1.30	0.14	1.73	0.12	0.28	0.40	0.64
−0.50	−1.06	0.21	−0.55	0.06	0.09	−0.14	0.40
1.91	2.29	0.60	0.98	0.11	0.18	0.14	0.19
2.52	2.42	1.07	1.89	0.12	0.24	0.17	0.25
0.98	1.09	−1.51	−0.42	0.06	0.08	−0.16	0.06
1.26	1.39	0.39	0.22	0.07	0.12	0.05	0.11
−0.24	0.71	1.27	−0.37	0.03	0.20	−0.03	0.34
1.87	−0.30	0.92	0.70	0.02	0.06	0.02	0.06
0.88	1.29	0.45	−0.17	0.10	0.17	0.02	0.15
3.97	2.36	1.83	3.92	0.23	0.49	0.17	0.15
2.81	2.31	0.21	0.64	0.05	0.12	0.08	0.16
3.99	5.09	2.82	4.04	0.25	0.37	0.56	0.54
0.68	−0.06	0.05	2.06	0.12	0.16	0.03	0.28
1.10	2.27	−0.01	−0.43	0.15	0.23	0.16	0.32
0.92	2.03	0.18	−1.09	0.05	0.09	0.10	0.19
4.72	7.93	−2.51	−7.95	0.09	0.11	0.51	0.07
1.47	2.34	1.20	0.11	0.10	0.15	0.05	0.33
1.51	5.80	0.54	0.74	0.09	0.15	0.18	0.67
1.02	0.91	0.12	−0.26	0.10	0.12	0.20	0.28
0.61	0.72	−1.59	−0.69	0.33	0.57	0.04	−0.02
0.47	1.18	0.37	−0.18	0.30	0.31	0.29	0.37
1.85	2.54	−0.68	0.41	0.15	0.05	0.15	0.08
1.61	1.82	1.22	0.75	0.07	0.15	0.09	0.38
−0.35	4.75	0.99	−0.69	0.09	0.30	0.89	0.35

(continued)

Table A-1. *Sources of Change in Output per Worker, 1987–2001,*
Least Squares Trend Growth (Continued)

SIC code	Industry	Growth in output per worker 1987–95	Growth in output per worker 1995–2001	Capital 1987–95	Capital 1995–2001
	Service-producing industries	1.26	2.41	0.25	0.64
	Transportation	1.91	0.75	−0.12	0.39
40	Railroad transportation	6.22	2.14	0.31	0.27
41	Local and interurban passenger transit	−1.71	−0.61	−0.43	0.04
42	Trucking and warehousing	3.45	0.78	−0.04	0.19
44	Water transportation	1.74	1.01	−0.20	−0.15
45	Transportation by air	−0.02	0.42	−0.09	0.79
46	Pipelines, except natural gas	−0.67	1.15	0.75	1.84
47	Transportation services	1.99	3.53	0.05	1.80
48	Communications	4.12	6.68	1.59	1.60
	Telephone and telegraph	5.49	7.95	1.58	1.11
483-484	Radio and television	0.01	1.77	1.93	3.23
49	Electric, gas, and sanitary services	2.14	2.05	0.75	0.81
50-51	Wholesale trade	3.43	4.19	0.63	1.78
52-59	Retail trade	1.27	3.44	0.35	0.30
	Finance and insurance	1.82	3.60	0.88	1.40
60	Depository institutions	2.91	3.12	1.46	1.36
61	Nondepository institutions	2.44	1.86	0.38	1.78
62	Security and commodity brokers	7.17	10.35	0.50	0.35
63	Insurance carriers	−0.63	−1.66	0.57	0.87
64	Insurance agents, brokers, and service	−3.35	2.79	0.10	0.54
65	Real estate (excluding owner-occupied housing)	2.74	1.71	0.29	0.06
	Other service industries	0.42	1.54	0.16	0.53
70	Hotels and other lodging places	1.02	−0.57	0.38	0.29
72	Personal services	1.00	1.54	0.27	0.28
73	Business services	2.86	3.56	0.03	1.00
75	Auto repair, services, and parking	0.85	1.46	1.03	0.25
76	Miscellaneous repair services	1.90	1.81	0.20	0.57
78	Motion pictures	0.12	0.26	0.36	0.32
79	Amusement and recreation services	1.57	−0.41	−0.31	0.31
80	Health services	−0.69	0.92	0.19	0.48
81	Legal services	0.00	1.49	0.07	0.28
82	Educational services	0.19	−0.95	0.01	0.05
83-87	Other services	−0.44	1.95	0.05	0.22

Source: Authors' computations. The reported values are the least squares trend coefficients from
cumulative summations of the log changes.

Contribution of				Contribution of			
Intermediate inputs		MFP		IT capital		Non-IT capital	
1987–95	1995–2001	1987–95	1995–2001	1987–95	1995–2001	1987–95	1995–2001
0.85	0.89	0.16	0.88	0.23	0.59	0.02	0.04
0.83	0.33	1.21	0.03	0.13	0.31	−0.26	0.09
2.50	0.33	3.42	1.54	0.03	0.04	0.28	0.22
−0.31	−1.94	−0.97	1.29	0.01	0.04	−0.44	−0.00
2.57	0.68	0.92	−0.10	0.10	0.08	−0.14	0.11
0.38	0.99	1.56	0.17	0.03	0.05	−0.23	−0.21
−2.38	0.08	2.45	−0.45	0.09	0.52	−0.18	0.27
1.35	−2.33	−2.78	1.64	0.61	0.91	0.14	0.93
2.23	1.56	−0.29	0.17	0.70	1.56	−0.65	0.24
0.86	5.11	1.68	−0.04	0.86	1.29	0.73	0.32
2.22	5.63	1.69	1.21	0.89	0.97	0.69	0.14
−3.56	3.07	1.64	−4.53	1.03	2.31	0.90	0.92
0.85	1.84	0.54	−0.60	0.25	0.25	0.51	0.56
1.31	−0.66	1.49	3.07	0.49	1.42	0.14	0.35
0.72	0.23	0.20	2.92	0.11	0.26	0.24	0.04
0.99	0.58	−0.06	1.61	0.62	1.09	0.26	0.31
1.27	0.30	0.19	1.47	0.85	1.24	0.60	0.12
2.31	−2.04	−0.25	2.12	1.10	1.61	−0.72	0.17
3.55	3.37	3.12	6.63	0.06	0.20	0.44	0.15
−1.08	−2.56	−0.13	0.03	0.31	0.63	0.26	0.24
0.13	2.35	−3.58	−0.10	0.07	0.25	0.02	0.29
2.01	0.24	0.44	1.41	−0.01	0.02	0.30	0.03
0.87	1.45	−0.61	−0.43	0.14	0.47	0.02	0.06
0.63	0.47	0.01	−1.33	0.06	0.13	0.32	0.16
1.64	0.88	−0.91	0.38	0.12	0.11	0.14	0.17
1.93	3.17	0.90	−0.60	0.15	1.08	−0.12	−0.09
1.24	−0.18	−1.41	1.39	0.04	0.11	0.99	0.14
2.81	2.84	−1.11	−1.60	0.16	0.34	0.04	0.23
0.96	−0.26	−1.21	0.20	0.20	0.14	0.16	0.19
1.74	0.40	0.14	−1.11	−0.04	0.07	−0.27	0.24
0.78	0.95	−1.66	−0.51	0.19	0.34	0.01	0.14
0.76	0.29	−0.82	0.91	0.14	0.28	−0.07	−0.00
0.42	−0.22	−0.24	−0.79	0.02	0.07	−0.01	−0.01
−0.19	1.87	−0.30	−0.13	0.10	0.25	−0.05	−0.03

Table A-2. *Sources of Change in Value Added per Worker, 1987–2001, Least Squares Trend Growth*

SIC code	Industry	Growth in value added per worker 1987–95	Growth in value added per worker 1995–2001
	Private nonfarm business	1.01	2.46
	Goods-producing industries	1.81	2.28
	Agricultural services, forestry, and fishing	–0.72	1.39
	Mining	3.39	–0.36
10	Metal mining	7.62	16.25
12	Coal mining	10.30	9.30
13	Oil and gas extraction	2.28	–4.00
14	Nonmetallic minerals, except fuels	1.28	4.35
15-17	Construction	0.22	–0.09
	Manufacturing	2.42	3.84
	Durable goods	3.50	6.34
24	Lumber and wood products	–3.88	–0.71
25	Furniture and fixtures	1.33	1.21
32	Stone, clay, and glass products	3.04	0.42
33	Primary metal industries	3.34	2.88
34	Fabricated metal products	1.33	0.34
35	Industrial machinery and equipment	5.23	11.91
37	Motor vehicles and other transportation equipment	1.07	3.02
36,38	Electronic equipment and instruments	7.74	11.75
39	Miscellaneous manufacturing industries	0.41	4.79
	Nondurable goods	0.96	0.44
20	Food and kindred products	1.30	–2.99
21	Tobacco products	–3.63	–17.22
22	Textile mill products	4.00	1.85
23	Apparel and other textile products	2.14	4.77
26	Paper and allied products	1.22	0.40
27	Printing and publishing	–2.68	–0.33
28	Chemicals and allied products	2.38	1.21
29	Petroleum and coal products	–2.00	2.41
30	Rubber and miscellaneous plastics products	4.14	3.81
31	Leather and leather products	3.68	0.36

| Contribution of | | | | Contribution of | | | |
| Capital | | MFP | | IT capital | | Non-IT capital | |
1987–95	*1995–2001*	*1987–95*	*1995–2001*	*1987–95*	*1995–2001*	*1987–95*	*1995–2001*
0.44	1.02	0.56	1.44	0.36	0.85	0.08	0.17
0.58	0.96	1.23	1.31	0.30	0.48	0.27	0.49
0.40	0.84	−1.12	0.56	0.14	0.19	0.27	0.65
1.27	1.21	2.12	−1.57	0.18	0.42	1.09	0.78
−1.02	2.44	8.64	13.81	0.68	0.57	−1.70	1.87
0.60	2.81	9.70	6.48	0.33	0.57	0.27	2.24
1.46	0.16	0.82	−4.15	0.13	0.38	1.33	−0.23
0.96	1.54	0.32	2.81	0.22	0.47	0.74	1.07
−0.15	0.85	0.37	−0.95	0.11	0.16	−0.26	0.69
0.72	1.06	1.70	2.77	0.32	0.53	0.40	0.54
0.74	1.30	2.76	5.04	0.31	0.65	0.43	0.66
−0.29	0.37	−3.59	−1.07	0.14	0.21	−0.42	0.16
0.31	0.61	1.02	0.60	0.18	0.32	0.13	0.29
−0.01	1.29	3.05	−0.87	0.07	0.47	−0.08	0.82
0.14	0.43	3.20	2.45	0.06	0.22	0.08	0.21
0.28	0.74	1.05	−0.40	0.23	0.38	0.05	0.36
0.90	1.68	4.34	10.23	10.51	1.29	0.38	0.39
0.45	0.90	0.62	2.13	0.18	0.40	0.27	0.49
1.71	2.15	6.03	9.61	0.52	0.87	1.19	1.28
0.28	0.85	0.14	3.94	0.24	0.33	0.04	0.52
0.99	1.69	−0.03	−1.25	0.48	0.70	0.52	0.99
0.61	1.12	0.69	−4.11	0.20	0.36	0.41	0.75
2.37	0.78	−5.99	−18.00	0.35	0.42	2.02	0.35
0.47	1.50	3.53	0.35	0.31	0.46	0.16	1.03
0.70	2.48	1.45	2.29	0.23	0.45	0.47	2.02
0.89	1.16	0.33	−0.77	0.30	0.34	0.59	0.82
0.81	1.22	−3.49	−1.55	0.73	1.29	0.08	−0.07
1.50	1.65	0.88	−0.44	0.77	0.74	0.73	0.90
1.60	0.80	−3.60	1.61	0.80	0.31	0.80	0.49
0.50	1.58	3.64	2.23	0.22	0.45	0.28	1.13
1.86	1.62	1.82	−1.26	0.18	0.68	1.68	0.94

(continued)

Table A-2. *Sources of Change in Value Added per Worker, 1987–2001,*
Least Squares Trend Growth (Continued)

SIC code	Industry	Growth in value added per worker	
		1987–95	1995–2001
	Service-producing industries	0.75	2.56
	Transportation	2.19	0.84
40	Railroad transportation	6.25	3.21
41	Local and interurban passenger transit	−2.69	2.09
42	Trucking and warehousing	2.02	0.20
44	Water transportation	3.85	0.23
45	Transportation by air	4.21	0.54
46	Pipelines, except natural gas	−2.52	4.51
47	Transportation services	−0.20	3.18
48	Communications	5.09	3.41
	Telephone and telegraph	5.08	5.00
483-484	Radio and television	6.24	−1.75
49	Electric, gas, and sanitary services	2.26	0.51
50-51	Wholesale trade	3.39	6.81
52-59	Retail trade	0.98	4.95
	Finance and insurance	1.47	5.14
60	Depository institutions	2.38	3.85
61	Nondepository institutions	0.49	9.68
62	Security and commodity brokers	6.08	12.39
63	Insurance carriers	1.03	1.38
64	Insurance agents, brokers, and service	−5.31	0.71
65	Real estate (excluding owner-occupied housing)	1.50	2.67
	Other service industries	−0.68	0.20
70	Hotels and other lodging places	0.72	−1.64
72	Personal services	−0.99	1.14
73	Business services	1.39	0.66
75	Auto repair, services, and parking	−0.51	2.79
76	Miscellaneous repair services	−1.69	−2.03
78	Motion pictures	−1.86	1.15
79	Amusement and recreation services	−0.20	−1.47
80	Health services	−2.19	−0.02
81	Legal services	−0.97	1.59
82	Educational services	−0.40	−1.29
83-87	Other services	−0.43	0.18

Source: Authors' computations. The reported values are the least squares trend coefficients from cumulative summations of the log changes.

Contribution of				Contribution of			
Capital		*MFP*		*IT capital*		*Non-IT capital*	
1987–95	*1995–2001*	*1987–95*	*1995–2001*	*1987–95*	*1995–2001*	*1987–95*	*1995–2001*
0.41	1.08	0.33	1.48	0.38	1.01	0.04	0.07
−0.24	0.78	2.43	0.06	0.27	0.61	−0.52	0.17
0.51	0.48	5.74	2.73	0.04	0.08	0.47	0.40
−0.83	0.04	−1.86	2.05	0.02	0.07	−0.84	−0.03
−0.11	0.45	2.13	−0.25	0.22	0.18	−0.32	0.26
−0.61	−0.49	4.46	0.72	0.08	0.16	−0.69	−0.66
−0.19	1.34	4.40	−0.80	0.18	0.89	−0.37	0.45
1.10	2.50	−3.61	2.01	0.89	1.24	0.20	1.26
0.08	2.86	−0.28	0.33	0.99	2.47	−0.91	0.39
2.52	3.01	2.56	0.40	1.36	2.42	1.16	0.59
2.43	2.22	2.65	2.78	1.37	1.93	1.06	0.29
3.47	5.28	2.76	−7.03	1.85	3.78	1.63	1.50
1.32	1.45	0.93	−0.94	0.44	0.45	0.89	1.00
1.00	2.72	2.38	4.09	0.79	2.19	0.22	0.54
0.58	0.49	0.40	4.46	0.19	0.43	0.39	0.06
1.54	2.42	−0.07	2.71	1.07	1.89	0.46	0.53
2.02	1.87	0.36	1.98	1.19	1.70	0.83	0.16
1.09	4.75	−0.60	4.93	2.43	4.33	−1.34	0.41
0.74	0.66	5.35	11.74	0.06	0.37	0.67	0.28
1.51	1.74	−0.48	−0.36	0.81	1.28	0.70	0.46
0.15	0.86	−5.46	−0.15	0.11	0.40	0.04	0.47
0.50	0.11	1.00	2.56	−0.02	0.04	0.52	0.06
0.25	0.86	−0.93	−0.67	0.22	0.76	0.03	0.10
0.66	0.49	0.06	−2.13	0.11	0.23	0.55	0.26
0.45	0.48	−1.45	0.66	0.20	0.20	0.25	0.29
0.04	1.54	1.35	−0.88	0.22	1.67	−0.18	−0.13
1.85	0.45	−2.36	2.34	0.08	0.20	1.77	0.24
0.42	1.26	−2.11	−3.29	0.34	0.75	0.08	0.51
0.84	0.75	−2.70	0.40	0.47	0.32	0.36	0.43
−0.56	0.61	0.35	−2.08	−0.08	0.14	−0.48	0.47
0.29	0.74	−2.48	−0.77	0.28	0.52	0.01	0.23
0.08	0.37	−1.06	1.22	0.17	0.37	−0.09	−0.00
0.02	0.09	−0.42	−1.38	0.03	0.12	−0.01	−0.02
0.09	0.39	−0.52	−0.22	0.18	0.45	−0.09	−0.06

Table A-3. *Sources of Change in Output per Worker, 1987–2001,*
Average Annual Rates of Change

SIC code	Industry	Growth in output per worker		Capital	
		1987–95	1995–2001	1987–95	1995–2001
	Private nonfarm business	1.35	1.96	0.19	0.52
	Goods-producing industries	2.05	1.76	0.18	0.38
	Agricultural services, forestry, and fishing	−0.02	1.03	0.21	0.60
	Mining	3.32	1.34	0.61	0.41
10	Metal mining	4.68	5.69	−0.88	1.03
12	Coal mining	7.82	5.59	0.30	0.95
13	Oil and gas extraction	2.56	−0.42	0.84	−0.36
14	Nonmetallic minerals, except fuels	1.31	1.56	0.49	1.00
15-17	Construction	−0.85	−0.95	−0.12	0.40
	Manufacturing	2.81	3.22	0.21	0.38
	Durable goods	3.98	4.17	0.25	0.50
24	Lumber and wood products	−0.97	0.75	−0.17	0.19
25	Furniture and fixtures	1.34	1.33	0.10	0.26
32	Stone, clay, and glass products	0.85	0.37	−0.03	0.50
33	Primary metal industries	2.64	−0.01	−0.01	0.13
34	Fabricated metal products	1.22	1.34	0.06	0.37
35	Industrial machinery and equipment	7.00	6.40	0.34	0.63
37	Motor vehicles and other transportation equipment	2.93	2.56	0.12	0.29
36,38	Electronic equipment and instruments	8.13	9.18	0.77	0.91
39	Miscellaneous manufacturing industries	1.12	1.94	0.09	0.41
	Nondurable goods	1.44	2.21	0.29	0.55
20	Food and kindred products	1.43	0.88	0.14	0.26
21	Tobacco products	3.67	0.32	0.54	0.22
22	Textile mill products	2.40	2.96	0.15	0.48
23	Apparel and other textile products	2.18	7.16	0.28	0.78
26	Paper and allied products	1.47	0.57	0.27	0.42
27	Printing and publishing	−0.94	0.26	0.32	0.55
28	Chemicals and allied products	1.58	1.43	0.53	0.68
29	Petroleum and coal products	2.12	3.05	0.34	0.16
30	Rubber and miscellaneous plastics products	2.92	3.05	0.16	0.54
31	Leather and leather products	0.82	5.31	1.03	0.44

Contribution of				Contribution of			
Intermediate inputs		MFP		IT capital		Non-IT capital	
1987–95	1995–2001	1987–95	1995–2001	1987–95	1995–2001	1987–95	1995–2001
0.78	0.75	0.37	0.68	0.18	0.43	0.01	0.09
1.21	0.99	0.65	0.39	0.11	0.18	0.07	0.19
1.02	0.29	−1.24	0.14	0.10	0.13	0.12	0.47
0.85	1.80	1.83	−0.86	0.10	0.22	0.51	0.19
2.51	−2.58	3.02	7.39	0.30	0.30	−1.18	0.73
3.54	1.77	3.82	2.77	0.13	0.19	0.17	0.76
0.09	2.54	1.62	−2.54	0.08	0.20	0.75	−0.55
1.07	−1.37	−0.26	1.95	0.13	0.28	0.37	0.73
−0.92	−0.83	0.19	−0.52	0.06	0.09	−0.18	0.31
1.79	2.02	0.79	0.80	0.11	0.18	0.11	0.20
2.40	1.99	1.29	1.64	0.11	0.24	0.14	0.26
0.40	1.12	−1.20	−0.56	0.06	0.08	−0.22	0.11
1.04	0.92	0.19	0.15	0.07	0.12	0.04	0.14
−0.37	0.49	1.26	−0.61	0.03	0.19	−0.06	0.31
1.90	−0.79	0.73	0.66	0.01	0.06	−0.02	0.07
0.53	1.27	0.63	−0.30	0.09	0.17	−0.04	0.20
4.12	2.30	2.41	3.35	0.20	0.47	0.15	0.17
2.65	1.90	0.15	0.35	0.05	0.12	0.06	0.18
3.86	4.07	3.32	3.97	0.23	0.37	0.54	0.54
0.38	0.05	0.64	1.47	0.11	0.16	−0.02	0.25
1.03	2.17	0.12	−0.50	0.14	0.22	0.15	0.33
0.76	1.96	0.52	−1.32	0.05	0.09	0.09	0.17
4.75	7.68	−1.56	−7.03	0.09	0.11	0.45	0.11
1.35	2.36	0.89	0.11	0.10	0.14	0.05	0.34
1.25	5.42	0.64	0.86	0.09	0.15	0.19	0.63
1.50	0.29	−0.30	−0.14	0.10	0.11	0.18	0.31
0.28	0.69	−1.53	−0.98	0.31	0.54	0.01	0.01
0.65	0.83	0.39	−0.08	0.28	0.30	0.25	0.38
2.00	2.79	−0.22	0.09	0.14	0.06	0.20	0.10
1.53	1.83	1.21	0.67	0.07	0.15	0.09	0.39
−1.36	5.66	1.16	−0.76	0.10	0.31	0.93	0.13

(continued)

Table A-3. *Sources of Change in Output per Worker, 1987–2001,*
Average Annual Rates of Change (Continued)

SIC code	Industry	Growth in output per worker 1987–95	1995–2001	Capital 1987–95	1995–2001
	Service-producing industries	1.36	2.33	0.22	0.63
	Transportation	1.96	0.51	−0.12	0.39
40	Railroad transportation	6.54	2.62	0.27	0.33
41	Local and interurban passenger transit	−1.60	−0.98	−0.44	0.02
42	Trucking and warehousing	3.40	0.52	0.02	0.20
44	Water transportation	2.29	0.78	−0.20	−0.15
45	Transportation by air	0.01	0.19	−0.15	0.75
46	Pipelines, except natural gas	0.67	0.51	1.33	1.51
47	Transportation services	2.27	3.08	−0.01	1.84
48	Communications	4.35	6.94	1.55	1.62
	Telephone and telegraph	5.79	8.37	1.58	1.15
483-484	Radio and television	0.17	1.74	1.79	3.20
49	Electric, gas, and sanitary services	2.47	2.08	0.80	0.89
50-51	Wholesale trade	3.26	4.22	0.62	1.81
52-59	Retail trade	1.21	3.22	0.31	0.30
	Finance and insurance	2.17	3.17	0.93	1.38
60	Depository institutions	2.89	2.96	1.31	1.22
61	Nondepository institutions	4.78	2.17	0.95	1.78
62	Security and commodity brokers	7.19	9.10	0.59	0.39
63	Insurance carriers	0.02	−0.92	0.60	0.89
64	Insurance agents, brokers, and service	−3.27	1.19	0.11	0.51
65	Real estate (excluding owner-occupied housing)	2.97	2.29	0.19	0.06
	Other service industries	0.63	1.49	0.15	0.49
70	Hotels and other lodging places	0.68	−0.90	0.31	0.37
72	Personal services	1.66	1.14	0.31	0.26
73	Business services	2.98	3.71	0.04	0.91
75	Auto repair, services, and parking	1.40	1.05	0.93	0.20
76	Miscellaneous repair services	2.62	0.91	0.18	0.55
78	Motion pictures	−0.30	0.12	0.33	0.33
79	Amusement and recreation services	1.91	−0.33	−0.31	0.35
80	Health services	−0.46	0.88	0.21	0.44
81	Legal services	0.13	1.60	0.06	0.26
82	Educational services	0.50	−0.97	0.01	0.04
83-87	Other services	−0.13	1.91	0.03	0.21

Source: Authors' computations. The reported values are average annual percent changes.

| Contribution of | | | | Contribution of | | | |
| Intermediate inputs | | MFP | | IT capital | | Non-IT capital | |
1987–95	1995–2001	1987–95	1995–2001	1987–95	1995–2001	1987–95	1995–2001
0.93	0.85	0.21	0.83	0.23	0.58	−0.01	0.05
1.09	0.13	0.99	−0.00	0.14	0.31	−0.27	0.08
2.91	0.39	3.25	1.89	0.03	0.04	0.24	0.29
−0.11	−1.83	−1.06	0.84	0.01	0.04	−0.45	−0.01
2.85	0.55	0.51	−0.22	0.11	0.08	−0.08	0.12
1.04	0.46	1.44	0.47	0.03	0.05	−0.24	−0.20
−2.34	−0.17	2.57	−0.38	0.10	0.53	0.00	0.00
3.23	−2.58	−3.76	1.63	0.69	0.94	0.64	0.57
2.86	1.17	−0.56	0.05	0.72	1.59	−0.74	0.25
1.09	5.10	1.65	0.13	0.85	1.30	0.69	0.32
2.53	5.61	1.58	1.44	0.91	1.00	0.67	0.15
−3.44	3.16	1.92	−4.43	0.98	2.30	0.81	0.89
0.81	2.21	0.84	−1.01	0.26	0.26	0.54	0.63
1.50	−0.61	1.11	3.00	0.51	1.42	0.11	0.38
0.54	−0.05	0.36	2.96	0.12	0.25	0.19	0.05
1.25	0.13	−0.01	1.64	0.64	1.06	0.29	0.32
1.11	0.49	0.45	1.22	0.78	1.14	0.52	0.08
4.17	−2.05	−0.36	2.48	1.32	1.58	−0.37	0.20
3.70	0.67	2.76	7.96	0.13	0.20	0.46	0.18
−0.53	−1.56	−0.05	−0.25	0.33	0.64	0.27	0.26
−0.00	1.13	−3.37	−0.44	0.08	0.23	0.02	0.27
2.04	1.06	0.72	1.16	−0.01	0.02	0.20	0.04
0.99	1.43	−0.51	−0.43	0.15	0.44	−0.00	0.06
0.29	−0.10	0.07	−1.16	0.06	0.13	0.26	0.24
1.94	0.72	−0.58	0.16	0.12	0.10	0.19	0.16
2.18	3.16	0.75	−0.37	0.20	1.00	−0.16	−0.10
1.46	−0.18	−0.98	1.03	0.05	0.11	0.88	0.09
2.90	2.54	−0.45	−2.13	0.17	0.34	0.01	0.21
0.57	−0.56	−1.20	0.36	0.20	0.13	0.13	0.20
2.09	0.41	0.13	−1.08	−0.04	0.07	−0.27	0.28
0.89	0.89	−1.55	−0.44	0.19	0.32	0.02	0.12
0.38	0.88	−0.31	0.46	0.14	0.26	−0.08	−0.00
0.64	−0.16	−0.15	−0.85	0.02	0.06	−0.00	−0.02
0.06	1.91	−0.21	−0.21	0.10	0.24	−0.07	−0.04

Table A-4. *Sources of Change in Value Added per Worker, 1987–2001,*
Average Annual Rates of Change

SIC code	Industry	Growth in value added per worker	
		1987–95	1995–2001
	Private nonfarm business	1.12	2.32
	Goods-producing industries	2.11	1.94
	Agricultural services, forestry, and fishing	−1.32	1.02
	Mining	4.37	−0.66
10	Metal mining	4.94	16.86
12	Coal mining	10.85	10.03
13	Oil and gas extraction	3.97	−4.52
14	Nonmetallic minerals, except fuels	0.57	4.94
15-17	Construction	0.12	−0.19
	Manufacturing	2.83	3.40
	Durable goods	4.00	5.82
24	Lumber and wood products	−3.21	−0.92
25	Furniture and fixtures	0.77	1.09
32	Stone, clay, and glass products	2.98	−0.25
33	Primary metal industries	2.56	2.74
34	Fabricated metal products	1.58	0.16
35	Industrial machinery and equipment	6.62	10.87
37	Motor vehicles and other transportation equipment	0.83	2.14
36,38	Electronic equipment and instruments	9.03	12.02
39	Miscellaneous manufacturing industries	1.52	3.67
	Nondurable goods	1.26	0.20
20	Food and kindred products	2.62	−3.88
21	Tobacco products	−1.10	−14.35
22	Textile mill products	3.11	1.89
23	Apparel and other textile products	2.48	5.13
26	Paper and allied products	−0.09	0.82
27	Printing and publishing	−2.66	−0.95
28	Chemicals and allied products	2.26	1.42
29	Petroleum and coal products	0.51	0.79
30	Rubber and miscellaneous plastics products	4.19	3.67
31	Leather and leather products	4.14	−0.14

Contribution of				Contribution of			
Capital		MFP		IT capital		Non-IT capital	
1987–95	1995–2001	1987–95	1995–2001	1987–95	1995–2001	1987–95	1995–2001
0.37	1.01	0.75	1.29	0.36	0.83	0.01	0.18
0.45	0.96	1.66	0.97	0.28	0.47	0.17	0.49
0.30	0.84	−1.61	0.18	0.13	0.19	0.16	0.66
1.15	0.66	3.19	−1.31	0.19	0.38	0.96	0.28
−1.80	2.19	6.86	14.36	0.68	0.65	−2.47	1.54
0.85	2.81	9.92	7.03	0.36	0.55	0.49	2.26
1.43	−0.79	2.51	−3.75	0.15	0.30	1.28	−1.10
0.92	1.69	−0.34	3.20	0.23	0.47	0.68	1.22
−0.22	0.69	0.35	−0.88	0.11	0.16	−0.33	0.54
0.59	1.09	2.22	2.28	0.30	0.51	0.30	0.58
0.63	1.33	3.35	4.43	0.29	0.63	0.34	0.70
−0.43	0.53	−2.79	−1.44	0.14	0.22	−0.57	0.30
0.27	0.68	0.50	0.41	0.18	0.32	0.10	0.36
−0.08	1.20	3.06	−1.44	0.07	0.45	−0.15	0.75
−0.04	0.46	2.60	2.28	0.04	0.21	−0.08	0.24
0.13	0.84	1.45	−0.67	0.22	0.38	−0.09	0.46
0.77	1.65	5.81	9.07	0.44	1.22	0.33	0.43
0.38	0.93	0.45	1.20	0.18	0.38	0.20	0.55
1.63	2.16	7.27	9.65	0.48	0.88	1.15	1.28
0.18	0.77	1.34	2.87	0.23	0.32	−0.05	0.45
0.92	1.71	0.34	−1.48	0.45	0.68	0.47	1.03
0.58	1.03	2.02	−4.86	0.20	0.34	0.38	0.69
2.12	0.91	−3.15	−15.12	0.34	0.40	1.77	0.50
0.47	1.52	2.63	0.37	0.32	0.45	0.15	1.07
0.74	2.38	1.73	2.68	0.23	0.45	0.51	1.93
0.80	1.25	−0.88	−0.42	0.28	0.34	0.52	0.91
0.70	1.23	−3.34	−2.16	0.69	1.22	0.01	0.01
1.35	1.66	0.90	−0.24	0.71	0.73	0.64	0.93
1.77	0.93	−1.23	−0.14	0.75	0.35	1.02	0.59
0.49	1.63	3.68	2.02	0.22	0.44	0.27	1.19
1.95	1.21	2.15	−1.34	0.18	0.68	1.76	0.53

(continud)

Table A-4. *Sources of Change in Value Added per Worker, 1987–2001, Average Annual Rates of Change (Continued)*

SIC code	Industry	Growth in value added per worker	
		1987–95	1995–2001
	Service-producing industries	0.78	2.49
	Transportation	1.78	0.75
40	Railroad transportation	5.92	3.95
41	Local and interurban passenger transit	−2.81	1.35
42	Trucking and warehousing	1.31	−0.07
44	Water transportation	3.62	1.07
45	Transportation by air	4.36	0.55
46	Pipelines, except natural gas	−2.81	4.27
47	Transportation services	−0.59	3.03
48	Communications	5.11	3.79
	Telephone and telegraph	5.04	5.59
483-484	Radio and television	6.72	−1.77
49	Electric, gas, and sanitary services	2.82	−0.07
50-51	Wholesale trade	2.88	6.94
52-59	Retail trade	1.14	5.04
	Finance and insurance	1.65	5.20
60	Depository institutions	2.57	3.36
61	Nondepository institutions	1.77	10.92
62	Security and commodity brokers	5.65	15.09
63	Insurance carriers	1.41	0.98
64	Insurance agents, brokers, and service	−4.94	0.10
65	Real estate (excluding owner-occupied housing)	1.81	2.36
	Other service industries	−0.53	0.14
70	Hotels and other lodging places	0.66	−1.30
72	Personal services	−0.42	0.72
73	Business services	1.18	0.88
75	Auto repair, services, and parking	0.06	2.05
76	Miscellaneous repair services	−0.42	−3.22
78	Motion pictures	−1.96	1.51
79	Amusement and recreation services	−0.17	−1.34
80	Health services	−1.99	0.01
81	Legal services	−0.34	0.98
82	Educational services	−0.22	−1.41
83-87	Other services	−0.30	0.02

Source: Authors' computations. The reported values are average annual percent changes.

Contribution of				Contribution of			
Capital		*MFP*		*IT capital*		*Non-IT capital*	
1987–95	*1995–2001*	*1987–95*	*1995–2001*	*1987–95*	*1995–2001*	*1987–95*	*1995–2001*
0.37	1.07	0.41	1.41	0.39	0.98	−0.02	0.09
−0.24	0.77	2.02	−0.02	0.29	0.61	−0.52	0.16
0.44	0.59	5.46	3.35	0.05	0.07	0.39	0.51
−0.84	0.01	−1.99	1.33	0.02	0.06	−0.86	−0.05
0.04	0.46	1.27	−0.53	0.23	0.19	−0.19	0.28
−0.61	−0.49	4.25	1.56	0.10	0.15	−0.70	−0.63
−0.31	1.29	4.69	−0.73	0.19	0.91	0.00	0.00
1.99	2.14	−4.71	2.08	1.02	1.29	0.98	0.84
0.02	2.91	−0.61	0.12	1.03	2.50	−1.02	0.41
2.48	3.08	2.57	0.69	1.36	2.47	1.11	0.61
2.44	2.34	2.53	3.17	1.41	2.02	1.04	0.32
3.28	5.26	3.33	−6.68	1.77	3.77	1.51	1.49
1.40	1.60	1.40	−1.64	0.45	0.48	0.95	1.13
1.00	2.79	1.86	4.03	0.82	2.20	0.18	0.59
0.52	0.50	0.62	4.52	0.20	0.42	0.32	0.08
1.63	2.38	0.02	2.75	1.12	1.83	0.52	0.55
1.82	1.69	0.73	1.65	1.10	1.58	0.72	0.11
2.40	4.81	−0.61	5.83	2.99	4.31	−0.59	0.50
0.86	0.72	4.75	14.26	0.16	0.38	0.70	0.34
1.59	1.80	−0.18	−0.80	0.86	1.29	0.73	0.50
0.17	0.81	−5.10	−0.70	0.13	0.38	0.04	0.43
0.33	0.10	1.48	2.25	−0.02	0.04	0.36	0.07
0.24	0.81	−0.78	−0.66	0.25	0.72	−0.00	0.10
0.54	0.62	0.12	−1.91	0.10	0.22	0.44	0.40
0.53	0.46	−0.94	0.26	0.20	0.18	0.33	0.28
0.05	1.41	1.13	−0.52	0.28	1.55	−0.23	−0.15
1.69	0.34	−1.60	1.71	0.09	0.19	1.60	0.15
0.37	1.21	−0.79	−4.38	0.35	0.75	0.02	0.46
0.76	0.76	−2.70	0.75	0.46	0.30	0.29	0.46
−0.57	0.70	0.40	−2.02	−0.08	0.14	−0.49	0.56
0.31	0.67	−2.29	−0.66	0.29	0.49	0.02	0.18
0.08	0.34	−0.42	0.65	0.18	0.34	−0.10	−0.00
0.03	0.08	−0.25	−1.49	0.03	0.11	−0.01	−0.03
0.05	0.37	−0.35	−0.35	0.17	0.43	−0.12	−0.06

Table A-5. *Industry Contributions to Growth in Nonfarm Labor Productivity, 1987–2001*

Least squares trend growth[a]

Industry	Aggregate	Value added weight	Value 1987–1995	Value 1995–2001	Value Change	Materials reallocation 1987–1995	Materials reallocation 1995–2001	Materials reallocation Change	Labor reallocation 1987–1995	Labor reallocation 1995–2001	Labor reallocation Change
Nonfarm business (BLS published)			1.45	2.32	0.88						
Nonfarm business (direct calculation)			1.01	2.46	1.45						
Intermediate inputs reallocation			−0.48	0.14	0.62						
Labor reallocation			−0.44	−0.31	0.13						
Nonfarm business (aggregated)	Yes	100.0	1.93	2.63	0.70	−0.48	0.14	0.62	−0.60	−0.50	0.10
Goods-producing industries	Yes	29.6	0.77	0.71	−0.06	−0.10	0.01	0.11	−1.13	−0.98	0.15
Agricultural services, forestry, and fishing	No	0.6	−0.00	0.01	0.01	−0.01	0.00	0.01	−0.08	−0.04	0.04
Mining	Yes	1.9	0.07	0.01	−0.06	−0.00	−0.03	−0.03	−0.15	0.08	0.24
Metal mining	No	0.1	0.01	0.00	−0.00	0.00	0.01	0.01	−0.02	−0.01	0.01
Coal mining	No	0.2	0.02	0.01	−0.01	0.01	0.01	−0.00	−0.06	−0.01	0.05
Oil and gas extraction	No	1.4	0.04	−0.00	−0.05	−0.01	−0.05	−0.04	−0.00	−0.00	0.00
Nonmetallic minerals, except fuels	No	0.2	0.00	0.00	−0.00	−0.00	0.00	0.01	−0.07	0.11	0.18
Construction	No	5.3	−0.01	−0.06	−0.05	0.03	0.06	0.02	−0.31	−0.23	0.09
Manufacturing	Yes	21.7	0.72	0.76	0.04	−0.12	−0.02	0.10	−0.58	−0.79	−0.21
Durable goods	Yes	12.3	0.58	0.60	0.02	−0.08	0.15	0.23	−0.47	−0.57	−0.10
Lumber and wood products	No	0.7	−0.00	0.01	0.01	−0.02	−0.01	0.01	−0.01	−0.01	0.01

Industry											
Furniture and fixtures	No	0.3	0.01	0.01	−0.00	−0.00	−0.00	−0.00	−0.03	−0.02	0.00
Stone, clay, and glass products	No	0.5	0.01	0.01	−0.00	0.01	−0.00	−0.01	−0.02	−0.02	0.00
Primary metal industries	No	0.8	0.02	0.01	−0.02	0.00	0.01	0.01	−0.05	−0.05	−0.01
Fabricated metal products	No	1.5	0.02	0.02	−0.00	−0.00	−0.02	−0.01	−0.09	−0.04	0.05
Industrial machinery and equipment	No	2.3	0.15	0.15	0.00	−0.02	0.11	0.13	−0.11	−0.06	0.05
Motor vehicles, other transportation equipment	No	2.5	0.08	0.08	−0.01	−0.05	−0.00	0.05	−0.00	−0.01	−0.00
Electronic equipment and instruments	No	3.3	0.28	0.31	0.04	0.00	0.05	0.04	−0.14	−0.32	−0.18
Miscellaneous manufacturing industries	No	0.4	0.00	0.01	0.01	−0.00	0.01	0.01	−0.02	−0.03	−0.02
Nondurable goods	Yes	9.4	0.14	0.16	0.02	−0.04	−0.16	−0.12	−0.10	−0.22	−0.12
Food and kindred products	No	2.0	0.02	0.02	−0.00	0.00	−0.07	−0.07	−0.01	−0.03	−0.01
Tobacco products	No	0.3	0.01	0.00	−0.01	−0.02	−0.04	−0.02	−0.02	−0.04	−0.02
Textile mill products	No	0.4	0.02	0.01	−0.01	0.01	−0.00	−0.01	−0.01	−0.03	−0.02
Apparel and other textile products	No	0.5	0.01	0.03	0.01	−0.00	−0.01	−0.01	−0.02	−0.03	−0.02
Paper and allied products	No	0.9	0.01	0.01	−0.01	−0.00	−0.00	−0.00	−0.03	−0.05	−0.02
Printing and publishing	No	1.5	−0.00	0.01	0.01	−0.03	−0.01	0.02	−0.02	−0.02	−0.00
Chemicals and allied products	No	2.4	0.04	0.04	0.01	0.02	−0.01	−0.04	0.00	−0.02	−0.02
Petroleum and coal products	No	0.6	0.01	0.01	0.01	−0.03	−0.01	0.02	−0.01	−0.01	−0.00
Rubber and miscellaneous plastics products	No	0.8	0.02	0.02	0.00	0.01	0.01	−0.00	0.02	0.02	−0.01
Leather and leather products	No	0.1	0.00	0.00	0.00	0.00	−0.00	−0.01	−0.02	−0.01	0.01

(continued)

Table A-5. *Industry Contributions to Growth in Nonfarm Labor Productivity, 1987–2001 (Continued)*
Least squares trend growth[a]

Industry	Aggregate	Value added weight	Value			Materials reallocation			Labor reallocation		
			1987–1995	1995–2001	Change	1987–1995	1995–2001	Change	1987–1995	1995–2001	Change
Service-producing industries	Yes	70.4	1.16	1.92	0.76	-0.38	0.13	0.51	0.53	0.48	-0.05
Transportation	Yes	4.0	0.08	0.04	-0.04	0.01	0.00	-0.01	-0.07	0.16	0.23
Railroad transportation	No	0.4	0.03	0.01	-0.02	-0.00	0.00	0.00	-0.00	-0.00	0.00
Local and interurban passenger transit	No	0.2	-0.00	-0.00	0.00	-0.00	0.01	0.01	0.02	0.02	-0.00
Trucking and warehousing	No	1.6	0.04	0.01	-0.03	-0.02	-0.01	0.01	-0.00	-0.00	-0.00
Water transportation	No	0.2	0.00	0.00	-0.00	0.00	-0.00	-0.01	0.01	-0.00	-0.01
Transportation by air	No	1.1	0.00	0.01	0.00	0.04	0.00	-0.04	-0.04	0.07	0.11
Pipelines, except natural gas	No	0.1	-0.00	0.00	0.00	-0.00	0.00	0.01	-0.05	0.07	0.12
Transportation services	No	0.4	0.01	0.01	0.01	-0.01	-0.00	0.01	0.00	0.01	0.01
Communications	Yes	3.4	0.15	0.22	0.07	0.03	-0.11	-0.13	-0.08	-0.13	-0.05
Telephone and telegraph	No	2.6	0.15	0.21	0.05	-0.01	-0.08	-0.07	-0.07	-0.09	-0.02
Radio and television	No	0.7	0.00	0.02	0.01	0.04	-0.03	-0.07	-0.01	-0.04	-0.03
Electric, gas, and sanitary services	No	3.4	0.07	0.06	-0.01	0.00	-0.05	-0.05	-0.08	-0.03	0.05
Wholesale trade	No	8.5	0.31	0.36	0.05	-0.00	0.23	0.23	-0.08	-0.03	0.05
Retail trade	No	11.3	0.15	0.38	0.23	-0.03	0.17	0.20	-0.11	-0.10	0.01
Finance and insurance	Yes	8.7	0.18	0.31	0.13	-0.03	0.19	0.22	0.42	0.25	-0.17
Depository institutions	No	4.0	0.12	0.13	0.01	-0.02	0.03	0.06	-0.01	-0.03	-0.02

Nondepository institutions	No	0.6	0.01	0.01	-0.00	-0.01	0.06	0.08	-0.00	-0.01	-0.01
Security and commodity brokers	No	1.4	0.09	0.18	0.10	-0.01	0.04	0.05	-0.05	-0.05	-0.00
Insurance carriers	No	1.9	-0.01	-0.04	-0.02	0.03	0.07	0.04	0.48	0.33	-0.15
Insurance agents, brokers, and service	No	0.8	-0.02	0.02	0.05	-0.02	-0.02	-0.00	-0.00	0.00	0.01
Real estate (less owner-occupied housing)	No	6.6	0.16	0.11	-0.05	-0.08	0.06	0.14	0.00	-0.01	-0.01
Other service industries	Yes	24.6	0.05	0.43	0.38	-0.27	-0.36	-0.10	0.53	0.37	-0.16
Hotels and other lodging places	No	1.0	0.02	-0.01	-0.02	-0.00	-0.01	-0.01	0.00	0.00	0.00
Personal services	No	0.8	0.00	0.01	0.01	-0.02	-0.00	0.01	-0.00	-0.01	-0.01
Business services	No	5.2	0.11	0.22	0.11	-0.07	-0.18	-0.12	0.01	0.00	-0.01
Auto repair, services, and parking	No	1.1	0.01	0.02	0.01	-0.01	0.02	0.03	0.03	0.01	-0.02
Miscellaneous repair services	No	0.4	0.01	0.01	0.00	-0.01	-0.01	0.00	0.18	-0.02	-0.19
Motion pictures	No	0.4	0.00	0.00	0.00	-0.01	0.00	0.01	-0.01	-0.01	-0.01
Amusement and recreation services	No	0.9	0.01	-0.00	-0.02	-0.02	-0.01	0.01	0.01	0.01	0.00
Health services	No	7.1	-0.07	0.06	0.14	-0.11	-0.07	0.04	0.11	0.09	-0.02
Legal services	No	1.7	-0.01	0.02	0.03	-0.02	0.00	0.02	0.25	0.32	0.07
Educational services	No	0.9	-0.00	-0.01	-0.01	-0.01	-0.00	0.00	-0.54	-0.33	0.21
Other services	No	4.9	-0.02	0.10	0.13	-0.00	-0.09	-0.09	0.49	0.31	-0.18

Source: Computed by authors using equation (2-3) of chapter 2. The basic data are the same as used to construct table A-1.
a. Based on gross output.

Table A-6. *Industry Contributions to Growth in Nonfarm Multifactor Productivity, 1987–2001*

Least squares trend growth

| | | | Multifactor productivity | | |
| | | | | Contribution | |
Industry	Aggre-gate	Domar weight	1987–95	1995–2001	Change
Nonfarm business (direct calculation)			0.56	1.44	0.88
Input reallocation			−0.09	−0.14	−0.04
Nonfarm business (aggregated)	Yes	186.9	0.66	1.58	0.92
Goods-producing industries	Yes	73.1	0.39	0.38	−0.01
Agricultural services, forestry, and fishing	No	0.9	−0.01	0.00	0.01
Mining	Yes	3.1	0.04	−0.03	−0.06
Metal mining	No	0.2	0.01	0.01	0.00
Coal mining	No	0.5	0.02	0.01	−0.01
Oil and gas extraction	No	2.1	0.00	−0.05	−0.05
Nonmetallic minerals, except fuels	No	0.3	−0.00	0.00	0.00
Construction	No	9.3	0.02	−0.05	−0.07
Manufacturing	Yes	59.7	0.34	0.45	0.11
Durable goods	Yes	31.7	0.35	0.59	0.23
Lumber and wood products	No	1.7	−0.03	−0.01	0.02
Furniture and fixtures	No	0.9	0.00	0.00	−0.00
Stone, clay, and glass products	No	1.3	0.02	−0.00	−0.02
Primary metal industries	No	2.9	0.03	0.02	−0.01
Fabricated metal products	No	3.4	0.01	−0.01	−0.02
Industrial machinery and equipment	No	5.5	0.10	0.22	0.12
Motor vehicles and other transportation equipment	No	7.9	0.01	0.05	0.04
Electronic equipment and instruments	No	7.2	0.20	0.29	0.09
Miscellaneous manufacturing industries	No	0.8	0.00	0.02	0.01
Nondurable goods	Yes	28.1	−0.01	−0.13	−0.12
Food and kindred products	No	7.6	0.01	−0.07	−0.09
Tobacco products	No	0.7	−0.02	−0.05	−0.03
Textile mill products	No	1.3	0.02	0.00	−0.02

(continued)

Table A-6. *Industry Contributions to Growth in Nonfarm Multifactor Productivity, 1987–2001 (Continued)*
Least squares trend growth

| | | | Multifactor productivity | | |
| | | | | Contribution | |
Industry	Aggre-gate	Domar weight	1987–95	1995–2001	Change
Apparel and other textile products	No	1.3	0.01	0.01	–0.00
Paper and allied products	No	2.6	0.00	–0.00	–0.01
Printing and publishing	No	3.3	–0.06	–0.02	0.04
Chemicals and allied products	No	5.9	0.02	–0.01	–0.03
Petroleum and coal products	No	2.8	–0.03	0.00	0.03
Rubber and miscellaneous plastics products	No	2.3	0.03	0.02	–0.01
Leather and leather products	No	0.2	0.00	–0.00	–0.00
Service-producing industries	Yes	113.8	0.27	1.20	0.93
Transportation	Yes	7.8	0.10	0.01	–0.10
Railroad transportation	No	0.7	0.03	0.01	–0.02
Local and interurban passenger transit	No	0.4	–0.00	0.00	0.01
Trucking and warehousing	No	3.4	0.03	–0.00	–0.03
Water transportation	No	0.6	0.01	0.00	–0.01
Transportation by air	No	1.9	0.05	–0.01	–0.06
Pipelines, except natural gas	No	0.1	–0.00	0.00	0.01
Transportation services	No	0.6	–0.00	0.00	0.00
Communications	Yes	5.6	0.09	0.00	–0.09
Telephone and telegraph	No	4.3	0.07	0.06	–0.01
Radio and television	No	1.2	0.02	–0.06	–0.08
Electric, gas, and sanitary services	No	5.6	0.03	–0.03	–0.07
Wholesale trade	No	12.4	0.18	0.38	0.20
Retail trade	No	17.4	0.04	0.50	0.46
Finance and insurance	Yes	14.8	0.01	0.34	0.32
Depository institutions	No	5.6	0.01	0.09	0.08
Nondepository institutions	No	1.4	–0.01	0.04	0.05
Security and commodity brokers	No	2.4	0.06	0.21	0.15
Insurance carriers	No	4.1	–0.00	0.00	0.00
Insurance agents, brokers, and service	No	1.3	–0.04	–0.00	0.04

(continued)

Table A-6. *Industry Contributions to Growth in Nonfarm Multifactor Productivity, 1987–2001 (Continued)*

Least squares trend growth

Industry	Aggre-gate	Domar weight	Multifactor productivity		
			Contribution		
			1987–95	1995–2001	Change
Real estate (excluding owner-occupied housing)	No	11.2	0.05	0.16	0.11
Other service industries	Yes	39.1	−0.23	−0.15	0.08
Hotels and other lodging places	No	1.7	0.00	−0.02	−0.02
Personal services	No	1.4	−0.01	0.01	0.02
Business services	No	7.8	0.06	−0.07	−0.12
Auto repair, services, and parking	No	1.9	−0.03	0.03	0.05
Miscellaneous repair services	No	0.7	−0.01	−0.01	−0.00
Motion pictures	No	0.9	−0.01	0.00	0.01
Amusement and recreation services	No	1.6	0.00	−0.02	−0.02
Health services	No	10.7	−0.18	−0.06	0.13
Legal services	No	2.2	−0.02	0.02	0.04
Educational services	No	1.6	−0.00	−0.01	−0.01
Other services	No	8.5	−0.03	−0.01	0.01

Source: Computed by authors using equation (2-4) of chapter 2. The contributions to the aggregate are computed using Domar weights at the industry level and aggregating up to the subsector and sector level. The industry data are the same as for table A-1. The target values for the total nonfarm sector are based on value added data.

Table A-7. *Industry Distribution of Value Added and Capital Income,*
1995–2001

Average percent share

Industry	Value added	Capital income	IT-capital income
Nonfarm business	100.0	100.0	100.0
Goods-producing industries	27.9	31.2	21.6
Agricultural services, forestry, and fishing	0.7	0.6	0.3
Mining	1.6	3.9	1.3
Metal mining	0.1	0.1	0.1
Coal mining	0.2	0.1	0.1
Oil and gas extraction	1.2	3.3	1.1
Nonmetallic minerals, except fuels	0.2	0.3	0.1
Construction	5.4	3.1	1.0
Manufacturing	20.2	23.6	18.9
Durable goods	11.6	11.8	9.4
Lumber and wood products	0.6	0.6	0.2
Furniture and fixtures	0.3	0.3	0.1
Stone, clay, and glass products	0.5	0.6	0.3
Primary metal industries	0.7	0.7	0.3
Fabricated metal products	1.4	1.7	0.7
Industrial machinery and equipment	2.1	1.6	2.4
Motor vehicles and other transportation equipment	2.4	2.5	1.5
Electronic equipment and instruments	3.1	3.4	3.7
Miscellaneous manufacturing industries	0.4	0.5	0.2
Nondurable goods	8.6	11.8	9.5
Food and kindred products	1.8	2.6	1.2
Tobacco products	0.3	0.3	0.1
Textile mill products	0.4	0.3	0.2
Apparel and other textile products	0.4	0.3	0.2
Paper and allied products	0.8	1.1	0.6
Printing and publishing	1.4	1.2	2.0
Chemicals and allied products	2.3	4.3	4.2
Petroleum and coal products	0.5	0.9	0.6
Rubber and miscellaneous plastics products	0.8	0.7	0.4
Leather and leather products	0.1	0.1	0.0

(continued)

Table A-7. *Industry Distribution of Value Added and Capital Income,*
1995–2001 (Continued)

Average percent share

Industry	Value added	Capital income	IT-capital income
Service-producing industries	72.1	68.8	78.4
Transportation	4.0	4.0	3.0
Railroad transportation	0.3	0.4	0.1
Local and interurban passenger transit	0.2	0.2	0.1
Trucking and warehousing	1.6	1.5	0.7
Water transportation	0.2	0.2	0.1
Transportation by air	1.2	1.0	1.1
Pipelines, except natural gas	0.1	0.3	0.1
Transportation services	0.4	0.4	0.9
Communications	3.4	6.4	17.9
Telephone and telegraph	2.6	4.7	14.1
Radio and television	0.8	1.7	3.8
Electric, gas, and sanitary services	3.0	6.7	4.3
Wholesale trade	8.6	7.1	14.4
Retail trade	11.2	8.5	4.8
Finance and insurance	9.7	8.5	16.0
Depository and nondepository institutions	5.0	6.1	11.9
Depository	4.2	2.9	4.6
Nondepository	0.8	3.2	7.3
Security and commodity brokers	1.8	0.7	0.9
Insurance carriers	2.1	1.6	2.9
Insurance agents, brokers, and service	0.8	0.2	0.3
Real estate (excluding owner-occupied housing)	6.3	16.1	0.6
Other service industries	25.8	11.5	17.4
Hotels and other lodging places	1.1	1.1	0.3
Personal services	0.8	0.6	0.4
Business services	6.2	3.0	8.3
Auto repair, services, and parking	1.2	1.6	0.3
Miscellaneous repair services	0.3	0.2	0.2
Motion pictures	0.4	0.3	0.4
Amusement and recreation services	1.0	0.7	0.1
Health services	7.1	2.8	4.5
Legal services	1.7	0.3	0.7
Educational services	1.0	0.1	0.0
Miscellaneous other services	5.2	0.9	2.0

Source: Computed by the authors from the BEA industry data file.

Workshops in the Brookings Program on Output and Productivity Measurement in the Services Sector

Two Topics in Services:
CPI Housing and Computer Software (May 23, 2003)

Authors

Theodore M. Crone, Federal Reserve Bank of Philadelphia
Antonia Diaz, Universidad Carlos III, Madrid
John Greenlees, Bureau of Labor Statistics
Kent Kunze, Bureau of Labor Statistics
Maria Jose Luengo Prado, Northeastern University
Jonathan McCarthy, New York Federal Reserve Bank
Leonard I. Nakamura, Federal Reserve Bank of Philadelphia
Richard Peach, New York Federal Reserve Bank
Marc Prud'homme, Statistics Canada
Dimitri Sanga, Statistics Canada
Jack Triplett, Brookings Institution
Richard Voith, Econsult Corp.
Kam Yu, Lakehead University

Discussants

Ana Aizcorbe, Brookings Institution and Federal Reserve Board
Ellen Dulberger, IBM
Robert J. Gordon, Northwestern University

Robert Martin, Federal Reserve Board
Patrick McMahon, IBM
Brent Moulton, Bureau of Economic Analysis
Steven Sharpe, Federal Reserve Board
Randal Verbrugge, Bureau of Labor Statistics

Two Topics in Finance:
Measuring the Output of Nonbank Financial Institutions and Alternative Measures of Corporate Profits (November 1, 2002)

Authors

Barry Bosworth, Brookings Institution
Irwin Gerduk, Bureau of Labor Statistics
Michael Holdway, Bureau of Labor Statistics
Ken Petrick, Bureau of Economic Analysis
Paul Schreyer, Organization for Economic Cooperation and Development
Steven Sharpe, Federal Reserve Board
Jack Triplett, Brookings Institution

Discussants

Larry Goldberg, Miami University
Kevin Stiroh, New York Federal Reserve Bank
Kim Zieschang, International Monetary Fund

Panel

Joel Demski, University of Florida
Pierre Jinghong Liang, Carnegie Mellon University
Brent Moulton, Bureau of Economic Analysis
George Perry, Brookings Institution

Services Industry Productivity:
New Estimates and New Problems (May 17, 2002)

Authors

Martin Baily, Institute for International Economics
Barry Bosworth, Brookings Institution
Mun Ho, Resources for the Future

Robert Inklaar, University of Groningen,
  The Netherlands, and the Conference Board
Dale Jorgenson, Harvard University
Robert McGuckin, The Conference Board
Someshwar Rao, Industry Canada
Andrew Sharpe, Center for the Study of Living Standards
Kevin Stiroh, Federal Reserve Bank of New York
Jianmin Tang, Industry Canada
Jack Triplett, Brookings Institution
Bart Van Ark, Yale University
Alan Webb, McKinsey Global Institute

Discussants

Stephanie Aaronson, Federal Reserve Board
Carol Corrado, Federal Reserve Board
Robert Gordon, Northwestern University
Michael Harper, Bureau of Labor Statistics
Charles Hulten, University of Maryland

Hedonic Price Indexes:
Too Fast, Too Slow, or Just Right? (February 1, 2002)

Authors

Ernst Berndt, Massachusetts Institute of Technology
Jorgen Dalen, Eurostat and Statistics Sweden
Bart Hobijn, New York Federal Reserve Bank
Christopher Mackie, National Academy of Sciences
Dietmar Moch, ZEW (Center for European Economic Research)
  and University of Mannheim, Germany
William Nordhaus, Yale University
Ariel Pakes, Harvard University
Charles Schultze, Brookings Institution
Mick Silver, Cardiff University, Wales
Jack Triplett, Brookings Institution

Discussants

Paul Chwelos, University of British Columbia
Iain Cockburn, Boston University
Ellen Dulberger, IBM
John Greenlees, Bureau of Labor Statistics
Charles Hulten, University of Maryland
Dietmar Moch, ZEW (Center for European Economic Research)
    and University of Mannheim, Germany
Bart Van Ark, University of Groningen, The Netherlands, and Yale University

The Adequacy of Data for Analyzing and Forecasting the High-Tech Sector (October 12, 2001)

Authors

Judy Dodds, Census Bureau
John Gates, Census Bureau
Irwin Gerduk, Bureau of Labor Statistics
Bruce Grimm, Bureau of Economic Analysis
David Gunter, Brookings Institution
Michael Holdway, Bureau of Labor Statistics
Katherine Levit, National Health Accounts
Sumiye Okubo, Bureau of Economic Analysis
Philip W. Swan, IBM
Stacey Tevlin, Federal Reserve Board
Jack Triplett, Brookings Institution
David Wasshausen, Bureau of Economic Analysis

Discussants

Martin Baily, Institute for International Economics
Carol Corrado, Federal Reserve Board
Ellen Dulberger, IBM
Daniel Sichel, Federal Reserve Board
Kevin Stiroh, Federal Reserve Bank of New York

Transportation Output and Productivity (May 4, 2001)

Authors

Barry Bosworth, Brookings Institution
Thomas Hubbard, University of Chicago
M. I. Nadiri, New York University
Robin Sickles, Rice University
Robert Yuskavage, Bureau of Economic Analysis

Discussants

Robert Gordon, Northwestern University
John Greenlees, Bureau of Labor Statistics
Michael Harper, Bureau of Labor Statistics
Scott Stern, MIT and Brookings Institution
Jack Triplett, Brookings Institution
Cliff Winston, Brookings Institution

Communications Output and Productivity (February 23, 2001)

Authors

Ana Aizcorbe, Federal Reserve Board
Mark Doms, Federal Reserve Board
Kenneth Flamm, University of Texas
Christopher Forman, Northwestern University
Douglas Galbi, Federal Communications Commission
Irwin Gerduk, Bureau of Labor Statistics
Shane Greenstein, Northwestern University
Marc Prud'homme, Statistics Canada
Daniel Sichel, Federal Reserve Board
Kam Yu, Statistics Canada and University of British Columbia

Discussants

Barry Bosworth, Brookings Institution
Robert Crandall, Brookings Institution
Kenneth Flamm, University of Texas
Robert Gordon, Northwestern University
Bruce Grimm, Bureau of Economic Analysis
Scott Stern, MIT and Brookings Institution
Jack Triplett, Brookings Institution

Measuring the Output of the Education Sector (April 7, 2000)

Authors

Ronald G. Ehrenberg, Cornell University
Barbara Fraumeni, Bureau of Economic Analysis
Stephen Heffler, Health Care Financing Administration
Clinton P. McCully, Bureau of Economic Analysis
Steven Rivkin, Amherst College
Benjamin P. Scafidi, Georgia State University
Amy Schwartz, New York University

Discussants

John Bishop, Cornell University
Barry Bosworth, Brookings Institution
Charles Hulten, University of Maryland
Julian Pettengill, Medicare Payment Advisory Commission
Jack Triplett, Brookings Institution

Panel

Mark Freeland, Health Care Financing Administration
Anne Harrison, Organization for Economic Cooperation and Development
Steven Heffler, Health Care Financing Administration
Richard I. Murnane, Harvard University Graduate School of Education
Solomon W. Polachek, State University of New York at Binghamton

Measuring Health Care (December 17, 1999)

Authors

Ernst R. Berndt, MIT
Li Wei Chao, University of Pennsylvania
Patricia M. Danzon, University of Pennsylvania
Irwin B. Gerduk, Bureau of Labor Statistics
Gregory G. Kelly, Bureau of Labor Statistics
Abigail Tay, Columbia University
Jack Triplett, Brookings Institution

Discussants

Henry J. Aaron, Brookings Institution
David Cutler, Harvard University
Dennis J. Fixler, Bureau of Labor Statistics
Robert Helms, American Enterprise Institute
Frank R. Lichtenberg, Columbia University

Measuring E-Commerce (September 24, 1999)

Authors

B. K. Atrostic, Bureau of the Census
Ernst R. Berndt, MIT
Erik Brynjolfsson, MIT
G. Christian Ehemann, Bureau of Economic Analysis
Barbara Fraumeni, Bureau of Economic Analysis
Austan Goolsbee, University of Chicago
John Haltiwanger, University of Maryland
Ronald Jarmin, Bureau of the Census
Ann Lawson, Bureau of Economic Analysis
Thomas Mesenbourg, Bureau of the Census
Al Silk, Harvard University
Andrew Whinston, University of Texas

Panel

Kenneth Flamm, University of Texas
Robert Gordon, Northwestern University
Nancy Rose, MIT
Richard Simpson, Industry Canada

Measuring the Output of Business Services (May 14, 1999)

Authors

Ellen Dulberger, IBM
Irwin Gerduk, Bureau of Labor Statistics
Robert Gordon, Northwestern University
John Greenlees, Bureau of Labor Statistics
Shane Greenstein, Northwestern University
Frank Levy, MIT
Llilach Nachum, Cambridge University
Roslyn Swick, Bureau of Labor Statistics
Andrew Wyckoff, Organization for Economic Cooperation and Development
Robert Yuskavage, Bureau of Economic Analysis

Measuring Banking Output (November 20, 1998)

Authors

Peter Hill, United Nations Economic Commission for Europe
Kent Kunze and Mary Jablonski, Bureau of Labor Statistics
Jack Triplett, Brookings Institution

Discussants

William Lang, Comptroller of the Currency
Brent Moulton, Bureau of Economic Analysis

Panel

Allen Berger, Federal Reserve Board
Dennis Fixler, Bureau of Labor Statistics
Diana Hancock, Federal Reserve Board
David Humphrey, Florida State University
Loretta Mester, Federal Reserve Bank of Philadelphia
Carl Obst, Organization for Economic Cooperation and Development
Thomas Rymes, Carleton University
Kim Zieschang, International Monetary Fund

Measuring the Output of Retail Trade (September 18, 1998)

Authors

Carole Ambler, Bureau of the Census
Roger Betancourt, University of Maryland
Barry Bosworth, Brookings Institution
Robert Lussier, Statistics Canada
Walter Oi, University of Rochester

Discussants

Martin Baily, McKinsey and Company
Robert Gordon, Northwestern University
Marshall Reinsdorf, Federal Deposit Insurance Corporation

Measuring the Output of Government Data Sets (June 11, 1998)

Authors

Carole Ambler, Bureau of the Census
Edwin Dean, Bureau of Labor Statistics
Louis Marc Ducharme, Statistics Canada
John Galvin, Bureau of Labor Statistics
John Haltiwanger, Bureau of the Census
Mary Jablonski, Bureau of Labor Statistics
Kent Kunze, Bureau of Labor Statistics
Robert Yuskavage, Bureau of Economic Analysis

Discussants

Martin Baily, McKinsey and Company
Ernst Berndt, MIT
Barry Bosworth, Brookings Institution
Ralph Monaco, University of Maryland

Measuring the Price and Output of Insurance (April 21, 1998)

Authors

Erwin Diewert, University of British Columbia
Peter Hill, United Nations Economic Commission for Europe
Mark Sherwood, Bureau of Labor Statistics

Discussants

George Akerlof, Brookings Institution
Jeffrey Bernstein, Carleton University
J. David Cummins, Wharton School, University of Pennsylvania

Panel

John Astin, Eurostat
Arlene Dohm, Bureau of Labor Statistics
Deanna Eggleston, Bureau of Labor Statistics
Robert Parker, Bureau of Economic Analysis
Krishna Sahay, Statistics Canada

References

Abel, Jaison R., Ernst R. Berndt, and Alan G. White. 2003. "Price Indexes for Microsoft's Computer Software Products." Working Paper 9966. National Bureau of Economic Research.

Aizcorbe, Ana, Carol Corrado, and Mark Doms. 2000. "Constructing Price and Quantity Indexes for High Technology Goods." Industrial Output Section, Division of Research and Statistics, Board of Governors of the Federal Reserve System, July 19.

Aizcorbe, Ana, Kenneth Flamm, and Anjum Khurshid. 2002. "The Role of Semiconductor Inputs in IT Hardware Price Decline: Computers vs. Communications." Finance and Economics Discussion Paper 2002-37. Board of Governors of the Federal Reserve.

Allen, Franklin, and Anthony M. Santomero. 1997. "The Theory of Financial Intermediation." *Journal of Banking and Finance* 21 (December): 1461–85.

———. 2001. "What Do Financial Intermediaries Do?" *Journal of Banking and Finance* 25 (February): 271–94.

Association of American Railroads. 2002. *Railroad Facts*. Washington.

Australian Bureau of Statistics. 2003. *Measuring Learning in Australia: A Framework for Education and Training Statistics*.

Baily, Martin N. 2002. "The New Economy: Post Mortem or Second Wind?" *Journal of Economic Perspectives* 16 (2): 3–22.

Baily, Martin N., and Robert Gordon. 1988. "The Productivity Slowdown, Measurement Issues, and the Explosion of Computer Power." *Brookings Papers on Economic Activity* 1988(2): 347–420.

Baily, Martin N., and Robert Z. Lawrence. 2001. "Do We Have a New E-conomy?" Working Paper 8243. Cambridge, Mass.: National Bureau of Economic Research.

Baily, Martin N., and Eric Zitzewitz. 2001. "Service Sector Productivity Comparisons: Lessons for Measurement." In *New Developments in Productivity Analysis*, vol. 63, NBER

Studies in Income and Wealth, edited by Charles Hulten, Edward R. Dean, and Michael J. Harper, 419–64. University of Chicago Press.

Bakos, Yannis. 2001. "The Emerging Landscape for Retail E-Commerce." *Journal of Economic Perspectives* 15 (1): 69–80.

Baltensperger, Ernst. 1980. "Alternative Approaches to the Theory of the Banking Firm." *Journal of Monetary Economics* 6 (1): 1–37.

Barnett, William A. 1980. "Economic Monetary Aggregates: An Application of Index Number and Aggregation Theory." *Journal of Econometrics* 14 (1): 11–48.

Basu, Susanto, and John G. Fernald. 1995. "Are Apparent Productive Spillovers a Figment of Specification Error?" *Journal of Monetary Economics* 36 (1): 165–88.

Basu, Susanto, and others. 2003. "The Case of the Missing Productivity Growth: Or, Does Information Technology Explain Why Productivity Accelerated in the United States but Not the United Kingdom?" Working Paper 10010. Cambridge, Mass.: National Bureau of Economic Research.

Baumol, William J. 1967. "Macroeconomics of Unbalanced Growth: The Anatomy of Urban Crisis." *American Economic Review* 57 (3): 415–26.

Berger, Allen N., and David B. Humphrey. 1997. "Efficiency of Financial Institutions: International Survey and Directions for Future Research." Board of Governors of the Federal Reserve System (Monetary and Financial Studies Section) and Florida State University, Department of Finance (February).

Berger, Allen N., and Loretta J. Mester. 1997. "Inside the Black Box: What Explains Differences in the Efficiencies of Financial Institutions?" *Journal of Banking and Finance* 21 (7): 895–947.

Berndt, Ernst R., Susan Busch, and Richard G. Frank. 2001. "Treatment Price Indexes for Acute Phase Major Depression." In *Medical Care Output and Productivity*, vol. 59, NBER Studies in Income and Wealth, edited by David Cutler and Ernst Berndt, 463–505. University of Chicago Press.

Berndt, Ernst R., and David Cutler, eds. 2001. *Medical Care Output and Productivity.* Vol. 62, NBER Studies in Income and Wealth. University of Chicago Press.

Berndt, Ernst R., Zvi Griliches, and Joshua G. Rosett. 1993. "Auditing the Producer Price Index: Micro Evidence from Prescription Pharmaceutical Preparations." *Journal of Business and Economic Statistics* 11 (3): 251–64.

Berndt, Ernst, and others. 2000. "Medical Care Prices and Output." In *Handbook of Health Economics* 1A, edited by Anthony J. Culyer and Joseph P. Newhouse, 119–80. Amsterdam: Elsevier.

Bernstein, Jeffrey I. 1999. "Total Factor Productivity Growth in the Canadian Life Insurance Industry: 1979–1989." *Canadian Journal of Economics* 32 (2): 500–17.

A. M. Best Company. 2001. "Glossary of Insurance Terms"(www.ambest.com/resource/glossary.html).

———. 2003. "Best's Aggregates & Averages—Property/Casualty—United States & Canada." Oldwick, N.J.

Betancourt, Roger R. 1998. "Draft Chapter on Retail Supply." Paper prepared for "Measuring the Output of Retail Trade," a Brookings workshop, September 18.

Betancourt, Roger R., and David A. Gautschi. 1993. "The Outputs of Retail Activities: Concepts, Measurements, and Evidence from U.S. Census Data." *Review of Economics and Statistics* 75 (2): 294–301.

Betancourt, Roger R., and M. Malinoski. 1999. "An Estimable Model of Supermarket Behavior: Prices, Distribution Services, and Some Effects of Competition." *Empirica* 26: 55–73.

Bishop, John H. 1994. *The Economic Consequences of Schooling and Learning*. Cornell University.

———. 2002. "Comment on Estimation of Productivity Growth in Education." Paper presented at "Measuring the Output of the Education Sector," a Brookings workshop, April 7, 2000.

Bodie, Zvi. 1999. "Investment Management and Technology: Past, Present, and Future." *Brookings-Wharton Papers on Financial Services*: 343–73.

Bodie, Zvi, and Robert C. Merton. 2000. *Finance*. Upper Saddle River, N.J.: Prentice-Hall.

Bonds, Belinda, and Tim Aylor. 1998. "Investment in New Structures and Equipment in 1992 by Using Industries." *Survey of Current Business* (December): 26–51.

Born, Patricia, and others. 1998. "Organizational Form and Insurance Company Performance: Stocks versus Mutuals." In *The Economics of Property-Casualty Insurance*, edited by David F. Bradford, 167–92. University of Chicago Press.

Bosworth, Barry P., and Jack Triplett. 2003. "Services Productivity in the United States: Griliches' Services Volume Revisited." Paper presented at a CRIW Conference in Memory of Zvi Griliches, Bethesda, Maryland, September 19–20.

Bowman, Raymond, and Richard Easterlin. 1958. "Comment: A Conceptual Basis of the Accounts: A Re-Examination." In *A Critique of United States Income and Product Accounts*, vol. 22, NBER Studies in Income and Wealth, 127–40. Princeton University Press.

Bradford, David F., and Kyle D. Logue. 1998. "The Effects of Tax Changes on Property-Casualty Insurance Prices." In *The Economics of Property-Casualty Insurance*, edited by David F. Bradford, 29–79. University of Chicago Press.

Brynjolfsson, Eric, and Lorin Hitt. 2000. "Beyond Computation: Information Technology, Organizational Transformation, and Business Performance." *Journal of Economic Perspectives* 14 (4): 23–48.

Bureau of Economic Analysis. 1996. "The Measurement of Property and Casualty Insurance Output: View of the Majority of the Members." Insurance and Pensions Modernization Work Team (June 27).

Bureau of Labor Statistics. 1997. *BLS Handbook of Methods*. Bulletin 2490 (April).

———. 2003. "Technical Note: Multifactor Productivity Index, Air Transport Industry, NAICS 481." Mimeograph, Industry Productivity Program.

Bureau of Transportation Statistics. 1993. *National Transportation Statistics: Historical Compendium: 1960–1992*.

Calomiris, Charles W., and Joseph R. Mason. 1999. *High Loan-to-Value Mortgage Lending*. Washington: AEI Press.

Cardenas, Elaine M. 1996. "Revision of the CPI Hospital Services Component." *Monthly Labor Review* 119 (12): 40-48.

Carr, Roderick M., J. David Cummins, and Laureen Regan. 1999. "Efficiency and Competitiveness in the U.S. Life Insurance Industry: Corporate, Product, and Distribution Strategies." In *Changes in the Life Insurance Industry: Efficiency, Technology and Risk Management*, edited by J. David Cummins and Anthony M. Santomero, 117–57. Norwell, Mass.: Kluwer Academic Publishers.

Catron, Brian, and Bonnie Murphy. 1996. "Hospital Price Inflation: What Does the New PPI Tell Us?" *Monthly Labor Review* 120 (7): 24–31.

Centers for Medicare and Medicaid Services. 2004. "National Health Accounts: Historical and Current Years" (www.cms.hhs.gov/statistics/nhe/default.asp).

Chen, Baoline, and Dennis J. Fixler. 2003. "Measuring the Services of Property-Casualty Insurance in the NIPAs: Changes in Concepts and Methods." *Survey of Current Business* 83 (10): 10–26.

Christensen, Lauritis R. 1971. "Entrepreneurial Income: How Does It Measure Up?" *American Economic Review* 61 (4): 575–85.

Clemons, Erick, Il-Horn Hann, and Lorin M. Hitt. 2002. "Price Dispersion and Differentiation in Online Travel: An Empirical Investigation." *Management Science* 48 (4): 534–49.

Cole, Roseanne, and others. "Quality Adjusted Price Indexes for Computer Processors and Selected Peripheral Equipment." *Survey of Current Business* 66 (1): 41–50.

Collins, Richard. 1993. "A Model Survey for Insurance." In *Papers and Final Report*, Eighth Annual Meeting, Voorburg Group on Service Statistics. Oslo, Norway, September.

Commission of the European Communities and others. 1993. *System of National Accounts 1993*.

Copeland, Morris A. 1932. "Some Problems in the Theory of National Income." *Journal of Political Economy* 40 (1): 1–51.

Copeland, Morris A., and Edwin M. Martin. 1938. "The Correction of Wealth and Income Estimates for Price Changes." Vol. 2, NBER Studies in Income and Wealth, 85–19. New York: National Bureau of Economic Research.

Corrado, Carol, and Lawrence Slifman. 1999. "Decomposition of Productivity and Unit Costs." *American Economic Review* 89 (May, *Papers and Proceedings*): 328–32.

Cummins, J. David. 1999. "Efficiency in the U.S. Life Insurance Industry: Are Insurers Minimizing Costs and Maximizing Revenues?" In *Changes in the Life Insurance Industry: Efficiency, Technology and Risk Management*, edited by J. David Cummins and Anthony M. Santomero. Norwell, Mass.: Kluwer Academic Publishers.

Cutler, David M., Mark B. McClellan, and Joseph P. Newhouse. 1999. "The Costs and Benefits of Intensive Treatment for Cardiovascular Disease." In *Measuring the Prices of Medical Treatments*, edited by Jack E. Triplett, 34–71. Brookings.

Cutler, David M., and others. 1998. "Are Medical Prices Declining? Evidence from Heart Attack Treatments." *Quarterly Journal of Economics* 113 (4): 991–1024.

Dean, Edward, and Kent Kunze. 1992. "Productivity Measurement in the Service Industries." In *Output Measurement in the Service Sectors*, vol. 56, NBER Studies in Income and Wealth, edited by Zvi Griliches, 73–101. University of Chicago Press.

Denison, Edward. 1985. *Trends in American Economic Growth 1929–1982*. Brookings.

Denny, Michael. 1980. "Measuring the Real Output of the Life Insurance Industry: A Comment." *Review of Economics and Statistics* 62 (1): 150–52.

Diewert, W. Erwin. 1980. "Aggregation Problems in the Measurement of Capital." In *The Measurement of Capital*, vol. 45, NBER Studies in Income and Wealth, edited by Dan Usher, 433–528. University of Chicago Press.

———. 1995. "Functional Form Problems in Modeling Insurance and Gambling." *Geneva Papers on Risk and Insurance Theory* 20: 135–150. Geneva, Switzerland.

Dohm, Arlene, and Deanna Eggleston. 1998. "Producer Price Indexes for Property/Casualty and Life Insurance." Paper presented at "Measuring the Price and Output of Insurance," a Brookings workshop, April 21.

Domar, E. D. 1961. "On the Measurement of Technological Change." *Economic Journal* 71 (December): 709–29.

Doms, Mark. 2003. "Communications Equipment: What Has Happened to Prices?" In *Measuring Capital in the New Economy*, NBER/CRIW, University of Chicago Press.

Doms, Mark, and Christopher Forman. 2003. "Prices for Local Area Network Equipment." Working Paper 2003-13. Federal Reserve Bank of San Francisco (June).

Doms, Mark, Ron S. Jarmin, and Shawn D. Klimek. 2003. "IT Investment and Firm Performance in U.S. Retail Trade." Working Paper 2003-19. Federal Reserve Bank of San Francisco.

Duke, John, Diane Litz, and Lisa Usher. 1992. "Multifactor Productivity in Railroad Transportation." *Monthly Labor Review* 115 (8): 49–58.

Dulberger, Ellen R. 1989. "The Application of a Hedonic Model to a Quality-Adjusted Price Index for Computer Processors." In *Technology and Capital Formation*, edited by Dale W. Jorgenson and Ralph Landau, 37–75. Massachusetts Institute of Technology Press.

Ehrenberg, Ronald G. 2000. "Why Can't Colleges Control Their Costs?" Paper prepared for "Measuring the Output of the Education Sector," a Brookings workshop, April 7.

Eurostat. 1997. *Methodological Manual for Insurance Services Statistics*. Luxembourg: European Commission, Statistical Office of the European Communities.

———. 1999. "Harmonisation of Price Indices." *Compendium of HICP Reference Documents* (January).

Evans, Richard. 2002. "INSEE's Adoption of Market Intelligence Data for Its Hedonic Computer Manufacturing Price Index." Presented at the Symposium on Hedonics at Statistics Netherlands, October 25.

Fabricant, Solomon. 1969. "Comment: Alternative Measures of the Real Output and Productivity of Commercial Banks." In *Production and Productivity in the Service Industries*, vol. 34, NBER Studies in Income and Wealth, 197–99. Columbia University Press.

Fama, E. 1985. "What Is Different about Banks?" *Journal of Monetary Economics* 15: 5–29.

Federal Communications Commission. 2003. *Trends in Telephone Service: 2003* (www.fcc.gov/wcb/iatd/stats.html).

Fisher, Franklin M., John J. McGowan, and Joen E. Greenwood. 1983. *Folded, Spindled, and Mutilated: Economic Analysis and U.S. v. IBM*. MIT Press.

Fixler, Dennis J., Marshall B. Reinsdorf, and George M. Smith. 2003. "Measuring the Services of Commercial Banks in the NIPAs: Changes in Concepts and Methods." *Survey of Current Business* 83 (9): 33–44.

Fixler, Dennis J., and Kim Zieschang. 1991. "Measuring the Nominal Value of Financial Services in the National Income Accounts." *Economic Inquiry* 29: 53–68.

———. 1999. "The Productivity of the Banking Sector: Integrating Financial and Production Approaches to Measuring Financial Service Output." *Canadian Journal of Economics* 32 (2): 547–69 (April).

Foster, Lucia, John Haltiwanger, and C. J. Krizan. 2002. "The Link between Aggregate and Micro Productivity Growth: Evidence from Retail Trade." Working Paper 9120. Cambridge, Mass.: National Bureau of Economic Research.

Fraumeni, Barbara. 2000. "The Output of the Education Sector as Determined by Education's Effect on Lifetime Income." Paper presented at "Measuring the Output of the Education Sector," a Brookings workshop, April 7.

Fraumeni, Barbara, and Sumiye Okubo. 2002. "R&D in the National Income and Product Accounts: A First Look at Its Effect on GDP." Paper presented at "Measuring Capital in the New Economy," NBER Conference on Research in Income and Wealth, Washington, April 26–27 (Revised September 2003). Forthcoming in *Measuring Capital in the New*

Economy, NBER Studies in Income and Wealth, edited by Carol Corrado, John Halti-wanger, and Dan Sichel. University of Chicago Press.

Fuchs, Victor R., and H. C. Sox Jr. 2001. "Physicians' Views of the Relative Importance of Thirty Medical Innovations." *Health Affairs* 20 (September/October): 30–42.

Galbi, Douglas. 2000. "Growth in the 'New Economy': U.S. Bandwidth Use and Pricing across the 1990s." Paper presented at "Communications Output and Productivity," a Brookings workshop, February 23, 2001 (www.brook.edu/es/research/projects/productivity/workshops/20010223/02_galbi.pdf).

Gerduk, Irwin B. 1999. "Producer Price Indexes for Accounting Services, Legal Services, and Advertising Agency Services." Paper presented at "Measuring the Output of Business Services," a Brookings workshop, May 14.

———. 2001. "Producer Price Indexes for Wired and Wireless Telecommunications." Paper prepared for "Communications Output and Productivity," a Brookings workshop, February 23. BLS mimeograph (www.brook.edu/es/research/projects/productivity/workshops/20010223/20010223.htm).

Gilder, George. 2000. *Telecosm : How Infinite Bandwidth Will Revolutionize Our World.* New York: Free Press.

Gold, Marthe R., and others. 1996. *Cost-Effectiveness in Health and Medicine.* Oxford University Press.

Gollop, Frank. 1979. "Accounting for Intermediate Input: The Link between Sectoral and Aggregate Measures of Productivity Growth." In *The Meaning and Interpretation of Productivity*, edited by Albert Rees and John Kendrick, 318–33. Washington: National Academy of Sciences.

Good, David H., Robin C. Sickles, and Jessie C. Weiher. 2001. "A Hedonic Price Index for Airline Travel." Paper presented at "Issues in Measuring Price Change and Consumption," a BLS conference, June 5–8, 2000 (revised June 26, 2001). Rice University mimeograph.

Gordon, Robert.1990. *The Measurement of Durable Goods Prices.* University of Chicago Press.

———. 1992. "Productivity in the Transportation Sector." In *Output Measurement in the Service Sectors*, vol. 56, NBER Studies in Income and Wealth, edited by Zvi Griliches, 371–422. University of Chicago Press.

———. 1999. "Management Consulting Firms: Some Approaches to Output Measurement." Paper presented at "Measuring the Output of the Business Sector," a Brookings workshop, May 14.

———. 2000. "Does the 'New Economy' Measure up to the Great Inventions of the Past?" *Journal of Economic Perspectives* 14 (4): 49–74.

———. 2002. "The United States." In *Technological Innovation and Economic Performance*, edited by Benn Steil, David G. Victor, and Richard R. Nelson, 49–73. Princeton University Press.

Gorman, J. A. 1969. "Alternative Measures of the Real Output and Productivity of Commercial Banks." In *Production and Productivity in the Service Industries*, vol. 34, NBER Studies in Income and Wealth, edited by Victor R. Fuchs, 155–189. Columbia University Press.

Griliches, Zvi, ed. 1992. *Output Measurement in the Service Sectors*, vol. 56, NBER Studies in Income and Wealth. University of Chicago Press.

———. 1994. "Productivity, R&D, and the Data Constraint." *American Economic Review* 84 (1): 1–23.

Grimm, Bruce. 1996. "A Quality Adjusted Price Index for Digital Telephone Switches." Working Paper. Bureau of Economic Analysis.

———. 1998. "Price Indexes for Selected Semiconductors: 1974–96." *Survey of Current Business* (February): 8–24.

Gullickson, William, and Michael J. Harper. 1999. "Possible Measurement Bias in Aggregate Productivity Growth." *Monthly Labor Review* 122 (2): 47–67.

———. 2002. "Bias in Aggregate Productivity Trends Revisited." *Monthly Labor Review* 125 (3): 32–40.

Gurley, G., and E. S. Shaw. 1960. *Money in a Theory of Finance.* Brookings.

Haavelmo, Trygve. 1960. *A Study in the Theory of Investment.* University of Chicago Press.

Haltiwanger, John, and Ron Jarmin. 2000. "Measuring the Digital Economy." In *Understanding the Digital Economy: Data, Tools, and Research*, edited by Erik Brynjolfsson and Brian Kahin, 13–33. MIT Press.

Hancock, Diana. 1985. "The Financial Firm: Production with Monetary and Non-Monetary Goods." *Journal of Political Economy* 93: 859–80.

———. 1991. *A Theory of Production for the Financial Firm.* Boston: Kluwer Academic Publishers.

Hanushek, Eric A. 1986. "The Economics of Schooling: Production and Efficiency in Public Schools." *Journal of Economic Literature* 24 (3): 1141–77.

Hill, Peter. 1996. "The Services of Financial Intermediaries, or FISIM Revisited." Paper presented at "Measuring Banking Output," a Brookings workshop, November 20, 1998.

———. 1998. "The Treatment of Insurance in the SNA." Paper presented at "Measuring the Price and Output of Insurance," a Brookings workshop, April 21.

Hirshhorn, Ron, and Randall Geehan. 1977. "Measuring the Real Output of the Life Insurance Industry." *Review of Economics and Statistics* 59 (2): 211–19.

———. 1980. "Measuring the Real Output of the Life Insurance Industry: A Reply," *Review of Economics and Statistics* 62(1): 152–54.

Hodgman, Donald R. 1969. "Comment: Alternative Measures of the Real Output and Productivity of Commercial Banks." In *Production and Productivity in the Service Industries*, vol. 34, NBER Studies in Income and Wealth, edited by V. R. Fuchs, 189–95. Columbia University Press.

Holdway, Michael, and Irwin B. Gerduk. 2001. "PPI Quality Improvement Initiative: Responses to New Item Bias in IT Equipment." Paper presented at "The Adequacy of Data for Analyzing and Forecasting the High-Tech Sector," a Brookings workshop, October 12.

Hornstein, Andreas, and Edward Prescott. 1991. "Insurance Contracts as Commodities: A Note." *Review of Economics Studies* 58 (October): 917–28.

Hubbard, Thomas. 2001. "Information, Decisions, and Productivity: On-Board Computers and Capacity Utilization in Trucking." Working Paper 8525. Cambridge, Mass.: National Bureau of Economic Research (October).

Hulten, Charles R. 1978. "Growth Accounting with Intermediate Inputs." *Review of Economic Studies* 45 (3): 511–18.

———. 1990. The Measurement of Capital. In *Fifty Years of Economic Measurement: The Jubilee*, vol. 54, NBER Studies in Income and Wealth, edited by Ernst R. Berndt and Jack E. Triplett, 119–52. University of Chicago Press.

Humphrey, David, and others. 2003. "Cost Savings from Electronic Payments and ATMs in Europe." Working Paper 03-16. Federal Reserve Bank of Philadelphia.

International Monetary Fund. 1994. *Balance of Payments Manual*, 5th ed. Washington: International Monetary Fund.

International Working Group on Price Indices. 1994. *International Conference on Price Indices: Papers and Final Report*. Ottawa, Canada: Statistics Canada (November).

Jaszi, George. 1958. "The Conceptual Basis of the Accounts: A Re-examination." In *A Critique of United States Income and Product Accounts,* vol. 22, NBER Studies in Income and Wealth, 13–127. Princeton University Press.

Jorgenson, Dale W. 1989. "Capital as a Factor of Production." In *Technology and Capital Formation*, edited by Dale W. Jorgenson and Ralph Landau, 1–35. MIT Press.

Jorgenson, Dale W., and Barbara Fraumeni. 1992a. "Investment in Education and U.S. Economic Growth." *Scandanavian Journal of Economics* 94 (supplement): S51–70.

———. 1992b. "The Output of the Education Sector." In *Output Measurement in the Service Sectors*, vol. 56, NBER Studies in Income and Wealth, edited by Zvi Griliches, 303–38. University of Chicago Press.

Jorgenson, Dale W., Frank M. Gollop, and Barbara M. Fraumeni. 1987. *Productivity and U.S. Economic Growth*. Harvard University Press.

Jorgenson, Dale W., Mun S. Ho, and Kevin J. Stiroh. 2002. "Growth of U.S. Industries and Investments in Information Technology and Higher Education." Paper presented at "Measuring Capital in the New Economy," NBER Conference on Research in Income and Wealth, Washington, April 26–27. Forthcoming in *Measuring Capital in the New Economy*, NBER Studies in Income and Wealth, edited by Carol Corrado, John Haltiwanger, and Dan Sichel. University of Chicago Press.

Jorgenson, Dale W., and Frank C. Lee, eds. 2001. *Industry Level Productivity and International Competitiveness between Canada and the United States*. Ottawa: Industry Canada.

Jorgenson, Dale W., and Kevin J. Stiroh. 2000. "Raising the Speed Limit: U.S. Economic Growth in the Information Age." *Brookings Papers on Economic Activity* (2): 125–211.

Kunze, Kent. 2003. "Productivity in the Prepackaged Software Industry, SIC7372: 1987–2000." Paper presented at "Two Topics in Services: CPI Housing and Computer Software," a Brookings workshop, May 23.

Lent, Janice, and Alan Dorfman. 2002. "A Transactions Price Index for Air Travel." Bureau of Labor Statistics mimeograph.

Lequiller, Francois, and others. 2003. "Report of the OECD Task Force on Software Measurement in the National Accounts." Working Paper 2003/1. Paris: OECD Statistics Directorate (March).

Lerner, Abba P. 1934. "The Concept of Monopoly and the Measurement of Monopoly Power." *Review of Economic Studies* 1 (June): 157–75.

Lim, Poh Ping, and Richard McKenzie. 2002. "Hedonic Price Analysis for Personal Computers in Australia: An Alternative Approach to Quality Adjustments in the Australian Price Indexes." Presented at Center for European Economic Research conference, Mannheim, Germany, April.

Lippman, Steven, and John McCall. 1981. "The Economics of Uncertainty." In *Handbook of Mathematical Economics,* vol. 1, edited by Kenneth Arrow and Michael Intriligator, 211–84. Amsterdam: Elsevier Science Publishers.

Litan, Robert, and Alice Rivlin. 2001. *Beyond the Dot.coms: The Economic Promise of the Internet*. Brookings.

Lozano, Ana V., and David B. Humphrey. 2002. "Bias in Malmquist Index and Cost Function Productivity Measurement in Banking." *International Journal of Production Economics* 76 (2): 177–88.

Lucking-Reiley, David, and Daniel F. Spulber. 2001. "Business-to-Business Electronic Commerce." *Journal of Economic Perspectives* 15 (1): 55–68.

Lum, Sherlene K. S., and Brian C. Moyer. 1998. "Gross Product by Industry: 1995–97." *Survey of Current Business* 78 (11): 20–40.

Lum, Sherlene K. S., Brian C. Moyer, and Robert E. Yuskavage. 2000. "Improved Estimates of Gross Product by Industry for 1947–98." *Survey of Current Business* 80 (6): 24–54.

Lum, Sherlene K. S., and Robert E. Yuskavage. 1997. "Gross Product by Industry: 1947–96." *Survey of Current Business* 77 (11): 20–34.

Marimont, Martin L. 1969. "Measuring Real Output for Industries Providing Services: OBE Concepts and Methods." In vol. 34, *Production and Productivity in the Service Industries*, NBER Studies in Income and Wealth, edited by Victor Fuchs, 15–52. Columbia University Press.

McKinsey Global Institute. 2001. "United States Productivity Growth 1995–2000: Understanding the Contribution of Information Technology Relative to Other Factors." Washington (October).

Mesenbourg, Thomas. 2001. "Measuring the Digital Economy." Discussion Paper. Bureau of the Census (www.census.gov/eos/www/papers/umdigital.pdf).

Messinger, P., and C. Narasimhan. 1997. "A Model of Retail Formats Based on Consumers' Economizing on Shopping Time." *Marketing Science* 16 (1): 1–23.

Morrison, Steven A., and Clifford Winston. 1986. *The Economic Effects of Airline Deregulation.* Brookings.

———. 1995. *The Evolution of the Airline Industry.* Brookings.

Moulton, Brent R., and Karin E. Moses. 1997. "Addressing the Quality Change Issue in the Consumer Price Index." *Brookings Papers on Economic Activity* (1): 305–49.

Moulton, Brent R., Robert P. Parker, and Eugene P. Seskin. 1999. "A Preview of the 1999 Comprehensive Revision of the National Income and Product Accounts: Definitional and Classificational Changes." *Survey of Current Business* 79 (8): 7–20.

Moulton, Brent R., and E. Seskin. 2003. "Preview of the 2003 Comprehensive Revision of the National Income and Product Accounts: Changes in Definitions and Classifications." *Survey of Current Business* (June).

Moyer, Brian, Marshal Reinsdorf, and Robert Yuskavage. 2004. "Aggregation Issues in Integrating and Accelerating BEA's Accounts: Improved Methods for Calculating GDP by Industry." Paper presented at "Architecture for the National Accounts," NBER Conference on Research in Income and Wealth. Washington, April 16–17.

Moyer, Brian C. and others. 2004. "Preview of the Comprehensive Revision of the Annual Industry Account." *Survey of Current Business* 84 (3): 38–51.

Nachum, Lilach. 1999. "Measuring the Productivity of Professional Services: A Case Study of Swedish Management Consulting Firms." Paper presented at "Measuring the Output of Business Services," a Brookings workshop, May 14.

National Center for Education Statistics. 2003. *Digest of Education Statistics 2002* (http://nces.ed.gov/programs/digest/).

National Research Council. 2002. *At What Price? Conceptualizing and Measuring Cost-of-Living and Price Indexes.* Panel on Conceptual, Measurement, and Other Statistical Issues in Developing Cost-of-Living Indexes. Committee on National Statistics, Division of Behavioral and Social Sciences and Education. Washington: National Academy Press.

Nordhaus, William D. 2002. "Productivity Growth and the New Economy." *Brookings Papers on Economic Activity* (2): 211–44.

Oi, Walter Y. 1992. "Productivity in the Distributive Trades: The Shopper and the Economies of Massed Reserves." In *Output Measurement in the Service Sector*, vol. 56, NBER Studies in Income and Wealth, edited by Zvi Griliches, 161–91. University of Chicago Press.

———. 2000. "Retail Trade in a Dynamic Economy." Paper prepared for "Measuring the Output of Retail Trade," a Brookings workshop, September 18, 1998.

Okamoto, Masato, and Tomohiko Sato. 2001. "Comparison of Hedonic Method and Matched Models Method Using Scanner Data: The Case of PCs, TVs, and Digital Cameras." Paper presented at the Sixth Meeting of the International Working Group on Price Indices, sponsored by the Australian Bureau of Statistics, April 2–6.

Oliner, Stephen D., and Daniel E. Sichel. 2000. "The Resurgence of Growth in the Late 1990s: Is Information Technology the Story?" *Journal of Economic Perspectives* 14 (Fall): 3–22.

———. 2002. "Informational Technology and Productivity: Where Are We Now and Where Are We Going?" *Economic Review* 87 (3): 15–44. Federal Reserve Bank of Atlanta.

O'Mahony, Mary, and Philip Stevens. 2003. "International Comparisons of Performance in the Provision of Public Services: Outcome-Based Measures for Education." London: National Institute of Economic and Social Research (July).

O'Mahony, Mary, and Bart van Ark. 2003. *EU Productivity and Competitiveness: An Industry Perspective.* Luxembourg: Office for Official Publications of the European Communities.

Organization for Economic Cooperation and Development. 1999. *Strategic Business Services.* Paris.

Oum, Tae Hoon, and Chungyan Yu. 1998. *Winning Airlines: Productivity and Cost Competitiveness of the World's Major Airlines.* London: Kluwer Academic Press.

Pan, Xing, Brian T. Ratchford, and Venkatesh Shankar. 2001. "Why Aren't the Prices of the Same Item the Same at Me.com and You.com? Drivers of Price Dispersion among E-tailers." Working Paper. Center for Electronic Markets and Enterprises, University of Maryland.

Panel to Study the Design of Nonmarket Accounts. 2003. "Designing Nonmarket Accounts for the United States: Interim Report." Committee on National Statistics, Division of Behavioral and Social Sciences and Education, National Research Council. Washington: National Academies Press.

Panzar, J., and J. Rosse. 1987. "Testing of Monopoly Equilibrium." *Journal of Industrial Economics* 35 (4): 443–56.

Parker, Robert. 1998. "Treatment of Insurance in U.S. National Accounts." Paper presented at "Measuring the Price and Output of Insurance," a Brookings workshop, April 21.

Pieper, Paul E. 1990. "The Measurement of Construction Prices: Retrospect and Prospect." In *Fifty Years of Economic Measurement: The Jubilee of the Conference on Research in Income and Wealth*, vol. 54, NBER Studies in Income and Wealth, edited by Ernst R. Berndt and Jack E. Triplett, 239–68. University of Chicago Press.

Pitt, Ivan L., and John R. Norsworthy. 1999. *Economics of the U.S. Commercial Airline Industry: Productivity, Technology and Deregulation.* Boston: Kluwer Academic Publishers.

Popkin, Joel. 1992. "The Impact of Measurement and Analytical Issues in Assessing Industry Productivity and Its Relationship to Computer Investment." Paper prepared for IBM. Washington: Joel Popkin and Company (October).

Pritchard, Alwyn. 2003. "Understanding Government Output and Productivity." *Economic Trends* (July 2003): 27–40.

Prud'homme, Marc, and Kam Yu. 2002. "A Price Index for Computer Software Using Scanner Data." Paper presented at "Two Topics in Services: CPI Housing and Computer Software," a Brookings workshop, May 23, 2003.

Ratchford, Brian T. 2003. "Has the Productivity of Retail Food Stores Really Declined?" *Journal of Retailing* 79 (3): 171–82.

Ratchford, Brian T., M. Lee, and D. Talukdar. 2003. "The Impact of the Internet on Search for Automobiles." *Journal of Marketing Research* 40 (May): 193–209.

Ratchford, Brian, and T. N. Srinivasan. 1993. "An Empirical Investigation of Returns to Search." *Marketing Science* 12 (Winter): 73–87.

Reinsdorf, Marshall. 1993. "The Effect of Outlet Price Differentials on the U.S. Consumer Price Index." In *Price Measurements and Their Uses*, edited by Murray F. Foss, Marilyn Manser, and Allan H.Young, 227–54. University of Chicago Press.

Rivkin, Steven G. 2000. "The Estimation of Productivity Change in Education." Paper presented at "Measuring the Output of the Education Sector," a Brookings workshop, April 7.

Ruggles, Richard. 1983. "The United States National Income Accounts, 1947–1977: Their Conceptual Basis and Evolution." In *The U.S. National Income and Product Accounts: Selected Topics*, vol. 47, NBER Studies in Income and Wealth, edited by Murray Foss, 15–96. University of Chicago Press.

Ruggles, Richard, and N. D. Ruggles. 1982. "Integrated Economic Accounts for the United States: 1947–1980." *Survey of Current Business* (May).

Santomero, Anthony M. 1984. "Modeling the Banking Firm: A Survey." *Journal of Money, Credit, and Banking* 16(4): 576–602. Bank Market Studies (November).

Schreyer, Paul. 2001. *Measuring Productivity: Measurement of Aggregate and Industry-Level Productivity Growth: OEDC Manual*. Paris.

Schreyer, Paul, and Philippe Stauffer. 2002. "Measuring the Production of Financial Corporations." OECD Task Force on Financial Services (Banking Services) in National Accounts.

Scott Morton, F., F. Zettelmeyer, and J. Silva-Risso. 2001. "Internet Car Retailing." *Journal of Industrial Economics* 49 (4): 501–20.

———. 2003. "The Effect of Information and Institutions on Price Negotiations: Evidence from Matched Survey and Auto Transaction Data." Working Paper. Yale University.

Seskin, Eugene P. 1999. "Improved Estimates of the National Income and Product Accounts for 1959–98: Results of the Comprehensive Revision." *Survey of Current Business* (December): 15–43.

Shapiro, Matthew P., and David W. Wilcox. 1996. "Mismeasurement in the Consumer Price Index: An Evaluation." *NBER Macroeconomics Annual* 11: 93–142. MIT Press.

Sherwood, Mark K. 1994. "Difficulties in the Measurement of Service Outputs." *Monthly Labor Review* (March): 11–19.

———. 1999. "Output of the Property and Casualty Insurance Industry." *Canadian Journal of Economics* 32 (2): 518–46. Presented at "Measuring the Price and Output of Insurance," a Brookings workshop, on April 21, 1998.

Sieling, Mark, Brian Friedman, and Mark Dumas. 2001. "Labor Productivity in the Retail Trade Industry: 1987–99." *Monthly Labor Review* 124 (12): 3–14.

Silver, Mick, and Saeed Heravi. 2002. "Why the CPI Matched Models Method May Fail Us: Results from an Hedonic and Matched Experiment Using Scanner Data." Presented at "Hedonic Price Indexes: Too Fast, Too Slow, or Just Right?" a Brookings workshop, February 1.

Smith, Michael D., Joseph Bailey, and Eric Brynjolfsson. 1999. "Understanding Digital Markets: Review and Assessment." Working Paper 140. Center for E-Business @MIT.

Statistics Netherlands. 1999. "A Volume Index for the Output of the Dutch Banking Industry Based on Quantity Indicators." Conference paper. Chateau de la Muette, Paris, Organization for Economic Cooperation and Development, September.

Stiroh, Kevin. 2002a. "Information Technology and U.S. Productivity Revival: What Do the Industry Data Say?" *American Economic Review* 92 (5): 1559–76.

———. 2002b. "Are ICT Spillovers Driving the New Economy?" *Review of Income and Wealth*, 48 (1): 33–57.

Stone, Richard. 1947. "Definition and Measurement of the National Income and Related Totals." Appendix to *Measurement of National Income and the Construction of Social Accounts*, Studies and Reports on Statistical Methods 7, Sub-Committee on National Income Statistics of the League of Nations Committee of Statistical Experts. Geneva: United Nations.

Sunga, Preetom S. 1984. "An Alternative to the Current Treatment of Interest as Transfer in the United Nations and Canadian Systems of National Accounts." *Review of Income and Wealth* 30 (4): 385–402.

Surface Transportation Board. 2000. "Rail Rates Continue Multi-Year Decline." Office of Economics, Environmental Analysis, and Administration (www.stb.dot.gov/econdata.nsf).

Swick, Roslyn B. 1999. "Producer Price Indexes for Engineering Services." Paper presented at "Measuring the Output of Business Services," a Brookings workshop, May 14.

Trajtenberg, Manuel. 1990. *Economic Analysis of Product Innovation: The Case of CT Scanners*. Harvard University Press.

Triplett, Jack E. 1990. "The Theory of Industrial and Occupational Classifications and Related Phenomena." 1990 *Annual Research Conference Proceedings*: 9–25. U.S. Bureau of the Census (August).

———. 1992. "Banking Output." In *The New Palgrave Dictionary of Money and Finance*, vol. 1, edited by Peter Newman, Murray Milgate, and John Eatwell. New York: Stockton Press.

———. 1996a. "High-Tech Industry Productivity and Hedonic Price Indices." In *OECD Proceedings: Industry Productivity: International Comparison and Measurement Issues*: 119–42. Organization for Economic Cooperation and Development.

———. 1996b. "Depreciation in Production Analysis and in Income and Wealth Accounts: Resolution of an Old Debate." *Economic Inquiry* 34 (January): 93–115.

———, ed. 1999a. *Measuring the Prices of Medical Treatments*. Brookings.

———. 1999b. "A Real Expenditure Account for Mental Health Care Services, 1972–95." Paper presented at "Measuring Health Care," a Brookings workshop, December 17 (www.brook.edu/dybdocroot/es/research/projects/productivity/workshops/19991217.htm.

———. 2001a. "Should the Cost-of-Living Index Provide the Conceptual Framework for a Consumer Price Index?" *Economic Journal* 111 (June): 311–34.

———. 2001b. "Price, Output, and Productivity of Insurance: A Review of the Measurement Issues." Brookings Discussion Paper.

———. Forthcoming. *Handbook on Hedonic Indexes and Quality Adjustments in Price Indexes for Information and Communication Technology Products.* Directorate for Science, Technology, and Industry. Paris: OECD.

Triplett, Jack E., and Barry P. Bosworth. 2002. "Baumol's Disease Has Been Cured: IT and Multifactor Productivity Growth in U. S. Services Industries." Paper presented at "Services Industry Productivity: New Estimates and New Problems," a Brookings workshop, May 17 (www.brook.edu/es/research/projects/productivity/workshops/20020517.htm).

Triplett, Jack E., and David Gunter. 2001. "Medical Equipment." Presented at "The Adequacy of Data for Analyzing and Forecasting the High-Tech Sector," a Brookings workshop, October 12.

U.S. Census Bureau. 2001. *1997 Economic Census: Manufacturing, Subject Series, Product Summary.* EC97M31S-PS.

———. 2003. *Current Industrial Reports: Communication and Other Electronic Equipment 2002.* MA334P (www.census.gov/cir/www/334/ma334p.html).

U.S. Department of Commerce. 2001. "2001 E-Commerce Multi-Sector Report." *E-Stats* (www.census.gov/eos/www/ebusiness614.htm).

United Nations. 1968. *A System of National Accounts.* New York.

Van Mulligen, Peter H. 2003. *Quality Aspects in Price Indices and International Comparisons: Application of the Hedonic Method.* Voorburg: Statistics Netherlands.

Voorburg Group on Services Statistics. 1992. "Report." Seventh Annual Meeting, Williamsburg, Va., October (http://stds.statcan.ca/english/voorburg/1992%20williamsburg/other/1992-report.pdf).

———. 1993. "Papers and Final Report." Eighth annual meeting, Oslo, Norway, September.

Walton, John. 1993. "Enterprise-Based Statistics in the Macro-Economic Framework: With Reference to Insurance." In "Papers and Final Report," Voorburg Group on Services Statistics. Eighth annual meeting, Oslo, Norway, September.

Warburton, Clark. 1958. "Financial Intermediaries." In *A Critique of United States Income and Product Accounts*, vol. 22, NBER Studies in Income and Wealth. Princeton University Press.

Wernerfelt, B. 1994. "On the Function of Sales Assistance." *Marketing Science* 13 (Winter): 68–82.

Winston, Clifford, and others. 1990. *The Economic Effects of Surface Freight Deregulation.* Brookings.

———. 1998. "U.S. Industry Adjustment to Economic Deregulation." *Journal of Economic Perspectives* 12 (Summer): 89–110.

Yntema, D. B. 1947. "National Income Originating in Financial Intermediaries." In Conference on Research in Income and Wealth, Studies in Income and Wealth, vol. 10. New York: National Bureau of Economic Research.

Yuskavage, Robert E. 1996. "Improved Estimates of Gross Product by Industry: 1959–94." *Survey of Current Business* 76 (8): 133–55.

———. 1999. "Measurement of Business and Professional Services in BEA's Gross Product Originating Series." Paper presented at "Measuring the Output of Business Services," a Brookings workshop, May 14, 1999 (www.brook.edu/es/research/projects/productivity/workshops/19990514.htm).

———. 2000. "Priorities for Industry Accounts at BEA." Presented at the Bureau of Economic Analysis Advisory Meeting, November 17.

————. 2001. "Issues in the Measure of Transportation Output: the Perspective of the BEA Industry Accounts." Paper presented at "Transportation Output and Productivity," a Brookings workshop, May 4.

Zieschang, Kim. 2002. "Measuring the Production of Financial Enterprises: Comments on the Schreyer and Stauffer Progress Report of the OECD Task Force on Financial Services." Paper presented at "Two Topics in Finance: Measuring the Output of Nonbank Financial Institutions," a Brookings workshop, November 1.

Index